LOUISVILLE

In Celebration of
LOUISVILLE

Martin E. Biemer

Partners in Progress by Gene Williams

Produced in cooperation with the
Louisville Chamber of Commerce

Windsor Publications, Inc.
Northridge, California

Windsor Publications, Inc.—History Books
 Division
Editorial Director: Teri Davis Greenberg
Director, Corporate Profiles: Karen Story
Design Director: Alex D'Anca

Staff for *In Celebration of Louisville:*
Manuscript Editor: Karl Stull
Photo Editor: Laura Cordova
Assistant Director, Corporate Profiles: Phyllis Gray
Editor, Corporate Profiles: Judith Hunter
Senior Proofreader: Susan J. Muhler
Editorial Assistants: Didier Beauvoir, Brenda
 Berryhill, Thelma Fleischer, Alyson Gould, Kim
 Kievman, Michael Nugwynne, Kathy B. Peyser,
 Pat Pittman, and Theresa Solis
Sales Representative, Corporate Profiles: Glenn
 Edwards
Layout Artist, Corporate Profiles: Mari Catherine
 Preimesberger

Library of Congress Cataloging-in-Publication Data
Biemer, Martin E., 1938-
In celebration of Louisville/Martin E. Biemer.
 Partners in progress/by Gene Williams. — 1st ed.
 p. cm. 23 x 31
"Produced in cooperation with the Louisville
 Chamber of Commerce."
Bibliography: p. 366
Includes index.
ISBN: 0-89781-239-5
1. Louisville (Ky.)—Economic conditions. 2.
 Louisville (Ky.)—Economic conditions—
 Pictorial works. I. Williams, Gene. Partners in
 progress. 1988. II. Title. III.
 Title: Partners in progress.
HC108.L6B54   1988
 330.9769'44—dc19   88-1594 CIP

©1988 Windsor Publications, Inc.
All rights reserved
Published 1988
Printed in the United States of America
First Edition

Windsor Publications, Inc.
Elliot Martin, Chairman of the Board
James L. Fish III, Chief Operating Officer
Hal Silverman, Vice President/Publisher

To Barry Bingham, Sr.,
who did so much
to help make Louisville
a great place to live.

*Previous page: Dramatic lights reflect off the
river. Photo by C. J. Elfont*

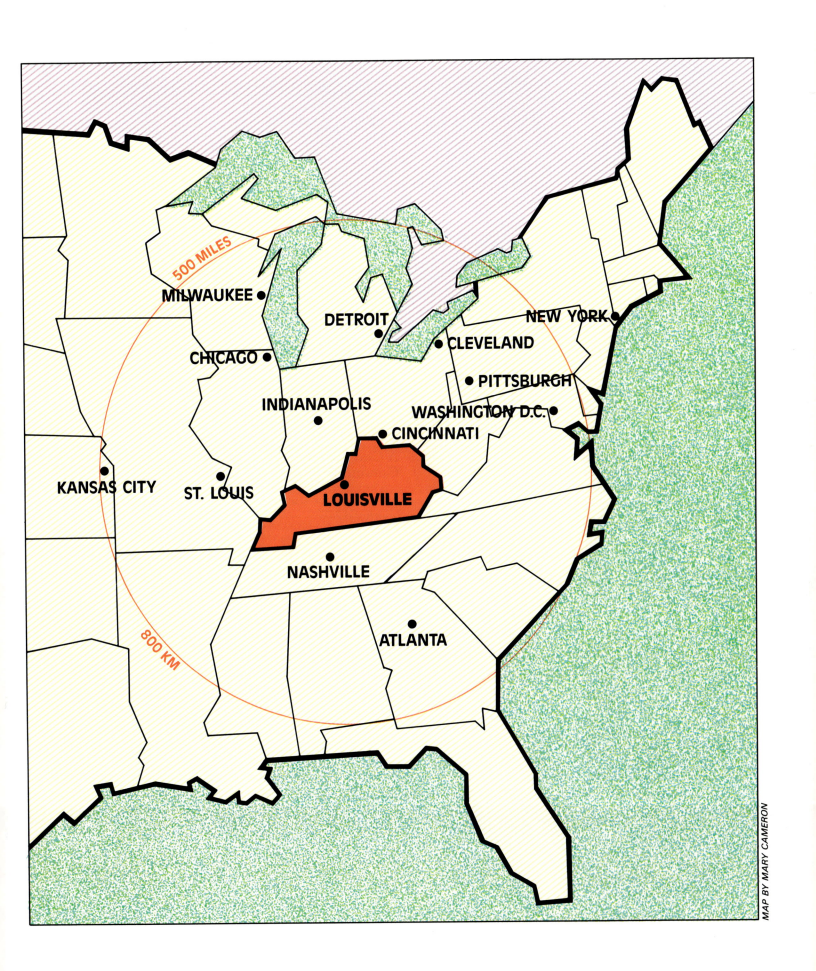

Contents

Part One *A Riverside Metropolis*

Prologue   **The Setting**   21

Chapter I   **A Riverside Metropolis**   27

Louisville became the new nation's first port of entry in the West–a place where trade would enter from the territories.

Chapter II   **More Than a Gateway**   49

For more than two centuries, Louisville's growth has been shaped by transportation.

Chapter III   **A Community of Communities**   67

One of the Louisville area's most attractive features is the people's strong sense of place–of pride in their neighborhoods.

Chapter IV   **A Blend of Cultures, A Love of Culture**   89

Louisville's culture is a lot like Louisville burgoo–a hearty stew in which individual flavors and textures stand out, sometimes providing surprises with each spoonful.

Chapter V **A Tradition of Learning** 117

When September comes to Louisville, more than one person out of four celebrates the season by going back to school.

Chapter VI **Festivals and Fun** 137

Louisvillians love the outdoors and almost every form of outdoor recreation, from waterskiing to snow skiing, swimming to ice skating, sunbathing to jogging, bird-watching to golfing, hiking to horseback riding, and family picnics to community festivals.

Chapter VII **A Center for Services** 157

By tradition Louisville is a city of services, a good place to live and do business, and a community that can adapt intelligently to social and economic change.

Chapter VIII **A Tradition of Craftsmanship** 171

Those who wonder about the future of manufacturing in the United States might do well to look to Louisville.

Epilogue **The Past and the Future Are Part of the Present** 185

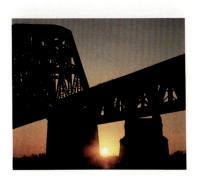

Part Two *Partners in Progress*

Chapter IX   **Networks**   190

Louisville's energy, communication, and transportation providers keep products, information, and power circulating inside and outside the area. South Central Bell 192; WAVE 3/Cosmos Broadcasting Corp. 194; WHAS-TV 198; WLKY-TV 200; Louisville Gas and Electric Company 202; The Courier-Journal 204

Chapter X   **Manufacturing**   206

Producing goods for individuals and industry, manufacturing firms provide employment for many Louisville area residents. Reliance Universal Inc. 208; Rohm and Haas 210; Corhart Refractories 212; Porter Paint Co. 214; Philip Morris U.S.A. 215; United Catalysts Inc. 216; American Synthetic Rubber Corporation 220; Carrier Vibrating Equipment, Inc. 222; Devoe & Raynolds Co. 224; E.I. du Pont de Nemours & Company 226; SEAMCO 228; Louisville Manufacturing Company, Inc. 230; Whip Mix Corporation 231; Louisville Stoneware Company 232; Brown-Forman Corporation 234; Kurfees Coatings, Inc. 237; Digital Equipment Corporation 238; GE Appliances 240; Borden Chemical 242; DCE, Inc. 244; American Air Filter 246; Louisville Bedding Company 247

Chapter XI   **Business**   248

Louisville's business and financial institutions offer a strong base for the city's growing economy. Louisville Chamber of Commerce 250; Citizens Fidelity Bank and Trust Company 251; Future Federal Savings Bank 252; BATUS, Inc. 254; The Cumberland Federal Savings Bank 258; Capital Holding Corporation 260; Commonwealth Life Insurance Company 262; Great Financial Federal 264; Health Data Network 266; Cowger & Miller Mortgage Company 268; Mercer-Meidinger-Hansen Inc. 270

Chapter XII   **Professions**   276

Greater Louisville's professional community brings a wealth of service, ability, and insight to the area. Wyatt, Tarrant & Combs 278; Eskew & Gresham, PSC 280; Peat Marwick Main & Co. 282; Goldberg & Simpson 284; Stites & Harbison 286; Barnett & Alagia 288; Brown, Todd & Heyburn 290

Chapter XIII **Building Greater Louisville** 292

From concept to completion, Louisville's building industry shapes tomorrow's skyline. NTS Corporation 294; Brandeis Machinery & Supply Corporation 298; RESCO 299; Henderson Electric Company Inc. 300; Hilliard Lyons 302; Sturgeon-Thornton-Marrett Development Company 304; Silliman Development Company, Inc. 308; Ready Electric Company 310; C&I Engineering, Inc. 312; US Ecology, Inc. 314; Paragon Group, Inc. 316; Harold W. Cates & Co., Inc. 318

Chapter XIV **Quality of Life** 320

Medical and educational institutions contribute to the quality of life of Louisville area residents. Department of Surgery, University of Louisville School of Medicine 322; University of Louisville 324; Bellarmine College 325; Medical Center Anesthesiologists 326; Louisville Hand Surgery 328; Medical Imaging Consultants 332; University Medical Associates, PSC 334

Chapter XV **The Marketplace** 336

Louisville's retail establishments, service industries, and products are enjoyed by residents and visitors to the area. J. Bacon & Sons Company 338; Hunt Tractor, Inc. 340; Galt House, Galt House East, Executive Inn, Executive West 341; Fashion Shops of Kentucky 342; Kroger Co. 344; Kentucky Fried Chicken 346; Ehrler's Stores 348; Winn-Dixie Stores, Inc. 350; The Paul Schultz Companies 352; A. Arnold & Son Worldwide Moving & Storage 354

Chapter XVI **Recreation and Leisure** 356

Thoroughbred and harness racing, major college and professional sporting events, conventions, concerts, and the annual Kentucky State Fair–all are at home in Louisville. Churchill Downs 358; Kentucky Fair & Exposition Center/Louisville Convention and Visitors Bureau 360; Louisville Downs 364

Bibliography 366

Index 368

Foreword

Louisville speaks for itself. No matter what the topic, Louisville speaks to it. Education. The arts. Business vitality. Growth. When you're speaking of a city recognized as one of the best places to live in America, you're speaking of Louisville. When you're speaking of a city alive with economic growth and new vision, Louisville speaks for itself.

This is a city rich in heritage and bathed in innovation. Each of this community's generations has passed along to the next a way of life that embraces the best of both worlds: big-city hustle and small-town hospitality. North and South meet here, where folk art and the fine arts mesh in a blend of tradition and technology.

The Louisville Chamber of Commerce celebrates all that is best about Louisville. We are both proud and honored to play a leading role in the development of a city that boasts corporate headquarters, healthy young businesses, and solid industries. We are equally honored to sponsor this book, which celebrates all that is best about how we have matured and how we continue to grow.

In Celebration of Louisville takes you on a tour of the rise of Louisville. From the days when the mighty Falls of the Ohio forced travelers to visit our shores, to the years of industrial revolution, to this era of renaissance, *In Celebration of Louisville* shares the secrets of how one community rose from a fort on the river to a thriving metropolis.

Many of the stories included in this book you've heard before: George Rogers Clark, the bustle of Fourth Street, the Kentucky Derby. Others may surprise you: the role of pigs in our development, Louisville's link to Saks Fifth Aveneue, the truck capital of the world, the parent of presidential china patterns.

From the start, the plan for this book has been to share Louisville. To help visitors get to know us. To help citizens get to know us better. Now that the book is in your hands, we hope you will sit back and enjoy. And listen as Louisville speaks for itself.

James O. Roberson
President
Louisville Chamber of Commerce

Right: Fourth Avenue was still thriving and the Seelbach Hotel was a center of activity in the late 1940s. Courtesy, The University of Louisville Photographic Archives

Toys and children's furniture from the early nineteenth century are watched over by a Sheraton period secretary/bookcase in the sitting room at Farmington. Photo by John Nation

Above: New Albany's 1869 Culbertson mansion, restored to its former glory, is a state historic site open to the public. Photo by Ted Wathen/Quadrant

Left: The chapel at the Louisville Presbyterian Theological Seminary stands at the crest of a hill overlooking Cherokee Park. Photo by Ted Wathen/Quadrant

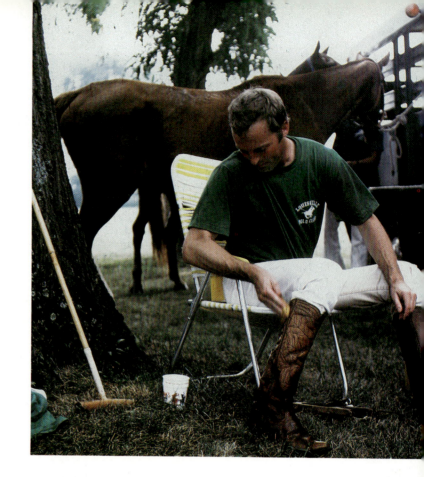

Right: This polo player takes a break on the Oxmoor Estate grounds. Photo by John Nation

Below: Dogwoods in bloom are an early sign of spring. Photo by John Nation

An elegant Victorian fountain graces the park-like strip down the middle of St. James Court in Old Lousville. Photo by John Nation

15

The Lions Eye Research Institute is part of Louisville's downtown medical center complex. Photo by C.J. Elfont

The glass atrium at the downtown Louisville Galleria shopping center encloses an area that was once part of Fourth Avenue. Photo by Ted Wathen/Quadrant

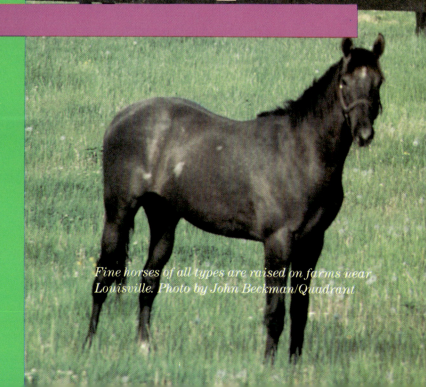

PART 1
A Riverside Metropolis

Fine horses of all types are raised on farms near Louisville. Photo by John Beckman/Quadrant

Green trees and rolling fields mark the rural countryside east of Louisville. Photo by John Beckman/Quadrant

Prologue
The Setting

Louisville in Kentucky has always been a favourite place of mine. The beauty of its situation, on the banks of La Belle Riviere, *just at the commencement of the famed rapids, commonly called the Falls of the Ohio, had attracted my notice, and when I removed to it, immediately after my marriage, I found it more agreeable than ever. The prospect of the town is such that it would please even the eye of a Swiss. It extends along the river for seven or eight miles, and is bounded on the opposite side by a fine range of low mountains, known by the name of the Silver Hills. The rumbling sound of the waters, as they tumble over the rock-paved bed of the rapids, is at all times soothing to the ear. Fish and game are abundant. But, above all, the generous hospitality of the inhabitants, and the urbanity of their manners, had induced me to fix upon it as a place of residence.*

—*John James Audubon*
Wildlife artist, naturalist
from Audubon Reader

The beauty of the area is still one of Louisville's main attractions, for visitors and residents alike. *La Belle Riviere*, the Ohio River, sprawls nearly a mile wide at the riverfront, a rippling mirror for city skylines, misty sunrises, and russet sunsets. The Silver Hills, now known as The Knobs,

THE SETTING

stand watch on the western horizon, looking like a distant range of Appalachians. Wildlife is still abundant, from the legions of waterfowl that stop at the river to the cardinals and raccoons that haunt the neighborhoods. Fish are abundant again in the Ohio River, recently declared safe for recreation and fishing after generations of dangerous pollution. And even though the population is 50 times larger than it was in 1808, when Audubon moved to Louisville, he would still find the hospitality, the gracious manners, and the love of culture that attracted him.

But the broad, rumbling rapids have changed, their sound no longer audible from the shoreline of Louisville. Walled off by a Z-shaped dam more than a mile-and-a-half long, most of The Falls now lie under more than 20 feet of water. The remainder—a National Wildlife Conservation Area in the midst of a metropolis—lies a half-mile away from the Louisville riverbank. To reach the spot, you take the George Rogers Clark Bridge to Indiana, turn right three times until you're headed west on Riverside Drive, then drive past some industries and through a gateway in the massive concrete floodwall. It takes a bit of determination to get there, but it's worth the trip.

Wooded parkland lies between the road and the river as you drive to the west. The downtown Louisville skyline shimmers in the distance, a mile or more away. Soon you hear the rush of water as it gushes through the massive gates of McAlpine Dam, built atop the old Falls.

If the river is moderately high, the rush becomes a roar as the water cascades over the top of the dam—creating a waterfall 8,000 feet long, zigzagging out of sight to the south and west. As the river rises further, the water "piles up" below the dam, and doesn't have as far to fall. At flood stage, most of the dam is marked only by a long, zigzag disturbance on the fast-flowing surface.

But when the water is low, perhaps three months out of the year, you'll be able to go back to the beginning. Find a path down the bank below the dam, through the driftwood washed up during the wet season, and you'll come to the bedrock that created the rapids.

This is no ordinary rock. Its surface is crowded with fantastic patterns—patterns that look like fans, stems, buffalo horns, slices of kiwi fruit, and bananas. They're the fossil remains of a vast coral reef that grew here more than 350 million years ago, when the area was covered by a tropical sea. More than 600 types of coral grew in that warm, ancient sea, each type building its distinctive stony skeleton.

Scattered atop this vast bed of rock are pools and potholes that retain their water, even when the river is low. Billions of water creatures live here, and millions of birds visit here to feast on them. Around 250 different species of birds have been spotted, including the endangered bald eagle and Arctic peregrine falcon. Some of them stay the year around.

The story of Louisville begins underfoot, in the jumble of fossils trapped in the rock. As the ancient continents moved and the seas changed, the coral reef was covered by shells, skeletons, debris, and silt. Layers of limestone formed around and above the reef; layers of shale, sandstone, and more limestone formed above them. The land rose higher and the sea drained away. The bedrock cracked and shifted, and the hills that became The Knobs were formed. To the east of The Knobs, a river flowed northward into what would become Indiana; to the west, another river flowed southward into what would become Kentucky.

Then the Ice Age arrived. The glaciers moved south at least three times, eventually damming the northbound river. The trapped water rose higher and higher, then flowed over The Knobs and cut a new river channel. When the glaciers melted, floods of water cut a broad, deep valley. When the glaciers returned, they filled that valley with boulders, gravel, sand, and dirt.

The flood of glacial water found resistance when it battered the fossilized coral reef. The softer limestone around it wore away; the reef became a large, stony hill. After the last glacier retreated, sand and gravel filled the bottom of the valley, and the coral hill became a high point in the bedrock below the new surface. When the modern Ohio River came meandering down the valley, it chose a course directly over the reef—setting the stage for today's Louisville.

The Falls of the Ohio became the only place where the 981-mile river flowed over bedrock. Rushing and tumbling, the water dropped 26 feet in three miles. When the river was high, the falls became swirling, furious rapids; when the river was low, the rapids became a series of waterfalls.

The spot had a special attraction for animals, and then for mankind. Woolly mammoths forded the river there in prehistoric times. Later, vast herds of migrating bison waded across. Mankind followed about 10,000 years ago, hunting the animals. Early Indians settled nearby, harvesting the abundant fish and shellfish.

The forces that created the river also created the rest of the landscape. Broad, flat areas of rich soil flank the river; higher plateaus overlook the bottomlands; and rugged hills and cliffs edge the ancient river valley. While people today may smile at Audubon's description of Louisville's "mountains," the tallest hills do rise more than 500 feet above river level. In places, they're rugged enough for practicing mountain-climbing skills.

The bedrock under Louisville tips downward to the west, so even the hills show variety. In the east, they're mostly limestone; in the west, they have layers of shale and sandstone. In the limestone plateaus to the east,

Facing page: Puffy white clouds and puffy white sails: a prescription for fun on the Ohio River.
Photo by John Nation

small caves and underground streams are common. On the hills of shale in the south and west, small-scale landslides are not unknown.

And wherever there's a bit of soil, plants take root and grow—usually abundantly. They owe their vigor to the soil and the weather, both legacies of the past.

The weather? Guidebooks usually mention the well-defined seasons and add that they can be variable and unpredictable. When people drive open convertibles at Christmas and New Year's, or retreat behind their air conditioners in July and August, the weather may bring thoughts of the ancient tropical sea. But when a 10-inch snowfall snarls traffic, or the Ohio River freezes from bank to bank, it may seem (for a while) that the Ice Age returneth.

Actually the weather is relatively mild, with enough sharp variations to make it interesting. There's usually plenty of rainfall, and no month on record has been completely dry. Summers are hot and humid, with an occasional cool spell for variety. Snowfall varies widely: in some winters there's never enough for good sledding; in other winters it lingers for weeks.

The valley influences the weather; you can watch the effect when the edge of a cloudbank stalls directly over the river. When the air is calm, humid air lies in the lowlands, and the trees send up a mist that makes The Knobs look like the Smoky Mountains.

Nearly half the days of the year are cloudy, and a third of the days bring rain. But one-fourth of the days are sunny, helping plants to grow luxuriantly. This makes most of the area a gardener's paradise—or a gardener's nightmare, depending on your outlook. A government

manual says one of the problems can be "intense plant competition." The plants grow so well that you have to fight them back!

Spring is Louisville's glorious time of year, with blossoms practically everywhere. The flowering trees and shrubs of the North thrive here, along with the hardier types from the South. Southern magnolias do well, although an occasional severe winter will give them pause. The variety of azaleas can be astounding. Spring wildflowers grow in city and suburban lawns, and seem to be everywhere in the parks.

The parks are Louisville's grandest tribute to its setting. Many of them were designed nearly a century ago by Frederick Law Olmsted, the father of American landscape architecture. Together the parks preserve examples of practically every type of natural attraction the

Above left: Dogwoods in bloom are an early sign of spring. Photo by John Nation

Above: Life on the river can be tranquil at sunset. Photo by John Nation

area has to offer: hills, cliffs, valleys, meadows, woodlands, brooks, and riverbanks.

And after decades of discussion, government leaders have gotten together to start work on a project to preserve the wildlife habitat and the ancient coral reef at the Falls of the Ohio. Audubon, who made more than 200 bird sketches here, would be pleased.

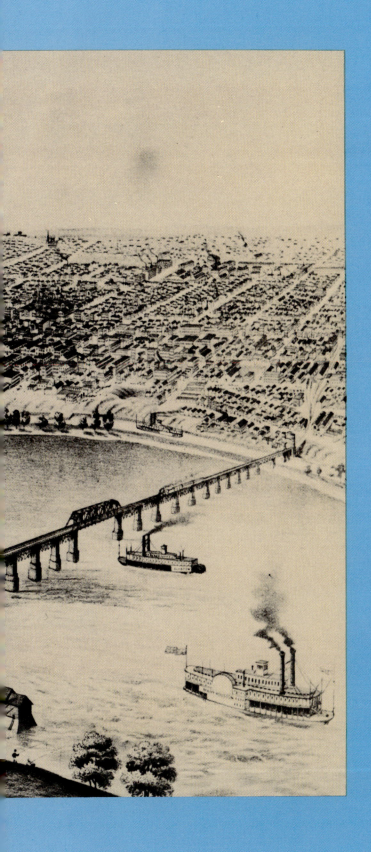

Chapter I

A Riverside Metropolis

THE SETTLEMENT AT THE FALLS

Forests blanketed most of eastern North America when the first Europeans arrived. The woods were so dense, and often so dangerous, that the best way to travel was usually by water. The French, exploring southwestward from the mouth of the St. Lawrence River, "discovered" the Ohio River about 1669. The broad water highway had been used by the Indians for centuries.

The British, exploring westward from the coast, crossed the Appalachians and clashed with the French. War erupted in 1754; France officially surrendered its territory nine years later.

But French settlers and their Indian allies continued to resist. In 1766 the British sent a 17-boat expedition down the Ohio and Mississippi rivers to help secure the territory. When the party reached the Falls of the Ohio, the boats had to be unloaded and the freight carried around the rapids. The expedition's leaders recommended that a military post be set up at The Falls to secure the spot for the British. But the area was remote, and the post wasn't established.

It took the American Revolution to bring permanent settlers to The Falls. In May 1778 George Rogers Clark arrived from Pennsylvania with orders to drive the British from the Illinois country. He had about 150 soldiers, perhaps 10 boats, and some 10 to 20 civilian families.

Clark established a camp on an island just above The

This view from the north shows Louisville in 1876. The river is high, allowing steamboats to pass over the old dam; a train leaves the south end of the area's first Ohio River bridge and enters Indiana. Steamboats line the wharf on the other side of the river, and downtown Louisville sprawls south of the wharf. The castellated gateway at the end of the bridge is not for defense against possible Confederte revival; it's simply for decoration. Courtesy, The University of Louisville Photographic Archives

Falls, near the southern bank of the river—the first permanent settlement in what became Louisville. The group cleared a large plot of ground, planted corn and vegetables, and built a wooden blockhouse and cabins. Then Clark set out for the Illinois country.

The settlers tended their crops, hunted game, and looked for good sites for homesteads. In late summer they built a new fort on the mainland and talked about building a town.

King Louis XVI of France decided to back the Revolution that year, and word reached Clark as he moved into Illinois. The news helped him gain the support of the French-speaking settlers. When he returned victorious to The Falls the next spring, he helped organize the new town—and suggested it be named Louisville.

(Clark spelled it "Lewisville," which hints at the variety of pronunciations surviving to this day. The "Lewisville" pronunciation is obsolete. "Loo'-ee-ville" is common in areas away from the city, and in some local circles. But most residents of the area pronounce it "Loo'-uh-vul," with a slur that newcomers find challenging to imitate.)

The site was a natural location for a town in the wilderness. The Falls were practically impassable most of the year, forcing travelers to come ashore. The river above The Falls was broad and calm, and its banks offered good places to land. Beargrass Creek entered the river a little above The Falls, forming a natural harbor. The land south of the river was broad and flat, its ponds and marshes posing the only major obstacles to a townsite.

Kentucky, then part of Virginia, was one of the earliest goals for pioneers heading west. Settlers trickled into the area in 1779; the spring of 1880 brought them in a rush. Nearly 300 boats had arrived by early May.

These early settlers came from both the North and the South—from Pennsylvania and New Jersey as well as Maryland and Virginia. Most were rugged pioneers, eager to work hard to build their fortunes.

But there were also settlers who had been awarded large land grants for their service in the French and Indian War, or who had bought land grants from the original owners. John Floyd was one of these; he bought 1,000 acres each from two Virginia officers. When he arrived in 1779 to claim his land, he found that 11 cabins had been built there already. He allowed the occupants to stay, as tenants.

The spring of 1880 also brought an escalation of the war. The British and Indians in Detroit were planning a major invasion of Kentucky. Indian attacks increased. "Stations"—fortified settlements—were built along Beargrass Creek and into the interior; their memory lingers today in the names of places and roads.

But the Indians refused to attack the little town of Louisville, perhaps because of the fort and the number of settlers. By the end of the year there were more than 800

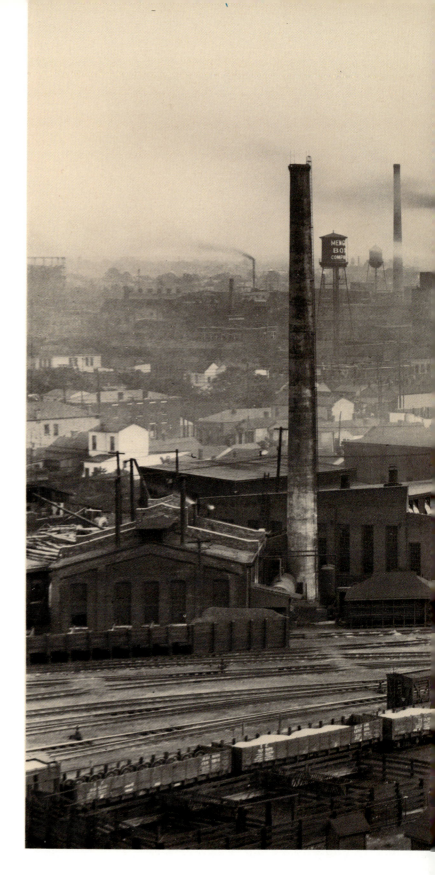

settlers in the area, and the Virginia legislature granted the new town a charter.

The British recognized the new nation in 1782, but Indian troubles continued for another decade. One of the many victims was Abraham Lincoln, grandfather of the future president, who was shot and killed in 1786 on his claim east of Louisville.

A BUSTLING YOUNG RIVERPORT

With the end of the Revolution, settlers flooded west, of-

ten coming down the Ohio with all their possessions on flatboats. And as river traffic grew, so did Louisville. The wharf spread eastward along the river, and the town stretched beside it. A new settlement formed at the lower end of The Falls, and soon became the town of Shippingport.

Shipyards built and repaired boats. Teamsters hauled cargo around The Falls. Warehouses were built for temporary storage. Merchants bought and sold goods. Businessmen wrote insurance on cargo and boats. Banks were formed to handle the money.

The Illinois Central Railroad serviced its steam locomotives in this roundhouse in the early 1920s. Courtesy, The University of Louisville Photographic Archives

Other settlements arose at The Falls: Portland, on the Kentucky bank downstream from Shippingport; and Clarksville, Jeffersonville, and New Albany, on the Indiana bank of the river.

Louisville became the new nation's first port of entry

in the West—a place where trade would enter from the territories held by the British, French, and Spanish. But the little town didn't thrive at first. The Spanish closed traffic on the Mississippi River and refused to trade with the new nation; the ban wasn't lifted for years. And even then, most of the traffic moved downriver. The cumbersome flatboats could only float downstream. Keelboats could be paddled and poled upstream, but the work was hard and travel was slow. It took three to four months for a keelboat to journey from New Orleans to Louisville.

Then came the machine that changed the nation. The *New Orleans* docked at Louisville in October 1811—the town's first steamboat, bound for her namesake city. Louisvillians were surprised at her ability to paddle upstream. And they were amazed 40 months later when the *Enterprize*, the first steamer to arrive from New Orleans, made the trip in 25 days—then paddled up the rain-swollen Falls and went on to Pittsburgh.

The steamboat reduced transportation costs by as much as 80 percent and brought prosperity to the entire river system. Louisville's population more than tripled between 1810 and 1820, then doubled again each decade through 1850. Louisville became Kentucky's largest city in the 1820s, and the nation's 10th largest in 1850. For a time New Albany was the largest city in Indiana.

Area boatyards were quick to adopt the new technology. The first steamboat built in Louisville was launched in 1816. During the river's golden age, the cities at The Falls built nearly one-fourth of the nation's steamboats.

The new prosperity brought new pride to Louisville. Downtown ponds and marshes were drained and filled, and the mysterious epidemics that had plagued the city began to fade. Streets were paved, fire engines bought, night watchmen hired. Musical and theatrical entertainments became common. The first hospital opened in 1825; Louisville became a city in 1828; and the first public school opened in 1829.

Manufacturing became important, although trade still dominated. Foundries made steam engines and other heavy machinery. Factories made soap, candles, sugar, flour, and rope; others processed tobacco and distilled whiskey.

The steamboat emphasized the problems on the river. A canal around The Falls had been proposed as early as 1783, but financing and regional rivalries stalled plan after plan. The project finally blossomed during the national canal craze of the 1820s. The canal, with three locks, was completed in 1830.

The river economy made Louisville slow to adopt the new transportation revolution—the railroad. Eastern Seaboard cities started building railroads in the 1830s to strengthen trade with the countryside; Louisville depended on the traditional toll roads called turnpikes. When riverless Lexington, Kentucky, proposed a railroad to the Ohio River at Portland, many Louisvillians saw the project as a threat.

New Albany started building a railroad north in 1848; Jeffersonville started building a railroad to Indianapolis about 1849. In 1850 Louisvillians organized the Louisville & Nashville Railroad (L&N).

The line from Lexington was completed the next year, terminating in Louisville instead of Portland. The L&N was completed to Nashville in 1859, connecting with another line that went on to Atlanta. The L&N route to Memphis was completed in 1861, on the day Fort Sumter surrendered.

The tensions that led to the Civil War were especially painful in Louisville. A border city on a major trade route, it had people and ideas from both the North and the South.

Slavery, of course, was the main issue. One of Louisville's first settlers was a slave, and blacks provided much of the city's labor. In the 1840s many occupations were dominated by blacks—including barbers, cooks, draymen, general laborers, hack drivers, waiters, wharf roustabouts, and well diggers. Blacks, slave and free, manned many of the factories.

But slaves were a declining part of Louisville's population. While their numbers increased until 1850, their proportion of the total population declined steadily after 1820. During the decade before the Civil War, Louisville's slave population actually declined as some were freed and others were sold to owners further south. Slave auc-

Facing page: The Louisville wharf was still a busy place in 1870, as horse-drawn carriages and wagons went down to meet the steamboats. Courtesy, The University of Louisville Photographic Archives

Electric trolley cars, like this one pulling a trailer formerly drawn by a horse, brought modern transportation to Louisville in the 1880s. Courtesy, The University of Louisville Photographic Archives

IN CELEBRATION OF LOUISVILLE

tions were still held at Louisville's courthouse by day, but abolitionist meetings were held there at night. The number of free blacks increased slowly but steadily.

"Foreigners" were another issue. In the late 1840s, revolution in Europe and famine in Ireland set off a tremendous migration to America, and many immigrants settled in Louisville. Established residents often feared their ideas, their religion, and their potential political power. Gangs began harassing "foreigners," occasionally stoning and beating them. The tensions exploded on August 6, 1855, an election day. Supporters of the "Know Nothing" party kept the Germans and Irish from voting, then rioted through the immigrant neighborhoods. At least 22 people were killed; the day became known as "Bloody Monday." The incidents dampened the city's growth for years to come.

THE GATEWAY TO THE SOUTH

Kentucky tried to remain neutral when the Civil War began. Louisville's city council voted $50,000 to protect the city, from both the North and the South, and vowed not to take sides.

River traffic to the South practically vanished, as gunboats patrolled the Ohio and Mississippi. But rail traffic boomed that first spring and summer, as the South built a stockpile of supplies.

Confederate forces moved into Kentucky in September, and the newly-elected legislature sided with the Union. Louisville quickly became a major Union supply point. Trains brought goods south to Jeffersonville, where they were ferried across the river to the railheads in Louisville. General William T. Sherman said later that the Atlanta campaign would have been impossible without the railroad from Louisville. Confederate raiders reached the outskirts of Louisville, but never invaded the city.

Lincoln freed the slaves in Confederate states, but slavery continued in Kentucky. Slaves could win their freedom by joining the army, and many left their homes to enlist. The rest of Louisville's slaves were freed after the war by the 13th Amendment to the U.S. Constitution.

The war had proved Louisville's value as a major trading center, and the city moved quickly to rebuild trade with the South. Agents for Louisville wholesalers saturated the area. Many were former Confederate officers, who emphasized the city's southern traditions.

Business leaders promoted all sorts of transportation improvements, from regularly-scheduled packet boats to new railroads and rail-river connections. Louisville's first bridge over the river was completed to Clarksville in 1870, providing the first rail service between Kentucky and Indiana. Two years later the canal was enlarged, allowing larger boats to bypass The Falls.

A TIME OF CHANGE

In 1880 the national *Frank Leslie's Illustrated Newspaper* called Louisville "one of the four great cities of the West which chiefly control the collection and distribution of produce of the soil and the mine, and the counter-movement of merchandise from the East and from foreign countries." The other "great cities": Chicago, Cincinnati, and St. Louis.

The growing railroad network weakened the natural trade advantage created by The Falls, but it expanded the avenues of trade. By the late 1880s rails connected Louisville with practically every city of importance. They also brought easy access to coal, iron ore, timber, and other raw materials. Louisville industry expanded and diversified greatly. By World War I, industry had edged past trade to become the predominant business in Louisville.

Growth and prosperity brought improvements to the

Louisville's Kosair Shrine chartered a special train for a trip to Chicago in 1920. Courtesy, The University of Louisville Photographic Archives

city, both physical and cultural. The arts became increasingly important: theater, opera, and music of all types. Louisville writers and painters gained national prominence. A well-landscaped park system was built in the 1890s; the parks were connected by boulevards ringing the outskirts of the city. Main Street became a tribute to trade, lined on both sides with ornate wholesale houses. The area south of Broadway, a mile south of the river, became an affluent suburb, with stone and brick mansions.

The area's second Ohio River bridge was opened to New Albany in 1886, with roadways for wagons alongside its railroad tracks. It provided the first way to drive across the river; for more than 40 years, it was the only way.

In 1889 Louisville became one of the first cities in the nation with electric trolley cars; their fast, reliable, and economical transportation stimulated rapid growth in the suburbs. Electric interurban railroads followed as the new century began, providing easy access to nearby towns.

The downtown business district stretched southward along Fourth Street, which became the city's new retail axis. And the turn of the century brought a series of new "skyscrapers," climaxed with the 19-story Kentucky Home Life building in 1913. One of the grandest was the 10-story Seelbach Hotel, completed in 1905.

The boom was over in 1915. Population growth had slowed considerably. The city's distilleries were declining as the nation moved toward Prohibition. Trade had reached a plateau; industrial development lagged. The war in Europe was creating new business for factories in

A RIVERSIDE METROPOLIS

northern cities, and Louisvillians were moving north to seek higher-paying jobs.

AN INDUSTRIAL POWER

Louisville quickly revived after Congress declared war on Germany in 1917. Factories expanded and started producing war materiel. New factories were attracted by the city's supplies of labor, power, water, and transportation facilities. The war provided one last surge of prosperity for Louisville's wagon-manufacturing business—and gave a boost to the new Ford assembly plant.

Camp Zachary Taylor was built at a cost of $10 million and trained about 150,000 soldiers before the war ended. Camp Knox was established 30 miles southwest of the city; later, as Fort Knox, it became a major training

Above left: The old Stitzel Distillery, one of many that dotted Louisville before and after Prohibition, is seen here during one of its many busy days. Courtesy, The University of Louisville Photographic Archives

Above: The Brown Hotel and Theater at Fourth and Broadway became Louisville's new center of elegance in the mid-1920s. Courtesy, The University of Louisville Photographic Archives

center and the depository for the nation's gold.

World War I ended late in 1918; Prohibition started in 1920. More than 30 distilleries and a dozen breweries were closed in Louisville; more than 6,000 jobs were lost. The economy stumbled and spurted for a couple of years, and then took off with the Roaring Twenties.

Manufacturing diversified into practically every field, from candy to drugs and from minnow buckets to pipe organs. Eighteen Louisville companies were the largest of their kind in the world; seven more were the largest in the United States; fourteen more were the largest in the South.

Downtown Fourth Street became a shopper's and pleasure-seeker's paradise, lined with stores, restaurants, and the new movie palaces. Broadway became the focus of new downtown development, with skyscrapers replacing the old mansions. When J. Graham Brown's 16-story hotel opened at Fourth and Broadway in 1923, former British Prime Minister David Lloyd George was the first to sign the register, and Paul Whiteman's Orchestra entertained.

Utilities were brought up-to-date. Sewers replaced the remaining open drainage ditches in the city; new sewers served new neighborhoods. The water company extended its pipes to serve the entire city. Louisville Gas and Electric Company built a new coal gas plant, developed an underground gas storage field, and constructed a hydroelectric power plant at The Falls. Competing telephone companies merged, making it possible for anyone with a phone to call anyone else with a phone.

Louisville got its first airport, first radio station, first intercity motor bus service, and first intercity truck line. The locks in the canal were enlarged in 1921, allowing larger boats and tows of barges to pass. A new dam was

completed in 1927, making the river navigable the year around. And the first bridge designed exclusively for highway traffic was opened in 1929, putting the last ferryboats out of business.

There was even an attempt to improve racial opportunity. The Kentucky branch of the Commission on Interracial Cooperation, supported by both races, found tremendous differences in education, hospital facilities, swimming pools, city parks, police protection, and other areas. It urged that blacks be offered facilities that were equal to those available to whites.

And blacks showed their growing political power. When the all-white, city-owned University of Louisville asked for a bond issue to build a new campus, black voters helped defeat it. Five years later the university proposed a new plan, including a college for blacks, and the new bond issue was approved overwhelmingly.

By the time the black college opened, in 1931, Louisville and the rest of the nation were deep in the Depression. Banks and businesses failed; jobs vanished. The end of Prohibition brought new work at the distilleries and breweries, but it helped only a little. By 1932 more than one-fourth of Louisville's workers were unemployed.

There were a few high spots. The Kentucky Derby Festival began in 1935, capitalizing on the world-famous

Facing page: Fine Kentucky bourbon mellows in these oaken casks in the mid-1930s. Louisville's distilleries boomed after the end of prohibition. Courtesy, The University of Louisville Photographic Archives

Above: Basketball has a long tradition in Louisville. Courtesy, The University of Louisville Photographic Archives

horse race to bring gaiety to the city. Federal projects gave Louisville new libraries, more sewers, expanded hospitals, improved parks, and elevated railroad lines that eliminated dangerous crossings. Public housing projects helped poor people move out of the slums.

But the major event of the Depression was a tragedy—the great flood of 1937. Torrential rains fell throughout the Ohio River valley, beginning in early January. When the flood peaked on January 27, it covered more than three-fourths of the city. Nearly 250,000 people were evacuated; 90 people died; damage was estimated at $50 million. Flood cleanup and repair helped create a surge in business that year; the upcoming war would create a boom.

A CITY REVIVED

While Louisville was suffering from its worst flood in history, Adolf Hitler repudiated the treaty that had ended World War I. Japan had already invaded China; Nazis would begin their spread through Europe a year later.

The Louisville area became a vital part of the "Arsenal of Democracy." A huge gunpowder plant was built across the river near Charlestown, Indiana, and soon employed nearly 32,000. A new airport was built south of Louisville, flanked by two aircraft plants. The world's largest synthetic-rubber complex was built at the southwest edge of the city; a plant to make naval guns was built along the L&N railroad.

Distilleries made the industrial alcohol needed to manufacture synthetic rubber. The Ford plant built jeeps. Other factories made parts and shell casings. The woodworking industry made parts for gliders; Hillerich and Bradsby turned from baseball bats to gunstocks. The shipyard in Jeffersonville made landing ships, submarine chasers, and other specialized boats.

As industry was growing, Louisville's young men were leaving—many for basic training at Fort Knox, which became a major training center in 1940. The Depression's shortage of work turned into a shortage of labor; women and blacks found job opportunities they'd never imagined. But the tragedy of the war was brought home when a 150-building, 1,000-bed temporary army hospital was built at the south edge of Louisville.

Newly prosperous Louisville found entertainment in nightclubs, hotels, movie houses, events to raise money for war charities, and at home over the radio. The Kentucky Derby Festival was suspended, but the Derby itself was continued. Travel restrictions prevented out-of-town

ticket sales in 1943; that year's race became known as the "Street Car Derby."

The end of the war brought an explosion of growth—of a type that no one had clearly foreseen. The automobile opened up tremendous opportunities for land development, just as the electric streetcar had done a half-century before. Most of the growth would take place outside the old cities. And in most cases, the industries and residents who moved to the suburbs would fight all attempts at annexation.

One result was a proliferation of small cities in Jefferson County outside Louisville—a trend that started in the late 1930s. Small cities multiplied after World War II. By the early 1980s the county had nearly a hundred of them.

Another result was the demand for new highways, which were crowded soon after they had opened. The

Above left: Police patrolled downtown streets in motorboats during the 1937 flood. Courtesy, The University of Louisville Photographic Archives

Above: "Lit up like Levy's" is an old Louisville expression, inspired by the Levy Brothers department store at Third and Market. The store, shown in its heyday, has closed, but the building has been restored to its former elegance. Courtesy, The University of Louisville Photographic Archives

first section of the new belt highway was opened in 1949, and within two years the traffic was twice as heavy as the planners had predicted it would be after two decades.

Downtown would suffer, but that trend wasn't evident at first. There was a brief flurry of new construction on Fourth Street in the early 1950s, then a period of slow decline. By the late 1950s downtown retailers were noticing the effect of the new suburban shopping areas.

These forces were at work in most major cities, but there was an additional factor in Louisville: the memory of the flood. Families that could afford new homes fled the neighborhoods that were flooded. The city's new floodwall, delayed by the war, wasn't completed until 1956; by then the flight to the suburbs was well established.

Louisville built on its new industrial base. Rubbertown prospered. International Harvester bought the large aircraft plant at Standiford Field to make tractors and farm machinery. The field itself became Louisville's new commercial airport.

The biggest boost of the postwar era was General Electric's decision to move its home-appliance manufacturing to the area. In the early 1950s, the company built six separate factories on a 1,000-acre plot south of the

Facing page: The 17-story Reyburn Building, shown near completion in 1927, was the last "skyscraper" built in Louisville until the 1950s. Located at Fourth and Broadway across from the Brown Hotel, it was a major part of the "south downtown." Courtesy, The University of Louisville Photographic Archives

Above: This stalwart crew made iron wheels for railroad cars in the early 1930s. Courtesy, The University of Louisville Photographic Archives

city. Appliance Park would employ nearly 23,000 people by the early 1970s.

One tradition hurt development for a time—eastern Jefferson County's role as an enclave for affluent suburbs and picturesque farms. When Reynolds Metals Company proposed a research-and-development park near Anchorage in the mid-1950s, opposition from residents stopped the project. When a second site southeast of the city was also opposed, Reynolds built the complex

41

in Virginia. Commercial and industrial development didn't move into the area until the mid-1960s.

The 1960s were a time of prosperity, grand projects, and grander dreams. Housing developments swallowed old farms; commercial centers with high-rise buildings blossomed at expressway interchanges. Expressway plans threatened parks and historic neighborhoods, and sparked interest in preservation. Urban renewal cleared old slums and brought a new medical center, government center, riverfront development, and public housing.

In 1955, the Commonwealth Building at Fourth and Broadway reached 21 stories—the tallest building completed in Louisville since 1919. By the mid-1960s, 20-story buildings were no longer unusual; in the early 1970s the first 40-story building was completed. The boom lasted until the mid-1970s, when energy problems jolted the nation's economy. Projects continued, but at a slower pace.

The postwar era also brought changes in the old social order. At the end of the war Louisville was still segregated, although blacks had been voting for decades.

The barriers fell slowly. Louisville elected its first black city alderman in 1945. The downtown library was desegregated in 1948, and two Catholic hospitals admitted their first black patients. Colleges and universities were desegregated in 1950; public golf courses and a fishing lake in 1952; the parks in 1955. And in 1956, after the U.S. Supreme Court overturned the "separate but equal" doctrine, public and Catholic schools desegregated peacefully.

Early 1961 brought a series of sit-ins. Some restaurants and entertainment businesses desegregated voluntarily; the city passed an open-accommodation ordinance in 1963. A long struggle, highlighted by a visit from Dr. Martin Luther King, Jr., brought an open-housing ordinance in 1967.

King was shot in Memphis the following April, and within two weeks there was racial violence in more than 120 cities across the nation. In Louisville, the violence erupted at the end of May.

SOLVING PROBLEMS

The violence was a vivid reminder that Louisville had problems—problems that couldn't be solved simply by

Facing page: When the old main post office was razed in 1943, the land was cleared and used to create this temporary downtown park. Courtesy, The University of Louisville Photographic Archives

Above: World War II saw one of Louisville's early efforts to bring peace between labor and management. Courtesy, The University of Louisville Photographic Archives

Left: Reynolds Aluminum used this large press to make boats out of aluminum sheets after World War II. Courtesy, The University of Louisville Photographic Archives

encouraging development and growth. Attention needed to be focused on racial relations, quality of education, labor relations, pollution, local government fragmentation, and—especially after the Arab oil embargo—coping with economic change.

The problem of racial relations was difficult to face. The early 1970s brought efforts to provide better opportunities for blacks—in housing, job opportunities, and education. But attitudes built over many generations were slow to change.

National attention focused on Louisville in 1975 when the federal courts found that the public schools were illegally segregated, and ordered them integrated in less than three months. Protesters marched in downtown streets and gathered at shopping centers. A few of the suburban protests turned into riots. And some parents who opposed the plan sent their children to private schools, or moved outside the county.

After a few weeks, the community settled into an uneasy peace, but strains continued. A year later, teachers went on strike, seeking a greater voice in education. Declining enrollment forced many schools to close.

Then, after several years of turmoil, attention turned to educational quality. Test scores began rising, especially among black students. By the early 1980s, the average test scores in Louisville's public schools were moving ahead of national averages.

Racial progress was evident in other areas. Blacks moved into higher-paying jobs and became accepted as equals in many businesses. Apartment complexes welcomed people of different races, and middle-class blacks moved quietly into formerly white suburbs. Legal barriers disappeared; social and economic barriers were yielding.

Labor relations posed real problems in the 1970s; the teachers' strike was only one example. Strikes disrupted production repeatedly at Appliance Park; bitter strikes erupted in violence at several factories; city fire fighters walked out and left Louisville in jitters.

By the late 1970s, business and labor leaders agreed that something had to be done. With behind-the-scenes groundwork and help from government mediators, labor relations gradually improved. By the early 1980s, Louisville's reputation as "strike city" was fading, and labor and management were cooperating in many programs.

The environment had posed problems from the beginning. Air settles and stagnates in the Ohio River valley, trapped by the surrounding hills. The Ohio River has

always been muddy, and the wastes from civilization made it worse. Farm animals, then septic tanks and small sewage-treatment plants, polluted every stream in the area.

Smoke was one of the first problems to gain attention; travelers commented on it 150 years ago. Coal fires created the problem; the World War II industries and multiplying automobiles aggravated it to the point that it was no longer tolerable.

In 1937, Louisville Gas and Electric Company installed one of the nation's first electrostatic precipitators to reduce the smoke from one of its power plants. But most of the city's sources of air pollution remained uncontrolled.

The city established an air-pollution agency in 1952, and started making progress toward reducing visible

Facing page: By the late 1930s, the skyscrapers of Fourth and Broadway were at the center of the "south downtown." Courtesy, The University of Louisville Photographic Archives

Above: Soldiers from nearby Fort Knox found welcome entertainment in Louisville during World War II. Courtesy, The University of Louisville Photographic Archives

pollution. The agency gained new clout with the environmental movement of the 1970s. It banned open burning and imposed pollution restrictions on businesses and industries. It supported the gas and electrical company's pioneering efforts to remove sulfur pollution from coal emissions. And it put together an automobile-emissions inspection program that became a national model of effectiveness. By the mid-1980s, Louisville met practically every federal standard for air quality.

Water pollution was recognized from the start; Louisvillians refused to drink water from the river. City water didn't become potable until 1909, when the Louisville Water Company installed and perfected one of the nation's earliest sand-filtration systems. More and more treatment was required as the river became more polluted.

Until the late 1950s, city sewers simply dumped wastewater into the river. Then the first major sewage-treatment plant was built, and the situation improved. But suburban expansion outdistanced the sewer system, and streams became polluted with the effluent from septic tanks.

The large sewage-treatment plant was brought up to the latest federal standards in the early 1980s. In the mid-1980s, a major expansion program started eliminating many septic-tank systems and inefficient small sewage-treatment plants.

Cities upstream also cleaned up their water. In 1986, the river at Louisville was declared safe for recreation and fishing—for the first time since standards were set.

Local government fragmentation had been a problem since the late 1930s. Small cities were incorporated to thwart annexation by larger cities; many small cities didn't have the resources to offer meaningful services.

One proposed solution was metropolitan government. But plans to merge Louisville and Jefferson County failed in 1956, 1970, 1982, and 1983.

Finally, in 1986, the city and county signed a compact to consolidate some operations and cooperate on others. Annexations and incorporations were suspended for 12 years, and the method of allocating local tax income was revised. One of the first concrete results was the establishment of a county-wide drainage authority, consolidating storm drainage and flood protection efforts that had been scattered among many government agencies.

The economy remained a continuing challenge. The industrial base was fading in the 1970s and early 1980s because of changing national trends, and Louisville became known as a "city in transition."

The city's last brewery closed in the late 1970s, along with several major cigarette factories. International Harvester closed all operations at the old aircraft plant at the airport. Many other factories closed or cut back production. Belknap Inc., once the world's largest hardware wholesaler, faded and died as the wholesale business changed.

One way to cope with the new economic challenges was to increase productivity. General Electric's new highly automated assembly line gained national attention. The number of jobs was reduced, but lower labor costs kept the appliances competitive with imports. Ford Motor Company gained union support for many improvements at its two major truck plants.

Other firms branched out in new directions. Humana Inc., based in Louisville, is one of the nation's leading operators of for-profit hospitals. Other health-related businesses, and service industries in general, were growing. And there was a growing movement to encourage entrepreneurs to open small businesses.

Cultural activities expanded greatly in the past few decades; the only real "problems" were the challenges of growth. Backed by volunteers and supported by local businesses, the Louisville Orchestra, Actors Theatre, and the annual Bluegrass Music Festival won international

attention. Opera and ballet companies offered several attractions each season.

The 1970s brought a public performing arts school to prepare middle- and high-school students for careers in music, dance, drama, and technical theater. The 1980s brought a modern two-auditorium performing-arts center to showcase local productions and present high-quality traveling shows. Museums and art schools expanded dramatically.

Those seeking entertainment could find everything from bluegrass to Broadway, Shakespeare to experimental theater, rock music to classical, folk music to jazz.

In 1922 you could still see the Falls of the Ohio in a relatively natural state. Courtesy, The University of Louisville Photographic Archives

Chapter II

More Than a Gateway

We reached Louisville in time—at least the neighborhood of it. We stuck hard and fast on the rocks in the middle of the river, and lay there four days.

—Mark Twain
Life on the
Mississippi

A NATURAL CROSSROADS

Transportation in our new nation's wilderness was a matter of following the path of least resistance. Often this was a river or stream—the larger and more peaceful, the better. Where waterways weren't convenient, people followed the trails established over the ages by deer and buffalo.

Major wilderness pathways, both water and land, came together and crossed at the Falls of the Ohio, a natural barrier and a natural gateway. Louisville was born to serve those who traveled those pathways. And for more than two centuries, Louisville's growth has been shaped by transportation.

For most of Louisville's first century, the community thrived on a contradiction in transportation: convenience built on inconvenience. People and goods traveling by boat usually had to go around The Falls by land; people and goods traveling by land usually had to take a boat to get across the river.

If you think of a gateway as a passage through a barrier—a passage that must be opened by a gatekeeper—then Louisville was truly a gateway at The Falls. The Louisville area made its living on transportation: by han-

A towboat passes westward beneath the Sherman Minton bridge, Louisville's newest bridge over the Ohio River. The American Institute of Steel Construction named it the nation's most beautiful long-span bridge of 1961. Photo by Ted Wathen/Quadrant

dling and storing freight; by accommodating, entertaining, and transporting people; and by servicing, repairing, and building all types of land and river vehicles.

As the wilderness was settled, the city and its transportation network grew. Wharves spread for miles along the riverbanks, above and below The Falls. The trails that connected the little riverport with the interior settlements became dirt roads; the roads were often improved by private companies and converted into turnpikes which charged tolls.

The city's gatekeeper role gave much of early Louisville a vested interest in the status quo. Transportation improvements were often opposed vigorously, and the opposition made Louisville slow to adapt to new developments.

The proposed canal around The Falls, for instance, was seen as a threat by Louisville draymen, and by some warehousemen and wholesalers. They fought it bitterly,

claiming it would allow riverboats to pass Louisville without stopping, giving Cincinnati an advantage in downstream trade.

Railroads posed an even greater threat. The city's first, a small railroad from Louisville to Portland, was designed to speed travel around The Falls. It opened in 1838—and was opposed so vigorously that it was closed five months later. The railroad to Lexington was delayed for nearly two decades, mostly because of the fear that it would allow traffic to bypass Louisville. New Albany and Jeffersonville both built railroads to the north several years before Louisville started building railroads to the south.

Once the railroads did arrive, the city tried to preserve its traditional business by forbidding them to connect. Goods and people still had to change vehicles, usually several times, to travel around the barriers at Louisville.

Facing page: A towboat pushing three barges heads west from the Conrail drawbridge on the Louisville and Portland Canal—the waterway that bypasses the Falls of the Ohio. Photo by Ted Wathen/Quadrant

Above: Small buses dressed as trolleys provide frequent service along downtown Louisville's Fourth Avenue. The buses were dubbed "Toonerville II" in honor of the old comic strip "Toonerville Trolley," created by Louisvillian Fontaine Fox. Photo by Ted Wathen/Quadrant

Bridges across the river were another threat, to river traffic in general and the ferryboat business in particular. The city was nearly a century old before the first bridge was opened in 1870; it carried only trains. Another 16 years passed before the second bridge was opened—

with roadways for people, horses, and wagons alongside its railroad tracks. And *that* was the only way to drive across the river for the next 43 years!

While established businesses opposed direct connections *through* Louisville, they supported direct connections *between* Louisville and other cities in the South. The Louisville and Nashville Railroad (L&N), completed just before the Civil War began, quickly proved the value of the new mode of transportation. Louisville thrived on war traffic.

In the years following the Civil War, the L&N built a transportation empire. Controlled by Louisville interests, it solidified the city's hold on the markets of the middle South. It dominated transportation in Kentucky and Tennessee, and was a major power in Alabama and northern Georgia. Louisville and L&N interests influenced Kentucky's General Assembly to delay Cincinnati's attempts to build a railroad through Kentucky to the South.

But the rapid expansion of the L&N took more money than Louisville could provide. Capital had to be raised in the money markets in the East. As the city entered its second century, control of the railroad was passing into "outside" hands. This shift of ownership brought a significant shift in emphasis. The railroad, once operated for the good of Louisville, was now operated for the good of itself.

The L&N became one of the major powers in the railroad wars of the late nineteenth century. Other railroad empires were attracted to the territory; competition lowered rates. Individual railroads sought strength

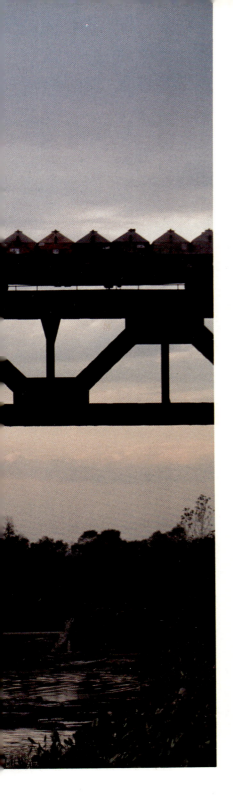

through friendly connections with lines outside their territories. Artificial obstructions erected by cities like Louisville were overcome and eliminated.

One result of this new railroad era was standardization. Before the Civil War, railroads were built to different "gauges"—different distances between the rails. Equipment designed for one gauge couldn't run on another. Most northern railroads were built to "standard gauge": 4 feet, 8 1/2 inches between the rails. Most southern railroads, including the L&N, were built with rails 5 feet apart.

This meant that passengers had to change trains when they crossed the border between North and South. It meant that freight had to be moved from one railroad car to another—or that the wheels under the car had to

Above left: A late afternoon freight train crosses the Indiana end of the Conrail bridge, which replaced Louisville's first Ohio River bridge. Photo by C.J. Elfont

Above: The Southern Railway, now part of the Norfolk Southern system, is one of the major railroads serving Louisville. Photo by John Beckman/Quadrant

be changed. Louisville capitalized on this when it required the L&N to be built to the southern gauge and the railroad to Lexington and Cincinnati to be built to the northern gauge.

IN CELEBRATION OF LOUISVILLE

Clear skies and autumn colors make it a great time for sailboating and steamboating on the Ohio River. Photo by John Nation

THE ERA OF CONVENIENCE

The new era arrived in 1886, when the L&N and other railroads throughout the South narrowed their rails to the northern gauge. Freight and passengers could now pass from North to South without tedious changes.

Another result of the new era was competition. Louisville's second railroad bridge over the Ohio River, completed in 1886, was built to bring competitive rates. The third railroad bridge, completed in 1895, increased competition even more. North met South at Louisville—and had several attractive alternatives for doing so!

By the end of the nineteenth century, Louisville had become a gateway of a different sort. The major railroads of the North—including the Pennsylvania, Baltimore & Ohio, and New York Central—joined the major railroads of the South—including the L&N, Chesapeake & Ohio, and Southern—offering quick transportation to every major city in the nation. In many cases there was a choice of more than one route, with competitive rates. On the river, steamboat traffic bypassed The Falls easily and without cost, using the toll-free canal and locks operated by the federal government. Low rates on the river offset longer distances and slower speeds, offering important competition for the railroads.

Louisville became known for convenience of transportation, not inconvenience. And its location, near the center of the eastern half of the United States, was to be its major strength throughout the twentieth century.

The evolving transportation network both helped the city grow and shaped the city's growth. Major industries, at first confined to the strip along the river, located along the railroad lines. Street railways and electric interurban railroads extended out the old turnpikes, providing cheap, reliable service that opened up land for development. Louisville's residential streets followed the expanding railroads and turnpikes, without regard for the compass.

The twentieth century and the internal combustion engine brought new transportation revolutions. Automobiles appeared in Louisville before the new century began, and Ford started assembling Model Ts in the city in 1914. A Wright flying machine entertained crowds at Churchill Downs in 1910, and Louisville's first airfield opened in 1918.

As automobiles multiplied during the 1920s, pavement crept out the old turnpikes to accommodate them. Louisville's first Ohio River bridge designed solely for automobiles opened in 1929, the year after the city's first scheduled airline service began.

The new modes of travel generally followed estab-

lished routes. Paved highways replaced the old nineteenth century turnpikes, connecting communities originally joined by trail. Airline pilots followed railroads and highways on their flights between cities.

The new modes of transportation also connected with the old. Louisville's first airport was built on a farm beside one of the major old turnpikes, which was paralleled by an electric interurban railroad. Louisville's second airport was built near the L&N's main yards, providing easy rail access for delivering material to the World War II aircraft plants. And Louisville's first major belt expressway connected these two airports with nearly all of the highways radiating south and east of the city.

AN INTEGRATED NETWORK

Today the Louisville area is blessed with a transportation network that offers quick, easy access to nearly every major city in the nation—with a choice of ways to get there. Freight travels by air, highway, rail, and river, and Louisville offers multiple ways to transfer freight from

Facing page: The Belle of Louisville *(top) gets the jump on the* Delta Queen *at the start of the Kentucky Derby Festival's Great Steamboat Race. Photo by John Nation*

Above: This is the business end of Louisville's authentic steamboat and river-going historic landmark, the Belle of Louisville. *Photo by Mark E. Gibson*

one mode to another.

Passengers can travel by air, bus, or car, but can take only nostalgic rides by river or rail. The city's historic *Belle of Louisville* steamboat provides a taste of the river passenger service that dwindled to nothing just after World War II. And while Louisville's last regular passenger train disappeared in the 1970s, the Kentucky Railway Museum offers occasional steam-powered train excursions to nearby cities.

Louisville's streets and highways were designed with direct transportation in mind, and the pattern serves well to this day. Major streets and roads radiate from the three highway bridges across the Ohio River, fanning out through the suburbs to nearby towns. Interstate highways head north, south, east, west, and northeast, connecting directly with every major city within 200 miles. Other interstate highways fan out from these cities, stretching from coast to coast and from Canada to Mexico.

A major belt route, Interstate 264, circles the city on the east, south, and west, connecting with every major highway and both of Louisville's airports. The Riverside Expressway along the north edge of the city completes the loop.

Much of Interstate 264 was built before the interstate system and its standards of design were established. The local route's design flaws became a serious problem as traffic increased. A major redesign was undertaken in

the late 1970s and reconstruction began in the early 1980s; the work is scheduled to be finished before the end of the decade.

An outer belt route, Interstate 265, was recently completed, connecting and bypassing the suburban areas. Most of the other interstates were started in the 1950s and 1960s; many miles were rebuilt in the 1970s and 1980s.

Facing page: Traffic is always busy on the Watterson Expressway. Photo by Christina M. Freitag

Below: Sun sets behind three of Louisville's Ohio River bridges: the Big Four, John F. Kennedy and George Rogers Clark. Photo by John Nation

IN CELEBRATION OF LOUISVILLE

Many of the streets and highways were designed to show off the area's natural beauty. Interstate 64 winds through scenic Beargrass Creek valley and tunnels under a major park on its way through the city. Interstate 71 thrusts across the bottomland along the river, in the shadow of 400-foot bluffs topped by historic mansions. Interstate 65's John F. Kennedy Memorial Bridge and U.S. 31's George Rogers Clark Memorial Bridge offer beautiful views of the city's skyline to southbound travelers. A system of scenic parkways circles the city, and many of the major highways wind through historic neighborhoods and natural areas.

The Transit Authority of River City provides bus service throughout the metropolitan area, on both sides of the river. Intercity bus lines connect Louisville with other major cities. Several major truck lines have terminals in the Louisville area; many others offer service direct to the customer's location.

Mergers and cutbacks changed the nation's railroad map tremendously during the 1960s and 1970s, but Louisville remains an important point on the lines of major carriers.

The L&N, no longer headquartered in Louisville, officially doesn't even exist. It's part of CSX Transportation, a multi-mode conglomerate that transports goods by rail, river, highway, and pipeline. CSX rail lines stretch from New York State to Florida and from Illinois to Louisiana, serving much of the territory in between. Lines through Louisville extend to St. Louis, Chicago, Detroit, Philadelphia, Miami, New Orleans, and (of course) Nash-

ville and Atlanta. Louisville's computerized Osborn Yard is a major point for assembling CSX trains—and a major point for transferring piggyback trailers and standard freight containers between highway and rail.

CSX faces strong competition throughout most of its territory from Norfolk Southern (NS), the other rail giant centered in the South. Louisville is on the main NS line from the southeast to St. Louis and Kansas City. And the railroad's acquisition of the old Kentucky and Indiana Terminal Railroad has given the NS access to most of Louisville's major industries. Both railroads pass through Louisville on their way north of the Ohio River—and both connect at Louisville with Conrail, the giant of the Northeast.

Two other railroads deserve mention. One is the Pa-

Facing page: Well-maintained railroads are a vital link in Louisville's transportation network. Photo by Christina M. Freitag

Below: Gold stripes and numbers decorate the sand dome of former Louisville and Nashville Railroad steam locomotive 152, lovingly restored by the Kentucky Railway Museum. Photo by C.J. Elfont

ducah and Louisville, which bought the old Illinois Central line between the two cities. It serves many Louisville industries, and does a good business hauling Western Kentucky coal to power plants and river terminals. The other is part of the Soo Line, which bought an old Milwaukee Road branch line into southern Indiana. The mergers of the 1970s gave the line a direct connection into Louisville, providing rail competition to the northwest.

Steamboat days may have ended shortly after World War II, but river traffic is still a vital part of the nation's transportation system. River barges haul tremendous amounts of heavy, bulky freight, such as coal, chemicals, salt, grain, oil, steel, and machinery. On the Ohio River, one 5,000-horsepower towboat can handle up to 17 barges, lashed together in a block nearly 110 feet wide and 1,200 feet long. Each barge can carry a load of 1,500 tons—as much as 15 railroad cars or 60 semi-trailers.

These towboats and barges roam a 15,000-mile river and waterway system that serves 19 states, from Pennsylvania to Minnesota and from Florida to Texas. American Commercial Barge Lines, headquartered in Jeffersonville and owned by CSX Corporation, is the largest barge transportation company in the world.

The American Commercial family also includes major river terminals, and boatyards for building and repairing boats and barges. Three of the company's terminals are in Louisville, handling coal and all sorts of raw materials and bulk merchandise. The Jeffboat boatyards in Jeffersonville, which traces its history back to the early steamboat days, repairs towboats and barges.

(Jeffboat built a tremendous number of military boats during World War II, and everything from simple barges to the *Mississippi Queen* steamboat during the 1970s. The early 1980s brought a depression in riverboat construction, and much of the Jeffboat plant was put into mothballs, awaiting the next upturn in the boat construction business.)

Louisville's air service offers some unusual advantages. The major commercial airport, Standiford Field, is only five miles from downtown—and located at the junction of Interstate 264 (the inner belt loop) and Interstate 65 (the major north-south expressway).

A dozen airlines serve Standiford Field, with more than 100 flights on a typical weekday—enough to offer convenient service to most major cities, but not enough to cause problems with congestion and delays. And

Facing page: A long barrel-vault skylight illuminates the main concourse, Pegasus sculpture, and escalators at Standiford Field's new terminal. Photo by John Beckman/Quadrant

Above: Private airplanes find a convenient port at Bowman Field, Louisville's first airport. Photo by John Beckman/Quadrant

while Louisville's weather can vary considerably, it's hardly ever bad enough to close the airport.

The weather and Louisville's location were the major factors cited by United Parcel Service when it established its nationwide overnight delivery service hub at Standiford Field in 1981. By the mid 1980s, UPS was

scheduling 75 flights each weeknight into Louisville—and handling about 300,000 packages a night.

Louisville's first airport, Bowman Field, was the busiest airport in the nation during World War II. It is still an important base for private and corporate planes, and hosts special guests (like the Goodyear blimp) and air shows.

The Indiana communities are served by the Clark County Airport, located just north of Clarksville at the junction of Interstates 65 and 265. Only minutes away from downtown Louisville, it's a base for planes owned by businesses and individuals on both sides of the river.

THE CONNECTIONS

The Louisville area is dotted with spots where people and freight can move from one form of transportation to another. At the airports, of course, people moved from highway to air—the only choices available for passenger travel. Express and mail also make the transition at Standiford Field.

Freight is another matter. The choices are broader and more varied, and usually depend on a combination of cost, convenience, and speed. Air, of course, is fastest, and usually most expensive. Highways are slower, usually more convenient, and usually less expensive. Rail is slower still—but much less expensive for large amounts of heavy material. Barges are slowest, and usually least expensive.

Public river terminals are where the three forms of surface transportation usually join. They're also good

Facing page: Fishermen test their skills in the rushing water of the Falls of the Ohio, just downstream from the gates of McAlpine Dam and in the shadow of the Conrail bridge. Photo by John Beckman/Quadrant

Above: Bowman Field, Louisville's first airport, was once the busiest airport in the United States. Its Art Deco terminal building is a historic landmark. Photo by C.J. Elfont

locations for industrial development.

The two major public riverports in the Louisville area are the Louisville and Jefferson County Riverport, just downstream from Louisville, and the Clark Maritime Centre, just upstream from Jeffersonville. Both feature rail and highway connections; both were beginning to grow in the early 1980s.

One advantage of these river-to-land terminals is the versatility they offer for unusually large and heavy loads. Machinery that could never travel by rail or ordinary highway can be hauled on barges—and then taken by special heavy-duty trucks to its final location.

Private river terminals also handle transitions. They include several locations where coal is dumped from railroad cars (and sometimes trucks) into barges, and where sand, stone, salt, oil, and chemicals are transferred from barges to trucks (and sometimes railroad cars).

Chapter III

A Community of Communities

One of the Louisville area's most attractive features is the people's strong sense of place—of pride in their neighborhoods. The numbers tell part of the story. Jefferson County, Kentucky, has more than 90 incorporated cities in addition to Louisville. Even more communities are shown on the map, but are not incorporated. Louisville itself is divided into more than 70 official neighborhoods, encouraged in their self-improvement efforts by the city's neighborhood development office. There are many more communities on the Indiana side of the river, and on the Kentucky side outside Jefferson County.

But more important than numbers is the identity of these areas; the often-distinctive cultures and ways of life. Tell a Louisvillian you're going to Shively, or St. Matthews, or Butchertown, or Old Louisville, or Portland, or Fern Creek, or Floyds Knobs—and you'll give more than a clue to what you'll see and what type of people you'll meet.

Part of the reason for this is the Louisville area's historic pattern of growth, along with Louisvillians' love of tradition. In the early days, there were many small, scattered settlements. Most of them have retained their identities, even after being swallowed by larger communities.

Another part of the reason is a basic spirit of independence. Louisville-area people like to fend and provide for themselves.

Yet another part of the reason is rivalry, often noticeable between the people who live north and south of the Ohio River. Hoosiers and Kentuckians compete in basketball, football, economic development, rhetoric, storytelling, and regional jokes—then join each other in work and play, like in-laws who enjoy each other's company but don't want to become too close. On their own sides of the river, neighborhoods and communities often compete like members of some large, noisy family.

Whatever the reasons, Louisvillians' focus on homes

The tranquil, tree-shaded Cherokee Triangle neighborhood lies just a short drive away from bustling downtown Louisville. Photo by John Nation

A COMMUNITY OF COMMUNITIES

Facing page: Sparkling fall colors bring a hint of northern forests to the edge of Cave Hill Cemetery along Grinstead Drive. Photo by John Nation

Above: Polished brass doors open into the lobby of the historic 300 building, erected in 1891 at the corner of Third and Main streets. Photo by C.J. Elfont

and neighborhoods has made the area truly a community of communities—each with its own history, traditions, and attractions.

THE SPECTRUM

There are many types of communities in the Louisville area, from downtown high-rise neighborhoods to rural crossroads, and from suburban office complexes to midtown clusters of small, historic homes. The interstate highway system has put many of these communities within easy reach of each other and has created a few of its own. Skyscrapers are no longer confined to the central city, for instance; clusters of them have arisen near several major interchanges, creating suburban villages with a wide range of shopping and services. And semiwilderness areas are not far removed from the city; there are deer crossing signs within a 15-minute drive of downtown Louisville.

One feature of Louisville's neighborhoods impresses visitors soon after they arrive: the number of historic landmarks and historic neighborhoods. So many Louisville neighborhoods have historic significance that nearly two dozen of them have been designated historic preservation districts, with special tax credits for restoration. Most of them are listed in the National Register of Historic Places. And tucked between and around these preservation areas are many more neighborhoods, developed mostly after the turn of the century, that retain the atmosphere of the eras when they were built.

Fine old farmhouses, many over a century old, have become centerpieces for suburbs and city neighborhoods alike. And the assortment of scattered historic landmarks, often nestled among modern buildings, must number in the hundreds.

Another striking feature is the contrast and diversity. For example: Harrods Creek, a community of private estates along the Ohio River northeast of Louisville, was the nation's second-wealthiest ZIP Code area in the 1980 census; Utica, just across the river, has a waterside community of rugged individualists living in an assortment of old mobile homes and small cottages.

THE DOWNTOWN NEIGHBORHOODS

In many cities, the terms "downtown" and "neighborhood" are mutually exclusive. Few people live downtown; even fewer feel like neighbors. In Louisville, however, there are neighborhoods downtown—neighborhoods where people live, as well as visit, work, and shop. They're apartment neighborhoods, tucked around and among the stores, hotels, restaurants, theaters, and high-rise office buildings. And they range from the historic to the ultramodern.

Louisville's downtown is a study in contrasts. Approach it from the north—across the George Rogers Clark Memorial Bridge—and you'll see a cluster of tall, modern buildings, in black and gold and gray and pink, reflected in the rippling waters of the river. But once you cross the bridge and glance up and down Main Street, you'll discover the mix of history and modernism that distinguishes much of Louisville.

Ignore, for the moment, the intriguing rows of nineteenth-century buildings to your left; the network of one-way streets forces you to turn right. The 11-story concrete and stone Farm Credit Banks building to your right dates from the urban renewal projects of the late 1960s; the construction project on your left will become one of the major office buildings of the late 1980s.

The next block features two of Louisville's gems of

Photo by C.J. Elfont

A COMMUNITY OF COMMUNITIES

Top: The matinee crowd leaves the Actors Theatre in one of Louisville's frequent showers. Photo by Christina M. Freitag

Left: Cast iron details distinguish a nineteenth century commercial building on Main Street. Photo by John Nation

historic architecture: the ornate, limestone-faced 300 Building at the southwest corner of Third and Main, built in 1891 for the old Kentucky National Bank; and the classic, columned Actors Theatre of Louisville building at 316 West Main, built in 1835 for the old Bank of Louisville.

The next block is a monument to urban renewal. On the right are the high-rise and low-rise office and hotel buildings of the early 1970s riverfront development. On the left is the 40-story, dark grey, boxlike, glass and steel First National Tower, Louisville's tallest building since the early 1970s.

Then comes the block that truly celebrates Louisville's blend of architecture. The massive, pink and gray granite, detail-rich, "post modern" Humana Building of the early 1980s rises on the left, followed by a row of restored commercial buildings from the previous century. On the right is the many-angled, sometimes-curved, silvered glass Kentucky Center for the Arts, which joyously mirrors the mix of buildings across the street.

Now the serious preservation begins. The next three blocks include the largest collection of cast-iron front commercial buildings in the nation, outside of New York

City. Most of them were built from 1880 to 1900, when Main Street was the bustling hub of the "Gateway to the South." Neglected for decades, and mostly spared from "modern" face-lifts, the buildings started attracting the attention of preservationists in the late 1960s. When the Museum of History and Science was created out of five old buildings in 1977, winning architectural awards in the process, Main Street's revival really gained momentum. Today the old retail, wholesale, and warehouse buildings contain shops, restaurants, offices, and apartments, all capitalizing on the spaciousness and graciousness of the Victorian designs.

How could all this history and modern development exist side-by-side? It's a result of the curious heritage of downtown Louisville—a heritage that gave the city two downtowns, a north and a south, and set up a creative tension between them.

An unintentional "urban renewal" project, a tornado, churned into the west end of Louisville's first downtown in 1890. Many old buildings were demolished; many new ones were damaged heavily. Businesses started rebuilding immediately, and the West Main commercial area became one of the most modern in the city.

But as the river's golden age ended and the twentieth century began, downtown development shifted southward along Fourth Street, away from Main Street. Soon it reached Broadway, a mile from the river. By the 1920s Broadway was the major focus of the new downtown,

with the best hotels, restaurants, stores, theaters, and high-rise apartment buildings close by.

The two downtowns were connected by Fourth Street, a bustling thoroughfare with just enough room for two lanes of parking, two lanes of traffic, and two rather narrow sidewalks. The congestion added to the air of busy prosperity, especially toward the Broadway end.

But the Depression brought an end to downtown development. The 17-story Heyburn Building, begun in 1926 at the southeast corner of Fourth and Broadway, was the last "skyscraper" built in Louisville until the 21-story Commonwealth Building was completed on the opposite corner nearly 30 years later.

With such a large and spread-out downtown area,

Above left: Downtown skyscrapers are reflected in the pools of the riverfront Belvedere plaza. Photo by John Nation

Above: The entrance to the Humana Building shows just a few of the geometric patterns of its design. Photo by C.J. Elfont

Louisville largely avoided the major development tool of more compact cities: tearing down the last generation's commercial buildings to make space for the next generation. Many of Louisville's old buildings survived and drifted into genteel poverty. By the late 1950s, much of

the old downtown—especially the part that escaped damage in the 1890 tornado—was dying or dead.

By that time, too, the move to the suburbs was in full swing, and shopping centers were drawing retail business away. The new Broadway downtown also drifted into a slow decline.

Louisville leaders were concerned, but action came slowly. Major plans for downtown redevelopment were proposed in 1931 (when there was no money for new investment) and 1942 (when there were no materials because of World War II). New buildings arose in scattered locations downtown in the immediate postwar years, but it wasn't until the mid-1950s that business and government leaders began to seriously consider a comprehensive redevelopment plan.

Action began in the 1960s, in several areas scattered around the traditional downtowns. Urban renewal helped clear acres of dilapidated buildings in three major areas: along Main Street; in a strip to the west of the old Fourth Street corridor; and in a large tract several blocks to the east.

The showcase development arose along Main Street, from Second to Sixth and stretching north almost to the river. The Riverfront Plaza/Belvedere—an elegant elevated plaza with grassy areas, cascading fountains, and reflecting pools—was built overlooking the river; a parking garage and an interstate highway are hidden below it. The Galt House Hotel and an office tower were built along the east side of the plaza; a shorter office building was built along the south side. The First National Tower arose across the street; a savings and loan association built a new headquarters near the tower. To the south and east of this area, the state built a new convention center and parking garage—and subsidized a new 17-story hotel, the Hyatt Regency Louisville, complete with a 17-story atrium. The projects brought new focus to the old downtown and encouraged the preservation efforts around them.

The second major project involved a long strip of dilapidated buildings to the west of Fifth and Sixth streets and from Main Street nearly to Broadway. It became the focus for new local, state, and federal government buildings, along with office buildings and acres of parking lots.

And the large tract east of downtown, separated from the business district by the north-south Interstate 65, became a new medical center—with five major hospitals, the University of Louisville Schools of Medicine and Dentistry, several medical office buildings and clinics, and the Board of Health offices.

During all this redevelopment, Fourth Street led several lives under several different names. In 1972 the half-mile north of Broadway became a landscaped pedestrian mall, dubbed the River City Mall. The new look failed to stop the changes in the old retail and theater district, but it did provide a focus for redevelopment and for trans-

Above: Strong, simple concrete shapes dominate the University of Louisville's buildings in the downtown medical center. Photo by C.J. Elfont

Facing page: Stairways zig-zag to the top of one of downtown Louisville's newest parking garages; there are elevators behind the stairs for those who don't need the exercise. Photo by Ted Wathen/Quadrant

forming the old downtowns.

The elegant 1905 Seelbach Hotel at Fourth and Walnut, which closed in 1975 after a long decline, was restored to its former glory and reopened as the 1970s came to an end. The 1902 Kaufman-Straus department store building, midway between the Main Street and Broadway downtowns, became the focus for the new Galleria—a shopping complex that covered part of the mall with a multi-story glass atrium. Elevated walkways lead to two new glass office towers, then to other nearby buildings.

The landmark Starks Office Building next to the Galleria, built in 1911 with a major addition in 1930, was restored and renovated. Its interior air shaft was turned into an atrium ringed with shops. Other old office buildings in the area were restored, some of them quite elegantly.

The Brown Hotel, built in 1923 at Fourth and Broadway, was restored in the early 1980s, after spending more than a decade as a public-school office and classroom building. It became the centerpiece for the redevelopment of the south downtown, which includes the new Theater Square restaurant and shopping area and a large new apartment complex. These projects inspired

A COMMUNITY OF COMMUNITIES

restoration of several of the area's tall office and apartment buildings, which date back to the golden age of the Broadway downtown.

And in the late 1980s, the mall itself was rebuilt with special lanes for small buses dressed as trolleys, bringing motorized transportation (and a name change) to Fourth Street again. Now it's the Fourth Avenue Mall.

THE RIVERFRONT

The late 1980s brought new focus to the old wharf areas along the riverfront, largely ignored through the decades.

Above left: The Brown and Williamson Tower, seen through the glass atrium spanning Fourth Avenue, is one of two tall office buildings attached to the downtown Louisville Galleria. Photo by C.J. Elfont

Above: Louisvillians and visitors crowded the lobby of the historic Brown Hotel for its grand re-opening in 1985. Photo by Christina M. Freitag

A COMMUNITY OF COMMUNITIES

The river's history as an avenue of commerce had a lot to do with it: Louisvillians seemed to think of the downtown riverbank as an industrial area with little potential for beauty. When the railroads arrived, tracks were built along the riverside to avoid existing buildings; when the interstate highways arrived, the pattern was repeated. The elevated Belvedere, centerpiece of the Main Street development of the early 1970s, was a concession and exception to this; it soared above the railroad and highway to overlook the river. A reconstructed portion of the old wharf, designed as a docking place for the steamboat *Belle of Louisville,* was tucked into a tangle of highway ramps, reached from the Belvedere by pedestrian stairways that zigzagged their way down to waterside.

The railroad tracks were abandoned and removed in the early 1980s, and riverfront action finally picked up a few years later. The National Headquarters of the Presbyterian Church (U.S.A.) accepted an offer of free space in the old Belknap warehouse complex; city officials agreed to build a new parking garage and landscape the surroundings. The wharf was modified and expanded to accommodate a floating restaurant; the city built parking lots close at hand. Officials began to find new locations for the remaining downtown riverfront industries.

And Mary and Barry Bingham, Sr., who had sold their

Facing page: The Belle of Louisville *and its "steepled" wharf boat lie at rest at the municipal wharf in downtown Louisville. Interstate 64, the Riverside Expressway, passes between the Ohio River and the downtown skyscrapers. Photo by John Nation*

Above: Farmers still offer their own produce for sale at Louisville's Haymarket. Photo by C.J. Elfont

media empire in 1986, donated $2.6 million to build the world's tallest floating fountain, to be placed in the river midway between Kentucky and Indiana, in full view of the Belvedere.

THE OLDER NEIGHBORHOODS

Drive in practically any direction from downtown Louisville, and you'll pass through an intriguing old neighborhood. Many of them have been restored in recent years; nearly all of them boast examples of Louisville's ubiquitous nineteenth-century working-class home, the shotgun house.

All shotgun houses are one room wide, several rooms deep, and one story tall at the front. From there,

Above right: Flowering dogwood accents a rainbow of slate, tile, and shingle roofs in the Cherokee Triangle neighborhood. Photo by John Nation

Above: Victorian elegance survives along the streets of Old Louisville. Photo by John Nation

Facing page: Potted impatiens march up the steps to the front door of an elegant Victorian home on Belgravia Court in Old Louisville. Photo by John Nation

the variations seem endless. Many shotguns have a wider room toward the back, with a front-facing door and a walk leading to the street. And many of these have a second story above the wider room. (Legend has it that this variation, called the "camelback," was inspired by an early tax law that set lower rates for one-story houses, and based the assessment on the height of the front of the house. Louisville historians haven't been able to confirm this; the pattern may have developed elsewhere.)

Most shotguns are wooden, but a good many are brick and a few are stone. The facades display almost every imaginable variation of architectural design—a tribute to early efforts to add distinction and a touch of elegance to virtually identical houses.

There are at least two theories about the origin of the name. One is based on the floor plan, which put all the interior doors in line with the front and back doors. Wags said you could fire a shotgun through the front door and the charge would go out the back, without doing any damage.

The second theory, proposed by folklorist John Vlach in the February 1977 issue of *Natural History* magazine, traces the name and the design back to Africa, where a similar house in southern Dahomey was called a "to-gun." Vlach says the design came to the New World with African slaves, moving from Haiti to New Orleans and on up the Mississippi River system.

The shotgun was well suited to the narrow city lots of the nineteenth century, and it provided residents with more privacy and independence than the connected row houses of eastern cities. Many of Louisville's shotguns have become jewels of restoration, often complete with

their original leaded- and stained-glass windows, fine woodwork, and elegant decorative touches.

Portland, the old riverport community at the foot of the Falls of the Ohio, is where Louisville's shotgun-house tradition appears to have started. The inexpensive, sturdy houses were ideal for the families of the men who worked in the factories and railroad yards in the area.

Portland is still a hard-working neighborhood, with many buildings dating back a century or more. It's also the home of the south end of McAlpine Dam, which tamed The Falls, and the Louisville and Portland Canal and McAlpine Locks, which provide riverboats with a route around The Falls. Visitors are welcome at the dam and locks, the best place to get a close-up view of the huge towboats and barges.

Butchertown, one of the city's earliest suburbs, is another haven for restored shotguns, many of them quite elegant. Originally a German settlement, it still has an Old World air—especially around St. Joseph's Catholic Church, a twin-spired Gothic structure that hovers over the neighborhood like a cathedral over a medieval village. The church is as elegant inside as it is without, and still has brass nameplates—engraved with German lettering—on many of its pews.

The neighborhood's name comes from the primary business of its early German settlers. Slaughterhouses, canneries, cooperages, harness and wagon shops, and soap and tallow factories thrived there from the middle nineteenth century to the middle twentieth century. Many of the old commercial and factory buildings have been restored for use by modern businesses, including a charming firehouse across the street from the church.

Germantown and Schnitzelberg, southeast of the downtown area, were also settled by Germans, many of them employed in nearby factories and breweries. Some of the most immaculate rows of shotgun houses can be found in Germantown, where many residents still scrubbed their front stoops and sidewalks, and even swept their streets with brooms, until after World War II. Here, too, are old-worldly neighborhoods of small houses, stores, and taverns surrounding large churches. Many of the traditional corner groceries and drug stores, with living quarters upstairs, are still around; some of them have been converted into specialty shops.

Old Louisville is a modern name, coined to describe the area of large houses and mansions that began spreading south from Broadway during the late nineteenth century. This was the prestige neighborhood of the Victorian era, with homes ranging from solid brick structures for professionals and businessmen to elegant mansions for the rich.

The area started a long, slow decline with the onset of the automobile. During World War II, the federal government encouraged owners to divide the large old homes into apartments to help ease the housing shortage.

Many of the well-built houses survived the changes and neglect without major structural damage, providing a rich assortment of opportunities when the preservation movement began in the 1960s. Old Louisville became one of the first of the city's historic-preservation districts. Today many of the houses have been restored and renovated as spacious, often elegant residences; others have become gracious quarters for many types of professional offices.

A COMMUNITY OF COMMUNITIES

St. James Court, extending south from Central Park, is the most elegant street in Old Louisville, with a stunning variety of Victorian mansions. Divided by a grassy, tree-lined parkway complete with a fountain, the street is illuminated by gaslights.

Belgravia Court, which crosses St. James Court at its southern end, doesn't even allow for vehicles. The houses and apartments face a parklike strip of grass with a broad walkway down the center, also illuminated by

Fishermen try their luck below the gates of McAlpine Dam, which tamed the mighty Falls of the Ohio. Photo by C.J. Elfont

IN CELEBRATION OF LOUISVILLE

A COMMUNITY OF COMMUNITIES

gaslights. It's a tranquil respite from the traffic-filled streets nearby.

Cherokee Triangle, south of Cave Hill Cemetery and about a mile-and-a-half east of downtown, is another preservation district—a virtually intact example of a wealthy "streetcar suburb," developed between the late nineteenth century and World War I.

It's also the starting point for a neighborhood—actually, a strip of neighborhoods—that deserves mention because of its unique evolution: Bardstown Road and the areas alongside. One of the area's earliest major roads, it began as a trail and soon became a turnpike. Development followed the horse, then the streetcar, and finally the automobile out the road to the suburbs; the buildings offer a cross-section of the rings of Louisville's growth.

Unlike many such thoroughfares, Bardstown Road never "died." Small stores and neighborhood shopping areas have passed from owner to owner and occupant to occupant. During the 1960s, the stretch through the Highlands became a center for Louisville's counterculture and artisans, with shops offering handmade goods and antiques. The 1970s and 1980s brought fine restaurants in old buildings, and night spots offering live entertainment from bluegrass to jazz to rock. Stores range from the simple to the elegant, and offer practically everything from high fashion to used clothing, from stained-glass windows to hardware, from fine furniture to "junque," and from fine wines to handmade ice cream. And there are still corner drugstores and a neighborhood movie house.

THE SUBURBS

Many of Jefferson County's incorporated suburbs weren't suburbs to begin with; they were self-sufficient communities far from the city. Jeffersontown, for example, was incorporated in 1797, far out the road to Taylorsville. Suburban sprawl from Louisville finally reached it in the 1970s, blending with Jeffersontown's own smaller suburban sprawl toward the city. The central business district in "J-Town" still has a friendly small-town feel, contrasting sharply with the bustling, high-tech atmosphere of nearby Bluegrass Industrial Park. Anchorage, incorporated in 1878 at a major railroad junction, and Middletown, a bit south along the road to Shelbyville, have also been surrounded by suburbs.

On the other hand, most of the smaller cities in Jefferson County were incorporated either to provide services for suburban developments far from the city, or to prevent Louisville from annexing them. Strathmoor Vil-

Fall comes to a tranquil country lane on the outskirts of Louisville. Photo by Christina M. Freitag

85

lage, Strathmoor Manor, Seneca Gardens, and Audubon Park were developed and incorporated before World War II, then were eventually surrounded by the growing city. Shively, at the south edge of Louisville, was incorporated in 1938 to keep the city from annexing several major distilleries. Older communities such as St. Matthews, and new subdivisions by the dozens, followed Shively's example after World War II.

Then there are the communities where the people are so independent they've never incorporated. Valley Station and Pleasure Ridge Park, along Dixie Highway southwest of Louisville, are two of the major ones. Glenview and Harrods Creek, northeast of the city, are two more. Fairdale, south of Louisville, even won a special state law declaring it an official "unincorporated urban place."

West Buechel is an incorporated community, but Buechel itself isn't. And Newburg residents voted to incorporate, then tried to disincorporate, and wound up in a long battle in the courts.

SOUTHERN INDIANA

Less than a mile of river separates Louisville from southern Indiana, but the psychological distance is greater. The Hoosier side has more of a small-town and rural atmosphere, enhanced by The Knobs (the low range of mountains Audubon described), with their rugged woodlands and small farms.

In some areas, the contrasts are striking. Tranquil, isolated bottomland farms lie in southern Indiana directly across the river from the industrial complex of southwestern Jefferson County; less than 10 minutes apart by boat, they're more than an hour apart by bridge and highway.

Nearer the bridges, however, small farms are less than 15 minutes away from downtown Louisville. Indiana and Kentucky city-dwellers flock to the pick-it-

yourself farms and orchards in the late summer and fall, carrying home fresh fruits and vegetables. A bit farther into the hills are farms where you can cut your own Christmas tree.

New Albany, once the largest city in Indiana, is still the largest city in southern Indiana. Its shipyards once produced some of the nation's fastest steamboats, including the *Robert E. Lee* and the *Eclipse*. The shipyards are long gone—but the mansions built by the steamboat captains and river barons still line Main Street, many of them restored.

Shotgun houses are found in New Albany, along with every style of house popular since before the Civil War. The feeling is a bit more spacious than in the older areas of Louisville. The downtown shopping area retains the two-, three-, and four-story brick business buildings that are so typical of a Hoosier county seat. Some of the finest views in the area can be enjoyed from the bluffs overlooking the city.

Jeffersonville, the second-largest city at the north side of The Falls, is another tranquil county-seat town with comfortable homes. Its riverfront looks directly across at Louisville's industrial riverfront. Since the Jeffersonville riverbank is far from the heavily-traveled commercial channel (which swings to the Louisville side), there's more room for pleasure boats and waterside recreation.

Below left: The bluffs above New Albany, Indiana, offer sweeping panoramic views of the Ohio River and the cities at the Falls of the Ohio. Photo by Ted Wathen/Quadrant

Below: Jeffersonville, Indiana, retains its small-town atmosphere. Photo by Ted Wathen/Quadrant

Chapter IV

A Blend of Cultures, A Love of Culture

A SPICY STEW

Louisville's culture is a lot like Louisville burgoo—that chunky, spicy, and somewhat indescribable stew that everyone eats at Kentucky Derby time. Every meat and vegetable you can imagine may go into the mix. And while it's cooked long enough to blend the flavors and aromas, individual flavors and textures still stand out—sometimes providing surprises with each spoonful.

The recipe for burgoo varies considerably from cook to cook. And people's view of Louisville culture varies considerably, depending on their backgrounds.

Southerners look at the office buildings, the factories, and the occasional snow, feel the somewhat quickened pace, listen to the accents, and usually conclude that Louisville is a northern city. Northerners and westerners look at the landscape, feel the moist summer heat, sense the relaxed pace, listen to the accents, and seem to know instinctively that it's a southern city.

And Kentuckians from outside the metropolitan area may declare that Louisville isn't *really* a part of Kentucky. It seems to them to be more like a special place, somewhere apart from the commonwealth.

A good example of the Louisville cultural burgoo is the variety of accents spoken in the city. Linguists have identified several distinct patterns.

One way of speaking goes back to Colonial Virginia: people say "tomahto" for tomato and "aboot" for about. It's a graceful, lilting southern accent, often with a touch of gentle refinement.

Another accent originally comes from the rural areas of Kentucky and states further south; linguists call it the "south midland" language. People may say "cain't" for can't and "mahl" for mile—and their speech may have a

Anyone can join in an ethnic dance at one of downtown Louisville's Heritage Weekend festivals. Photo by John Beckman/Quadrant

A BLEND OF CULTURES, A LOVE OF CULTURE

relaxed but very definite rhythm. It's a southern accent of a much different sort.

In business and professional circles, where newcomers are common and where Louisvillians have more contacts with people in other areas, the accents are less pronounced. Sometimes they seem vaguely southern; sometimes they seem as universal as the language of network television. Cadence is often the key to the speaker's origin: a rapid talker is almost definitely a newcomer to Louisville.

Customs also overlap, in sometimes subtle ways. The "grits line"—which divides those who serve grits with their breakfast eggs from those who don't—is somewhere to the south, near the Tennessee border. You can find a restaurant that serves grits in Louisville, but it may take some searching. Chili, however, isn't automatically served over spaghetti, the style of the North and East. In Louisville, you can order your chili "with" or "without," and if you forget to specify, your server may ask your preference.

Lifestyle cultures vary widely as well. For many people, Louisville means the Ohio River. They may live along its banks—in movable house trailers; in two-story houses with the main living quarters upstairs so that floods won't cause much damage; and sometimes in houses on stilts. The river is a year-round force in their

Facing page: Louisvillians flocked to a downtown street rally at the Kentucky Center for the Arts in 1987 to help attract the headquarters of the Presbyterian Church (U.S.A.) to Louisville. Photo by John Nation

Above left: Colorful, authentic costumes often highlight Louisville's ethnic festivals. This man is dressed in the style of the Ukraine. Photo by John Beckman/Quadrant

Above right: When the dancer's button says "Kiss Me, I'm Italian," there's no doubt about the focus of this Heritage Festival. Photo by John Beckman/Quadrant

lives. Others live on higher ground bordering the river, in homes ranging from modest cottages to mansions. The river is at hand, but poses less of a threat. And in every residential area bordering the river, docks line the banks from spring to fall—with everything from rowboats to yachts lining the docks.

Some people focus their lives on horses: Thoroughbreds, Arabians, quarter horses, and other breeds. They raise them on land ranging from two-acre plots to handsome estates. They get together with their friends and their horses for events ranging from ultra-formal dressage competitions to steeplechases to rodeos—and of course the Thoroughbred and trotting-horse races at the two major tracks.

The more universal lifestyles are scattered throughout Louisville's metropolitan area: rural regions with small farms and orchards; small towns; sprawling suburbs and suburban office complexes; city neighborhoods of all types; a somewhat scattered colony of artists, performers, and writers; and even a taste of big-city downtown. Central Louisville has penthouses and elegant apartments; the rugged hills near the city have secluded woodland cabins. The view from the penthouses nearly always includes the hills; the view from the cabins sometimes includes the skyscrapers.

There is ethnic diversity as well. Although census figures show that more than 98 percent of the residents were born in the United States, Louisvillians have a natural interest in ancestry and customs. Heritage festivals have spotlighted the food, costumes, dances, music, and crafts of many peoples, including Africans, Arabians, Asians, British, Caribbean islanders, Filipinos, French, Germans, Greeks, Hungarians, Indians, Irish, Italians, Jews, Latin Americans, and Ukrainians. The mixtures at some of these festivals can rival an entire year of *National Geographic.*

German influence is strong in a community where nearly 19 percent of the residents claim some ancestor from Deutschland. Large neighborhoods take pride in their German traditions. There are annual Strassenfests and Oktoberfests. German societies promote athletics, dancing, and song. Bratwurst is a favorite food. One "oom-pah" band, with a delightful play on words, calls itself the "Hot Brats."

United Kingdom ancestry, at nearly 18 percent, is second only to German. The English heritage is so pervasive that it's simply normal in Louisville. Shakespearean festivals and British-style equestrian events emphasize the tradition.

The Irish are a close third, at 16 percent, a figure that swells considerably during the St. Patrick's Day parade. Politics in Louisville often follows patterns that seem distinctively Irish.

While foreign-born residents are a small part of the population, Louisville welcomes people from around the globe. There are refugees from the world's troubled lands, including Iran, Southeast Asia, and Latin America.

A BLEND OF CULTURES, A LOVE OF CULTURE

There are Jewish immigrants from Russia, and recent arrivals from every continent except Antarctica.

And while most Louisville-area residents were born in America, more than one-fifth of them were born in other states. Once they settle in, the northerners become more southern, and the southerners become more northern.

One result of all this diversity is a wide range of opinions. Louisvillians hold strong beliefs, and they're not shy about expressing them. Intense debate may surround public and private issues, and factions form easily. In the short run, this makes decision-making seem complex and laborious. But in the long run, it assures that all viewpoints are heard and considered—and that the culture of Louisville remains spicy and varied.

THE PERFORMING ARTS

The performing arts, in their many forms, are some of Louisville's greatest assets. Few other metropolitan areas of less than a million people can boast an internationally respected regional theater, an equally respected symphony orchestra, professional opera and ballet companies, and a major performing-arts center. Few have their own high school devoted to the performing arts, with its own modern theater, and with a schedule of European tours. Few can support three public radio stations and two public television stations.

And none but Louisville can boast a combination like this: one of the world's largest annual bluegrass music festivals (on the downtown riverfront), one of the nation's best-known annual festivals of new plays (at Actors Theatre), and one of the world's largest annual awards in music composition (the University of Louisville's Grawemeyer Award).

Of course, there's also a lively variety of attractions for those just seeking an evening's entertainment—from sophisticated big-city cabaret acts to honky-tonk country-and-western saloon bands. A typical week finds live music played by country, blues, bluegrass, soul, jazz, rock, fusion, pop, big band, folk, and ethnic groups. There are frequent concerts by choral and classical groups as well.

The Kentucky Center for the Arts, opened in 1983, is the area's jewel-like showcase for live entertainment. With a traditional-style main hall seating more than 2,400, a semicircular theater seating 626, and an experimental "black box" theater seating 91 to 135, it can handle everything from grand opera to folk singers—and from film festivals to meetings. It is the setting for many of Louisville's performing-arts groups, and for a variety of visiting attractions from Broadway musicals and big-name performers to ethnic dancers and blues singers.

Producers, directors, agents, and critics from Europe started joining their counterparts from New York and California in the late 1970s for a new kind of pilgrimage—to a significant festival of new American plays at Actors Theatre in Louisville. The first festival, in 1976, was a sleeper. Only three critics viewed the two new productions. But one of the plays, D.L. Coburn's *The Gin Game*, went on to win the Pulitzer Prize. When Beth Henley's *Crimes of the Heart* also won the Pulitzer after premiering at Actors in 1978, the theatrical world took serious notice.

The festival is part of a wide-ranging and often experimental concept brought to the theater by Jon Jory, who became producing director in 1969. Under his lead-

Above: Actors Theatre of Louisville puts on year-round performances.

The Louisville Orchestra performs on the main stage at the Kentucky Center for the Arts. Photo by John Nation

ership, Actors became the first organization to win the "Triple Crown" of American theater: the Margo Jones Award, the James N. Vaughan Memorial Award for Exceptional Achievement, and a special Tony award for Distinguished Achievement in Theatre.

With its own building—including a semicircular, 637-seat main auditorium and a smaller theater seating 159—Actors can present small to large productions in settings that let the audience feel close to the action. Offerings range from light comedies and musicals to heavy tragedies, and from historic dramas to (of course) some of the newest plays in America.

The Louisville Orchestra, which celebrated its 50th anniversary in 1987, is known widely for its support of contemporary classical composers. Since 1950 it has been commissioning and performing new works—and making recordings of them available on its own label, First Edition Records.

But it is also known in Louisville as the symphonic orchestra that can make music fun—from its Superpops concerts to special programs for children and for the entire family. As it entered its second half-century, it inaugurated a series of summer outdoor concerts, then scheduled a 10-day music festival featuring 20 musicians, composers, and critics from throughout the world. While scheduling a full season of its own performances, the orchestra also provides musicians for Louisville's opera and ballet companies.

The Kentucky Opera, founded in 1952, is one of the nation's respected regional opera companies. Scheduling performances in three different theaters, it can present a variety of types of operas in settings that show them to best advantage.

Offerings have ranged from traditional grand operas, such as *Aida*, *The Barber of Seville*, and *Carmen*, through operettas like *The Merry Widow* and *The Mi-*

A BLEND OF CULTURES, A LOVE OF CULTURE

kado, to new works such as Philip Glass' *The Fall of the House of Usher*. Leading roles are filled by major singers from Louisville and elsewhere, and the chorus is a troupe of outstanding Louisville-area singers.

The Louisville Ballet burst into national prominence in 1978, when it became the first regional ballet company to attract Russian dancer Mikhail Baryshnikov as a guest soloist. Louisvillians who had seldom been to a ballet went to see the Russian artist—and discovered they liked ballet, even without him. The Louisville group, which had been a poor but dedicated semiprofessional company since 1952, found new audiences and new support.

Alun Jones, who became the company's artistic director in 1978 and was responsible for attracting Baryshnikov, is also credited with expanding the company's repertoire and its expertise. He has added ballets by many of the world's foremost choreographers and has

Above: The Louisville Ballet, a respected regional company, schedules a wide variety of performances. Photo by Christina M. Freitag

Above left: Members of the Kentucky Opera are seen in production. Courtesy, Kentucky Opera

premiered original ballets of his own.

Stage One: The Louisville Children's Theatre is one of the nation's few professional theaters for youngsters. With special productions for school groups and family audiences, and with a wide range of educational programs, it reaches over 100,000 people a year.

Shakespeare in Central Park has been producing free outdoor performances of Shakespeare for more

IN CELEBRATION OF LOUISVILLE

than 25 years. The group sponsored a special Shakespearean "Rap Contest" one summer to bring the Bard to a hip assortment of high school students.

The Iroquois Amphitheater Association, which produces Broadway musicals and all types of concerts at an outdoor amphitheater, opened in 1938.

The Louisville Theatrical Association was organized in 1938 to bring first-rate Broadway entertainment to Louisville. Attractions, usually scheduled into the Kentucky Center for the Arts, include Broadway musicals, and concerts and shows by major stars.

All of these organizations, and many more, are part of a major fund-raising effort called the Greater Louisville Fund for the Arts. The fund collects nearly $3 million a year from corporations, employees, and individual contributors. The money helps support a dozen major performing arts groups, two art galleries, and a host of smaller efforts in the performing and fine arts.

Louisville musical groups get additional exposure through FM stereo broadcasts over the three local public radio stations. The oldest, WFPL and WFPK, are owned and operated by the Louisville Free Public Library. WFPL

A BLEND OF CULTURES, A LOVE OF CULTURE

specializes in jazz and information, including National Public Radio and American Public Radio programs; WFPK specializes in classical music.

WFPL has played a key role in encouraging Louisville's jazz scene, which was practically moribund in the early 1970s. From a weekly jazz show in the mid-1970s, WFPL advanced in 1980 to five-hour shows five nights a week. By 1987 jazz programming had more than doubled, to more than 52 hours a week.

The station broadcasts live performances by local jazz and folk artists, and it played a major part in helping

Below left: The audience brings its own seating arrangements for outdoor performances of Shakespeare in Central Park. Photo by John Nation

Below: Theatergoers crowd the multi-story, multi-balcony lobby at the Kentucky Center for the Arts. Photo by John Nation

to organize the Louisville Jazz Society, which sponsors live performances. The station's daily "Jazz Calendar" lets listeners know where and when live jazz is being played.

Sister-station WFPK broadcasts live classical performances, including concerts by the Louisville Orchestra. And both stations broadcast interviews with visiting artists.

WUOL, owned and operated by the University of Louisville, got its start in 1976 when a commercial FM station abandoned its classical format and gave its library and equipment to the university. The station broadcasts classical music 24 hours a day—including live performances from the University of Louisville School of Music's recital hall.

THE VISUAL ARTS

While the performing arts have earned Louisville an international reputation, the other fine arts also play an important part in the city's culture. Sculpture graces the grounds of many public buildings, from the colleges and universities to the Kentucky Center for the Arts. Sculpture, paintings, drawings, and photographs enliven the halls and offices of businesses, and small galleries have been set up in the lobbies of banks and television stations. Four-year colleges and universities have fine-arts programs, with space to exhibit the work of their students and faculties.

The J.B. Speed Art Museum is the area's oldest and largest museum. Established in the late 1920s at the edge

of the University of Louisville campus, it has been expanded three times to offer a variety of settings for an even larger variety of works.

The Speed made local history in 1977 when it raised $1.5 million to buy and protect a single painting, Rembrandt's *Portrait of a Woman*. And it raised local eyebrows in 1983 when it bought sculptor John DeAndrea's life-size and lifelike sculpture of two clothed men and a nude woman lounging at a picnic, patterned after an Edouard Manet painting of 1863.

The museum also has works by masters including Rubens, Monet, Picasso, Brancusi, Henry Moore, and Leonardo da Vinci. It offers a schedule of special exhibits and special programs—and it has a gallery where visitors may rent or buy works by local and big-name artists.

The Water Tower Art Association schedules 10 major exhibitions each year, plus classes and workshops that include free art classes for children. Its exhibits feature works by local and regional artists, and its shop offers regional art and handicrafts for sale. The association makes its home in the Louisville Water Company's first pumping station—a neoclassic building completed in 1860 at the edge of the river.

The Louisville Art Gallery, located in the main downtown library, features contemporary art (including computer art), educational programs, workshops, and theme exhibits—many of them designed specifically for children. Its "Art and Special Needs" programs provide art experiences for children with hearing, sight, and other impairments.

The University of Louisville Photographic Archives

Facing page: The downtown Kentucky Center for the Arts is a mixture of angles and curves, clear glass and mirrors, steel and concrete. Photo by John Nation

Below: "Reclining Figure: Angles," by British artist Henry Moore, is one of many pieces of sculpture at the J.B. Speed Art Museum. Photo by John Nation

offers exhibits of historic and contemporary photographs, many drawn from its own vast collection. It also sells prints made from its collection of negatives.

In addition, several private galleries offer a wide variety of artworks for sale. The largest concentration is in a complex called "ArtsSpace," once the home of the Kentucky Industries for the Blind. Galleries there offer works ranging from contemporary to traditional, done by artists of the present and past.

SPIRITUAL LIFE

Religion plays a vital part in the cultural life of Louisville. The National Council of Churches' 1980 nationwide report on church membership (the latest available) shows that nearly 60 percent of the residents of the Louisville

Facing page: Classic statues look down from the balustrade at the historic Water Tower, completed in 1860. Photo by John Beckman/Quadrant

Above: The J.B. Speed Memorial Museum is Louisville's oldest and largest museum of art. Photo by R. Hower/Quadrant

A BLEND OF CULTURES, A LOVE OF CULTURE

area are adherents of a religion. That's considerably more than the national average of about 50 percent, as well as Kentucky's average of 54 percent and Indiana's average of 45 percent.

The institutions tell more of the story: the new national headquarters of the Presbyterian Church (U.S.A.), the Southern Baptist and Presbyterian seminaries, the two Catholic colleges, and the large Catholic school system. But there's more to the story than that. Louisville is also one of the nation's leaders in religious tolerance and cooperation.

The Kentuckiana Interfaith Community became one of the first ecumenical groups in the nation to include Jews when it welcomed Louisville's Jewish congregations in 1979. Among its many cooperative programs is the Faith Channel, which opened on Louisville's cable-television system in 1987. The channel offers a full-time schedule of religious programs—from the Catholic and Southern Baptist satellite networks and from Jewish and Protestant sources.

Louisville is also known for its network of community ministries, one of the most extensive in the country. Churches in individual neighborhoods band together to share their facilities and offer services for all the neighborhood's residents. Programs can include day care, counseling, employment services, youth activities, food closets, social events, handicraft classes—practically anything that might help people, spiritually and socially. Almost every part of the metropolitan area is served by one of these community ministries. The movement is so strong that in 1983 Louisville hosted the first national conference on neighborhood ministries.

Religion was a part of Louisville's cultural life from the beginning. The first settlers scheduled services in their homes; later they got together in meetinghouses. The first church was erected by Methodists in 1809; the first Catholic church was built two years later.

The Catholic Archdiocese of Louisville is the ancestral home of most of the nation's Catholic churches. In 1808, the church subdivided the new nation into four dioceses, headquartered in New York, Philadelphia, Boston, and Bardstown, Kentucky. The Bardstown diocese served everyone west of the Appalachian Mountains. In 1841, its headquarters was moved to Louisville. As the

Far left: The Marcus Lindsey Methodist Church is one of several neighborhood churches in Butchertown. Photo by C.J. Elfont

Left: Stained glass windows grace Old Louisville's Walnut Street Baptist Church, which has one of the largest Southern Baptist congregations in the city. It moved to St. Catherine Street many years ago, but kept its old name. Photo by C.J. Elfont

years passed, the diocese was subdivided again and again, and now serves central Kentucky.

The Catholic church in Louisville was swelled rapidly during the early nineteenth century by refugees from the French Revolution, revolutions in Germany, and famine in Ireland. Ethnic parishes thrived, with services conducted in French, German, and Irish as well as English and Latin.

The vast immigration of "foreigners" caused increasing social and political tension in Louisville. The community reached its peak of intolerance with the "Bloody Monday" riots of 1855, aimed primarily at the Catholic immigrants. The calm response of Catholic Bishop Martin John Spalding helped the major religious leaders of the city to start building a spirit of tolerance that would distinguish Louisville a century later.

Today the Catholic church is the largest denomination in the Louisville area, with over one-third of the church members and about 22 percent of the total population (compared with 21 percent of the national population).

Southern Baptists, the nation's second-largest denomination in 1980, were also the second largest in the Louisville area, with about 16 percent of the local population. Formed in Augusta, Georgia, in 1845, the Southern Baptist Convention was a result of the great religious revivals of the early nineteenth century, plus the tensions between the North and the South. Northerners are often surprised to learn that one-third of the original 300,000 members were slaves.

The convention became a focus of religious struggle during the 1980s, as fundamentalists challenged the denomination's moderate element and demanded a return to a strict, literal interpretation of the Bible. Louisville's Southern Baptist Theological Seminary also came under attack from fundamentalists and responded by trying to mediate the differences between the two factions. Some Southern Baptists said the struggle might split the denomination; others said it would strengthen it spiritually. The ultimate impact on both the denomination and the seminary wasn't expected to be known until the early 1990s.

While the 1980s were a time of religious ferment for the Southern Baptists, they were a time of final healing for the nation's two largest Presbyterian denominations. The two had split when the Civil War began; they joined forces again in 1983, forming the Presbyterian Church (U.S.A.).

The split churches had been headquartered in New York and Atlanta; the combined church looked for a new

A BLEND OF CULTURES, A LOVE OF CULTURE

site without strong ties to the past. Louisville was the home of the only seminary recognized by both of the old churches, and Louisville-area Presbyterians were divided almost equally between them. After much debate, the combined church decided to establish its new headquarters in Louisville.

While the Catholics, Southern Baptists, Methodists, and Presbyterians are the largest denominations in Louisville, there is a great deal of diversity. The National Council of Churches listed 40 different active denominations, and there are others not included in the list.

Facing page: Students pause to talk on the spacious grounds of the Southern Baptist Theological Seminary. Photo by C.J. Elfont

Below: The old Gardercourt Mansion near Cherokee Park passed first to the University of Louisville, and then to the Presbyterian Seminary. Photo by Christina M. Freitag

THE LOVE OF HISTORY

Louisville's love of history is obvious to anyone who tours the area. The many neighborhoods of restored homes, churches, schools, and business buildings, where people go about their daily lives, is evidence enough. And historic markers seem almost as common as bus stops.

The *Belle of Louisville*, a steamboat built in 1914, is the area's most beloved historic attraction. She was bought by Jefferson County in 1962 after leading a succession of lives (river packet, ferryboat, towboat, and excursion boat) under other names (the *Idlewild* until 1948; then the *Avalon* until 1962).

The dilapidated, much-abused stern-wheeler was rebuilt to become the city and county's link with the river's glory days, and it is included in the National Register of Historic Landmarks. From Memorial Day through Labor Day, it offers excursions from Louisville's wharf each day except Monday. The *Belle* is available for charter cruises as well, and is the local favorite each year in the Great Steamboat Race at Kentucky Derby time.

The Kentucky Railway Museum's Locomotive 152, a thoroughbred of a steam passenger locomotive built for the Louisville and Nashville in 1904, is the area's other historic vehicle on the National Register. After a small group of volunteers worked 13 years to restore her, the locomotive started pulling excursion trains in 1985. The excursions have ranged throughout Kentucky and into nearby states.

For those with a deeper thirst for history, there are

many more attractions. Old homes of several eras have been restored, refurnished, and opened to the public. Many of them offer special programs on life of the past.

The Brennan House in downtown Louisville is an Italianate townhouse built in the 1860s, then occupied by the Brennan family for 90 years. The furnishings, mainly Brennan family heirlooms, show the home life of a wealthy family of the Victorian era.

Farmington is a country mansion built between 1808 and 1810, inspired by a design by Thomas Jefferson. Originally the focus of a 1,500-acre estate owned by the Speed family, the mansion now sits on 18 acres surrounded by city and suburbs. The furnishings depict life on a country estate before the Civil War; the grounds include an elaborate early-nineteenth-century garden, a

Above: The Belle of Louisville *sets her paddlewheel in reverse, and backs away from the wharf in a cloud of lighted steam. Photo by R. Hower/Quadrant*

Facing page, top: Trees shade the front of the Brennan House. Photo by C.J. Elfont

Facing page, bottom: The historic Brennan House in downtown Louisville preserves the surroundings of a wealthy Victorian family. It is open to the public for tours. Photo by C.J. Elfont

A BLEND OF CULTURES, A LOVE OF CULTURE

working blacksmith shop, and a reconstructed stone and timber barn.

Locust Grove, the last home of Louisville founder George Rogers Clark, features a Georgian-style plantation mansion begun about 1790 by Clark's brother-in-law, Major William Croghan. Meticulously restored, it is furnished in the style of the early nineteenth century. The grounds, now 55 of the original 693 acres, include a large formal garden, featuring flowering shrubs and trees known in Kentucky before 1818.

The Thomas Edison House in Louisville's Butchertown is a modest cottage where Edison rented a room in 1867 while he worked as a telegraph operator nearby. His room is furnished as it would have been when he lived there, and exhibits include many Edison inventions.

The Culbertson Mansion in New Albany was built in 1869 in the French Second Empire style, and it is typical of the grand homes of the steamboat age. An Indiana state memorial, it has been restored and furnished in the style of its era.

The Scribner House, in downtown New Albany, was built in 1814 by the city's founder, Joel Scribner. Restored in 1932, it includes many original furnishings and family portraits.

Facing page: Wool, spinning wheels, yarn and a loom – the basic ingredients and tools for pioneer cloth – are on display at historic Locust Grove. Photo by Mark E. Gibson

Above: The grounds of historic Locust Grove offer much the same view as they did when George Rogers Clark spent his last days there. Photo by C.J. Elfont

Several museums in the Louisville area concentrate heavily on history. The Louisville Museum of History and Science is centered in an iron-front commercial building, started on Main Street in 1878. The museum occupied the building a century later, after a renovation project that won several national and state architectural awards. Exhibits range from prehistoric to space age, with items ranging from fossils to an Egyptian mummy to an Explorer space capsule. Programs include classes and field trips designed for all ages, including tours of the nearby Falls of the Ohio.

The Portland Museum, in the community that grew up at the foot of The Falls, features exhibits and educational programs focused on the era when settlers first

IN CELEBRATION OF LOUISVILLE

arrived. It is located in a large house built in the early 1850s by John Graham, a poor Irish immigrant who became a wealthy Portland businessman.

The Howard Steamboat Museum in Jeffersonville is a Victorian mansion built in the early 1890s for Edmonds J. Howard, son of the founder of the Howard Shipyards. The Howard family operated the shipyards from 1834 to 1931, and the mansion became the family home for three generations. The house features many of the family's original furnishings, dating from 1893 through 1957. It also boasts a large collection of steamboat fittings, artifacts, models, photos, and drawings.

The Kentucky Railway Museum, along the L&N main line to Cincinnati and Lexington, has a good-sized collection of historic railroad equipment. It offers short train rides on summer weekends, in addition to the long steam excursions mentioned earlier. The Floyd County Museum in New Albany features a series of miniature animated dioramas based on life in Indiana in the nineteenth century.

A BLEND OF CULTURES, A LOVE OF CULTURE

HISTORICAL RESEARCH

Several of Louisville's historic organizations are widely recognized as resources for research. While their focus is on scholarship, they also have exhibits open to the public.

The Filson Club is named for John E. Filson, who published the first history of Kentucky in 1784. Organized more than a century ago, the club is a private society with a museum and an extensive library of books

Facing page: An antique violin and music score lie on the antique piano in the music room at Locust Grove. Photo by John Nation

Below: Luscious greenery characterize the grounds at Locust Grove. Photo by Marie E. Gibson

and old documents. Located in a historic mansion south of downtown Louisville, it is a valuable resource for authors and people researching their ancestry.

The University of Louisville Archives has many collections of historic documents, including a large amount of material from the headquarters of the old Louisville & Nashville Railroad. The university's separate Photographic Archives has a collection of more than a million photos, including the Roy Stryker collection of documentary photos covering American life in the 1930s and 1940s.

The Sons of the American Revolution has a special collection of information and materials concerning the Revolutionary War. The group has a museum and library in its national headquarters in Louisville.

THE SPIRIT OF GIVING

Many of Louisville's cultural assets wouldn't be possible without a basic trait of the Louisville character: a spirit of giving to make the community better. It's a trait shared by all levels of society, from the church groups that stage bazaars to help clothe the poor to the people who stage an elegant steeplechase to help the opera.

Much of the money comes from Louisville's leaders and their corporations. It's evident in the titles of many performing-arts events: the Humana Festival of New American Plays, the Yellowstone Superpops Concerts,

A BLEND OF CULTURES, A LOVE OF CULTURE

the Cumberland Coffee Concerts, and the Bingham Endowed Series at the Kentucky Center for the Arts. Practically every major production has a major corporate sponsor; some have several.

One of the strongest supporters of this philosophy, Barry Bingham, Sr., headed the media conglomerate that included The Courier-Journal and Louisville Times, WHAS radio and TV, and Standard Gravure Corporation. A strong believer in community service, Bingham set up a foundation in 1951 to contribute five percent of his companies' pre-tax profits to charitable, educational, and cultural organizations. In the 1980s, grants ranged from $700,000 to $1 million a year.

The foundation was dissolved in 1986, after the companies were sold. Bingham and his wife set up the Mary and Barry Bingham Sr. Fund—and awarded more than $18 million to more than 75 recipients during its first year. More than 90 percent of the grants went for projects and organizations in Kentucky and southern Indiana. "That's where the money from the companies was made," Bingham told *Courier-Journal* writer Glenn

Below left: The Floyd County Museum in New Albany was once a Carnegie Library, built in 1902. Photo by C.J. Elfont

Below: Seen here is the Scribner House in New Albany. Photo by C.J. Elfont

IN CELEBRATION OF LOUISVILLE

Rutherford. "That's where we wanted it to stay." Many of the projects, he said, had been on the couple's minds for years, and they hoped to see some of them come to pass during their lifetimes.

While many business leaders are very generous, individual contributions are just as important. Employee campaigns help raise money from individuals, and some businesses encourage the effort by matching employees' contributions.

The Fund for the Arts raises as much money from individual, professional, and employee contributions as it does from corporations. Established in 1949, it was the nation's first major local fund-raising organization for arts groups. Annual contributions increased from $700,000 in 1977 to $2.7 million in 1987, for the nation's second highest per capita contribution to a fund of its type.

The six-county Metro United Way provides money for more than 80 agencies in the Louisville area; together, they provide services for nearly one out of every three residents. The fund raised more than $13 million in 1987—more than twice the $5.5 million of a decade earlier. More than two-thirds of the money comes from individuals, through payroll deductions and individual contributions. Another fourth comes from corporations.

One of the area's strongest grass-roots campaigns is

the annual WHAS Crusade for Children, climaxed since the early 1950s by a telethon at the WHAS-TV studios. For several days before the telethon, uniformed volunteer fire fighters go door-to-door collecting contributions, and set up "road blocks" at major intersections to gather donations. On the day of the telethon, a parade of fire trucks arrives at the studios, sirens wailing and red lights flashing. The fire fighters, carrying the donations in firemen's boots and money sacks, dump the cash into a large box on stage. The crusade raises more than $2 million annually, and distributes the money among about 150 children's programs in Kentucky and southern Indiana.

Above: Residents of Louisville rallied on Main Street, in front of the Kentucky Center for the Arts, to attract the national headquarters of the Presbyterian Church (U.S.A.). Photo by Christina M. Freitag

Facing page: Louisville Cathedral of Assumption's lofty steeple rises into the sky. Photo by C.J. Elfont

115

Chapter V

A Tradition of Learning

THE LOW-KEY RESOURCE

When September comes to Louisville—when the mugginess of summer begins to fade and the flowers begin their last burst of bloom—more than one person out of four celebrates the season by going back to school. They include traditional students, from the nursery schoolers lining up for recess to the college students lining up to buy textbooks. They include the "non-traditional" students who've become almost traditional in recent years, from the office and factory workers taking courses to advance themselves to the midlife people studying for new careers. And they include a healthy smattering of surprises, like the retired newspaper editor who returned to college to earn his long-delayed bachelor's degree.

Thousands more don't show up on official enrollment figures. They're the people who take noncredit courses at high schools and colleges for fun and satisfaction—courses ranging from brass rubbing and wildflower identification to steamboat history and will-writing.

Education, it seems, is one of Louisville's low-profile assets. The variety is impressive; the quality is often excellent; but the reputation isn't widespread. Jefferson County's public school system is one of the 20 largest in the nation; the average achievement test scores in most subjects are above national averages. Private schools include a large Catholic system and several respected independent schools. Vocational and business schools offer training in practically every field imaginable. Colleges and universities offer outstanding programs in medicine, engineering, theology, business, and many other disciplines; one of the theological seminaries is among the world's three largest. And the area's seven major colleges and universities have joined in a coopera-

Students swarm the walks among the modern classroom buildings during a homecoming rally at the University of Louisville. Photo by C.J. Elfont

117

tive effort to make the resources of all of them available to the full-time students at any of them.

These are the types of assets that win friends, influence society, and launch careers—but not necessarily the type that attract national notice.

If educational progress made headlines, however, there could be a series of interesting stories about developments in Louisville.

First, there has been a tremendous increase over the past generation in higher education choices, both in quantity and quality. In the early 1960s, the Louisville area had one relatively small municipal university, a smattering of small colleges and community colleges, and a large seminary and a small one. Today there is a major urban university; a branch of a state university; the largest private college in Kentucky; and a large two-campus junior college. The large seminary has become one of the largest in the world; the smaller seminary has expanded.

The Jefferson County public school system made steady progress from the late 1970s to the mid-1980s. Average achievement-test scores improved from mostly below national averages to mostly above. The dropout rate was reduced 40 percent; disciplinary suspensions were reduced nearly three-fourths. Special programs are available for gifted and talented students; for students who want to pursue careers in the arts, the crafts, the trades, and business; and for students whose parents favor traditional discipline in education, and those whose parents prefer an open, lightly structured and innovative program.

There has been a great increase in educational opportunities for blacks. In mid-1987, the Courier-Journal and Times Company's Bluegrass State Poll showed that 65 percent of the black residents, and 81 percent of the whites, believed that blacks no longer faced discrimination in getting a quality education. And a University of Chicago study based on enrollment figures in the mid-1980s showed that Kentucky's public schools were among the most integrated in the nation—second only to Delaware's.

Kentuckiana Metroversity is an association of the seven major colleges, universities, and seminaries in the Louisville area. Qualified students at any Metroversity institution may take one course per semester at any other institution, greatly expanding their choices. Students may also use the libraries at any of the seven institutions, greatly expanding their resources. And the Metroversity cable television channel offers a range of educational programs, including correspondence courses for college credit.

PUBLIC EDUCATION

After the decade of trauma and turmoil in the 1970s, public education made a strong comeback in Louisville in the 1980s. The Jefferson County Public Schools improved their test scores, increased their offerings, reduced their reliance on desegregation busing, and reversed their enrollment decline. The University of Louisville learned to cope with a dramatically increased enrollment, launched a major campaign to improve programs and library resources, and watched some of its professors and programs gain national recognition for excellence and innovation. And University of Louisville graduate Sherleen Sisney, a teacher at Jefferson County's

A TRADITION OF LEARNING

Ballard High School, was named the national teacher of the year in 1984.

Much of Louisville's progress in public education in the 1980s can be credited to "the two Dons"—Donald W. Ingwerson, superintendent of the Jefferson County Public Schools, and Donald C. Swain, president of the University of Louisville. Both came to Louisville from California in 1981; both took over institutions left in disarray by the problems of the 1970s.

The similarities between the two are striking: tall,

Facing page: Another day, another trek to school. Photo by John Nation

Below: These inquisitive minds make use of their classroom computer. Photo by John Nation

IN CELEBRATION OF LOUISVILLE

somewhat slim, affable, quietly competent—and able to inspire confidence, resolve conflicts, and build teamwork. Both came from respected institutions; both concentrated on building community support as well as improving the quality of education. And by the mid-1980s, both had persuaded Louisville businesses to contribute substantial amounts of money for innovative programs.

Businesses and matching grants generated over $5 million, for instance, to help pay for 32-station computer labs in each of the Jefferson County school system's elementary and middle schools. Businesses contribute hundreds of thousands of dollars each year to support other public school programs.

And when Swain launched a $40-million "Quest for Excellence" campaign to improve the University of Louisville's libraries, faculty, and programs, and to attract outstanding students, business contributions helped boost the total to $49 million.

The challenges the two Dons faced, like many challenges in Louisville, were rooted in conflicting traditions. Their advantage as "outsiders" was their lack of identity with factions of the past; their advantage as leaders was their ability to win support from almost every faction.

TRAUMA AND PROGRESS

Louisville's major educational trauma came in 1975, when the federal courts ordered the public school system to desegregate. It was a sweeping order, setting specific standards for the proportions of black and white students in each school. And the school system, which had undergone a painful merger only a few months before, was given less than three months to put a desegregation plan into action. The court order was the result of a complex and sometimes bitter struggle that had been evolving for decades.

Louisville's first school opened in 1782, when the little village was still a cluster of cabins and dirt streets. Parents had to pay tuition; most children went without formal schooling. The first free public school opened in 1829, for all white children between the ages of 6 and 14. One-fourth of Louisville's population was black, but more than 90 percent of them were slaves. Education for black children would develop more slowly.

As the proportion of free blacks increased, the demand for education for black children grew. Louisville's first school for "colored people" opened in 1841—a private school with five pupils and one teacher. Blacks were still excluded from public schools. Finally, in 1870, a committee of black leaders tallied the amount of

A TRADITION OF LEARNING

school taxes that black citizens were paying and convinced the city to establish public schools for black children. The new Central Colored School opened for classes in 1873, the first building in Kentucky to be built with public funds for educating black children.

Louisville, like other cities in the North as well as the South, formed a segregated public school system that would endure for generations. Kentucky law formalized the situation in 1904 by forbidding blacks and whites to go to school together. The law was repealed in 1950, and Louisville's colleges and universities desegregated almost immediately. In the public schools, however, desegregation came more slowly.

In 1954 the U.S. Supreme Court ruled that racial segregation in public schools was unconstitutional. In 1956 Louisville's public school system became one of the largest to desegregate peacefully and one of the first to desegregate voluntarily. School attendance zones were redrawn without regard to race, and voluntary transfers were allowed as long as the schools could handle them.

Facing page: University of Louisville students take time out to study. Photo by John Nation

Below: High school dancers go through their exercises at the Youth Performing Arts School. Photo by Ted Wathen/Quadrant

121

Louisville's 45,000 students, 27 percent of them black, were free to attend the schools of their choice. Tradition still had its place, however: transfers were requested by 45 percent of the blacks assigned to formerly white schools, and 85 percent of the whites assigned to formerly black schools.

(The "open enrollment" plan had an interesting side effect: many high school coaches emulated their college counterparts and recruited promising young athletes from throughout the city. High school athletics reached a new level of competition in the Louisville area.)

Jefferson County's separate public school system also officially desegregated in 1956, but without much fanfare. Of the 33,000 students, only 3 percent were black.

The social changes of the next two decades brought tremendous pressures to the two school systems. While the population of Louisville peaked and started to decline, the population tripled in Jefferson County outside the city. The city school system saw its tax base erode as many affluent families moved to the suburbs. The county school system had to schedule double sessions and build dozens of new schools to meet the demand.

While the city and county public schools were officially desegregated in 1956, they were still called "racially identifiable" at the end of the 1960s. Nearly all of them were mostly black or mostly white, reflecting the composition of their surrounding neighborhoods; hardly any of them reflected the proportionate mix of races in the community at large. Civil-rights activists filed desegregation suits against both school systems in the early 1970s.

The city school system, increasingly hard-pressed financially, merged with the county system in early 1975, while the suits were still pending. The federal desegregation order came less than three months later.

Because of the housing patterns in the community, thousands of children had to ride buses to schools outside their neighborhoods. In addition, hundreds of teachers had to be transferred to different schools to balance the teaching staffs.

Demonstrations erupted shortly after the desegregation order was issued and continued for months. Almost all of them involved whites who opposed what they called "forced busing." Some of the demonstrations turned into riots. National Guard troops and federal marshals joined local and state police to guard the children, schools, and buses.

Thousands of white parents withdrew their children from public schools; enrollment dropped about 10,000 — or nearly 8 percent — from the previous year. New private schools were organized to serve many of the children. Roman Catholic Archbishop Thomas J. McDonough declared that the Catholic schools would not become a haven from busing, and parochial school

Above: A young oboe player concentrates on his music at the Youth Performing Arts School. Photo by Ted Wathen/Quadrant

Facing page: Students stroll the broad walkway that passes through the Life Sciences Building at the University of Louisville. Photo by John Beckman/Quadrant

enrollment increased only slightly. (Desegregation opponents boycotted the archdiocesan development fund that year).

Desegregation was only one of the challenges facing the newly-merged public school system. The former city and county schools had different organizational structures, different pay scales and personnel policies, and vastly different educational programs. Population in Jefferson County had reached its peak. The post-World War II baby boom had ended, and the number of school-age children leveled off and began to decline. Many school buildings were old and expensive to maintain. Mergers allowed the school system to consolidate attendance districts and close some schools. Thirteen schools were closed as desegregation began.

Problems continued through the rest of the 1970s. Teachers became so frustrated that they went on strike for two weeks in December 1978. Between 1976 and 1980 nearly 30 more schools were closed. While some of the closed schools reopened for special programs, about two dozen were closed permanently, and many were sold. Public opinion polls showed a low opinion of the quality of education.

The healing process began in the fall of 1981, when Ingwerson became the new superintendent. He built on the school system's strengths, which included innovative programs that began before the mergers. And he started new programs tailored to the community's needs.

One policy, which began before Ingwerson's arrival and has been expanded greatly since then, has had sev-

eral important effects. "Magnet programs," designed to attract students, are being offered in selected schools serving every grade. These programs have increased student choices, improved the quality of education, and reduced the need for desegregation busing.

Shifting housing patterns have also helped reduce the need for desegregation busing. One result: all middle and high schools are now exempt from busing; only a few were exempt when desegregation began. Another result: black students face about seven years of desegregation busing today; when the program began, they faced an average of eight or nine years of busing.

As the last half of the 1980s began, the school system's enrollment started to climb. Part of the increase came as the number of private schools dwindled; part appeared to be caused by an increase in the number of school-age children.

Today's school system offers many special features.

The nation's first comprehensive computer education program for children in kindergarten through grade 12 was established in Louisville.

Every elementary and middle school has a computer lab, and high schools have computers for specific subjects. Students use computers to practice skills in spelling, math, and writing, and they use a special computer language to solve problems. Some schools have shown dramatic improvements in achievement-test scores since the program began.

The Advance Program offers special classes for gifted students (those in the top 3 percent academically), and there is an Honors Program for college-bound students in middle and high schools.

Louisville's Youth Performing Arts School, of the type made famous in *Fame*, offers special programs in acting, dance, instrumental music, theater techniques, and voice. Student performers have appeared in several states and started scheduling European tours in 1987.

High school magnet programs have been developed in business management, communications and media arts, computer technology, legal and government services, mathematics, medicine, science and technology, and visual arts. In addition, there is a middle-school magnet program emphasizing math, science, and technology.

An "open environment" program at the J. Graham Brown School provides opportunities for students of all grade levels to mix and learn in a relatively unstructured atmosphere. At the other end of the spectrum, traditional schools emphasize strict dress and discipline codes, intensive homework, academic achievement, and active involvement by parents.

An international studies program at Atherton High School emphasizes foreign languages and courses on the culture, government, and politics of other nations. It includes a program sanctioned by the International Baccalaureate Organization in Geneva, Switzerland.

Vocational education programs, in regular high

schools and at special vocational centers, cover practically all the skilled trades and specialized service occupations. And students can take part in a cooperative work program to build job skills.

The Jefferson County High School offers course schedules that are convenient for students who work. The school, designed to serve dropouts and potential dropouts of all ages, offers traditional courses and grants a high school diploma.

AN URBAN UNIVERSITY

The seal of the University of Louisville (U of L) bears the profile of Minerva, the Roman goddess of wisdom, invention, the arts, and martial prowess, and the date 1798, which marks the beginning of a dream. The dream, a great institution of higher education, was an ambitious one for a pioneer town of less than 400 people. It was a

Students amble between classes at the University of Louisville. Photo by John Beckman/Quadrant

dream that wouldn't even begin to come true until more than a century had passed.

By the late 1980s, U of L had become one of the nation's major urban universities. Its main campus, medical center, and several branch centers served more than 20,000 students—offering them a choice of three dozen undergraduate, graduate, and professional degrees and certificates in more than 100 fields of study. U of L graduates included more than two-fifths of Kentucky's physicians, four-fifths of its dentists, one-third of its lawyers, and nearly one-half of its engineers.

The National Commission on Educational Excellence has listed U of L's teacher education program as one of nine notable programs in the country. Medical school faculty members have been in the forefront of several experimental programs, including infant heart transplants. The business school was nationally recognized for its use of microcomputers. The Speed Scientific School, with a new $5-million center, was focusing on research and training in computer-aided engineering and factory automation.

Business support was helping turn the university into one of Kentucky's major research centers.

The School of Music contributed substantially to the success of the Louisville Orchestra, Ballet, and Kentucky Opera. The Grawemeyer Awards for music composition, education, and "improving world order," each worth $150,000, had earned international recognition.

The debate team had been to the national finals six out of eight years, and won the national championship in 1982. And the success of U of L's basketball team—NCAA national champions in 1980 and 1986—had

IN CELEBRATION OF LOUISVILLE

helped make the athletic program completely self-supporting. It was a far cry from the underfinanced and often under-respected municipal university of the early 1960s.

From the very beginning, U of L had grown slowly and erratically. While the Kentucky general assembly chartered a city seminary in 1798—the year on the U of L seal—the school didn't open for classes until 15 years later. Called the Jefferson Seminary, its courses were mostly at the high school level. After a 16-year struggle, it closed in 1829.

Nine years later, the city tried again—establishing the Louisville Medical Institute and the Louisville Collegiate Institute. The medical school thrived and would become the keystone of the university's later development. But the collegiate school closed after only six years.

In 1846 the University of Louisville was chartered. It took over the Louisville Medical Institute, established a law school, and tried to establish an academic department to replace the old collegiate institute. The medical and law schools were solid successes, but the academic department merely existed on paper for the next 60 years.

The late nineteenth century brought a boom in medical education to Louisville, and by 1900 the city had seven medical schools. Standards were lax, however, and there was increasing concern with quality of medical education throughout the country. A national reform movement soon brought new, tougher standards. In an effort to meet them, U of L absorbed most of its local competitors in 1907—and reestablished its academic unit, partly to provide good undergraduate training for future medical students. A few years later, city government began making annual appropriations for the university.

City support helped the university grow over the next four decades. The graduate school, dental school, scientific and engineering school, music school, and school of social work were established, one by one. The separate Louisville Municipal College for blacks was opened in 1931; it was absorbed into the university when Louisville's colleges desegregated 20 years later.

But progress was not assured. The voters' defeat of a $1-million bond issue in 1920 delayed hopes for a new campus for five years. The city paid a large part of the U of L's operating expenses during the 1910s and 1920s, but city support dwindled during the Depression and after World War II. Tuition rates climbed.

Over the years, U of L played a dual role as a private and municipal university. In the nineteenth century it was mainly a private institution, paying its own way from tuition and fees. In the twentieth century it became a semipublic institution, with its own endowment and administration but with appropriations from the city. The defeat of an important bond issue in 1960 and the city's dwindling appropriations dictated a new direction. After a decade of debate and political compromise, U of L joined the state higher education system in 1970.

The new status brought tremendous growth. Tuition rates dropped dramatically in the first few years to match the levels at other state schools. State money built a series of major new buildings, transforming the main campus and the Health Sciences Center. Enrollment doubled during the 1970s; U of L became one of the nation's fastest-growing universities.

But with the growth came growing pains. U of L had to compete with long-established state institutions for money and programs, and the competition became severe. One complicating factor was the establishment of a University of Kentucky junior college in Louisville just two years before U of L joined the state system.

The state Council on Higher Education—which oversees all state colleges and universities—decided that U of L should offer only selected Ph.D. programs, and several degree programs were dropped. The state also adopted an "open admissions" policy, admitting anyone with a high-school diploma; U of L had to establish remedial programs for students who weren't well prepared for college-level work.

Facing page: Hot air balloons rise behind the administration building at the University of Louisville. Photo by C.J. Elfont

Left: Students use the latest optical and electronic equipment to study small blood vessels in the University of Louisville Health Sciences Center physiology department. The department has been designated as Kentucky's Center of Excellence in applied microcirculatory research. Photo by C.J. Elfont

IN CELEBRATION OF LOUISVILLE

In 1977 the Council on Higher Education defined U of L's role in the state system, declaring it a "major university" which "shall meet the educational, research, and service needs of its metropolitan area" with a broad range of bachelor's and master's degree programs. In addition, the council decided that U of L would share a "statewide mission in medicine, dentistry, law, and urban affairs" with the University of Kentucky. And the council gave U of L permission to develop doctoral programs that were relevant to its urban mission and didn't unnecessarily duplicate degrees offered by other state institutions.

The directions of U of L's "urban mission" soon became clear. The school of business, established in 1953, expanded and moved into its own new building. The school of education, established in 1968, moved into its own new building and formed many cooperative and experimental programs with the public school system. The division of allied health and the school of nursing were established in the late 1970s, helping expand the university's health education programs. And the new college of urban and public affairs opened in 1983, combining the schools of social work and justice administration with the urban studies center and establishing a new school of urban planning and development.

The late 1980s brought a new phenomenon to the U of L—overcrowded dormitories and a long waiting list for student housing. This was a significant development for a university with a tradition of being a "commuter school," where more than three-fourths of the students live in the immediate area and more than two-fifths attend school part-time. President Swain called the development "a very nice problem" that indicated the university's increasing attraction for students outside the Louisville area. It also helped emphasize the need for his proposed new dormitory.

JEFFERSON COMMUNITY COLLEGE

Jefferson Community College (JCC) is the Louisville area's largest two-year college—and, with 7,750 students, its second-largest college of any kind. An outgrowth of the student population boom of the 1960s, JCC is one of 14 community colleges established as part of the University of Kentucky system. Opened in 1967, it brought state-supported higher education to Louisville while U of L was still a semiprivate municipal university.

With its low tuition rates, career-oriented courses, and classes scheduled for the convenience of working students, JCC expanded rapidly at its downtown campus. In 1980 a second campus was opened: a new, five-building complex in southwestern Jefferson County.

Fully accredited, JCC offers two-year associate degrees, with more than 50 majors in arts and sciences and nearly 20 career program majors in the applied sciences. Many graduates go on to earn four-year degrees at other colleges.

INDIANA UNIVERSITY SOUTHEAST

Indiana University Southeast (IUS) is the Hoosier state's major public institution for higher education in the Louisville area. One of eight campuses in the Indiana University system, it offers two-year, four-year, and master's degree programs. With more than 4,800 students, it is the Louisville area's third-largest college, and the largest educational institution in southeastern Indiana.

IUS began in 1941 as an extension center, offering nighttime courses in public schools and government buildings. Enrollment boomed during World War II, as

A TRADITION OF LEARNING

gasoline rationing made it impractical for part-time students to drive to Indiana's established colleges. The boom continued after the war; the center moved into its own building in 1945, established a full schedule of daytime classes in 1950, and began offering four-year degrees in the mid-1960s. It moved to its spacious campus north of New Albany in 1973. By the late 1980s, IUS offered seven associate degrees, 24 bachelor's degrees (in academic and technical areas), and three master's degrees.

From the beginning, IUS was designed as a commuter school, without housing for students. While about 70 percent of the students work at least part-time, more than 40 percent of them attend classes full-time.

THE CATHOLIC TRADITION

Catholic schools traditionally have played a strong role in education in Louisville. In the mid-1980s they included 55 elementary schools and 10 high schools in Jefferson County, handling nearly 20 percent of the county's students. Two colleges had their origins as Catholic institutions, and one of them is now the largest private four-

The administration building at Jefferson Community College was once part of the Louisville Presbyterian Theological Seminary. Photo by C.J. Elfont

year college in Kentucky.

Louisville's oldest Catholic school is also its oldest continuously operated high school—Presentation Academy, established for girls in 1831. Parish elementary schools were established later and were coordinated under a central system in 1925.

While the public schools faced trauma in the 1970s, Catholic schools faced dramatic changes in the 1960s. The number of teaching nuns, brothers, and priests declined, slowly at first and then rapidly. Lay teachers were hired to fill the vacancies, and costs escalated. Enrollment in elementary schools in the Archdiocese of Louisville dropped from a peak of over 41,000 in 1964 to less than 22,000 in 1972.

The decline slowed considerably in the 1970s, but enrollment continued to dwindle, falling below 20,000 in the early 1980s. Quite a few elementary schools were closed; so were a few high schools.

Enrollment figures confirm that Catholic schools did not become a "haven from busing" in the mid-1970s; the slow decline in enrollment continued. But the Reverend Thomas Duerr, superintendent of Catholic schools, said parochial schools were becoming a "value choice" for parents of many religions in the 1980s. In some schools, he said, many of the students were not Catholic. The attraction, he said, was education "in the traditional mold ... basic education, without a lot of frills ... good discipline...and a very caring atmosphere."

In 1987 the archdiocese began new programs to raise money for the schools and attract qualified students. A special Easter Sunday collection raised about $300,000 for educational programs; about a third of it went into a financial aid fund for families that needed help with elementary school tuition payments.

BELLARMINE COLLEGE

Louisville's second-largest four-year college is also its newest: Bellarmine College, founded in 1950 by the Archdiocese of Louisville. The small liberal-arts school served only men at first—but men of any religion and any race. In 1968 it merged with Ursuline College, a Catholic school for women founded in 1938, and became coeducational. By 1980 Bellarmine had become the largest private college in Kentucky.

Part of Bellarmine's success was based on its em-

A TRADITION OF LEARNING

phasis on a high-quality liberal-arts education, in a setting where students would know the faculty members personally. This emphasis on scholarship and quality reached out to the world at large in 1955, when the college established the Bellarmine Medal. The medal is awarded to people who have exemplified the virtues of justice, charity, and temperance in dealing with difficult and controversial problems of national and international scope. Recipients have included Henry Cabot Lodge, Sargent Shriver, William F. Buckley, the Reverend Jesse Jackson, Mother Teresa of Calcutta, and Walter Cronkite.

But this emphasis was not enough as the 1970s dawned. Enrollment was declining, and some officials were afraid the college might have to close.

Dr. Eugene V. Petrik, who became president in 1973, brought a new emphasis on practicality—a solid liberal-arts program with a good sprinkling of job-oriented skills. Internships were developed for students in most academic areas. When college students turned from activism to a concentration on careers, Bellarmine was ready.

Another key to the college's success was based on a shrewd assessment of the community's educational

Above left: Bellarmine College, Kentucky's largest private four-year college, perches on a hill in eastern Louisville. Photo by John Beckman/Quadrant

Above: The handsome buildings at Indiana University Southeast rose in the late 1960s in the rolling countryside north of New Albany. Photo by Ted Wathen/Quadrant

needs—and on offering special programs to meet those needs.

In 1975, for instance, Bellarmine started a graduate program in business administration, with classes scheduled after normal hours so working people could earn their master's degrees. It was the school's first graduate program, and by the mid-1980s it was the largest MBA program in Kentucky.

Another example: the music department offers a degree with a jazz emphasis, unique in the Louisville area. The college also offers jazz workshops open to students in high school and other colleges, with top jazz

IN CELEBRATION OF LOUISVILLE

performers teaching the students and performing in concerts.

By the early 1980s, enrollment had grown so much that Bellarmine raised more than $6 million to construct five new buildings and renovate others. By the late 1980s, enrollment stood at more than 2,600 students. Bachelor's degrees were offered in more than four dozen majors, and master's degrees were offered in business, education, nursing, and social administration.

SPALDING UNIVERSITY

Spalding University, located in an assortment of new and historic buildings at the south edge of downtown Louisville, is a source of surprises. There is no sprawling campus; the university's buildings are tucked between Old Louisville neighborhoods and a downtown business district. But the administration building surrounds the historic Whitestone Mansion, with its beautifully preserved Victorian rooms, and the gymnasium is the spot where former heavyweight boxing champion Muhammad Ali got his start.

The main buildings give the appearance of a Catholic women's college, harking back to the university's origins. But more than half the student body is non-Catholic, and men have been admitted for nearly four decades.

The general atmosphere is one of quiet scholarship. And yet the school is the home of the annual "Run for the Rodents," a delightful rat-race parody of the Kentucky Derby that kicks off the week-long Derby Festival.

A TRADITION OF LEARNING

Spalding is the only institution in Louisville to offer a bachelor's degree in social work, and both bachelor's and master's degrees in library science. And Spalding's Weekend College is the only program in Louisville that guarantees students they can earn a bachelor's degree solely by attending classes during weekends.

Spalding's current Louisville location was established in 1920 as Nazareth College for women. It was an extension of the educational activities of the Sisters of Charity of Nazareth, who had opened their first academy in a log cabin in Nelson County, Kentucky, in 1814. In 1952 the college started admitting men. In 1969 it absorbed Nazareth College of Nazareth, Kentucky, and became Spalding College. In 1984 it became a university.

From the beginning, Nazareth and later Spalding attracted local students who were striving to better themselves. Some of the first courses were offered at night and on weekends to help teachers and nurses pursue their degrees. In recent years, about 80 percent of Spalding's students have come from Jefferson County;

Below left: One of the major buildings at Spalding University, is pictured here while the institution was still a college. Photo by Ted Wathen/Quadrant

Below: Spalding University's administration building is one of many landmarks in Old Louisville. Photo by C.J. Elfont

IN CELEBRATION OF LOUISVILLE

about 90 percent commute to school, and about 80 percent have jobs. More than three-fourths receive some form of financial aid, and more than one-third are married. In 1987 Spalding was serving more than 1,400 students, and the school announced a $20-million fund drive for an expansion program to serve an eventual enrollment of 2,000.

THE SEMINARIES

Religious education has been important to Louisville for more than a century, since the Southern Baptist Theological Seminary moved in from South Carolina. And religious education played a key part in Louisville's riverfront development efforts in the late 1980s, when leaders of the Louisville Presbyterian Theological Seminary helped attract the national headquarters of the Presbyterian Church (U.S.A.). Both seminaries have played parts in Louisville's North-South tradition.

When the Southern Baptist Convention was formed in 1845, it was frankly a product of Southern culture. Fourteen years later, on the eve of the Civil War, the denomination opened the Southern Baptist Theological Seminary in Greenville, South Carolina. The new school faced hard times during the war and Reconstruction, and the trustees voted in 1872 to move north to Louisville. Money was scarce, and the move wasn't completed until five years later. But the new location not far from downtown Louisville was a good one.

By 1921 the enrollment had grown to 421, making it one of the world's largest seminaries, and the old complex was overcrowded. The school bought an old estate, along Lexington Road at the eastern edge of Louisville, and opened a new 100-acre campus there in 1926.

In the late 1980s, it was one of the three largest seminaries in the world, with more than 3,200 students. It was also the largest private graduate school in Kentucky. Students came from 45 states and two dozen foreign countries and held degrees from nearly 700 different colleges and universities.

The seminary offers seven master's degrees and five doctorates, with specialties including theology, ministry, education, social work, and music. An undergraduate division, the Boyce Bible School, offers diplomas in three areas.

For more than 80 years, the Louisville Presbyterian Theological Seminary had a unique distinction: it was the only institution supported by both the northern and southern branches of the denomination, which had split when the Civil War began.

The seminary began modestly in 1893, holding classes in the Sunday school rooms of the Second Presbyterian Church. Sponsored by the Presbyterian Synods of Kentucky and Missouri, it was aligned with the southern branch of the church.

The Danville (Kentucky) Theological Seminary, established in 1853, was aligned with the northern branch and fell on hard times in the years following the Civil War. In 1901 it merged with the Louisville Seminary and closed its Danville campus. The combined seminary became the only one to serve both branches of the church.

For 60 years the seminary made its home on a campus of Gothic buildings at the edge of downtown Louisville. In 1963 it moved to a new 38-acre campus on an old estate in the eastern part of the city, not far from the Southern Baptist seminary.

With an enrollment of about 250 students, it is an average-sized Presbyterian seminary, but one of Louisville's smallest institutions of higher education. The arrival of the church's national headquarters in the late 1980s, however, could give enrollment a modest boost.

The school offers master's degrees in divinity and religion, and a doctorate in ministry. In addition, it works with the University of Louisville and Bellarmine College to offer double degree programs in social work, law, education, criminal justice, and business management for non-profit institutions.

Brick walks, Colonial architecture and spacious grounds bring an air of tranquility to the Southern Baptist Theological Seminary. Photo by C.J. Elfont

Chapter VI

Festivals and Fun

CELEBRATING THE WEATHER

Louisvillians love the outdoors as only those who live in a changeable mid-latitude climate can love it: They take advantage of every reasonable opportunity to enjoy it. Appreciation of good weather is almost automatic in a place where rain (or sometimes snow) falls an average of one-third of the days each year, and where the sky is clear an average of one-fourth of the days of the year.

Practically every form of weather can be found in Louisville, in enough variety to keep people's attention and interest. Practically every form of outdoor playground can also be found, from rivers and lakes to meadows and forests to hills and cliffs. And almost every form of outdoor recreation is popular, from waterskiing to snow skiing, swimming to ice skating, sunbathing to jogging, bird-watching to golfing, hiking to horseback riding, and family picnics to community festivals.

The list of public recreation facilities sounds like a dream resort: a dozen golf courses, nearly 250 tennis courts, about 20 swimming pools, nearly 20 fishing lakes, nearly four miles of specially-paved bicycle trails, dozens of miles of hiking trails, dozens more miles of horseback-riding trails, a riding stable—all of them operated by state and local parks departments. Private facilities expand the list tremendously. And the frequent spells of good weather encourage a sparkling schedule of outdoor festivals and entertainment, for at least ten months out of the year.

January and February are usually the exceptions. They can be cold or warm, damp or dry, snowy or rainy, cloudy or sunny, and maybe all of the above within a few short days. Ice skating on artificially frozen outdoor rinks is popular when the weather permits, and there are even a few commercial ski slopes (with mostly artificial

A tightly packed field heads into the stretch at Churchill Downs. Photo by John Nation

FESTIVALS AND FUN

snow) in the southern Indiana hills. On the other hand, there can be days that are perfect for golfing or tennis. For the most part, it's a season for taking advantage of the weather as you find it—and not for making any long-range outdoor plans!

As for summer, well, there's good reason to advertise that Kentucky has the nation's largest air-conditioned state fair. But there's also a good reason why the Louisville Redbirds baseball team has broken all minor-league attendance records.

THE FESTIVAL SEASON BEGINS

The Irish, that hardy northern race and a traditional force in Louisville, launch the year's outdoor festival season with their annual parade on the Saturday closest to

Facing page: Strollers enjoy the autumn colors along Eastern Parkway, a legacy of Frederick Law Olmsted's master plan for Louisville's city park system. Photo by John Nation

Left: A fly fisherman practices his skills in Louisville's Beargrass Creek. Photo by John Beckman/Quadrant

Below: Visitors climb to the overlook at Iroquois Park in southern Louisville. Photo by C.J. Elfont

March 17, St. Patrick's Day. A green line is painted down Main Street, shamrocks appear everywhere, restaurants feature Irish stew, and a few pubs offer green beer. Since 16 percent of Louisville's residents have some provable Irish heritage, and since many more become Irish for a day, the event can be a big one. But since March is Louisville's rainiest month, and March weather can be as changeable as Irish humor, the paraders must be a hardy bunch—on occasion, much hardier than the spectators!

April, when the weather turns warmer and the flowers begin to bloom, is the real start of the outdoor season. One of the first events, naturally enough, involves horses: the Oxmoor Steeplechase, held for more than four decades on an estate now surrounded by the eastern suburbs. It's an event for family fun, with plenty of room for picnics. The horses and riders race cross-country, jumping fences and hedges and water hazards, in the finest equestrian tradition. There are also terrier races and often a classic automobile show. Proceeds go to charity.

Two neighborhood festivals also enliven the month. The City of Audubon Park's Festival of the Dogwood, the last weekend in April, celebrates the blooming of nearly 200 dogwood trees. Residents spotlight the trees on their lawns; young women dress as southern belles to greet visitors, and there is food and music in Wren Park. The Cherokee Triangle arts and crafts fair usually takes place the same weekend, with more than 100 artists and craftspeople displaying and selling their winter's handiwork—and with tours of some of the neighborhood's grand, historic homes. These neighborhood festivals usually coincide with the beginning of Louisville's annual rite of spring—the Kentucky Derby Festival.

THE KENTUCKY DERBY FESTIVAL

The Kentucky Derby, the world's most famous race for Thoroughbred horses, has been Louisville's annual salute to spring since 1875. Steeped in tradition, it retains

Below: Flowers grace the courtyard at the entrance to the grandstand at Churchill Downs. Photo by Mark E. Gibson

Facing page: Cheering crowds drown out the sounds of the horses' hooves as they round the first turn in the Kentucky Derby. Photo by John Nation

IN CELEBRATION OF LOUISVILLE

FESTIVALS AND FUN

many of its original features, along with a huge assortment of modern attractions.

For many decades, the Derby has been the highlight of the first week of the spring racing season at Churchill Downs, and a destination for lovers of horse racing from throughout the nation. In 1956 it inspired the beginnings of a citywide spectacle, when the Kentucky Derby Festival Parade first made its way down Broadway. The week's events started expanding tremendously in the early 1960s, when the newly renovated *Belle of Louisville* challenged Cincinnati's *Delta Queen* in the Derby week's first Great Steamboat Race.

Today the big celebration begins eight days before the race, and the festivities continue practically nonstop through the day after. There are so many activities it's impossible to attend them all. The tourist business booms, but other business activities may slow considerably. The Louisville verb "to derby" means "to party"—at any one of the scores of public events or the hundreds of private ones.

The schedule starts with a pair of high-toned (and high-priced) affairs on the Friday before the Friday before the race: the Kentucky Derby Festival "They're Off" luncheon and the Fillies Derby Ball. Saturday morning brings the first community-wide event, the Kentucky Derby Festival Great Balloon Race. It's open without charge to everyone, and it's liable to be seen by anyone, anywhere in the area. More than 51 colorful hot-air balloons take part in the "hare and hounds" event, which starts at the Kentucky Fair and Exposition Center grounds. The previous year's winner becomes the "hare," taking off early and landing at a spot the pilot chooses. The crew of the hare takes a large piece of fabric with an X on it, and drops the target to the ground; the rest of the pilots try to hit the center of the target with a bag of bluegrass seed. The pilot that comes closest wins.

The vagaries of Louisville's spring weather and wind make the outcome—and even the course—impossible to predict. The pack of balloons has drifted in practically every direction from the fairgrounds. Unusually bad weather conditions can delay the race, from a few hours to the next day.

Another major event for everyone, the 13.1-mile Kentucky Derby Festival mini-marathon, starts at Louisville's Iroquois Park and wends through the streets to the downtown riverfront. More than 5,000 runners usually take part, sounding like a herd of small rubber-shoed buffalo as they hit the pavement. It sometimes takes place at the same time as the balloon race—and it's even possible for their paths to cross.

This is the "hare" balloon's view of the still-earth-bound "hounds" at the start of the Kentucky Derby Festival's hot-air balloon race. Photo by John Nation

Wednesday afternoon brings the Kentucky Derby Festival Great Steamboat Race, the modern era's oldest annual match between authentic stern-wheel riverboats. It always features the *Belle of Louisville* and the *Delta Queen*, and sometimes welcomes a third boat as well. The steamboat captains, crews, and partisans start the war of bombast several days before the race, with broad hints about "secret weapons" and "dirty tricks." The winner enjoys the right to wear the Gilded Antlers, the symbol of supremacy on the river, throughout the coming year.

Crowds line every inch of publicly-owned riverbank on both sides of the river along the course, from downtown Louisville's riverfront upstream to Six Mile Island. There's a huge public party with music and refreshments on the Belvedere, which overlooks the start and the finish, and another one at the Water Tower Art Association's grounds along River Road, where the boats pass on their way upstream and again on their way back down. People with riverfront homes and businesses give their own race-watching parties.

And since tickets on the boats are sold out far in advance, the *Belle of Louisville* and the Kentucky Derby Festival offer a special, low-cost "Steamboat Race Trial" excursion the morning of the race, covering the course at a more tranquil pace.

Thursday afternoon brings the Kentucky Derby Festival Pegasus Parade, named for the flying horse of Greek mythology. With more than two dozen floats, dozens of marching bands, all types of horses, beautiful vehicles, and scores of clowns, it is nationally televised and often lasts two hours. Bleachers, grandstands, and refreshment booths line Broadway for more than a mile, helping make the parade a grand picnic and party.

Above: Keyed-up runners hit the street as the Kentucky Derby Festival Mini-Marathon begins. Photo by John Nation

Facing page: Outriders and their mounts are elegantly attired at the Hard Scuffle Steeplechase. Photo by John Nation

Friday brings the Derby's lesser-known counterpart, the Kentucky Oaks race at Churchill Downs for three-year-old fillies. It's an elegant dress rehearsal for the next day's big event—and a popular alternative for Louisvillians and visitors who can't get good seats for the Derby itself.

These are just the highlights. A typical schedule shows more than 75 events during the Kentucky Derby Festival, ranging from exclusive invitation-only receptions and dinners to massive outdoor concerts and barbecues. There are square-dancing, clogging, basketball, and body-building exhibitions; automobile and air shows; charity balls; horse shows; and a variety of runs, jogs, and walks. Some of the community-wide events even poke fun at the Derby and its nickname, the "Run for the Roses": there's the Run for the Rosé (waiters and waitresses race with wine-filled glasses on trays), the Ramble for the Roses (a walk through south Louisville), and the Run for the Rodents (a race for laboratory rats).

Race day itself is Louisville's biggest party day of the year. Those who have tickets often play host to or attend

FESTIVALS AND FUN

145

IN CELEBRATION OF LOUISVILLE

Facing page: An old limestone quarry has become an elegant swimming pool, ringed with vine-covered cliffs, at Lakeside Club in eastern Louisville. Photo by John Nation

Above: Flowers and pretty hats are part of the charm on the sidelines at the Hard Scuffle Steeplechase. Photo by John Nation

Derby breakfasts before leaving for the track. Those who don't have tickets may throw Derby parties during the afternoon, complete with racing paraphernalia (including lottery tickets and betting stands) and climaxed by watching "The Greatest Two Minutes in Sport" on television. (One of the advantages of living in Louisville: the city's greatest sporting event is broadcast locally, live.) And Louisville natives living in far-away cities may throw their own Derby parties, with decorations imported from back home.

THE KENTUCKY DERBY

The world's greatest horse race started modestly enough—as the highlight of the opening meet at a track designed to revive Kentucky's troubled Thoroughbred horse-racing business. Colonel Meriwether Lewis Clark suggested that Kentucky horsemen adopt the English pattern: racing horses by class and age, so they would be matched more evenly.

Backers organized the Louisville Jockey Club in 1874, and built a new one-mile track on a farm south of Louisville owned by John and Henry Churchill. In keeping with the English model, the prestige race was called the Kentucky Derby; soon the race track became known as Churchill Downs.

The organizers added $1,000 to the entry and other fees for that first Kentucky Derby; the $2,850 total winner's purse was phenomenal for the times. The precedent guaranteed participation by the finest horses, breeders, trainers, and jockeys. (By the mid-1980s, the winner's purse topped $600,000—still phenomenal.)

Tradition is everything at the Kentucky Derby. The original grandstand, a wooden structure with twin spires, has been replaced by a much larger grandstand—still largely wooden, with twin spires. The mounted officials wear red jackets and white riding trousers, patterned on British derby costumes. A herald in similar costume sounds the "Call to the Post" on a gleaming, four-foot-long brass trumpet. The crowd sings "My Old Kentucky Home," with a tear in many an eye. The horses are ceremoniously paraded in front of the grandstand, while an announcer describes their accomplishments, before being led to the gate. And the winning horse is draped in a blanket of more than 500 roses, arranged in the same design for nearly 60 years.

Since a full day at Churchill Downs includes about 10 two-minute races spread out over eight hours, there's a lot of activity besides watching the horses. Socializing and betting are the major attractions—along with people-watching and being watched.

In the high-priced boxes in the grandstands, the rich and the famous gather from around the nation to mingle and be seen. Louisvillians and guests show off their elegant spring outfits, including a few men's colors you'll probably see for less than two weeks out of the year.

Spectators study their programs and racing forms intently, follow their formulas or their hunches, and flock to the windows to place their bets. Portable bank money machines provide cash on their credit cards. Lunch can be anything from hot dogs sold at portable stands to fine cuisine served in an elegant dining room. And everywhere in the stands are the mint julep vendors, peddling their official concoctions of bourbon whiskey, sugar water, ice, and mint leaves.

While tradition and more-or-less dignified playfulness are the order in the grandstands, inhibitions are cast aside in the sprawling, grassy infield. Picnics and vast expanses of winter-pale skin are everywhere, and the "derbying" is much more evident than the racing. Since the track is practically invisible from many parts of the infield, battery-powered television sets sometimes offer the best views of the race.

Louisvillians usually relax and recover for a couple of weeks after the Derby. It's a time for personal pursuits, such as catching up on your gardening. Weather is only part of the reason that local folklore says you should set out your tomatoes the Saturday after Derby day.

Things stir again in late May with the Hard Scuffle Steeplechase, on an estate northeast of Louisville. This social and sports event is an elegant affair, designed to raise money for the Kentucky Opera.

INTO THE SUMMER...

June brings hot weather, and activities for those who enjoy the heat. There's a weekend festival or two on the Belvedere, the summer festival in Portland, and the riverfront festival in Jeffersonville. July brings several Independence Day festivals, with picnics, live entertainment, and fireworks.

August brings the Kentucky State Fair, along with a series of horse shows, including a world championship horse show, at the fairgrounds. Over half a million visitors attend the 10-day event, attracted by exhibits and entertainment that range far beyond agriculture. There are mock trials, spelling bees, pipe-smoking contests, military exhibits, marching bands, a zoo, college football practice, professional wrestling, racing pigs, fireworks, dart-throwing contests, and the traditional contests for farm animals, produce, and domestic arts. Much of this happens outside, of course, but the huge air-conditioned exhibition halls offer welcome shelter from the heat, humidity, and occasional showers. Music includes bluegrass, country, gospel, rock, dixieland, big band, and just plain pop—and the concerts feature some of the nation's top entertainers.

The schedule of festivals picks up in late August and early September, when the weather usually begins to moderate. Late August brings the downtown Strassenfest, with music, dance contests, a variety of German foods and wines, and (of course) beer.

The big event of early fall is the annual Bluegrass Music Festival on the Belvedere, with more than 30 hours of free entertainment over three days. There's a huge variety of top bluegrass bands, from as far away as Germany. The traditional highlight is a performance by the father of bluegrass music, Kentucky's Bill Monroe.

Community festivals also blossom in September—in Audubon Park, Jeffersontown, St. Matthews, Shively, Jeffersonville, and elsewhere. And there's the Corn Island Storytelling Festival, when storytellers spin their tales on the *Belle of Louisville*, at the historic Water Tower, and (for ghost stories) at Long Run Cemetery. (Corn Island, the site of Louisville's first settlement, disappeared under the Ohio River's waters many years ago—a story in itself.)

Early October brings the St. James Court Art Fair, a three-day event that brings arts and crafts exhibitors from more than 25 states to the elegant historic neighborhood in Old Louisville. Thousands browse the booths and nibble the snacks in good weather; buses shuttle many visitors back and forth from parking areas outside the neighborhood.

The same weekend usually brings the Oktoberfest (with games, beer, and bratwurst) to Butchertown, another historic neighborhood. And this weekend also usually marks the beginning of New Albany's week-long Harvest Homecoming Festival.

November can bring unpleasant weather to Louisville once again, but there's still one major festival left: Thanksgiving weekend's Light Up Louisville and Dickens on Main Street. The festivities start Friday evening, with a lighting ceremony at the huge community Christmas tree in Jefferson Square Park. When the signal is given, the holiday lights go on in the park, on City Hall and the courthouse, and throughout the downtown area—all at one time.

The Main Street historic area is draped with tiny lights. Business people, street vendors, actors, singers, and musicians wear costumes from the era of Charles Dickens, sell old English wares and food, and sing old English songs and Christmas carols. The weather can range from pleasantly warm to blustery cold to a bit of old English fog and drizzle—but the show always goes on.

THE PARKS

Louisville's metropolitan parks system is one of the oldest and largest in the nation. It traces its beginning to 1889, when Mayor Charles D. Jacob bought a large wooded tract on "Burnt Knob," four miles south of the city, with his own money—then went to the city treasurer for reimbursement. Opponents called the purchase "Jacob's Folly" and raised a storm of protest, but the city council agreed to make it a city park. The council also approved a grand 150-foot boulevard from the city limits

FESTIVALS AND FUN

to the new park, and property owners along the route donated the land.

An independent parks commission was established the next year, with plans and money to build several parks and a series of landscaped boulevards. For the designs, the commission hired the firm founded by Frederick Law Olmsted, the father of American landscape architecture and the architect-in-chief of New York's Central Park.

Olmsted's master plan included three major multipurpose parks, showcasing the area's three major types of natural landscape. Totaling nearly 1,000 acres (and expanded to more than 1,500 acres in the years that followed), they were named for the Indian tribes that once hunted in the area.

Burnt Knob became Iroquois Park, and eventually included nearly all of the rugged hill. An overlook at the crest offers one of the area's best sweeping views of the

A dancing water light show awes visitors at the Kentucky State Fair. Photo by Christina M. Freitag

Ohio River, its floodplain, and the city of Louisville.

A large tract along the riverbank west of Louisville became Shawnee Park, with low-lying bottomland bordered by a broad expanse of relatively flat, higher ground. It's the area's most beautiful riverside park.

East of the city, the small gorge cut by meandering Beargrass Creek, with its cliffs and woods and meadows, became Cherokee Park. The park's winding roads cross the creek repeatedly on a series of picturesque stone bridges.

The boulevards, called parkways, were designed to offer tranquil drives through the countryside to the parks. North Western, South Western, Algonquin, Eastern, and Cherokee parkways formed a broad loop around the western and southern edges of the city, connecting Shawnee Park with Cherokee Park. Southern Parkway extended far southward to Iroquois Park. The new boulevards provided attractive channels for the city's growth in the late nineteenth and early twentieth centuries, and became major thoroughfares in the automobile age. Despite heavy traffic, most of them are still beautiful, scenic routes through their neighborhoods.

Olmsted's firm eventually designed 14 more parks, scattered throughout the city. And by the time the expanded city-county park system neared its 100th anniversary, it included more than 130 parks, playgrounds, nature preserves, and other natural areas—from landscaped city plots of less than an acre, to the rugged 4,000-acre Jefferson County Memorial Forest.

This extensive park system was inspired, in part, by

the disastrous tornado of 1890. Louisville rallied to build a better city than before, and the parks became a major part of the plan. The city's next disastrous tornado ground through Cherokee Park in 1974, obliterating much of the dense old woodland. Louisville responded with an ambitious replanting program—and then noticed the deterioration in other fine old parks. By the mid-1980s, major restoration projects were under way in several parks, including Iroquois and Cherokee.

Louisville also has a city park located two counties away—about 30 miles southwest of the city along the Piomingo Bend on the Ohio River. Otter Creek Park was built by the federal government in the 1930s as an experimental mini-national park. It includes steep cliffs overlooking the river, dense woodlands, rugged gorges, grown-over farmland, the sites of two long-gone villages, and a cave once used as a storehouse by Confederate guerrilla General John Hunt Morgan and perhaps as a hideout by Jesse James.

Presented to the City of Louisville in 1947, the park now has a large modern restaurant with a sweeping view from atop the cliffs; a modern lodge with single and double rooms; two rustic lodges and an assortment of cabins; tent and trailer camping sites; and a large YMCA camp—along with a nature center, swimming pool, and boat-launching ramp.

The Louisville area is blessed with even more parks and natural areas, from E.P. "Tom" Sawyer State Park in eastern Jefferson County to parks owned and maintained by smaller cities, including New Albany, Jeffersonville, and Clarksville in Indiana.

Another Louisville treasure is parklike without being a park: Cave Hill Cemetery. Created in 1848, it is a showplace of classic monument sculpture and has a magnificent botanical garden, with nearly 300 species of trees. Ducks and swans live on the ponds the year around, and the trees, shrubs, and lawns are covered with blossoms in the spring.

OUTDOOR ENTERTAINMENT

Outdoor plays, musicals, and concerts are very popular in Louisville in the summertime. In addition to the events on the riverfront Belvedere, the city has long-established series in two of the Olmsted parks.

Iroquois Amphitheater was built in 1938 with federal help, and soon became one of the major stops on the old summertime "straw-hat circuit" for traveling operettas and Broadway musicals. Many of the top performers of the 1940s and 1950s played there, performing many of the top hits of the day.

The amphitheater fell on hard times in the late 1950s and early 1960s, hurt by the popularity of television and by several very rainy summers. Community and student groups still used it occasionally, but there was little income and maintenance suffered. Then, in the early 1970s, a grass-roots movement began among the park's nearby neighborhoods, and the amphitheater slowly came back to life. Refurbished, it now offers a heavy schedule of summer performances, including musical comedies directed and staged by local professionals, with casts made up of local performers. Classical, jazz, and choral concerts are among the other offerings.

Shakespeare in Central Park is another long-established series of outdoor programs. Several plays are performed each summer in the park in the midst of the Old

Autumn colors stand out at Shawnee Park. Photo by C.J. Elfont

IN CELEBRATION OF LOUISVILLE

Louisville historic preservation area.

And the Water Tower Art Association schedules outdoor jazz concerts on the grounds of the landmark 1860 pumping station along the Ohio River at the northeast edge of Louisville.

THE LOUISVILLE ZOO

The Louisville Zoological Gardens, opened in 1968, is one of the nation's newest major zoos—and one of the pioneers in breeding endangered animals. One experiment gained worldwide attention in 1984: the successful transplant of a zebra embryo into a 26-year-old quarter horse mare. It was the first birth of a wild equine to a surrogate mother. The zoo also has one of the world's few successful breeding colonies of endangered woolly monkeys, and is one of the few inland zoos to successfully breed gray seals.

Most of the animals are exhibited in naturalistic settings designed to simulate their native lands. And the zoo's lakes and ponds have become stops on the flyways for migratory water birds, which mix freely with flamingoes and other exotics and enjoy the abundant food.

The indoor "Metazoo," with natural displays and hands-on learning exhibits, is popular with adults as well as children. It was the first of its kind in the United States, and has served as a model for other zoos. A $2.1-million "HerpAquarium" for rare reptiles—including tropical crocodiles and giant tortoises—was scheduled to be completed in 1989.

The zoo is open throughout the year, with frequent special programs such as "Dawn with the Animals," "Hal-

FESTIVALS AND FUN

loween at the Zoo," and the elegant, formal "Zoofari" fund-raising ball.

SPORTS

Professional sports in Louisville centers on two major activities: horse racing (including harness racing) and baseball. But semiprofessional and amateur sports run the entire gamut; the only major blanks are in sports that require ice or snow.

Thoroughbred horses race at Churchill Downs, home of the Kentucky Derby, during a two-month schedule in the late spring and a one-month schedule in the fall. The historic track added a turf course in 1987, expanding its offerings. And whether the track is open or not, the Kentucky Derby Museum on the grounds offers a stunning multimedia show that captures the essence of Thoroughbred racing.

When the horses aren't running under jockeys at Churchill Downs, different types of horses are pulling sulkies at nearby Louisville Downs, the harness-racing

Below left: A hat, glove, and the home playing field of the Louisville Redbirds is seen here. The Redbirds were the first minor league baseball team to attract more than one million spectators to a season of home games. Photo by John Beckman/Quadrant

Below: This University of Louisville football player makes a run for the goal. Photo by Quadrant

153

track. Between the two of them, they keep horse racing (and pari-mutuel betting) going strong for most of the year.

Baseball returned to Louisville in 1982, after a long absence, when A. Ray Smith moved his American Association team from Springfield, Illinois, and named it the Louisville Redbirds.

Smith, a magnetic personality with a tremendous talent for marketing, promoted baseball as an event as well as a game. He spent $2 million to upgrade the state fairgrounds stadium. He said baseball is a game that leaves a lot of time to spare, so he provided extra activities that the whole family could enjoy. He brought in a fancy scoreboard, a dixieland band, a smorgasbord of reasonably-priced concessions, baseball greats to sign autographs, entertainers, and more.

He also arranged a full schedule of special nights for employees of local businesses and industries, with ticket discounts and giveaways financed partly by the employers. And Smith was always on hand, chatting joyfully with the fans and posing for pictures.

The results were spectacular. The Redbirds became the first minor-league team to attract more than a million spectators to a season of home games—setting a record of 1,052,438 in 1983. And that record was no fluke; the team posted five annual minor league attendance records in its first six years.

In late 1986, Smith sold 80 percent of his interest to a group of local investors, and went to St. Petersburg, Florida, to try to set up a major-league team. He said he couldn't resist the challenge. Louisville fans gave him a gigantic send-off, and continued to support their Redbirds.

Other professional sports have had less success in Louisville, perhaps because of the tremendous college and high school action. Basketball is to Kentuckians what basketball is to Hoosiers—the most important "academic" sport of them all.

When the University of Louisville won the National Collegiate Athletic Association basketball championship

in 1980, Louisvillians knew their team had arrived. And when the University of Kentucky finally agreed to meet U of L in season basketball four years later, Louisville fans enjoyed their greatest vindication. U of L followed up with another NCAA basketball championship in 1986.

The tremendous popularity of U of L basketball, and the tremendous income from ticket sales, led to a self-supporting athletic program in the mid-1980s. Athletic department finances went from annual losses of $500,000 to $1 million in the late 1970s to a profit of $2 million in 1985-1986. Basketball income financed a major push for an improved football program, and provided money for a wide range of minor sports (such as volleyball, soccer, and women's basketball).

High school basketball, while not much of a money-maker, is just as avidly played—and just as avidly followed by partisan groups of fans. Tourneys in Kentucky and Indiana are always sellouts. There is much less interest in football; U of L was still trying to field a strong team in the late 1980s. High school football is fiercely fought and avidly followed, but not as much as basketball.

Above: Golfers face the challenges of Iroquois Golf Course, one of many fine public courses in the Louisville area. Photo by C.J. Elfont

Above left: University of Louisville basketball's Mark Abrams, #34, positions himself to receive a pass. Photo by Carl Maupin/Quadrant

Miscellaneous spectator sports, amateur to professional, include swimming, tennis, golf, soccer, track and field events, polo, ballooning, motorcycle racing, and even tournament bass fishing. And as the 1980s draw to a close, Louisville, home of Indianapolis 500 winner Danny Sullivan, looks forward to the completion of a new $2.2-million motor speedway—its first since the old fairgrounds track closed in 1981.

Chapter VII

A Center for Services

THE TRENDS OF THE TIMES

When the Presbyterian Church (U.S.A.) decided in mid-1987 to move its headquarters to Louisville, it was more than an economic development coup for the city at The Falls. It was a reaffirmation of Louisville's tradition as a city of services, as a good place to live and do business, and as a community that can adapt thoughtfully to social and economic changes.

Louisville today is the center for business and professional services for most of Kentucky and a large part of southern Indiana. And many Louisville businesses have national and international operations, as well.

People throughout the world are familiar with the face and the recipe of Colonel Harland Sanders, founder of Kentucky Fried Chicken. But shoppers in New York and Chicago might be surprised to learn that Saks Fifth Avenue and Marshall Field's department stores are owned by a Louisville company. People who appreciate fine china and crystal might not realize that Lenox is a subsidiary of another Louisville company. And those who appreciate fine whiskey might be surprised to find that a Louisville company owns the Jack Daniel's Distillery in Lynchburg, Tennessee.

Kentucky's three largest banks are based in Louisville; so are more than half the state's 30 largest businesses. Louisville's medical community is known internationally for heart transplants, hand surgery, microsurgery, treatment of burns—and the innovations of Humana Inc., its national for-profit hospital and health-care chain. Louisville's law firms include the largest and most influential in the state.

Louisville is also a city of business in transition. After more than a century of emphasis on manufacturing, Louisville is moving back toward its tradition of service.

Business has been a major part of life at The Falls

Colorful flags, living trees and vendors' carts enliven the atrium in the downtown Louisville Galleria. Photo by John Beckman/Quadrant

since before Louisville was born. In April 1774, four years before the first settlement was established, John Campbell and John Connolly advertised lots for sale in a proposed town on their land grant at The Falls. The price was four Spanish dollars per lot. It was the first attempt at real-estate sales in the unborn community, and the advertisement emphasized the area's potential for business:

The advantageous Situation of that Place, formed by Nature as a temporary Magazine, or Repository, to receive the Produce of the very extensive and fertile Country on the Ohio and its Branches, as well as the necessary Merchandises suitable for the Inhabitants that shall emigrate into that Country (as Boats of fifty Tuns Burthen may be navigated from New Orleans up to the Town) is sufficient to recommend it ...

Indian trouble and the Revolution prevented settlement until George Rogers Clark's expedition arrived. Business began as soon as enough land was cleared and shelters were built; residents bought, sold, and bartered goods with travelers and newcomers.

Trader John Sanders became the settlement's first "banker," issuing certificates in exchange for furs and skins. The certificates promised to pay the bearer after Sanders could sell the goods. Since cash was scarce and the certificates were transferrable, they soon became a medium of exchange. Even when cash was available, it wasn't always the most valuable commodity—especially the currency issued by the Continental Congress. In the early 1780s, salt produced south of Louisville brought $2 a bushel in produce, but only $1.50 a bushel in cash.

And the economy could take violent swings on the frontier, creating business "opportunities." In the hard winter of 1779 to 1780, corn sold for $165 per bushel; that spring, it dropped to $30.

Louisville's first formal, full-time business was probably an inn: a simple log building offering shelter and meals. Warehousing and trade developed hand-in-hand, conducted out of the traders' homes and outbuildings. The landing at the mouth of Beargrass Creek became a formal harbor, governed by the town trustees; men found work unloading and loading boats, hauling cargo around The Falls, and piloting boats over the treacherous rapids. A public marketplace was established on what became Market Street.

The first true retail store was opened in 1783 in a

A CENTER FOR SERVICES

large log building on Main Street; proprietor Daniel Brodhead would accept cash, John Sanders' certificates, or goods he could sell to others. The following year a customs collection station was set up, recognizing the potential growth in trade with territories held by France and Spain. And in 1785 a log courthouse was built, giving Louisville's legal profession a more-or-less permanent focus.

Wholesale and retail trade expanded tremendously during the golden ages of the steamboat and railroad, building on the city's location as the "Gateway to the South." Financial, legal, and other service businesses grew apace. Manufacturing developed first as a supplement to business, and then became the city's major focus.

The city even played a major part in a reform movement that swept the American business community in the early twentieth century. The Associated Advertising Clubs of America held their fifth meeting in Louisville in 1909, and a major concern was the public's lack of faith in advertising. The meeting led to the formation of national and local vigilance committees, made up of ethical advertisers who pressured newspapers and magazines to reject misleading ads. In 1914 these vigilance committees became known as Better Business Bureaus, and Louisville's was the third in the nation.

The last quarter of the twentieth century has brought major changes to businesses and manufacturers throughout the nation. The attraction of the Presbyterian headquarters is just one example of Louisville's ability to adapt.

The headquarters' location is multi-symbolic. It fills two of the buildings in the complex built by Belknap Hardware and Manufacturing Company, once the nation's largest wholesaler of hardware. It overlooks the site of Louisville's first harbor, where pioneers tied up their flatboats. And it has become the focus of a restoration effort that is bringing late twentieth-century services to an area once dominated by nineteenth-century commerce.

Belknap, founded in 1840 at Third and Main streets, rose to prominence as Louisville became the "Gateway to the South." At its peak, the company stocked about 90,000 items on its 37 acres of floor space. "Someone who was building a house in Alabama could order everything" he needed from the company, recalled Jonathan Belknap, great-grandson of the founder.

Belknap thrived by supplying independent hardware stores with a full line of merchandise, including many hard-to-find items that weren't available elsewhere. But the mid-twentieth century brought the growth of large chains of hardware and building-supply stores that could buy directly from the manufacturers, bypassing traditional wholesalers. The new chains ate into the business of Belknap and its customers. After more than a decade of increasing problems, Belknap was sold in mid-1984 to Louisvillian David A. Jones, a cofounder of Humana Incorporated.

Jones' rescue efforts came too late. Belknap declared bankruptcy in late 1985, and closed in early 1986. Jones provided money to help satisfy creditors, and was given title to all of Belknap's real estate. He emerged controlling 17 acres of land between Main Street and the Ohio River, occupied by a dozen empty warehouses and office buildings.

While Jones was trying to save Belknap, he was also serving as cochairman of a committee formed to attract the church headquarters to Louisville. Early in 1987, he offered the church two of his empty buildings, virtually free, and offered to raise the money needed to renovate

Facing page: Seen in the midst of the Belle of Louisville's *paddlewheel is the city skyline. Photo by John Nation*

Left: American frontiersman and military leader, General George Rogers Clark is one of Louisville's historic patriots. Photo by John Nation

IN CELEBRATION OF LOUISVILLE

them. His proposal inspired pledges of help from businesses—pledges that eventually topped $7 million. And once the Presbyterians accepted, the project became the keystone in a plan to redevelop the entire warehouse complex, along with the rest of the historic area at the northeastern edge of the old downtown. The new church headquarters added a new cultural dimension to Louisville's traditional role as a major center for services.

The recent history of Louisville's BATUS Incorporated is another example of adaptation to change. BATUS is part of B.A.T. Industries of London, England, and the holding company for its American enterprises.

B.A.T. originally stood for British American Tobacco company; BATUS simply added "United States" to the name. BATUS, in turn, is the parent of Louisville's Brown & Williamson Tobacco Corporation, one of the nation's top tobacco companies.

But tobacco has been a declining business for more than a decade, and BATUS has diversified. Saks Fifth Avenue and Marshall Field's are two of its department-store chains. Ivey's department stores in the Southeast, Breuner's furniture stores in the West, and Thimbles fashion stores are also part of the company. So is Appleton Papers Incorporated of Wisconsin, the world's leading producer of carbonless copy paper and the nation's leading producer of thermal paper.

BATUS closed Brown & Williamson's cigarette factory in Louisville in 1982, consolidating production in a modern plant in another state. But BATUS kept its headquarters, and Brown & Williamson's headquarters and research facilities, in Louisville. Together, they're still one of the area's largest employers. As far as Louisville operations are concerned, Brown & Williamson has become a service company, not a manufacturing company.

THE BUSINESS OF TRADE

Through business cycle after business cycle, Louisville has been a major center for trade. Today the city attracts shoppers from throughout Kentucky and southern Indiana, and from as far away as Cincinnati, Indianapolis, and Nashville.

In many ways, today's retail scene is rather typical for a metropolitan area of a million people. Downtown merchants are coming up with new ways to attract shoppers from the suburbs; a series of major shopping centers rings the city; smaller shopping centers and small-town business districts fill in the gaps; neighborhood stores offer convenience and variety; and a few specialized shopping areas have grown almost by accident.

In downtown Louisville, the attractions range from the multistory Louisville Galleria, with its soaring glass atrium enclosing part of the Fourth Avenue Mall, to Lemon and Son Jewelers Inc., Louisville's oldest retail firm.

The Galleria, with its two connected office towers,

was the main focus of downtown redevelopment in the early 1980s. Clothing, jewelry, stationery, cards, cosmetics, records, books, computers, electronic components, toys, fast food, candy, imports, gifts, and knickknacks—all are available there, or in nearby buildings connected by enclosed walkways. In terms of floor space, the Galleria itself was the area's 10th largest shopping center in 1986. But when the additional stores along the walkways were taken into account, it rivaled the area's largest suburban centers.

Lemon and Son, on the Fourth Avenue Mall about two blocks south of the Galleria, has been owned by the same family since it was established in 1828. The carpeted showroom is lined with cherrywood cases and cabinets, and is lighted by crystal chandeliers from Czechoslovakia. Since 1924, the company has supplied

the gold and jade trophy for the winner of the Kentucky Derby. It has been in its present location in 1930, weathering the Depression, the 1937 flood, the Fourth Street business decline, and a 1987 fire.

Retailing is a dynamic business in Louisville. Lemon's is one of the rare companies that has remained under the same ownership for more than a few decades. The story of the Stewart Dry Goods Company, once Louisville's top local department store, is an illustration of recent trends.

Headquartered in an elegant downtown building erected in 1907, Stewart's established a chain of suburban branch stores after World War II. In the 1970s, it was sold to a large interstate department store chain, but kept its old name. In the early 1980s, the chain sold Stewart's (along with the L.S. Ayers stores in

Waterfalls, bubbling spurts of water, floodlights and soaring steel rods make a visual delight of the fountain at Jefferson Mall. Photo by C. Maupin/Quadrant

Indianapolis) to another interstate department store company; Stewart's was merged into Ayers. Then the new interstate owner offered the former Stewart's stores for sale. In mid-1987, a buyer was found: Louisville's last major locally-owned department store chain, Snyder's. But before the sale could be completed, Snyder's was bought by a chain based in Pennsylvania.

Through the changes, Stewart's reduced the retail space in its downtown store, remodeling the upper floors for offices. The location near the Galleria is a valuable

one, but the grand old department store, like similar stores in other cities, has changed forever.

Louisville also has a few unique shopping areas that attract visitors from other major cities. Antique hunters prowl the shops along Bardstown Road, Frankfort Avenue, and elsewhere. The historic preservation movement has helped establish several skilled artisans specializing in restoring and creating stained-glass windows and ornaments. A colony of art shops and antique stores along Frankfort Avenue offers everything from needlework and sketches to baskets and sculpture, and from Kentucky contemporary art to old masterworks. With around 5,000 retail establishments (according to the U.S. Census Bureau), the Louisville area offers plenty of places to shop.

Retail trade can't survive without suppliers, and Louisville is still a major wholesale center. Census Bureau figures show there are more than 1,600 wholesale businesses in the area, including about 100 dealing in hardware. Many of them specialize rather narrowly—in items like beer, chemicals, medical equipment, construction equipment, or water beds. Others offer broad ranges of products such as clothing, food, sporting and hobby goods, or building supplies.

Yet another type of trade has become big business in Louisville—a type undreamed of during the city's first century and a half. The automobile age made franchise restaurant chains possible; Colonel Harland Sanders made Kentucky internationally famous for fried chicken.

The colonel led a colorful life long before he came up with his famous recipe: farmer, streetcar conductor, 16-year-old soldier, railroad fireman, lawyer, steamboat operator, tire salesman, and service station operator. He started serving meals to travelers in 1930, in the dining room of his home at his service station in Corbin, Kentucky. Later he opened a restaurant, which did well, and Kentucky's first motel, which closed during World War II. In 1952 he sold the first franchise to make his special type of fried chicken. When the new interstate highway bypassed his restaurant in the mid-1950s, he was left with little more than his social security checks, his small franchise operation, and his enthusiasm.

By 1963 he had 600 outlets throughout the United States and Canada. The next year, he sold his United States operation for $2 million to a group of investors including John Y. Brown, Jr., of Louisville. The company issued its first stock in 1966, and moved into a new $2-million headquarters in Louisville two years later.

A CENTER FOR SERVICES

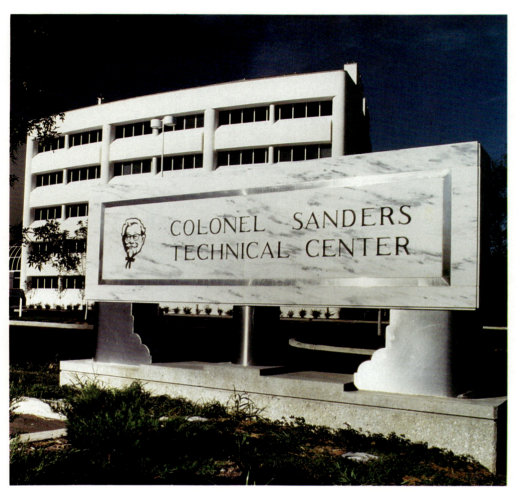

By mid-1971 there were more than 3,500 Kentucky Fried Chicken (KFC) restaurants in the United States and abroad; the company was sold to Hublein Inc. for $285 million. In 1982 KFC was sold to PepsiCo Inc., for $840 million. In the late 1980s, the company had more than 6,500 restaurants in 55 countries, including large operations in Japan, Australia, New Zealand, Great Britain, Puerto Rico, and Mexico. Annual sales topped $3.5 billion. And in 1987 KFC opened the first franchise restaurant in China, overlooking Mao Tse-Tung's mausoleum in Beijing.

The success of Kentucky Fried Chicken inspired other franchise operations in Louisville. Two of the most successful have been the Chi-Chi's Mexican-style restaurant chain, one of the top 20 Kentucky-based companies, and the Druther's International fast food chain, one of the largest companies based in the Louisville area.

HEALTH CARE

Thanksgiving weekend of 1984 brought the attention of the world to Louisville—and to Bill Schroeder, the man who was to live a record 620 days with the support of an artificial heart. Hourly bulletins reported on his progress

Above left: These people wait their turn on the Toonerville II. Photo by John Nation

Above: The success of Colonel Sander's Kentucky Fried Chicken is an inspiration to other local businesses. Photo by John Beckman/Quadrant

in the days following his operation; millions of people followed the reports, silently cheering and praying for his survival.

Two more men received artificial hearts in the following months; Schroeder outlived both of them. But Schroeder was only semimobile, tied to his mechanical heart's power supply, and further disabled by a series of strokes. After his death, the medical community confined artificial hearts to temporary uses, while continuing to analyze their potential.

The heart implants at Humana Hospital/Audubon were a dramatic illustration of Louisville's leadership in the field of medicine. But Louisville doctors and hospitals are leaders in other procedures, as well.

Patients have come from throughout the world to have fingers, hands, and entire limbs reattached at Louis-

Facing page: Modern architecture characterizes the Medical Tower Building. Photo by C.J. Elfont

Above: The Baptist Hospital East is one of Louisville's largest community hospitals. Photo by John Nation

ville's Jewish Hospital. Physicians have come from throughout the world to learn the techniques at the Louisville Institute for Hand and Microsurgery. Patients have come from a multistate area to receive organ transplants—sometimes multiple organ transplants—in Louisville hospitals. And critically ill children, suffering everything from severe burns to birth defects to cancer, are treated at Kosair Children's Hospital, one of the nation's 15 largest hospitals for children.

Health care has a long tradition at The Falls. The first hospital, Louisville Marine Hospital, opened in 1823, mainly to care for people who became sick while traveling. St. Joseph's Infirmary, the first religious hospital, opened in 1836. And the Louisville Medical Institute, the forerunner of the University of Louisville School of Medicine, opened in 1838.

The Marine Hospital is long gone, but its former site is in the middle of today's sprawling downtown Medical Center complex. Built around the U of L Schools of Medicine and Dentistry, the center includes five major hospitals, centers for cancer and eye research, a rehabilitation center for victims of strokes and neurological injuries, a drug- and alcohol-abuse center, Red Cross headquarters, and several large office buildings filled with doctors' offices, clinics, and laboratories.

Each hospital in this center has its specialties, along with facilities for general treatment. Many of the programs are operated in conjunction with the medical school, and many of the doctors are on the medical school faculty.

Jewish Hospital, internationally known for hand and microsurgery, also specializes in other types of complex surgery, including heart and organ transplants, plastic surgery, and neuroscience. Methodist Evangelical Hospital has a growing occupational medicine program, and one of the nation's first special facilities for decontaminating people who have come into contact with hazardous materials. Kosair Children's Hospital is equipped to handle practically every disease, injury, and birth defect in children. Norton Hospital, operated in conjunction with Kosair Children's Hospital, offers acute care, an advanced spinal center, cancer treatment, and a special pavilion for women.

Humana Hospital/University of Louisville, operated by Humana Incorporated for the university, is Kentucky's only level-one treatment center for adults with severe injuries. It also has an adult burn center, a diabetes center, and a center for geriatric research.

The concentration of hospitals in the medical center, along with the shift of population to the suburbs, helped force several of Louisville's older hospitals to move or to close in recent years. But the city is still served by three

other major hospitals: Sts. Mary and Elizabeth in the southwest, Humana Hospital/Audubon (which succeeded the old St. Joseph's Infirmary) in southern Louisville, and St. Anthony's in the Highlands.

The move to the suburbs began in 1970, when Extendicare built Suburban Hospital in the affluent area east of the city. Baptist Hospital East soon arose just across Interstate 64; a decade and a half later, Baptist Hospitals of Louisville completed the transition by phasing out its original hospital in the city's Highlands area. The late 1970s and early 1980s saw the construction of Humana Hospital/Southwest, in southwestern Jefferson County, and Humana Hospital/Audubon, in southern Louisville near the suburbs.

Suburban Hospital was a trend-setter. It was the area's first hospital operated for profit, and it brought a new type of competition to the hospital business. It was also one of the first hospitals built by Extendicare, Inc., a rapidly growing chain of nursing homes that would soon become one of the nation's largest hospital chains—and Louisville's largest home-based company.

In those days of expanding government health-care plans and generous hospitalization insurance benefits, the demand for hospital beds was growing rapidly. By 1973 Extendicare had sold all its nursing homes, and was concentrating entirely on hospitals. In 1974 it changed its name to Humana Inc. By 1986 the company had 86 hospitals in 21 states and three foreign countries.

Humana helped bring modern business practices and modern marketing techniques to a field long dominated by not-for-profit and charitable organizations. These practices became especially important in the 1980s, when the federal government, large insurance companies, and employers pressed for lower health-care costs and shorter hospital stays. As hospital occupancy rates declined, hospitals had to compete more aggressively for patients.

One of Humana's major techniques for attracting patients is to establish "centers of excellence" at selected hospitals—centers for research and education in medical specialties, which become regional referral centers for patients needing special treatment. Louisville's Humana Heart Institute International, with its heart transplant and artificial heart program, is one of these centers.

The company also established primary-care clinics with extended hours to treat patients who didn't need hospitalization, and to refer patients to Humana hospitals. Humana had 160 of these clinics in the early 1980s, but they didn't prove profitable. It sold the last of them in 1987.

A third technique was establishing health-care programs that would offer lower rates while referring patients to Humana hospitals. These programs included health maintenance organizations, regular group health plans, and medicare supplement plans. By late 1987, about 580,000 people were covered by Humana plans, providing a growing base of potential patients.

A CENTER FOR FINANCE

The mid-1980s brought a flurry of changes to the financial scene in the Louisville area and throughout Kentucky. The changes enhanced Louisville's position as the state's financial center—and made Louisville a power in southern Indiana banking, as well.

Revisions in national and state banking laws made the changes possible. The major changes came after Kentucky and Indiana passed laws that removed the old restrictions keeping banks from operating across county and state lines.

First, the holding companies that own Louisville's three biggest banks—Citizens Fidelity, First National,

and Liberty National—began buying banks in other cities in Kentucky. When the new laws allowed, they also began buying banks across the river in southern Indiana.

As the competition increased, Citizens Fidelity edged past First National Bank to become Kentucky's largest bank, in terms of assets. Then, in early 1987, Citizens became the first large Kentucky bank to be absorbed by a large multistate holding company: PNC Financial Corporation of Pittsburgh. Other Kentucky banks were also considered to be good targets for takeovers, and in 1988, First Kentucky National Corporation announced intentions to merge with Cleveland's National City Corporation.

One of the reasons Kentucky banks became targets was their overall sound management. A 1987 study by Professional Banking Services, a Louisville consulting firm, showed that Kentucky banks' average return on assets and equity was significantly higher than the national average. First Kentucky National Corporation, which owns First National Bank, had increased its stock dividends every year for 40 years.

But traditional banking isn't Louisville's only financial strength. The city has also become a national center for processing transactions—charge card slips from merchants, charge card payments from customers, airline ticket orders, and other modern substitutes for cash.

Below left: The Almstedt Brothers building, erected in the 1920s, is one of the elegant old bank buildings on Market Street. Photo by C.J. Elfont

Below: Here's an elegant welcome to the First National Bank. Photo by C.J. Elfont

In this business, time and efficiency are everything: the quicker an item can be processed, the quicker the money goes into the proper bank account. It's also a highly computerized business, transmitting millions of dollars a day over the Federal Reserve System's electronic banking network. Louisville's transportation network and location help; mail and express shipments arrive quickly from throughout the eastern half of the United States.

Louisville's National Processing Company, owned by First Kentucky National, is one of the nation's largest transaction processors, and one of the few companies approved by the U.S. Treasury Department to handle MasterCard and Visa slips. It has operations in Phoenix, Dallas, and Chicago as well as in Louisville. Together they handle over 200 million paper and electronic transactions a year. Weekly volume can top $100 million—and not one cent of it in cash!

Within months after PNC's merger with Citizens Fidelity, the Pittsburgh bank holding company announced it would consolidate its processing operations in Louisville—greatly increasing the amount of money passing through the city by mail and computer network.

INSURANCE

Two more large financial powers make their headquarters in Louisville. Both are insurance holding companies. Capital Holding Corp., Kentucky's third-largest home-based company in terms of revenue, owns insurance companies based in Kentucky and other states including California, Florida, Georgia, Pennsylvania, and North Carolina. It has a large work force in Louisville, mainly in the Commonwealth Building at Fourth Avenue and Broadway. Capital Holding stayed there throughout the business decline in the surrounding area, and became a key force in the revival of the Broadway-focused part of downtown. In late 1987 it gave the area another important boost by announcing plans to build a large new headquarters next to the Commonwealth Building.

I.C.H. Corporation, Kentucky's fourth-largest home-based company in terms of revenue, owns individual companies based in Colorado, Illinois, Pennsylvania, Texas, and elsewhere. It maintains a small corps of employees in Louisville; major offices are located at the home bases of the companies it owns.

THE MEDIA

January 1986 brought the end of an era in Louisville: The Bingham family, owner of the city's newspapers for more than 70 years, put its entire media empire up for sale.

The decision to sell ended local ownership of *The Courier-Journal*, winner of eight Pulitzer Prizes and often rated among the nation's top 20 newspapers. One of the nation's few major newspapers with a liberal editorial policy, it was also one of the few major newspapers not owned by a multicity chain. The sale also meant the breakup of a media conglomerate that included the area's leading television and radio stations, which had been a leader in cultural and charitable efforts throughout the area.

And for people throughout the nation, it brought the story of a family tragedy, headlined "The Fall of the House of Bingham" by *The New York Times*. The grandchildren of Robert Worth Bingham, who bought the newspapers in 1918, had developed such strong and conflicting interests that they could no longer work together to run the business. Their 79-year-old father, Barry Bingham, Sr., decided to sell the companies because of the conflict.

The sale included the morning *Courier-Journal;* the evening *The Louisville Times*, which attracted less national attention but drew more subscribers in Louisville; WHAS-TV, the city's leading television station; WHAS and WAMZ, two of the leading radio stations; Standard Gravure, a large printing company specializing in Sunday newspaper magazine and colored advertising supplements; and subsidiary companies that prepared computer network abstracts of articles from hundreds of technical journals, produced television commercials, and operated a chain of local computer stores.

Most of the empire went to multistate chains. Gannett Company bought *The Courier-Journal* and *The Louisville Times*, and later discontinued the *Times*. The Providence Journal Company of Rhode Island bought WHAS-TV; Clear Channel Communications of Texas bought radio stations WHAS and WAMZ. Only Standard Gravure emerged as a "family-owned" company; it was bought by Michael Shea, a native of Atlanta, who moved to Louisville soon after he took over.

The Courier-Journal calculated in mid-1987 that the total price for all the companies was nearly $443 million. More than $115 million went to Barry Bingham, Sr., and his wife, Mary; the rest was divided among his children, their spouses, and grandchildren.

The Bingham tradition of excellence in journalism made Louisville a highly competitive media market. Television stations developed news operations that were larger and better than in other cities of similar size. Large radio stations also developed strong news operations.

Small daily newspapers do a good business in Jeffersonville and New Albany, competing fiercely with Indiana editions of *The Courier-Journal*. Weekly neighborhood newspapers, however, had a hard time competing—especially after *The Louisville Times* developed weekly neighborhood sections, focusing on community news. Community weeklies survived, but often changed hands.

The area's major newspaper success story of recent years is *Business First*, a weekly newspaper established in 1984 by American City Business Journals of Kansas City. For a publisher, the company tapped Mike Kallay, former business editor and assistant managing editor of *The Louisville Times*. Kallay brought the Louisville tradition of excellence in journalism to the new paper, along with his own extensive knowledge of the business community. Within three years, the paper had a paid circulation of over 9,000, and was earning a profit.

Louisville magazine, a slick-paper monthly published by the Louisville Chamber of Commerce, covers all aspects of community life. Established in 1950, it has won a series of local and national awards for writing, design, photography, and overall content.

THE BROADCAST SCENE

The Louisville area has a national reputation as a competitive broadcast town, both in television and in radio. There are seven local television stations: three major network affiliates, two independents, and two stations affiliated with the Public Broadcasting System. The sale of WHAS-TV, the CBS affiliate and the traditional leader in area ratings, prompted a strong challenge by WAVE-TV, the NBC affiliate and strong second in the ratings. The two public television stations, WKPC and WKET, vary their schedules so that they rarely show the same PBS program at the same time.

The radio scene is even more active, with 21 stations in the immediate Louisville area and more on the fringes. Formats are targeted at nearly every imaginable interest and age group, from contemporary to nostalgic, rock to classical, religious to informational. Two public radio stations offer classical music; the third offers jazz, blues, folk, news, and information. Former Bingham stations WHAS (AM) and WAMZ (FM) led the ratings in early 1987, each with more than 15 percent of the total daytime listeners. But the ratings have been very volatile over the years as stations change ownerships, focus, and format. One noticeable trend: the public radio stations have been gaining audience; WFPL, the jazz station, rose from 13th to 8th place between 1986 and 1987.

Louisville's strong media tradition, and the variety of businesses and industries, have nurtured an active and competitive business in advertising and public relations. More than a dozen agencies had 10 or more employees in early 1987; at least three public relations firms also employed 10 or more. This field, like broadcasting, is quite volatile; alignments change as companies win and lose large accounts.

The Courier Journal *still holds its own amidst the competition. Photo by John Nation*

Chapter VIII

A Tradition of Craftsmanship

STRENGTH IN DIVERSITY

Those who wonder about the future of manufacturing in the United States might do well to look to Louisville.

Ford Motor Company has two large, modern plants in Louisville suburbs. One assembles Ranger pickup trucks and all of the company's Bronco II utility vehicles; the other assembles all of the company's U.S.-made medium and heavy trucks. Employees and union leaders are involved in programs to increase productivity and quality. And the Ranger/Bronco II plant boasts the fastest automotive assembly line in the United States.

General Electric's Appliance Park, in the suburbs south of the city, is one of the largest appliance manufacturing complexes in the world. Built in the early 1950s, it began undergoing major renovations in the early 1980s. Using the latest design and automation techniques, the company is making better appliances for less money, using fewer labor-hours per appliance.

Meanwhile, at two companies in the historic industrial areas just east of downtown, skilled potters and decorators make fine stoneware dishes and knickknacks using techniques passed down through the centuries.

And in an older industrial neighborhood in the southern part of the city, a small group of artists and craftsmen custom-builds fine pipe organs. Their instruments grace churches, music schools, and auditoriums from South Dakota to the Atlantic Ocean and the Gulf of Mexico.

Manufacturing, it seems, is headed in two directions. Large factories can thrive if they modernize, using technology and employee involvement to increase productivity and quality. Smaller factories and shops can thrive by relying on a high degree of craftsmanship to produce specialized equipment and goods, often custom-building their products to order.

Six major factories stand in a row at General Electric Appliance Park. Photo by R. Hower/Quadrant

IN CELEBRATION OF LOUISVILLE

Louisville, like other cities in the U.S., was stricken by a series of major factory cutbacks and closings in the 1970s and early 1980s. Manufacturing jobs declined from 26 percent of the area's employment in the mid-1970s to 20 percent in the mid-1980s.

But Louisville is attracting new industries, and is encouraging its established industries to modernize. In fact, while manufacturing jobs in general were in decline from the late 1960s to the mid-1980s, the number of manufacturing firms in the Louisville area actually increased. The key to this trend was a trimming down in the average size of manufacturing firms: in the late 1970s, nearly half the local manufacturers had more than 20 employees; in the late 1980s, less than 42 percent of them had more than 20.

A CHANGING ROLE

Manufacturing came early to Louisville, supplementing the community's role as a frontier center for transportation and trade.

Sawmills were set up almost immediately to turn the area's trees into lumber. Just two years after the settlement was established, George Rogers Clark proposed building boats in Louisville, noting "here is saw mills plenty." Lumber and boats would become two of the area's major products.

Salt works were another early industry, now vanished. Brine was drawn from wells southwest of Louisville, then cooked until the water boiled away and salt remained. For several decades the Louisville area was the frontier's primary producer of salt, which was important for preserving foods.

Distilling thrived from the beginning. Only two years after the first settlers arrived, three residents were making and selling whiskey, establishing a tradition that continues unbroken to this day. (During Prohibition, of course, it was officially produced only for medicinal purposes.)

By 1810 there were several small industries, most of them serving the settlers and their farms. They included a flour mill, a foundry, a soap and candle factory, a sugar refinery, and tobacco processors. In 1816 the city built its first steamboat; soon manufacturing was booming. It grew even more as the railroads arrived.

The industrial revolution brought a spirit of craftsmanship to the cities at The Falls. The world's most elegant steamboats were built here; they inspired a pride that carried over to humbler manufacturing enterprises—from heavy machinery to plows and from furniture to clothing. The European immigration brought skilled craftsmen to the area; many set up their own shops, and many of the shops grew into factories.

World War II brought a much heavier emphasis on manufacturing, based again on the transportation network. Louisville's location on the Ohio River and major

railroad lines gave it easy, safe access to oil, coal, and other raw materials. And its complex of distilleries gave it a tremendous capacity to produce industrial alcohol—one of the key ingredients in synthetic rubber.

A complex called "Rubbertown" grew rapidly along the river southwest of Louisville, making the city the world's largest producer of synthetic rubber during World War II. A naval gun plant arose in the southern part of the city. A new airport appeared nearby, flanked by aircraft plants. A major gunpowder plant was built at Charlestown, Indiana, northeast of Louisville. The old Howard Shipyards in Jeffersonville built landing craft and other small boats; the Ford plant in southwestern Louisville produced jeeps and military trucks.

Industrial expansion continued after the war. Rubbertown continued to grow, producing an increasing variety of plastics and synthetic rubber. International Harvester took over one of the aircraft factories and used it to produce farm equipment. The Cold War kept the naval gun plant and the powder plant in production.

A TRADITION OF CRAFTSMANSHIP

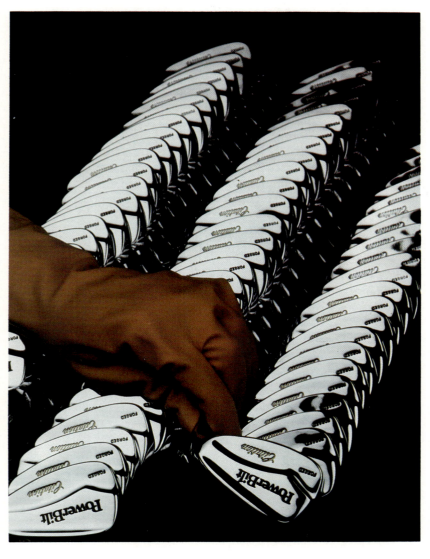

Ford built a new, larger facility to help meet the growing demand for cars—and then built another facility to produce heavy trucks. Appliance Park blossomed with the housing and baby booms, employing nearly 23,000 people by the early 1970s.

But industrial expansion was accompanied by sometimes-painful adjustments, as gains in new sectors came with losses in the old. Two of Louisville's three breweries closed in the 1960s; a major tobacco factory closed in 1970. Labor troubles grew through the 1960s and early 1970s as workers encountered the increasing demands and frustrations of high-pressure production. The Louisville area's manufacturing employment peaked in the late 1960s and early 1970s—then followed the national trend as manufacturing started to decline.

First came a series of production cutbacks and layoffs; then came plant shutdowns. Louisville's last brewery closed in 1978. Brown & Williamson closed its cigarette factory in 1982, eliminating more than 2,900 local jobs. Financially troubled International Harvester closed

Above: Powerbilt golf clubs are manufactured in Louisville. Photo by Quadrant

Above left: Tobacco plants flourish in the rich soil and wonderful climate of Louisville. Photo by John Nation

its factory in 1983 and its foundry in 1985; they had employed 6,500 at their peak. Lorillard phased out its cigarette factory beginning in 1985; another 1,000 jobs were lost. The old Louisville & Nashville shops were phased out as the railroad was absorbed into CSX Corporation; 3,000 jobs moved elsewhere. Jeffboat stopped producing new boats at the old Howard Shipyards in 1986, but kept the plant intact to do repairs—and to wait for the time when demand for new barges and towboats will return.

IN CELEBRATION OF LOUISVILLE

At the same time, jobs were being created by new and expanding industries. And in several instances, large-company pullouts became opportunities for local companies. Louisville Edible Oil Products Inc. produced soybean oil for a wide variety of food processors, using the old Durkee Foods plant. Thoroughbred Containers Inc. makes all kinds of cardboard containers in the old Mead Container Corporation plant—which was in one of the factories that Ford had outgrown. Carrier Vibrating Equipment Inc. is a world leader in making equipment to handle bulk material; its six local managers bought the company from Rexnord. Louisville Forge and Gear Works operates in part of the old International Harvester plant.

The changing economy also brought a change in Louisville's labor climate. Management and labor worked with federal, state, and local leaders to find new ways to solve their problems peacefully. Tobacco workers and building-trades workers approved no-strike clauses in some of their contracts. Louisville's strike record, which had been much worse than the national average in the 1970s, became better than the national average in the 1980s.

FROM MODEL T TO BRONCO II

Mid-1987 brought welcome news to Louisville: Ford Motor Company announced plans for a $260-million expansion of the Louisville Assembly Plant, birthplace of the popular Ranger pickup trucks and Bronco II utility vehicles. The expansion was expected to add at least 300 jobs to the payroll of the Louisville area's second-largest industrial employer—and a substantial increase in production capacity at the plant that claimed the nation's fastest automotive assembly line: 79 vehicles per hour in 1988.

The expansion includes a new wing of about 160,000 square feet. It was designed to add a new model to the utility vehicle line, and to provide for increased production. And it was a clear sign that Louisville's labor-management cooperation was working.

Labor problems had been common at the Louisville Assembly Plant in the 1970s. Quality and productivity suffered, and the company reportedly considered closing the facility. Alarmed at the prospect, local union leaders and plant management worked together to establish a new atmosphere of cooperation.

Employees were asked for their recommendations on improving quality and efficiency—and on improving the design of the vehicles. They were even asked to help design the plant layout when the assembly line was upgraded. Pride in their work increased so much that the employees themselves organized open houses at the plant. In 1986 the U.S. Department of Labor said that Ford was Louisville's "shining labor-management star."

Through the years, Ford has manufactured nearly every type of civilian vehicle in its Louisville plants—from the Model T to the LTD and from the compact pickup to huge tractors for semi-trailer rigs. Edsels were assembled here in the late 1950s; the last of the "big" family sedans were assembled here in the 1970s (requiring nearly two years of double shifts to meet the demand).

Production began modestly in 1913, in two small shops where workers assembled a dozen Model T Fords a day. The first factory opened three years later in southern Louisville; production climbed from 7,000 vehicles a year in 1916 to 56,000 a year by the mid-1920s. In 1925 production moved to a new, larger factory in western Louisville, with a daily capacity of 400 cars. It built the Model T, Model A, the Ford V-8, and a variety of trucks. In World War II it built military trucks and jeeps; after the war it returned to civilian production.

The present Louisville assembly plant, directly south of Louisville, opened in 1955. It was designed to produce 16 of Ford's 17 automobile body styles, and all 190 different truck models.

In 1969, truck production was shifted to the new Kentucky Truck plant east of Louisville. Medium, heavy, and extra-heavy trucks have been produced there ever since. The assembly plant continued to build passenger cars, and in 1973 resumed building light trucks.

Light trucks became the assembly plant's sole product in 1981. Ford's new compact pickup truck, the Ranger, was introduced there in 1982. And the Ranger-based Bronco II, which traces its concept back to the World War II jeep, was born there in 1983.

The new compact trucks were tremendously successful; the Ranger soon became America's best-selling compact pickup. The one millionth Ranger/Bronco was assembled in Louisville only three and a half years after production began.

At the Kentucky Truck Plant, production follows the national economy. Large trucks are built to order, often produced as bare chassis so bodies can be added elsewhere. Many medium trucks become school buses; other medium and heavy trucks become fire engines, dump trucks, large vans, tow trucks, garbage trucks, and anything else imaginable.

Since these trucks are expensive investments, sales follow overall economic trends. Ford began attacking economic downturns in the 1980s by setting up a leasing system for companies and government agencies that weren't prepared to buy new trucks.

GE'S APPLIANCE PARK

Southeast of downtown Louisville, on a 1,000-acre plot of former farmland surrounded by suburbs, lies the area's largest industrial employer: General Electric Company's Appliance Park.

To call it a factory would be gross understatement. Arranged in a neat north-south row are six factory buildings, each a unit unto itself. They produce washers, dryers, electric ranges, dishwashers, and refrigerators.

A foundry, the park's own railroad yards, and a 48-acre warehouse lie to the west of the factories. To the east, across a broad strip of grass, is a long row of parking lots. To the south are buildings for administrative offices, and for research and development.

This is the headquarters of GE's Appliance Business, with a global network of more than 35,000 employees. In 1987, about 13,000 of them worked at Appliance Park.

It's a place where each appliance is shipped with a printed letter "signed" by one of the employees who produced it, thanking the customer for buying it and telling how to get help if it isn't satisfactory. It's a place where employees proudly wear T-shirts proclaiming "GE is ME"—and are featured in newspaper and magazine advertisements if they make notable off-the-job contributions to the community. It's a place where union and

Facing page: A Ford Bronco II holds a place of honor on a pedestal outside its birthplace. Photo by John Nation

Left: Pride is part of the culture at General Electric Appliance Park, where workers often wear their "GE is ME" T-shirts on the job. Photo by John Nation

management representatives have been sitting down together, working out ways to improve production efficiency and product quality—even if it means major changes in work rules and sometimes a loss of jobs.

It's a place that has changed dramatically in recent years.

In the 1960s, GE had a national reputation for being tough with unions; labor responded with toughness of its own. Disputes over grievances often led to strikes. Appliance Park lost more than 500,000 man-hours a year because of walkouts; in one of the worst years, a federal mediator counted more than 40 strikes.

The situation began to change in the mid-1970s. Company and union officials realized that the atmosphere was damaging morale, productivity, and quality—and ultimately profits, jobs, and take-home pay. Mediators helped guide the company and unions through the delicate negotiations needed to start building labor peace.

The national economy emphasized the urgency of the task. Sales of major appliances dropped dramatically; Appliance Park announced layoff after layoff. From a peak of 23,000 in 1973, the work force zigzagged down to less than 14,000 by the early 1980s.

In 1981, at the height of a recession, GE decided to spend nearly $40 million to turn Appliance Park's dishwasher factory into a highly efficient, highly automated

Facing page: This tower, one of the first high-rise office buildings erected at a suburban freeway interchange in the area, is known throughout Louisville as the "wedding cake building." Photo by John Beckman/Quadrant

Above: Paint manufacturing is one of the important chemical related industries in Louisville. Photo by John Nation

operation. The company told the unions that the changes were necessary to remain competitive, increase sales, and save jobs. A union leader said later that labor was both afraid to automate and afraid not to.

The new dishwashers were more efficient and more reliable, earning top ratings from consumer testing organizations. GE's share of the nation's dishwasher sales increased by 10 percentage points, to 40 percent. And dishwasher sales increased as the national economy improved.

There were 1,500 jobs in the dishwasher factory before the modernization, and only 900 immediately afterward. But the increased sales brought increased employment, and by 1987 the number of jobs at the plant had climbed back to 1,500.

While the modernization was under way, management took steps to emphasize teamwork throughout Appliance Park. Quality circles were set up to give

employees a voice in improving operations. Management and labor became more frank with each other, discussing options and seeking ways to improve quality and productivity. Strikes became rare. In 1984, a decade after the effort for labor peace began, *Fortune* magazine named Appliance Park one of the 10 best-managed plants in the nation.

In the mid-1980s, GE started a $108-million program to modernize refrigerator assembly at Appliance Park. The goal once again was to make better and more efficient appliances for less money, with fewer labor hours.

FROM RUBBER TO PLASTIC TO...

The Rubbertown complex, with its acres of gleaming tanks and pipes and mysterious-looking structures, has given Louisville an important advantage in the age of synthetics. The government-built factories were sold to private businesses after World War II, and the range of materials produced there expanded dramatically.

Two of the well-known major chemical and rubber companies have large plants there: E.I. Dupont de Nemours & Company, and B.F. Goodrich. Dupont makes neoprene, the synthetic rubber used in products ranging from shoe soles to tires and adhesives to rocket fuels. B.F. Goodrich makes plastics, dry rubber, latex, and specialty materials.

Other companies produce raw materials for chemical processes. Airco Carbide, for instance, makes calcium carbide, then uses it to make acetylene, which in turn is used to make synthetic rubber. United Catalysts Inc. produces chemicals that make other chemical processes possible.

Also in the Rubbertown complex, companies turn the raw rubber and plastics into products that can be used in many ways. Rohm & Haas Kentucky Inc. produces acrylic emulsions, polyvinyl chloride modifiers, Plexiglas molding powder, and Acryloid coatings. These are vital ingredients in thousands of industrial and consumer items, including adhesives, greeting cards, light fixtures, outdoor signs, paints, phonograph records and compact disks, plastic bottles, plastic pipe, plastic wrapping, skylights, textiles, waxes, windows, and window frames.

A TRADITION OF CRAFTSMANSHIP

Some of the chemicals and materials produced in Rubbertown are passed on to other local industries. Paint manufacturing is one of the important chemical-related industries in Louisville. Porter Paint Company, one of the nation's top 20 paint companies, makes high performance coatings and resurfacing materials, as well as paint, at its two local plants. It sells its paint, along with wallpaper and other decorating supplies, at more than 115 company-owned Porter Paint stores and more than 400 independent dealers in the Midwest and Southeast.

Other Louisville paint and coating manufacturers with operations in Louisville include DeVoe & Raynolds, Reliance Universal Inc., and Kurfees Coatings Inc.

Another chemical plant from the World War II era, the Indiana Army Ammunition plant, continues to be a sizable industry in the late 1980s. Production has changed dramatically from wartime to peacetime. Employment peaked at nearly 30,000 during World War II, peaked at about 19,000 during the Vietnam war, and stabilized at more than 1,800 in the late 1980s. At that rate, it is the area's fifth largest manufacturer.

Above left: Bernhein Distillery Company represents a traditional Louisville industry. Photo by C. J. Elfont

Above: Skilled hands and traditional tools fashion a bowl in the Hadley Pottery factory. Photo by C.J. Elfont

HEAVY METAL, LIGHT METAL

The age of steam brought machinery manufacturers to Louisville, and they've been a vital part of the area's industry ever since. More than 160 plants in the area make machinery and metal products today, from steam boilers to saw blades and from truck trailers to conveyors.

The biggest today is the Naval Ordnance Station Louisville, another of the World War II plants. The station, owned and operated by the U.S. Navy, overhauls and repairs large naval guns and shipboard weapons systems, such as rocket launchers. At nearly 2,400 employ-

179

ees, it was the area's fourth largest manufacturer in 1987. The Henry Vogt Machine Company, another of the area's top 10 manufacturers, began as a small machine shop in the 1880s and has been family-operated ever since. Today it has more than 1,000 employees and a worldwide sales network. Products include steel valves and fittings for the oil, chemical, and power industries; steam boilers; thermal energy storage machines; refrigeration equipment; and ice-making machines.

American Standard makes plumbing fixtures and luxury baths. Kentucky Manufacturing Company makes truck trailers. Lantech Inc. makes stretch wrap equipment. Bunton Company makes commercial lawn and turf equipment, widely used by parks departments, golf courses, and businesses.

On the lighter side, Reynolds Metals Company has three plants in Louisville, making products ranging from aluminum foil to aluminum lamp posts. One plant makes aluminum powders and pastes used in paints and rocket fuel. With nearly 900 employees, Reynolds is one of the top 10 manufacturers in the area.

Alcan Aluminum, in addition to aluminum foil, makes foil-laminated paper used in cigarette packages, and light-gauge aluminum sheet used to make heat exchangers.

CRAFTSMEN AND CRAFTSWOMEN

One of Louisville's major industrial strengths is the number of small companies devoted to producing products of fine quality.

Louisville Stoneware Company and Hadley Pottery Company are two examples—similar businesses with different personalities. The basic technology has been known for thousands of years; modern improvements have made the quality more consistent. Both companies produce sturdy pieces admired for their simplicity, humor, and rustic charm.

Working with carefully selected clays at just the right moisture levels, artisans use their hands and simple tools to create dishes, pots, and curiosities. Other artisans add the decorative patterns, following standard designs but doing the painting by hand. The finished pieces are placed into kilns, then heated to temperatures that fuse the clay so thoroughly that it will be safe in dishwashers, ovens, microwaves, and freezers.

Louisville Stoneware, formerly the Louisville Pottery Company, has been in the business since 1905. It offers more than 170 different shapes of stoneware, from traditional dishes to dishes shaped like pineapples, and from simple door plaques to birdhouses. When these shapes are multiplied by the number of decorative patterns available, the Louisville Stoneware catalog swells to more than 1,800 items.

The company's artists add new shapes and patterns from time to time, and produce custom designs for businesses and individuals.

Hadley Pottery is a living memorial to Mary Alice Hadley, a Louisville artist who started designing pottery about 1940. Her custom designs were so popular that she and her husband set up for expanded production in the old Butchertown Candle Factory in eastern Louisville.

Mrs. Hadley added new designs through the 1960s to adorn a complete line of dishes, including egg cups, teapots, porringers, and bean pots. And there are a few knickknacks, including a cat, a catbird, and a quail, duck, and hen.

Mrs. Hadley's husband sold the business after she died, but the employees stayed on, producing the designs she created.

Steiner-Reck Inc., one of the few pipe-organ builders in the United States, is a relative newcomer to Louisville—and came here almost accidentally. Phares Steiner, an organ maker based in Cincinnati, needed more shop space. He searched the areas around Cincinnati, Dayton, and Pittsburgh, but couldn't find adequate facilities at a price he could afford. Finally he found the proper space in a building in Old Louisville, and moved there in 1962.

Four years later, Gottfried C. Reck, a journeyman organ builder from Germany, came to Louisville to work with Steiner. They shared an enthusiasm for "tracker" organs—organs with direct mechanical linkages between the keyboard and valves, instead of pneumatic or electrical connections. In 1968 they formed a partnership, and in 1983 it became a corporation.

Organ building requires the skills of an architect, cabinetmaker, musician, fine mechanic, pipe maker, and

A TRADITION OF CRAFTSMANSHIP

tuner. Steiner and Reck have divided the responsibilities to take advantage of their individual strengths: Reck in architecture, mechanical design, and construction; Steiner in musical design, installation, and "voicing" the instrument to its surroundings.

Each Steiner-Reck organ is custom designed for its location, blending visually and acoustically with the architecture. Design and construction can take several months to several years, depending on the size of the organ and the complexity of the project. Production varies but averages between four and five organs a year.

As the company approached its 30th anniversary, it had built and installed nearly 90 organs in 17 states; about one-sixth were in Louisville. The grandest of all, with 48 stops and 63 ranks of pipes, is the focal point above the stage in the recital hall at the University of Louisville School of Music. The smallest is the portable three stop, three rank instrument used by the Louisville Bach Society.

There are many other examples of fine craftsmanship in the Louisville area, from cabinetmakers to jewelers to tool-and-die makers. And no recitation would be complete without the story of John Andrew "Bud" Hillerich, son of a German-born woodworker who set up shop in Louisville just before the Civil War.

Bud liked woodworking, but he loved baseball. One day in 1884 he offered to make a new bat for baseball great Pete Browning, and unwittingly started a new tradition.

Pete stood by as Bud shaped the bat, testing it at intervals until it felt just right. The next day he got three hits in three times at bat, ending a slump. Other players found their way to Hillerich's shop, and Bud's custom bats became known as Louisville Sluggers.

The company added golf clubs in 1916, and changed its name to Hillerich and Bradsby Company. The plant moved to larger quarters in Jeffersonville in 1974, and now turns out about 1.5 million wooden baseball bats a year. It also makes about 750,000 aluminum bats a year at a plant in California, and turns out golf clubs at plants in

Facing page: An inspector carefully checks each drink-sized bottle of genuine Kentucky bourbon. Photo by John Nation

Below: He's rolling out the barrels at Early Times Distillery. Photo by C. J. Elfont

IN CELEBRATION OF LOUISVILLE

Kentucky, Indiana, and Ontario. The president, J.A. Hillerich III, is a passionate fan of the Louisville Redbirds.

OLD STANDARDS

One of Louisville's 10 largest manufacturers makes one of Kentucky's most traditional products: bourbon whiskey, that fiery and tasty liquid that begins as corn and other grains. Another makes products from one of Kentucky's most picturesque and profitable crops: tobacco, shredded and packed into paper tubes to become cigarettes.

Both industries are traditional mainstays in Louisville, and both are in a state of transition. Where whiskey is concerned, it's a trend toward lighter and less fiery alcoholic beverages, often based on wine and fruit juices. As for tobacco, it has experienced a continuing decline in domestic sales based on concerns for users' health. In both cases, the manufacturers have responded in a number of ways: developing new products; consolidating manufacturing facilities; merging with similar companies; and buying companies that produce totally different products.

Brown-Forman Corporation is an example of the changes in the bourbon industry. The Louisville area's sixth-largest industrial employer, it makes Early Times and Old Forester at its distillery in Shively, then bottles them at its plant in Louisville.

But the company's best-selling brands are California Cooler, a line of fruit-flavored drinks based on wine; Jack Daniel's, the legendary "sipping whiskey" distilled in Lynchburg, Tennessee; and Canadian Mist, the nation's best-selling Canadian whiskey. The company also makes Southern Comfort, and imports Scotch and Irish whiskeys, cognac, tequila, and liqueurs. It sells a variety of domestic and imported wines.

And in recent years, Brown-Forman has diversified into other fields, including Lenox china and crystal, and Hartmann luggage.

Glenmore Distilleries is Louisville's second-largest home-based distilling company. The home of Kentucky Tavern, Yellowstone, and Old Thompson bourbons, it also produces a traditional line of gins and vodkas. Glenmore is also the maker of the Mr. Boston line of spirits and liquors, and publishes the bible of the mixed drink field, the *Mr. Boston DeLuxe Official Bartender's Guide.*

Recently the company began producing Chi-Chi's Margarita, a pre-mixed drink licensed by Louisville's chain of franchised Mexican restaurants. And for those who like the taste of a margarita without the kick of tequila, Glenmore offers Tequita—a beverage on the order of a wine cooler.

Two decades ago, there were four major cigarette factories in Louisville, employing as many as 12,000 workers. Today, there is one, with a payroll of about 3,400 employees.

Philip Morris, which processes and stores tobacco and makes cigarettes in Louisville, is the area's third largest manufacturer. Its plant in the western part of the city was modernized at a cost of more than $100 million in the early 1980s. It is now one of the world's largest cigarette factories under one roof; its updated equipment can turn out 275 million cigarettes per day. Many of the brands it produces have become more famous than the company's namesake: Marlboro, the world's best-selling cigarette; Merit; Benson & Hedges; and Virginia Slims.

But cigarette sales in the United States have been dropping since 1981; per capita consumption has been declining longer than that. Although increasing exports are cushioning the decline, the overall trend is downward. Traditional tobacco companies are meeting this challenge in several ways. One way is diversification, into companies and products that have nothing to do with tobacco. Another is consolidation: combining production facilities from several plants into one modern plant.

Consolidation led American Tobacco Company to close its Louisville plant in 1970; Brown & Williamson to close its plant in the early 1980s; and Lorillard to close its plant in 1985. But consolidation is also what kept Philip Morris production in Louisville, helped by a precedent-setting nine-year no-strike contract negotiated with the old tobacco workers union in 1979. (The union has

undergone some consolidation of its own: it's now the Bakery, Confectionery and Tobacco Workers International Union.) Recent negotiations have extended the life of that no-strike agreement to 15 years, and Louisville's remaining tobacco workers are some of the highest-paid production workers in the nation.

THINGS TO EAT

Several years ago, a nervous turkey appeared on billboards and television throughout the Louisville area. Eat ham for Thanksgiving dinner, he pleaded: Fischer's ham.

At about the same time, Phyllis Diller was appearing in a series of advertisements for another old-line Louisville food processor. Paramount, she said, makes "the beautiful pickle."

Then there's Al and Bob Purnell's "Old Folks Whole Hog Country Sausage," promoted by Al himself in down-home television commercials. Their smiling pig symbol and their countrified commercials belie their sophistication: they were among the first to make whole-beef sausage, dietetic sausage, and sausage-and-biscuit packages for microwave ovens.

Fischer Packaging Company, Paramount Foods, Inc., and the F.B. Purnell Sausage Company are just three of the Louisville area's many food processing companies, national and local. Pillsbury makes prepared dough products (biscuits, dinner rolls, and cookies) in New Albany; Armour processes meats. Mother's Cookie Company's name doesn't quite say it all; it's a major producer of Girl Scout Cookies, as well as its own brands.

And Colgate-Palmolive Company's plant in Clarksville makes toothpaste and dishwashing liquids to clean up after you eat—along with laundry detergent in case you eat too vigorously.

The biggest food operation based in Louisville, however, is Dairymen, Inc.—the nation's third largest agricultural cooperative, and its fifth largest food processing company.

Dairymen's members include about 6,400 dairy farmers in 16 eastern and southeastern states, from southern Pennsylvania to southern Illinois to Florida to Louisiana. It processes milk in 14 dairy plants, and makes butter, cheese, and milk powder at four manufacturing plants. Most of its products are sold under the Flav-O-Rich and Farm Best brand names.

Facing page: The twin towers of the downtown Galleria flank the multi-story glass atrium that spans Fourth Avenue. Photo by John Nation

Below: Oaken barrels used for aging Kentucky bourbon stand in neat rows at Glenmore Distillery. Photo by Ted Wathen/Quadrant

Epilogue

The Past and the Future Are Part of the Present

Louisville today is a city of contrasts: northern energy and southern grace; big-city bustle and small-city convenience; complex sophistication and frank simplicity; high-rise apartments and comfortable homes; grand opera and low-down blues. Many eras and cultures exist in Louisville, side-by-side.

These differences inspire a kind of creative tension that adds excitement to the community. Louisvillians hold strong opinions, and aren't shy about expressing them. Major community decisions may bring long and noisy discussions. The solutions that result often show a special type of balance—like the mirrored walls of the Center for the Arts reflecting the nineteenth-century buildings across the street.

The Ohio River, at last, is receiving the attention it deserves. Long polluted, it is safe for recreation again. Long separated from downtown Louisville by a deteriorating industrial area, it's the focus of major redevelopment that will open its banks to the public.

Downtown Louisville is polishing its two faces, and the long strand of Fourth Avenue that connects them. Service jobs are attracting more people to the central city, both to work and to live. Shopping and entertainment are following them back.

While the mixture of service, technology, and history inspires the downtown revival, the suburbs are thriving as the highway network expands. Major industries, shopping centers, and office complexes are growing around the freeway interchanges; major communities are settling around them. The older small towns add spice to

The Belle of Louisville, *an authentic old steamboat, pulls away from the Louisville wharf for a nighttime cruise. Photo by C.J. Elfont*

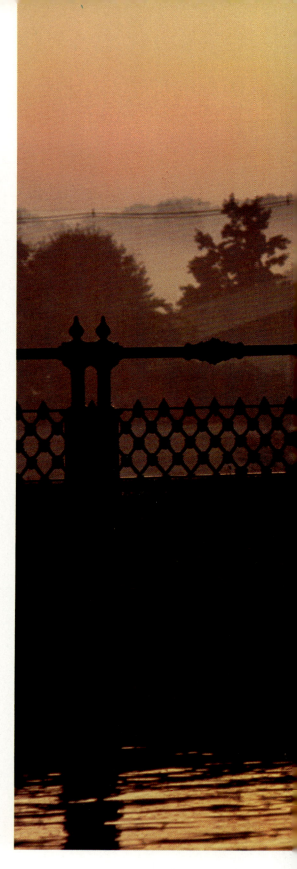

the scene, providing tranquil counterpoints in the hurry-up age.

Local government encourages the mixture. City programs help buyers who renovate old houses and businesspeople who renovate old commercial and industrial buildings. The "enterprise zone" designation offers special inducements for businesses that locate in areas of high unemployment and hire people from their neighborhoods. Special taxing districts encourage industrial development in the suburbs. A foreign trade zone offers special advantages for importers and exporters. And state and local governments have helped retrain workers for the new automated assembly lines.

Private enterprise is involved, as well. The Louisville Chamber of Commerce has programs to link promising businesses with investors, to encourage high-tech businesses, and to help new businesses and industries to locate in Louisville. Retired businesspeople offer help to struggling young businesses. The YWCA has a program to help low-income people go into business for them-

selves. And businesses of all kinds support cultural events of all kinds.

Louisville is a place where a rider on horseback can salute the pilot of a jet fighter; where a child can live in a 150-year-old home and use a computer at school; where anyone can enjoy a stunning sunset from the decks of a real old-time steamboat.

Nearly eight generations after John James Audubon, there's plenty to make Louisville "a favourite place of mine"…and perhaps of yours, as well.

Above left: "Light Up Louisville" turns City Hall and nearby Jefferson Square Park into a wonderland of lights. Photo by Christina M. Freitag

Above: Sunrise strikes the water in the historic reservoir at the Louisville Water Company's Crescent Hill treatment plant. Photo by John Nation

PART 2
Partners in Progress

Expressways and office buildings are agleam at dusk in this view. Photo by John Nation

Photo by Christina M. Freitag

South Central Bell 192-193

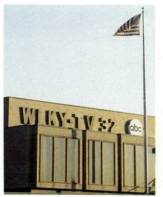

WLKY-TV 200-201

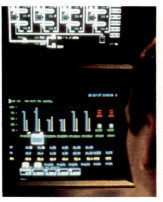
WAVE 3/Cosmos Broadcasting Corp. 194-197

WHAS-TV 198-199

Louisville Gas and Electric Company 202-203

The Courier-Journal 204

Chapter IX
Networks

Louisville's energy, communication, and transportation providers keep products, information, and power circulating inside and outside the area.

Photo by C.J. Elfont

IN CELEBRATION OF LOUISVILLE

SOUTH CENTRAL BELL

As the Information Age changes society, survival of businesses, government agencies, and schools will depend on their abilities to manage and transfer information. The telephones, switching centers, computers, and tiny glass fibers that make up the telecommunications network will give the user a competitive advantage.

In Louisville, South Central Bell is planning and building the telecommunications network of the future. The company is moving toward an Integrated Services Digital Network (ISDN) that allows video, facsimile, voice, and data to be transmitted by the same communications channel. For communities such as Louisville, ISDN will be a valuable resource for economic development.

From the somewhat inauspicious beginning in the laboratory of Alexander Graham Bell when he transmitted the now-famous "Mr. Watson, come here, I want you," has grown one of the most sophisticated, technically advanced parts of our modern society. Bell would no doubt be astounded by that progress, even though he witnessed major advances in his system before he died in 1922. But could he ever have dreamed of fiber optics, call forwarding, call waiting, three-way calling, WATS lines, and networking computers?

Progress has come swiftly over the past 30 or so years. Many of the changes seemed, at the time, to be the technological ultimate but became rather quickly commonplace or even obsolete. Without a doubt, many telephone service refinements will continue to flow to the public.

On the line for all of this is South Central Bell, one of two operating telephone systems in the BellSouth Corporation and the leading provider of telecommunications products and services in five states—Kentucky, Alabama, Louisiana, Mississippi, and Tennessee. In Kentucky alone South Central Bell, operating out of its headquarters in Louisville, employs 3,911 people and serves 771,469 customers.

In Louisville, there are more than 2,200 South Central Bell employees and more than 343,000 customers. A breakdown shows nearly 265,000 residential customers, roughly 82,000 business customers, and more than 6,000 coin stations.

That growth reached epic proportions in late 1987, when the latest in a series of Electronic Switching Systems went into service in the suburb of Shively, making Louisville the first metropolitan area in the South

Skilled central office technicians perform ongoing maintenance of the complex state-of-the-art telecommunications equipment, install new customer service procedures, and update equipment and procedures to ensure high-quality and failure-free customer service. Photo by C.M. Freitag

South Central Bell's service technicians, dispatched from 14 local work centers each morning and by phone throughout the day, are responsible for constructing, installing, and maintaining voice and data-transmission lines in the Louisville area. Photo by Bud Hunter

NETWORKS

Employees greet customers not only with a highly competent and confident attitude toward providing service but also with a warmth and a desire to place the customer first. Photo by C.M. Freitag

Central Bell system to become 100-percent electronic. Louisville began electronic switching in 1974 with its previous headquarters, a block to the east of its present headquarters. Over the intervening 13 years, 20 more offices were converted, making the entire program a $137-million investment.

Despite modern-times enthusiasm, the telephone in Louisville goes back to the beginnings of the Bell venture as a result of prominent Louisville resident James B. Speed's having seen Bell demonstrate his invention at the 1877 Philadelphia Exposition. Speed ordered two of the telephones and had them installed—one in his downtown office and the other in his cement plant in the Portland area of the city. That single line, providing communication between the two points, made Louisville one of the early dots on the nation's telephonic map.

It did not take long for that dot to grow, as Speed and some partners organized the American District Telegraph Company in 1879, beginning with 200 subscribers on multiparty lines. The Ohio Valley Telephone Company took over the business—retaining the original officers—in 1883, and the customer list grew to 1,400.

To solidify Louisville's position as an early telephone center, the firm in 1884 erected the first building in the world for the sole purpose of housing a telephone exchange. By 1886 telephone customers numbered 2,000.

Following a couple of sales and consolidations, Louisville telephone service came under Southern Bell Telephone and Telegraph Co. in 1926. Customers and service continued to grow, a new building was constructed in 1932, and Louisville continued to be the benefactor of the latest advances in the telephone business, always swimming in technology's mainstream.

Three major catches in that mainstream in recent years are services known as C.O. LAN, RingMaster, and Stylist.

C.O. LAN, which stands for Central Office Local Area Network, is a private data-communications network service for business or residential customers and is considered a link to the Integrated Services Digital Network, which allows simultaneous voice and data communications.

RingMaster provides many of the benefits of multiple-line telephones to single-line subscribers. With this service up to three telephone numbers ring on a single line, each having a distinctive ring to let the customer know who is being called.

Stylist service allows part of a telephone number to be listed as a word. For example, an automobile dealer might make what would have been the last four digits of his number the letters CARS.

The power of technology, the flexibility of the telecommunications network, and the imagination of South Central Bell employees are working to make life less complicat-

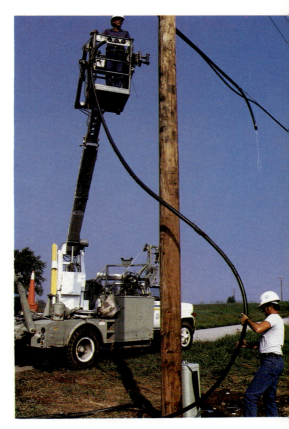

An important aspect of providing telecommunications service is being prepared for growth. To build new facilities correctly and without delay demands teamwork by all employees. Photo by C.M. Freitag

ed. Energy management systems, home education programs, home security, and home health-monitoring systems—all made possible by the telecommunications network—will help us juggle home, family, and career.

Even in the face of swift changes that make many new technologies obsolete in no time, South Central Bell and its employees continue a long tradition of being a model corporate citizen and giving individual service to the community. In this environment, special values flourish.

Those stated values of South Central Bell are customer first, respect for the individual, pursuit of excellence, positive response to change, and community mindedness. They have always been on the company's line, and they still ring true.

IN CELEBRATION OF LOUISVILLE

WAVE 3/COSMOS BROADCASTING CORP.

On Thanksgiving Eve 1948 WAVE-TV broadcast a two-hour show that featured civic officials and local entertainers on a set designed to look like a Kentucky barn. Today that telecast is remembered not for its content, but for its place in broadcast history; it was the first television show aired in Kentucky. The program was viewed by nearly every family in the area that owned a television receiver—all 2,000 of them.

Forty years and 1.1 million television sets later, WAVE 3 is building on the proud tradition that was born on that blustery November evening in 1948. As the first television station in the state, WAVE-TV's obligation to serve its community was an awesome responsibility—one that its owners recognized from the start.

In 1950 George W. Norton, Jr.,

WAVE 3's logo, a contemporary version of the station's logo in the 1950s, symbolizes WAVE 3's proud tradition as well as its promising future.

president and founder of WAVE, Inc., wrote about the station's first 16 months of operation: "Through the window of your television set can come anything from a high school game in which your boy is playing to a national event like the World Series, a dramatic hit on Broadway or an intimate musical review, a living room chat with the president of the United States or a prayer at the altar of a great cathedral."

Norton listed several of WAVE-TV's milestones during those first months: election coverage, a broadcast of a performance by the Louisville Symphony, and the area's first telecasts of hockey, boxing, baseball, football, and basketball. The station brought the World Series for the first time into the homes of area viewers in 1949, and had provided the state with the first television broadcast of the Kentucky Derby earlier that same year. Norton added that the responsibilities of broadcasters went beyond "alert showmanship." "Television," he concluded, "has a vital role to play during this critical era in world history, and we in TV must carry out faithfully our responsibility of good citizenship."

FORTY YEARS OF COMMUNITY SERVICE

George Norton's family not only had a long tradition of "good citizenship" in its community but also a tradition of progressive thinking. Within a year of its inaugural broadcast, the

News anchor Don Schroeder.

Meteorologist John Belski.

News anchor Jackie Hays.

Sports anchor Bob Domine.

WAVE 3 moved from its building on Broadway to this, its current facility, on Floyd Street in 1959. The building was dedicated with the broadcast of an opera commissioned by WAVE, Inc.

WAVE Television gave Kentucky viewers their first televised coverage of football, baseball, and basketball. Reprinted with permission from The Courier-Journal

station had installed television sets in the city's libraries and had broadcast a church service featuring sign language for the hearing-impaired. By 1950 WAVE-TV was airing English courses from the University of Louisville—the first broadcasts in the country that could be taken for college credit.

The 1950s saw WAVE-TV taking an active role in the growth of the community. Beneficiaries of the station's efforts were as diverse as the YMCA, the Department of Parks and Recreation, and Kentucky Educational Television. In 1956 the station broadcast its first telethon, "Bids for Kids," a fund-raising event for Children's Hospital. Over the next four years "Bids for Kids" raised $426,000 for the hospital.

As Louisville grew in the 1960s and 1970s, WAVE-TV's commitment to its community grew as well. The station was recognized for its contributions to the arts and to dozens of local civic and public service organizations. The owners of WAVE, Inc. (which was renamed Orion Broadcasting in 1969) recognized that as broadcasters they had the unique opportunity—and obligation—to educate their viewers through the world's most powerful medium, television.

So, in 1965, WAVE-TV's Special Projects Division was created to develop and produce documentary programs that explored the issues most important to the people in Kentucky and southern Indiana. For the next 20 years WAVE-TV produced award-winning programs on such topics as open housing, air quality, juvenile delinquency, preservation of local folk music, school dropouts, and the Ronald McDonald House. In 1970 "Tempo," a weekly program focusing on the issues and culture of Louisville's black community, premiered. "Tempo" evolved into today's "Urban Insight."

In 1981 Orion was purchased by Cosmos Broadcasting Corporation, a subsidiary of the Liberty Corporation in Greenville, South Carolina. Cosmos continued the Orion tradition of community service, and in 1983 the station teamed with the Salvation Army to collect donations of food, money, and toys at Christmastime. Since then WAVE-TV's Helping Hand has made the holiday season brighter for hundreds of area families. The following year the sta-

Special tours of the building are given on a regular basis. Seen here are WAVE 3 anchor, Don Schroeder, and Cub Scout Pack 42.

The WAVE "Live Eye" first hit the streets in 1977, increasing the station's capabilities for broadcasting live news events. Courtesy, Pat Pfister

IN CELEBRATION OF LOUISVILLE

Production Center 3 was built in 1986, giving the station a state-of-the-art production facility. It is used for production of commercials. Courtesy, Pat Pfister

From 1984 to 1987 WAVE 3 raised $1.136 million locally to fight muscular dystrophy. Courtesy, Pat Pfister

tion became the local broadcaster of the Jerry Lewis Telethon, and by 1987 had raised $1.136 million locally to fight muscular dystrophy. In 1985 another holiday tradition was born; WAVE-TV began broadcasting live reports from the annual Red Cross Donorama.

FORTY YEARS OF LOCAL NEWS COVERAGE

During its first months of operation, WAVE-TV broadcast six days a week and only during the evening hours; by early 1950 the station had expanded its broadcast day to seven hours and its broadcast week to seven days. By 1952 WAVE-TV's programming could be viewed from 7 a.m. until 11:30 p.m. Even in its early days the station scheduled regular daily coverage of local and national news.

The 1950s were a decade of innovation for WAVE-TV, as the new medium was discovering its place in Louisville-area homes. Early news broadcasts used Polaroid pictures to tell local stories; film later replaced the Polaroids, and kinescope recordings allowed the station to broadcast programs and events on a delayed basis. As technology grew so did the capabilities of WAVE-TV, and as the city grew so did the responsibilities of its broadcasters.

The owners of WAVE-TV recognized those responsibilities. In the 1960s the station was the city's first to open a news bureau in the state capital (1965), and in Washington, D.C. (1966). An Indiana bureau was set up in 1966, the same year the station sent a reporter to Vietnam to report on Kentucky servicemen in combat. In 1968 WAVE-TV was the first local station to broadcast regularly scheduled editorials and was the first station to install a television weather radar system. The city's first television meteorologist was hired by WAVE that same year.

By the 1970s WAVE-TV had enjoyed 20 years as the area's number-one choice for local news coverage. From its stories on the city's record-breaking blizzards (1971 and 1978) and its devastating tornado (1974) to its vigilant coverage of the city's court-ordered school busing (1975), WAVE-TV was the station Kentuckiana turned to for the latest news. During that same period WAVE-TV was the first local station to hire a full-time consumer-advocacy reporter, the WAVE Troubleshooter.

WAVE-TV firsts were commonplace in the 1980s as well. The station's hour-long newscast (Louisville's first) allowed time for in-depth coverage of the events and issues most important to its viewers. The area's first regularly scheduled health report, "Healthcast," aired in 1985, and "Positively Kentuckiana," a "good news" feature was added a year later. In 1987 the station broad-

WAVE Television's Fabulous Five celebrated the station's 10th anniversary in 1958. From left to right: Bill Gladden, Ed Kallay, Ryan Halloran, Livingston Gilbert, and Bob Kay.

cast the area's first entirely live satellite newscast. The station's news department continued its tradition of gathering first-place awards from the Society of Professional Journalists, Sigma Delta Chi, and the Kentucky News Press Photographers' Association.

FORTY YEARS OF LOCAL PROGRAMMING EXCELLENCE

Children today probably wouldn't go out of their way to watch "Junior's Club." However, when WAVE-TV's first "kiddie" show premiered in 1949, the locally produced program was a smash hit; and any Baby Boomer who grew up in Louisville has not likely forgotten eating lunch every day with Uncle Ed in the Magic Forest.

The scope of the station's locally produced programs was as broad as the interests of its viewers. The 1950s saw WAVE-TV broadcasting "TV Opera Theatre," as well as "Club Ebony," a program featuring local jazz performers. "Stop the Music," "The Pee Wee King Show," and "Music Place" were among the station's most popular music programs during the next 30 years. WAVE-TV brought local musicians back to the screen in the 1980s with "Front Row Center," the critically acclaimed series that showcased the talents of area pop music entertainers.

From "Farm" (in the 1950s and 1960s) to "Kentucky Afield" (1960s and 1970s) to "Parade of Champions" (1970s and 1980s), WAVE-TV has produced programs that address the interests of the station's rural viewers. Today "Urban Insight" and "Sing Ye" focus weekly on the black community, and "Close-Up" continues to examine public affairs of interest to all viewers. "Today in WAVE Country," which premiered in 1957 as "Today on the Farm," remains the city's only locally produced program that offers local news, weather, and entertainment five days a week.

Children and their interests have remained a priority for the station, though the focus has changed with the times. In 1986 WAVE-TV embarked on an ongoing project, "For Kids' Sake," a campaign that addresses the problems facing kids today. By broadcasting special programs and vignettes and sponsoring communitywide events, the station has addressed issues such as coping with divorce, planning for careers, family communication, and enjoyment of reading. In 1988 WAVE-TV joined forces with Junior Achievement to give recognition to adults who give their time to this worthwhile organization.

WAVE 3—BUILDING ON A PROUD TRADITION

In 1958 WAVE-TV adopted a sine wave as its logo, and until 1974 that logo symbolized the station's tradition of excellence. Then, in 1987, the station returned to that basic symbol, but with a contemporary design that will be utilized well into the 1990s. The return symbolizes WAVE 3's pride in its past and dedication to its future.

In 1950 George Norton wrote, "The crystal ball of television is a particularly tricky device for prophesying the future since TV is bounding beyond all new frontiers daily, surpassing in advances every new development that could be forecast." Norton died in 1964, but not before the TV station that he founded blazed the trail of broadcasting excellence in the community that he loved.

WAVE-TV has continued to explore frontiers that George Norton dared not even dream of. Today WAVE 3's crystal ball prophesies a promising future that will build on the proud tradition that made WAVE-TV the leader in Kentucky broadcasting.

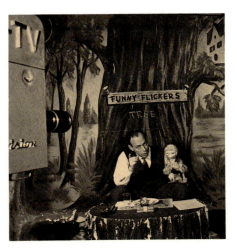

Ed Kallay hosted "Funny Flickers" from the Magic Forest during the 1950s. Today Louisville's Baby Boomers have fond memories of Uncle Ed, Sylvester, and Tom Foolery. Courtesy, University of Louisville Archives, Lin Caufield Collection

WAVE-TV was the first television station in Kentucky to broadcast in color; first, color pictures from NBC in 1954, then locally originated color pictures in 1962. Courtesy, Lin Caufield Photographers, Inc.

WAVE-TV gave Kentucky its first television coverage of the Kentucky Derby in 1949. Reprinted with permission from The Courier-Journal

IN CELEBRATION OF LOUISVILLE

WHAS-TV

Being number one has become a habit for WHAS-TV. A habit other Louisville television stations have been trying to break for some time.

Its philosophy? Being number one means maintaining and strengthening Action 11 News, the region's best since 1978. It means being the trendsetter in technical and entertainment fields in the highly competitive Louisville industry. Its WHAS Crusade for Children has had a tremendous impact on the market and has made the station the leader in community service over the past 34 years.

Committed to quality in both local and CBS network programming, WHAS-TV has opened the world to Kentuckiana. In addition to special issue-oriented programs over the years, WHAS-TV has become legendary in its coverage of the Kentucky Derby Festival, as well as the derby itself—two yearly highlights for Louisville. The station's all-day coverage on Derby Day has remained unmatched for more than 30 years, taking its on-air personalities into thousands of Kentucky and Indiana homes, where they become invited guests in a multitude of festive events on the first Saturday in May.

Public affairs programs such as "Doctors on Call," an informative medical program, and "2010 Fate or Future," an examination of potential problems and challenges relating to the future of Kentucky, are other examples of WHAS-TV's locally produced programming.

WHAS-TV's number-one status dates back to its conception, when, on September 19, 1946, it became the first commercial television station approved by the Federal Communications Commission for Louisville. It became the second television station to air, beaten by a short 16 months by rival WAVE-TV. The station went on the air as Channel 9 at 9,600 watts on March 17, 1950, as a CBS

The Action 11 News team (from left): Dave Conrad, Gary Roedemeier, Melissa Forsythe, Jim Mitchell, Melissa Swan, and Chuck Taylor.

affiliate. It was the brainchild of Louisville's renowned Bingham family, then owners of The Courier Journal and Louisville Times Company. Originally the station shared space with its already well established counterparts in the Courier Journal & Times Building at Sixth and Broadway.

Even though television was a mere fledgling, WHAS-TV was destined to fly high. It established its commitment to news immediately by producing a daily newsreel called "Today's News Today." Other early locally produced programs included "T Bar Ranch"; "Hayloft Hoedown"; "Hi Varieties"; "Good Living"; "Walton Calling" with host Jim Walton, who was to become the station's all-time favorite on-screen personality; and "Mr. Crusade." In February 1988, keeping with its drive to produce the finest news product, WHAS-TV announced the new "5:30 Action 11 News," giving Kentuckiana a new half-hour of news, combining local and national news features with weather, traffic,

WHAS-TV's Crusade for Children has made the station a leader in community service over the past 34 years.

business, consumer, health, and other news. Both programs will continue to give viewers instantaneous news via SatCam (Kentucky's only mobile television satellite newsgathering vehicle) and live aerial perspectives from SKY 11 (Kentucky's only full-time television news helicopter).

In 1979 WHAS-TV formed its own film and production company, Louisville Productions, to produce commercials and business communications programs. One of the premier production companies in the country, Louisville Productions maintains a full service, state-of-the-art facility, including uplinking facilities, a one-inch computer edit suite, and one of the most advanced electronic graphics and animation systems in the world. Louisville Productions is highly respected for quality commercial production by major corporations in Louisville and throughout the country.

In April 1987 WHAS-TV introduced Louisville's first satellite newsgathering (SNG) vehicle. SatCam brings a new dimension to the already comprehensive news coverage provided by Action 11 News. SatCam expands local, live coverage and allows Kentuckiana viewers to participate in news events unreachable before.

In 1954 WHAS-TV introduced its Crusade for Children, a giant community effort that has successfully raised more than $26 million in funds to aid in the care and treatment of handicapped children in Kentucky and southern Indiana. With more than 200 volunteer fire departments serving as the major collecting force, this two-day event in late May reflects regional concern for the children with a massive outpouring of money from firemen's efforts, churches, industry, and telephone pledges.

Ownership passed from the Bingham family in December 1986 to the Providence Journal Company of Rhode Island. Vice-president/Broadcasting for the Providence Journal Company, Jack C. Clifford, states his firm was attracted to the station through its reputation for quality and the potential for growth in the Louisville market. He sees Louisville as a city with a strong sense of community, vital to a station's success. Indeed, a community of which WHAS-TV is proud to be part.

WHAS-TV introduced Louisville's first satellite news gathering (SNG) truck in April 1987 to expand local, live coverage on Action 11 News.

WLKY-TV

On September 1, 1961, at 2 p.m., WLKY-TV signed on the air with a special program "Kick Off 32," introducing the new station, facilities, and programs. Following the special, WLKY presented college football (which remains a favorite even today). Since 1983 WLKY has been owned and operated by Pulitzer Broadcasting, a subsidiary of the Pulitzer Publishing Company, famed for its annual Pulitzer Prizes for distinction in journalism (both print and broadcasting), literature, drama, and music.

Louisville viewers have come to expect the highest standards and commitment to journalistic excellence that typify the Pulitzer name. WLKY's mission is to build a reputation, acceptance, and popularity based upon integrity and public service as well as the quality of entertainment.

WLKY is a large and important part of Pulitzer Broadcasting's seven-station group. The Pulitzer company sees WLKY as having more potential than any of its other stations—as a stand-alone business, a contributor to the company's corporate success, and a force in the local community. While some of the corporation's other stations are in smaller markets than Louisville, they are all dominant in their markets and very much committed to the communities they serve. That is the philosophy for all the Pulitzer properties.

Despite frugal beginnings WLKY-TV is now housed in an elaborate studio and administrative building on the northeast edge of Louisville atop a hill overlooking the beautiful Ohio River. The station moved into the present facility in October 1967. To add to the excitement of that fall season, WLKY also began broadcasting in color and added a new weather person to their staff in her first full-time television job. Her name: Diane Sawyer. Today the station is fully equipped with state-of-the-art news-gathering technology such as mini-cameras, and microwave and satellite capabilities that can bring Channel 32 News viewers late-breaking stories from wherever news is happening both live and on tape. WLKY also broadcasts in stereo and leads the way with the ABC Television Network in having the most closed captioned programming for the hearing impaired.

WLKY's commitment to community service is best demonstrated by the extremely successful feature of Channel 32 News "Wednesday's Child," the WLKY Spirit of Louisville's annual Bell Awards honoring outstanding volunteer work in Louisville, and the station's annual involvement in the Easter Seal Telethon.

Since August 1980 WLKY-TV has been finding adoptive parents

WLKY-TV, Channel 32, sits atop a hill near the Ohio River on Louisville's near northeast side.

for special needs children, temporarily placed in foster homes, in a program appropriately named after the nursery rhyme that depicts Wednesday's child as "full of woe." Each Wednesday, on both the 6 p.m. and 11 p.m. edition of Channel 32 News, a child or group of siblings who are victims of broken homes, parental neglect, abuse, or abandonment is featured. Many are older children with heavy emotional needs, but because of their ages are difficult to place in adoptive homes.

The program has been a gratifying success for the station, the adoptive parents, and the children themselves. More than 550 children have been successfully placed in permanent homes and are heading for the day they can be, like Sunday's child, "bonnie and blithe and good and gay." Many viewers, unable to adopt, have supported the program through financial gifts; a nonprofit, independent organization has been set up to administer donations for aiding adoptive family services.

The Bell Awards, administered by the station's Spirit of Louisville Foundation, Inc., a nonprofit organization founded in 1978, recognizes the unselfish, humanitarian volunteer service of up to 10 people per year. The recipients are honored at a ceremony that is hosted by WLKY-TV and televised in prime time. The program has featured such speakers over the years as Dale Evans, Frank Gifford, the DeBolt Family, and Dr. Norman Vincent Peale.

Since 1984 the Easter Seal Telethon has raised thousands of dollars for the Kentucky Easter Seal Society to help support the organization's rehabilitation programs for children and adults with communication, orthopedic, neurological, social, psychological, learning, and developmental disorders caused by congenital disabilities, traumatic accidents, or debilitating diseases. WLKY-TV believes its commitment to this project, as well as to its other community-spirited programs, not only helps raise much-needed funds but also heightens public awareness of the special needs within the community.

WLKY-TV has established itself in the area of news coverage as well. Numerous awards throughout the years have included honors from the statewide United Press International, Associated Press, Sigma Delta Chi (Society of Professional Journalists), and various national awards to anchors and reporters for excellence in news coverage. Sports coverage is of major importance in a sports-oriented community like Kentuckiana, and WLKY has excelled in this area as well. Along with the ABC Television Network, which has covered the Kentucky Derby on an exclusive basis since 1974, WLKY mounts more than 17 hours of Derby-related programming around the "most exciting two minutes in sports."

Viewers, advertisers, and community service organizations throughout Kentuckiana know they can depend upon the commitment, the services, and the resources of WLKY-TV. Many of the more than 100 employees of WLKY devote

Part of WLKY-TV's push into the live-reporting field is the station's Instacam, which can get a glimpse of breaking news just about anywhere in the station's viewing area.

This mounted bell is emblematic of the station's annual Bell Awards given for outstanding volunteer work by Louisville area citizens.

many hours a week to serve on boards and committees of various civic and charitable organizations, giving freely of their time and offering the powerful assistance of their television station to these organizations.

This is a station that looks toward a bright future, rather than dwelling on the past, in an industry where daily service and performance are the standards by which it is measured. That is the goal of each and every broadcast day at WLKY-TV, as the staff seeks to entertain, inform, and educate the viewing public of the Kentuckiana area.

LOUISVILLE GAS AND ELECTRIC COMPANY

Louisvillians sing the praises of Louisville Gas and Electric Company. The utility has been providing energy for 150 years—since the days of gaslights, during the time it was a gas and water company.

Even in those days the company made Louisville one of the brightest stops along the Ohio River's 1,800-mile passage from Pittsburgh to New Orleans. Things have not changed much in that regard for LG&E, which shares in the pride of Louisville's designation by Rand McNally as being among the nation's top 10 most desirable places to live, and by Partners for Livable Places as among the top 16 in North America.

Casting Louisville in a good light and supplying it with natural gas service are major parts of LG&E's mission, but that mission also extends to a larger region, one that covers approximately 700 square miles in parts of 17 counties, with an estimated population of 800,000, exclusive of the Fort Knox Military Reservation, which the firm serves with both electricity and gas. Along with adequate and reliable service, LG&E also can offer its more than 300,000 electrical customers and 235,000 gas customers rates that rank among the lowest in this part of the country.

Founded as the Louisville Gas and Water Company in 1838, the firm has witnessed myriad advances in technology and has survived two world wars, the Great Depression, the advent and growth of government regulation, and a couple of historic natural disasters.

In its beginnings it even created better days by making Louisville the first city west of the Alleghenies and only the fifth in the country to have manufactured gas, first delivering it to customers in 1839. The gas, manufactured from coal, was used only for lighting for more than 40 years; use for heating and cooking had to wait until electric lighting was developed in the late 1870s.

Since the company had not gotten into supplying water, the "and water" designation was dropped in 1842. However, the advent of electric lighting in the 1880s inspired the firm to obtain a new charter in 1888 and to have it amended two years later to grant it "the right to manufacture, distribute, and sell electricity" for illumination, and to buy stock in electric companies. The new charter allowed the company to gain controlling interest that same year in the Louisville Electric Light Company, thus paving the way for the eventual consolidation of a number of competing gas and electric operations into Louisville Gas and Electric on July 2, 1913.

The steady gains in sales, revenues, and earnings during the 1920s came to an abrupt end in the early years of the Great Depression, but no layoffs occurred and employees had to endure only one, three-month-long, 10-percent salary decrease during those years. Government regulation changed the rules of the utilities ball game during Franklin D. Roosevelt's New Deal days, but LG&E managed to stay in its league with a minimum of trouble.

Creating trouble of another kind, however, was Louisville's devastating flood in the winter of 1937, in which the company's entire generating capacity of 192,340 kilowatts was partly or entirely under water following the river's cresting 29 feet above flood stage. Electric service was discontinued on January 24, but an interconnection allowed LG&E to restore light to the eastern part of the city on January 28. However, it was not until February 22 that power began to be generated again by LG&E's own stations. The cost of

Electricity was introduced in Louisville in 1876. Soon a number of electric companies formed, several of which sold newfangled electric gadgets. In 1913 a number of competing gas and electric firms merged to form Louisville Gas and Electric Company.

On Christmas Day 1839 Louisville became the fifth city in the nation and the first west of the Allegheny Mountains to have gaslights, which were supplied by Louisville Gas and Electric's oldest ancestor, Louisville Gas and Water Company.

The dedication of employees, on their daily jobs and frequently in the face of danger and disaster, has enabled the company to serve its customers reliably for 150 years.

the flood to the company was estimated at $1.2 million, not including loss of revenue.

Thirty-seven years later disaster struck again, in the form of several tornadoes that swept through the Louisville area, including one that devastated Brandenburg in Meade County, which also is served by LG&E. The tornadoes severed all lines interconnecting LG&E with other electric utilities, but left all LG&E generating stations unharmed. Twenty-nine company substations were rendered inoperative, and some 84,000 customers were without power; two-thirds of those had power restored within three hours. The cost to the firm was $2 million.

LG&E's contemporary history has been involved with environmental matters and with the construction of a major power plant in nearby Trimble County, northeast of Louisville. In the environmental arena, LG&E helped to develop one of the nation's first efficient and full-scale sulfur-dioxide removal systems to handle stack effluent and to reduce emission so it would meet government limits. LG&E continues to be a leader in the so-called "scrubber" systems, and this year will complete a refurbishing of its seven systems to make certain they perform well and comply with the limits.

Construction on the $810-million, 495-kilowatt, coal-fired electric generating plant in Trimble County is continuing toward a 1990 start-up.

LG&E has been a pioneer in air-pollution control, receiving national and international recognition for its development and installation of scrubbers, which remove sulfur dioxide from the coal that is burned to produce electricity. Sophisticated computer equipment is used to operate the scrubbers at the Mill Creek and Cane Run generating stations.

At present LG&E's two steam stations have a rating of 2.1 million kilowatts, and its six combustion-turbine generators are rated at 108,000 kilowatts, for a total of a little more than 2.2 million kilowatts of power. The system, which has no nuclear power plants and has no plans for any, is further enhanced by its 80,000-kilowatt hydroelectric facility located on the Ohio River at Louisville.

Louisville Gas and Electric Company, only 10 years younger than the City of Louisville, takes pride in how its history of growth and sophistication has paralleled the city's. The city and the firm have grown together, worked together, suffered together, and rejoiced together. They have always seemed to go together, both parties seemingly knowing that they need each other—that neither could get along without the other.

Its lifetime of service to the area and its continuing vision of a greater Louisville is not something taken lightly by the Louisville Gas and Electric Company. It is, instead, a light that will not fail.

IN CELEBRATION OF LOUISVILLE

THE COURIER-JOURNAL

"It feels like winning the Triple Crown... Fittingly, Louisville is a sparkling jewel in that crown."

That statement in the city that bred the Kentucky Derby, the first of the three Triple Crown horse races, certainly seemed appropriate as Allen Neuharth, then president of Gannett Company, Inc., announced the sale in 1986 of *The Courier-Journal* and *The Louisville Times* operations to the media giant.

The sale solidified Gannett's move in about a year into the large-newspaper field, giving the firm, based in Arlington, Virginia, the *Detroit News,* the *Des Moines Register,* and the Louisville papers—the latter with their nearly 1,200 employees, and daily circulation of 240,000 and Sunday circulation of 330,000.

The sale also brought the Gannett chain—the largest in the world, with more than 90 newspapers—a historic newspaper company of unquestioned quality, integrity, and status in the world of journalism. It was in its third generation of ownership and operation by the Bingham family of Louisville, one of the few papers of stature in the United States still owned independently.

Judge Robert Worth Bingham, Barry Bingham, Sr., and Barry Bingham, Jr., carried proudly and well the mantle of journalistic excellence set forth when Judge Bingham purchased controlling interest in the papers in 1918. Not too long after that, Bingham laid down this credo: "I have always regarded the newspapers owned by me as a public trust, and have endeavored to conduct them as to render the greatest public service."

Those words are not only etched in bronze on a wall of the newspaper's front lobby but also in the minds and hearts of the parade of fine journalists who toiled for the Binghams. That parade has included the irascible but nonetheless legendary Henry Watterson, who became the first editor of *The Louisville Courier-Journal* in 1868, and Mark

The Courier-Journal's *airplane has covered more than 500,000 miles since 1977 throughout Kentucky and Indiana. The plane has FFA-equipped photo windows that can be removed in flight.* Courier-Journal *staff photo by Bill Luster*

Ethridge, who with a young Barry Bingham, Sr., in 1936 helped usher in a golden age for the newspapers.

The Courier-Journal resulted from the merger in 1868 of George D. Prentice's *The Louisville Daily Journal,* which was founded in 1830, and Walter N. Haldeman's *The Louisville Morning Courier,* founded in 1844. *The Louisville Times* was first published by the company in 1884. It ceased publication in 1987.

Watterson heads the list of recipients of the eight Pulitzer Prizes won by the Louisville papers. The list also includes reporter William "Skeets" Miller, whose heart-rending accounts of Floyd Collins—who was trapped and eventually died in a Kentucky cave—held the nation spellbound; editorial cartoonist Robert York; reporters John Fetterman, Richard Whitt, and Joel Brinkley; photographer Jay Mather; the photographic staff of both papers for coverage of school busing; and a public service award for a fight for stronger strip-mining controls.

The Pulitzer Prize-winning Courier-Journal *is enjoyed by 240,000 Louisville area residents daily and 330,000 on Sunday.* Courier-Journal *staff photo by Pam Spaulding*

204

Photo by Chuck Elfont

Photo by Chuck Elfont

Photo by Chuck Elfont

Reliance Universal Inc. 208-209

Rohm and Haas 210-211

Corhart Refractories 212-213

Porter Paint Co. 214

American Synthetic Rubber Corporation 220-221

Carrier Vibrating Equipment, Inc. 222-223

Devoe & Raynolds Co. 224-225

E.I. du Pont de Nemours & Company 226-227

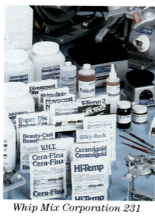
Whip Mix Corporation 231

Louisville Stoneware Company 232-233

Brown-Forman Corporation 234-236

Kurfees Coatings, Inc. 237

Borden Chemical 242-243

DCE, Inc. 244-245

American Air Filter 246

Louisville Bedding Company 247

Chapter X
Manufacturing

Producing goods for individuals and industry, manufacturing firms provide employment for many Louisville area residents.

Philip Morris U.S.A. 215

United Catalysts Inc. 216-219

SEAMCO 228-229

Louisville Manufacturing Company, Inc. 230

Digital Equipment Corporation 238-239

GE Appliances 240-241

IN CELEBRATION OF LOUISVILLE

RELIANCE UNIVERSAL INC.

An international company with its origin in Louisville, Reliance Universal Inc. has its headquarters in an office tower overlooking the eastern part of the city. The following scenario provides a quick review of only a few of the manufactured products that benefit from specialty coatings and polymers produced by Reliance Universal.

Scene: From attractively coated computer equipment a shopping list has been generated. As you leave home heading for the shopping mall in a brightly trimmed automobile, you glance admiringly at newly installed, factory-finished siding on your home. En route you observe business locations and an industrial complex comprised of handsome pre-engineered buildings, constructed and roofed with factory-painted metal building components. Purchases at the shopping center include canned foods and beverages, boxed cosmetics and personal care products, pet foods, books, and a host of other products packaged in coated paper wrap, paperboard cartons, and in coated metal containers.

Some of the dyes and pigments that are used as colorants in a variety of coatings.

Upon returning home the items will be stored in an attractively coated refrigerator/freezer and in beautifully finished kitchen and bath cabinets. The remaining areas of your home—the dining room, living room, and bedrooms—are furnished with stylish natural wood furniture, elegantly finished and protected with Reliance's wood coatings. End of scene.

In addition to supplying manufacturers with coatings for products that are used at home, Reliance is a major producer of coatings for office machines and equipment, institutional and commercial products, entertainment and recreational equipment, and for special industrial uses where high-performance, heavy-duty, and corrosion-control paints are required.

Founded in the city as Reliance Varnish Company in 1919 by Ben Robertson, Sr., the firm stands as one of the five leading U.S. manufacturers of specialty coatings and polymers. These products are used to decorate and protect a variety of industrial and consumer products, among them manufactured wood products for every purpose, paper and metal containers, major appliances, computers and office equipment, exterior siding, and metal surfaces on pre-engineered buildings and structures such as chemical plants, refineries, and offshore oil rigs.

Aside from its status as a U.S. producer, with 14 plants nationwide, Reliance Universal hangs its coat on the international rack with two plants in Canada and one in Belgium. In addition, through licensed international affiliates, the firm's technology and products are distributed worldwide.

Because markets for industrial coatings are diversified and specialized, and particular applications within each market demand specific properties, most of the products manufactured by Reliance are custom-made. The company is organized to serve its markets through operating divisions—the Wood Coatings Division, the Specialty Coatings Division, the High-Performance

It takes the 130 raw materials shown to make up the 12 end products needed to produce the finish on this chest.

MANUFACTURING

Coatings Division, and the International Division.

Reliance is the nation's leading supplier of coatings for wood products, the principal markets being furniture, home-entertainment cabinetry, prefinished wall paneling, kitchen and bath cabinets, decorative siding, exterior siding, and architectural mill work.

Sales in specialty coatings cover a broad range of industrial uses, the most prominent being computers and office equipment, coil-coated aluminum and steel for building products, major household appliances, metal furniture and fixtures, automotive specialties, bicycles, toys and recreational equipment, lawn and garden equipment, metal packaging, and paper and paperboard packages.

In addition, the corporation produces specialty corrosion-resistant, high-performance coatings for use on chemical storage tanks, cross-country pipelines, sanitary and waste-treatment plants, and other surfaces that require special protection from corrosive environments.

Reliance has pioneered several technological advances. Among them are: catalyst converting varnish, flat-line panel and door finishing on a continuous conveyor system, and fast-dry wood coating to utilize the high-velocity forced-air oven-drying principle.

At its first location, Ninth and Kentucky streets, just west of downtown, Reliance produced oleoresinous varnishes and japans (a varnish with a hard, brilliant finish) for the carriage trade. The company developed its business further by selling wood-furniture varnishes to the factories of Old Louisville and southern Indiana, eventually expanding its sales territory as far west as the Jasper-Huntingburg area of Indiana. By horse and buggy this represented nearly a week-long sales trip. Today it is approximately a two-hour drive.

In 1947 the firm moved its factory into new quarters at 4730 Crittenden Drive in the city's South End, and a few years later undertook its first expansion outside Louisville by buying Tomlinson Varnish Company of North Chicago, Illinois. Thus began a quarter-century of acquisition and new plant construction that helped reshape the corporate organization for its entry into the decade of the 1980s.

Along the way, in 1963, a name change was made to reflect Reliance's organizational growth and its expanded scope in the marketplace. Reliance Varnish Company then became Reliance Universal Inc., which became a wholly owned subsidiary of the Tyler Corporation in 1981.

In addition to its technological advances in the wood and varnish trade, Reliance—through its Robertson Research and Development Center at the Crittenden Drive location—has fostered several changes in the coatings industry. Among them are high solids liquid paints, radiation-curable coatings, water-based specialty finishes, and distinctive styling and color design for simulated wood reproduction and beautification.

As it has been since the open-kettle days, technological advances pursued at its Robertson Research and Development Center at the Crittenden Drive location remain an important facet of the corporation's industrial life. As more and more manufacturers come to rely on the company's products, Reliance Universal Inc. aims to provide the finest finishing touch in the industry.

Orange—Wood Coatings Division operations
Yellow—Specialty Coatings Division operations
Red—High-Performance Coatings operations
Blue—Corporate Headquarters and Research and Development Center in Louisville
Green—Company's operations in Belgium

This shows the application of Reliance coil coating on metal used to fabricate a variety of industrial aluminum and steel products.

209

ROHM AND HAAS

The message Rohm and Haas Kentucky Inc. has for the public is a simple one: "You don't know us, but you can't go through the day without coming in contact with a product that somehow incorporates something that Rohm and Haas makes." Examples include paints, caulking, textile applications, floor polishes, glue, automobile taillights, reflective letters on highway signs, Christmas ornaments, plastic bottles, vinyl window frames, automotive finishes, and coatings on greeting cards.

The Louisville plant, located in an area dubbed Rubbertown because of its ties to the synthetic-rubber industry, is a specialty chemical plastics manufacturer that employs 650 people. Its industry competition includes E.I. du Pont de Nemours, Monsanto, Union Carbide, and Dow Chemical.

Rohm and Haas—founded in 1909 in Philadelphia—has grown to eight plants in the United States and 25 worldwide, employing approximately 13,000 people. It has not tied itself to one market, preferring instead to sell to a variety of industries.

The firm's basic building-block chemicals are supplied by the petroleum industry. Those chemicals are converted by Rohm and Haas into bulk materials that are in turn changed into specialty forms such as acrylic emulsions, molding powder, Acryloid coatings, monomer products, plastic additives, and Plexiglas (developed by Otto Rohm in 1936).

Another factor in Rohm and Haas' low level of name identification with Louisvillians is the fact that almost all of its products are shipped outside the area. In order that residents, especially those in the nearby Rubbertown area, could become more acquainted and more comfortable with the chemical firm, Daniel Ash, president and plant manager since 1980, invited them to tour his plant in the summer of 1987 and get an idea of what happens there. He explains: "No industry talked about itself as recent as 20 to 25 years ago. But we said we need to get to know our neighbors better, we need to find out their concerns, and we need to try to provide the information that will give them the assurance that what we're doing here is not putting them in jeopardy. They need to know that we have the capability to handle emergencies and we test those capabilities." Naturally, Ash and his neighbors hope no such emergencies will arise.

The organization also has formed a citizens advisory council that meets once a month to express concerns and learn more about the company. The group includes representatives of neighborhood councils, a county commissioner, two legislators, a member of the medical community, an urban and public affairs expert, and a member of the Sierra Club.

Ash believes there are gains expected from this civic effort. "The chemical industry over the years said virtually nothing about itself to its neighbors," he says. "We felt that if we took care of things inside the fence and made sure we weren't creating a hazard for our neighbors, that's all we needed to do. They didn't need to know what chemicals

Rohm and Haas, founded in 1909 in Philadelphia, has eight plants in the United States and 25 worldwide. Shown here is the Louisville facility.

MANUFACTURING

we were handling—what we were making. That's the way we did business. We didn't cause problems for our neighbors—[but] we began asking if we were conducting ourselves in a manner appropriate with today's society."

Ash believes the advisory group, where there has been good attendance and lively dialogue, will help Rohm and Haas attain that goal.

The plant was built by the U.S. government during World War II and was leased to Union Carbide for the production of butadiene for the neighboring synthetic-rubber plants. It was acquired at auction from the government by Rohm and Haas in 1959 and put into production in 1962.

"We have put down some rather deep roots here," says Ash, a native Louisvillian who sets an example for community involvement by serving as the 1988 chairman of the Louisville Chamber of Commerce. Those roots include the approximately $160 million invested in the plant since 1959 and the projected investment of an additional $150 million in a five-year building and modernization plan now under way for the plant that already ranks as fourth largest in the company.

Physical growth is being matched by growth in employee relations, thanks to emphasis on sustained training, communication, and greater responsibility. Perhaps the premier effort is that of self-regulating work teams, through which team members learn and use leadership skills as the leadership role rotates among the members. Thus far the employees have responded enthusiastically.

Ash says he has seen people who have not been good employees turn into great ones as a result. "There's a new level of enthusiasm because they're making decisions they weren't allowed to make before," he notes. "I just think a much more committed, interested employee is evolving . . . we want to create an environment where attitudes can change."

To illustrate, Ash offers this anecdote: After a less-than-exemplary employee spent time with one of the work teams, his wife called and accused management of brainwashing him. "If you haven't," Ash quoted her as saying, "I want to know what you did to him. He can't say enough good things about you-all, after years of not saying anything nice about you."

That augurs well for Rohm and Haas, believes Ash. "Our intent," he says, "is to build on what we've already started in people involvement and in the quality of our products. We'll be taking a solid, strong facility and making it even stronger. This plant is in fine shape; it's healthy, it's vibrant, it's growing. But, the job's never done."

Rohm and Haas products touch the lives of nearly everyone on a daily basis as they are incorporated into a variety of products such as plastic pipe fittings, bottles, automotive coatings and automobile taillights, and coatings for various applications.

CORHART REFRACTORIES

Harry S. Truman gets the credit for popularizing the saying, "If you can't stand the heat, get out of the kitchen." Withstanding the heat—as in 3,900 degrees Fahrenheit—is exactly what Corhart Refractories and its products do best.

The firm has been credited with developing the state of the art of glass-industry refractories. Its products—heat-resisting ceramic materials made in the form of bricks, large blocks, or slabs—line glassmaking furnaces around the world, and, by withstanding ultrahigh temperatures, do their job of helping turn sand into molten glass.

As necessity is so often the mother of invention, so it was with refractories in the United States. Prior to World War I Corning Glass Works, Corhart's parent company for 58 years, depended on German clay for the fire-resistant pots in which its glasses were melted. When Germany was unable to recover satisfactorily from its wartime defeat, Corning set out to end its earlier dependence on the German clay as well as develop a refractory able to withstand a continuous glass-melting operation.

Researchers, noting that mullite remained unmelted in glass, reasoned that this material could be used for refractories. Discovery of this material, however, was only half the solution. The other half was how mullite could be melted and formed into a refractory block without also melting the container. The solution developed by the researchers was to electrically fuse the raw materials, using them as their own container. These "Electrocast" refractory blocks very quickly revolutionized glassmaking.

Molten refractory being poured into molds.

Finished and match-marked refractory blocks preassembled and ready for shipment to a glass manufacturer.

The Corhart story began on June 27, 1927, when Corning entered into a joint venture with Hartford-Empire, a company with strong ties to customers in glass manufacturing. A plant was built soon after at 16th and Lee streets, and the firm opened for business with an initial payroll of 30 employees. The plant site was chosen because of its central location for markets and incoming raw materials, and because of the availability of low-cost power and transportation.

The first Electrocast refractories produced by Corhart, called Corhart Standard, were an immediate success, and within 15 years 80 percent of the glassmaking industry was using the product. This success led to creation of the company's own research laboratory in 1936. Following World War II the firm developed refractories for use in the steel industry that continued until this decade, when the decline of U.S. steel making caused the company to leave that market.

Over the years there have been a

MANUFACTURING

Furnace designs are diagramed piece by piece using computer-aided design as a first step in ensuring quality.

number of corporate changes for Corhart. In mid-1985 a leveraged buyout from Corning was accomplished by Corhart's management team as Corning sold several businesses to generate capital for new ventures. The always-profitable Corhart continued to successfully serve its markets and has excelled particularly in international sales, exporting more than one-third of its products. This overall strength led to the acquisition of Corhart in 1987 by Societe Europeenne des Produits Refractaires (SEPR), the industrial ceramics division of the Saint-Gobain Group of France. This makes Corhart a strategic U.S. component in one of the world's largest industrial ceramics concerns.

Corhart has always been something of a silent presence in Louisville's industrial community because there are no glassmakers in the area; the company primarily serves cus-

Prototype refractory material being poured as part of product development activity.

tomers in other parts of the United States and worldwide.

In terms of community involvement, however, Corhart is a visible and active contributor. Principal among the firm's activities is its extensive involvement in Junior Achievement. The company maintains close ties to the University of Louisville's Speed Scientific School and School of Business. Corhart, which numbers about one of every seven of its 350 Louisville employees as an engineer, annually employs co-op students from the Speed School.

While the use of Corhart refractories ensures that glassmakers can run their furnace continuously from four to 10 years, the Louisville firm is looking to an even brighter future. The tradition of innovation and dedication to development of new and better products not only continues, but money for research and development has more than doubled in the past five years.

The impetus for this is a program setting the direction for the Corhart of the present and of the future, with enhanced problem-solving capabilities, new products, and, most important, error-free products and services as major goals.

Whatever directions Corhart Refractories pursues during its second half-century, it intends to remain committed to ideals and attitudes reflected in its logo, the pyramid. The original symbol carried the words "quality," "endurance," and "economy." Today the company remains committed to these same qualities and to continued preeminence in industrial ceramic technology.

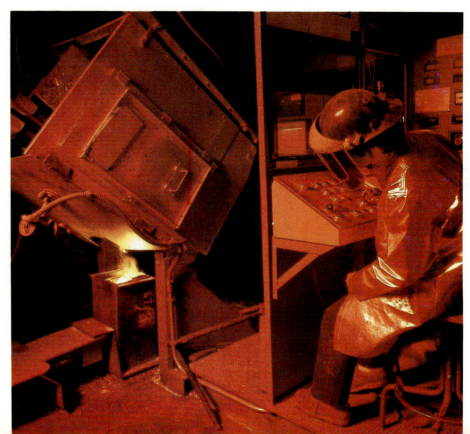

PORTER PAINT CO.

If you want to paint the town, Porter has what you want and will let you pick from a multitude of colors.

Porter Paint Co. has been doing that since 1923, when H. Boone Porter, who had purchased the year-old Becker-Tabb Paint Company in 1922, put his name on the paint-manufacturing plant in Louisville. Ever since, the orange-and-cream diagonal stripes that adorn Porter cans and trucks have been synonymous with the highest quality paint and coatings.

The firm, which employs 450 people in Louisville and about 1,000 nationwide, has painted itself into a quality corner of which it is extremely proud. Although its product is the most expensive in its market area, the company, because of that quality, offers a product that lasts many years while retaining its color and protective surface. As a result, Porter is in the top 15 among America's 1,000 paint companies.

Porter serves its contractors and do-it-yourself customers through more than 125 full-service decorating stores in 30 metropolitan areas and has 450 dealers in 23 states, primarily in the Midwest and Southeast. It entered the wall-covering business in 1943 and serves more than 6,000 independent dealers across 22 states.

The High Performance Coatings Division provides sophisticated products that beautify, but primarily protect, major industrial plants and civil engineering projects. With a direct sales force, selected distributors, and nationwide warehousing, this group operates across the United States, serving breweries; food, pharmaceutical, and chemical plants; paper mills; offshore drilling rigs; and many other industries.

Two recent moves have expanded Porter's base even further. Porter Corrosion Control Services Inc. was formed in Houston, Texas, to provide cathodic protection and high-performance coatings to protect reinforced concrete structures such as garages and bridges. The acquisition of Consumers Paint Factory, Inc., in Gary, Indiana, gave Porter the world's largest supplier of lettering enamels to the sign industry.

Porter's planned double-digit sales growth could paint a new economic chapter in an industry that has had sales growth of only about one percent in recent years and could easily brush past many of its competitors.

Physical growth took a big jump recently with construction of a 140,000-square-foot, $3.1-million warehouse adjacent to its second plant in Louisville just west of downtown. It consolidated national warehousing and distribution functions and allowed further expansion at its plants.

With a constant eye on market growth, Porter has turned its attention recently to fast-growing cities within its region, expecting to increase its home-painting and wall-covering businesses through more stores and dealerships. Already, professional painters decorate more than 400,000 homes annually with the Porter products.

As to growth, a Porter Paint official was quoted in a newspaper: "One of the biggest advantages Porter has is we're only in one-third of the United States. We have two-thirds of the United States in which to grow."

The familiar orange-and-cream-striped trucks crisscross the country providing dependable service to Porter customers.

The Porter Paint Co. corporate offices and plant number one, Louisville.

PHILIP MORRIS U.S.A.

The Louisville cigarette-manufacturing center of Philip Morris U.S.A. represents a source of civic pride, a spirit the community shares in having a local operation of a successful multinational corporation. Louisville can lay claim as the home of Marlboro, the world's most popular cigarette brand.

One-quarter of all Marlboros, as well as Merit, Virginia Slims, and Benson & Hedges, are made in Louisville using sophisticated technology and skilled labor. In one day the Philip Morris state-of-the-art equipment can turn out 5,000 cigarettes each minute, a total of 270 million in a three-shift, 24-hour period. That's a staggering annual capacity of 65 billion cigarettes that can originate in Louisville and move to points around the globe.

Philip Morris came to Louisville in 1944, when it purchased the Axton-Fisher Tobacco Company plant to produce its own brands. Operations grew rapidly. In just four decades Philip Morris has become a major manufacturing center covering 106 acres in the community's West End.

Today the five-building production center complements a primary processing addition capable of handling 500,000 pounds of cut tobacco filler a day. The administrative and technical annex supports these facilities, along with a shipping operation that moves some 22,500 cases a day. An additional 53 buildings, including 43 warehouses, house the stemmery, leaf department, and storage.

But Philip Morris is more than a work place for its 3,400 employees. As Louisville's largest industrial employer, Philip Morris takes its leadership role seriously and has been a nationwide model for effective labor/management relations. So firm is the commitment that the nine unions represented at Philip Morris in 1987 signed a six-year extension on a historic nine-year, no-strike agreement.

Philip Morris thrives on creating a hometown quality of life that provides for happy, productive workers. The Philip Morris mark of distinction can be found in creative solutions to civic problems and sponsorships for area education, arts, and entertainment projects.

The size and tremendous capabilities of the Louisville operation make Philip Morris a popular tourist attraction. Each weekday, guests trace the path of tobacco from seed to pack on free one-hour tours.

The Philip Morris presence in Louisville seems a perfect match of a product and its natural resources. The company is the largest purchaser of burley tobacco grown on more than 70,000 Kentucky farms. The "golden leaf" is the state's number-one cash crop. Directly or indirectly, the tobacco industry provides jobs for more than 81,000 Kentuckians who earn nearly one billion dollars each year.

But Philip Morris U.S.A. is only a part of the greater Philip Morris Companies, Inc., the world's largest producer of consumer goods. Sharing the corporation's global strategy are Philip Morris International (also manufacturing tobacco products), General Foods Corporation, Miller Brewing Company, and Mission Viejo Realty Group. The company touches us where we smoke, eat, drink, and live.

The familiar pylons in front of the Philip Morris U.S.A. manufacturing complex.

Guided one-hour tours tracing tobacco from seed to pack are a popular tourist attraction.

UNITED CATALYSTS INC.

United Catalysts Inc. is an affiliated company of Süd-Chemie AG of Munich, West Germany, and began as a manufacturer of specialty catalysts for the fertilizer, chemical, and petroleum-refining industries. Süd-Chemie, incorporated in December 1857, traces its beginnings to the famed German scientist Justus von Liebig, who developed the formula for superphosphate fertilizers, with production by the company of superphosphate and sulfuric acid beginning in 1860.

Over the years United Catalysts Inc. has diversified into other fields becoming, in addition to its position in the catalysts field, a leading producer of rheological additives, desiccants, and industrial minerals.

UCI was formed in 1977 by Süd-Chemie AG through the merger of Girdler Chemical, Inc., which goes back to the mid-1940s in Louisville as Girdler Engineering Co., and Catalysts and Chemicals Inc., which started operations in Louisville in 1957. There are four major divisions within United Catalysts Inc. The four divisions, which employ roughly 800 people, are the Catalyst Division, Rheological Division, Desiccants Division, and Clay and Minerals Division. The products that UCI supplies touch us all, from the food we eat to the clothes we wear to the cars we drive to the homes we live in.

The Catalyst Division of United Catalysts produces heterogeneous catalysts for the fertilizer, petroleum, and chemical industries. Catalysts speed up a chemical reaction, creating a chemical change in milliseconds that ordinarily might take years without the catalytic reaction. The catalysts are not consumed in this reaction, leaving them to work their magic for years before needing to be replaced.

Research and development on many of the major commercial catalytic applications are performed in this group as well as the engineering designs and field technical services. Catalyst manufacturing is the original activity of United Catalysts, and two manufacturing plants and laboratories are located in Louisville. The city also serves as headquarters for the group of companies that includes these affiliates: Catalysts and Chemicals Europe, located in Brussels, Belgium; Catalysts and Chemicals Inc., Far East, located in Tokyo, Japan; and United Catalysts India Inc., located in New Delhi, India.

A strong capability in research and development, coupled with extensive testing facilities, makes United Catalysts Inc. a complete and innovative catalyst supplier. Aside from producing its own catalysts, UCI also manufactures proprietary catalysts for many chemical manufacturers. These are developed in the laboratories of the various companies and require manufacture to precise specifications.

The Rheological Division began in 1979 with the importing of Tixogel organoclay products from the parent, Süd-Chemie, before UCI opened its own Tixogel plant in Louisville in 1980. Tixogel is the trade name for UCI's clay-based rheological additives for organic and aqueous solvents such as paints. Rheological additives control flow and are used to prevent sagging, slumping, and settling in products.

The main office building of United Catalysts Inc. in Louisville.

UCI, through its 1984 acquisition of The York Castor Oil Company of New Jersey, produces a line of organic rheological additives that perform the same function and are made from castor oil derivatives.

A representative sample of the various shapes, sizes, and types of catalysts manufactured at the Louisville catalyst plants.

MANUFACTURING

The Rheological Division's Louisville manufacturing facility.

Raw and processed castor oil also are sold. These rheological agents are sold to the paint and coatings, printing ink, cosmetics, adhesives, sealant, pharmaceutical, and lubricating-grease industries.

In addition to producing rheological additives, the division's Technical Service Laboratory in Louisville performs product evaluations and problem-solving functions. Its research laboratory works to develop new products.

In the Desiccants Division, United Desiccants-Gates mines and packages desiccants, including montmorillonite clay, activated carbon, silica gel, or molecular sieve. Desiccants are used to protect machinery, electronics, food, pharmaceuticals, military equipment, and other packaged products from moisture damage. These packaged desiccants will protect the contents of a sealed container until it is opened.

In 1983 United Catalysts built a plant in New Mexico for the processing and bagging of a high grade of activated montmorillonite clay from the United Desiccants-Gates' mine in Arizona. In 1985 UCI acquired the

United Desiccants-Gates' modern manufacturing facility in Belen, New Mexico.

Production of pharmaceutical desiccants at the Pennsauken, New Jersey, United Desiccants-Gates plant.

N.T. Gates Co., which was founded in 1952 and has been a supplier of desiccants to the pharmaceutical, military, textile, and food industries.

The N.T. Gates Company, responding to a demand for compact sizes in desiccants, came up with the innovative "drop in" desiccant packets. The major market for this was the pharmaceutical industry, including manufacturers of medical and diagnostic equipment. A demand for high-speed, automatic insertion of desiccants in packaging operations came in the late 1960s, and after intensive research, Gates responded with desiccant canisters, which were integrated into automated packaging lines.

The Clay and Minerals Division is made up of the Albion Kaolin Co. and the Southern Talc Co. Albion Kaolin, located in Hephzibah, Georgia, is the site of the oldest, continuously operating kaolin clay mine in the United States. The firm mines and produces high-purity kaolin clays for the paper, rubber, plastics, ceramic, refractory, fiberglass, chemical, and agricultural industries.

Albion Kaolin products are produced both by airfloat and by slurry processing. The airfloated products are high-purity, low-moisture kaolin powders that have undergone flash drying, roller-mill pulverizing, degritting, and final purification by passing through air-classification systems. Slurry items are produced by multiple wet-screening, selective blending, and chemical additions. All of the kaolin products are guaranteed to give consistent performance. In addition to its production, the company coordinates technical service, quality control, and product development for the division.

Southern Talc, founded in 1905, is located in Chatsworth, Georgia, and mines and processes intermediate-

The mining site of the Albion Kaolin Company in Hephzibah, Georgia.

and high-grade talc for the plastics, rubber, ceramic, pesticide, chemical, paint, and paper industries. Southern Talc also provides custom grinding and packaging services to its customers.

Zeochem, a joint venture of United Catalysts and Chemische Fabrik Uetikon of Switzerland, produces synthetic zeolites for dehydration, chemical processing, and catalytic applications.

Zeochem was formed in 1980 to manufacture and market molecular sieves as absorbents and catalyst supports for the chemical industries in the United States, other parts of the Western Hemisphere, and parts of the Orient. Products made in the Zeochem plant, which is adjacent to the United Catalysts' production facility in Louisville, are used in petroleum and petrochemical processing, in sealed insulating glass, in the paint and coatings industry, in ethanol production, in refrigeration, in drying and purifying air, and in air brakes.

At UCI, products are manufactured in both continuous and batch operations. Key steps in these operations are controlled to ensure uniformity of the products, mostly tiny things that pack quite a wallop and that come in several shapes, from

MANUFACTURING

Zeochem's office and plant in Louisville.

customers' requirements each and every time.

As new products are developed, the need for new or altered solutions will continue to expand. UCI welcomes that challenge, and expects to continue to grow right along with the needs, producing solutions to meet those new needs as they are identified.

Growth in all five business areas—Catalysts, Rheological, Desiccants, Clay and Minerals, and Zeochem—will act as a catalyst in creating and speeding action at UCI, with the ultimate goal being a continuation of swift and quality service for its customers. That is how United Catalysts Inc. keeps pace with rapidly changing chemistry, and how it contributes to those changes that mean so much to the lives of mankind.

pellets to spheres to raschig rings to tablets, depending on the application. In order to achieve uniformity and quality, all products are made to fixed formulations and procedures that are monitored by continuous process control. The techniques of manufacture are critical, and considerable emphasis is placed on process and quality-control tests.

All divisions of UCI are incorporating Statistical Process Control (SPC) programs into areas of manufacturing and service operations. UCI had a tremendously successful pilot SPC program in 1987, whereby a custom catalyst was manufactured in Louisville for a major chemical producer using a process that is statistically controlled. SPC provides all of UCI's employees with the knowledge and statistical tools to assist in the manufacture of quality products and services that meet all

An aerial view of United Catalysts Inc.'s South Plant operation on Crittenden Drive, Louisville.

AMERICAN SYNTHETIC RUBBER CORPORATION

The strains of that classic country and western song, "On the Road Again," no doubt is sweet music to the ears of employees and officials of American Synthetic Rubber Corp. The firm manufactures polybutadiene rubber, which goes toward making tires for such well-known names in the industry as Michelin, General, and Dunlop. And as long as people stay on the road, American Synthetic figures to have plenty of tread on its economy.

Much of that volume is expected to come from a new product, solution styrene-butadiene rubber, which the corporation, whose only plant is in Louisville's Rubbertown section, is making from a secret formula developed by Michelin, the largest of 16 shareholders in American Synthetic. This product, a company spokesman says, is a different kind of tire rubber, one that gives good grip, but at the same time offers good rolling resistance and good mileage.

In order to manufacture the solution styrene-butadiene rubber, American Synthetic has put in approximately $6 million worth of new equipment. But that is only part of an updating of the company's manufacturing strategies that began in 1979 as a result of the down-sizing of American automobiles, which meant the down-sizing of tires, and the consequent down-sizing of the synthetic rubber industry. Since 1979 American Synthetic has put $32 million into modernizing and keeping its plant up to date, which has helped the corporation rebound from those earlier problems. Another $6.5 million is earmarked for modernization during 1988, with an eye toward potential needs into the 1990s and beyond.

American Synthetic's Louisville plant, one of four manufacturers of polybutadiene rubber in the United States, got its start in September 1943 as one of 15 government-owned plants producing synthetic rubber for the nation's needs during World War II. The plant, which had an annual production capacity of 60 million pounds, operated until April 1947, when it was put on a standby basis by the government.

On September 1, 1950, the Kentucky Synthetic Rubber Corporation was established for the purpose of reactivating and operating the plant, which was put into production that December for the manufacture of "hot" rubber. However, by August 1952 "cold" rubber was being produced. In 1954, 29 companies formed American Synthetic Rubber Corporation, which took possession of the Louisville plant in April 1955.

Expansion and addition of new products brought the sales volume in 1958 to 75 million pounds in 24 types of rubber. Sales volume ran high throughout the decade of the 1960s, reaching a peak of 100 million pounds in 1964. Changes in the operation following the troubled 1970s have made the American Synthetic facility one of the most efficient and highest-quality plants in the industry. During that time the annual production capacity will have increased from 110 million pounds to 232 mil-

American Synthetic Rubber Corporation lights up the night in Louisville's Rubbertown.

MANUFACTURING

lion pounds by the end of 1988.

Aside from production of synthetic rubber, American Synthetic also has for several years manufactured a liquid polymer that has been used as a binder for solid fuel in America's missile program. The polymer was first used in Minuteman missiles and has since been used in several missile programs for the United States and its allies. In 1977 a plant was expanded specifically for the production of this polymer, whose largest use now is in the U.S. space shuttle program.

Diversification, as with most American manufacturers, has come to American Synthetic over the past several years as a way of keeping pace with U.S. economic shifts. The corporation has pursued three paths toward diversification: contract manufacturing for other companies, joint ventures with other firms or processes, and the develop-

The Louisville plant is one of four manufacturers of polybutadiene rubber in the United States, and has for several years produced a liquid polymer that is used as a binder for solid fuel in the missile program.

ment of new products or new uses for existing ones through research and development.

Officials believe the company's greatest strength lies in the experience, dedication, and versatility of its nearly 300 employees. The hourly work force, numbering almost 200, has an average tenure of 25 years with the firm. The salaried supervisors and managers are nearly as experienced in the rubber business, many of them having prior experience as line operators.

A 60-person maintenance and services department has the skills, tools, and equipment to take care of all types of plant repair and maintenance on an around-the-clock basis.

The company's technical staff, which has extensive experience in emulsion and solution polymerization, consists of research and development chemists, quality-control chemists, and technicians.

The engineering staff consists of numerous chemical and mechanical engineers, several of whom have more than 30 years' experience with the corporation. These engineers specialize in process engineering, energy conservation, environmental affairs, safety, project management, maintenance engineering, and mechanical design.

With its modernization program running full throttle, its diversification in gear, and the high potential seen for its newest rubber product, American Synthetic Rubber Corporation no doubt feels as if it is on a roll.

IN CELEBRATION OF LOUISVILLE

CARRIER VIBRATING EQUIPMENT, INC.

They have been called "shakers" or "oscillators." Carrier calls them "vibrating." And their conveyors respond with multifunctional performance that seems somewhat magical.

Vibrating equipment is designed and engineered at Carrier to solve world-class problems in the handling and processing of bulk materials. In fact, the more complex the problem the better the vibes Carrier gets when it's solved.

Most people think of conveying as moving products on belts, acknowledges company president Bob DeSpain, but there are many operations where conventional-type conveyors can't meet the need. Says DeSpain, "If the material is hot or real abrasive; if you want close transfer; need to enclose with dust-tight covers; classify materials; separate large particles from small; cool, dry, and leach; combine a process function with movement for related cost efficiencies—that's when vibrating conveyors, where the material rather than the equipment moves, are recommended."

In most cases a customer will come to Carrier with nothing more than a raw problem, and without a vague notion of how it can be solved. That's the kind of challenge on which Carrier thrives. On the way to a solution, the firm analyzes and interprets requirements, runs performance tests on the client's materials, then designs and builds the equipment for the specific installation.

Engineering has been the keynote for the company that was started in 1947 by three Louisville men, merged with a national conveyor giant, and then returned to Louisville ownership through a leveraged buyout in 1983 by the firm's local managers. That engineering has benefited the industries that provide the backbone of American manufacturing: chemicals, food, dairy, automotive, foundry, primary metals, steel, coal, glass, mineral, synthetics, rubber, wood, paper, scrap, and tobacco.

Carrier's impact goes beyond the boundaries of the United States. It

Molten glass, at 2,200 degrees Fahrenheit, is quenched and cooled in water-pool troughs for ease of handling and recycling.

is the leader in specialized bulk-material-handling worldwide, according to DeSpain, who came to the company in 1959 as a draftsman. Carrier, whose equipment can be small enough to sit on a desk or as large as 150 tons, has operations in Mexico and Canada and licensees in England, Belgium, Sweden, Japan, Australia, and India. However, all engineering is done in Louisville.

How does a Carrier product affect the average consumer? "If you eat cereal of any kind for breakfast," says DeSpain, "that cereal has been processed on our equipment." For example, in a sugared flake the producer wants uniformity; during the vibrating conveyance all of those flakes not measuring up will drop through a screen while the others move toward their packaging destination. Along the way, the sugar is added, and the product is gently conveyed and cooled so the sugar will adhere to the flake.

Salt is another subject for a Carrier conveyor, one which dries it and gets it into crystal form and ready for the kitchen or other applications, such as salting snowy roads.

Every time a person rides in an automobile, he or she is in touch with

Casting feeders on "smart cars" traverse to receive and charge blast units with loads of castings in cleaning areas of foundries.

MANUFACTURING

Fluid bed dryer/cooler systems process foods, confections, chemicals, synthetics, minerals, metals, and scrap.

Carrier—because 98 percent of the rubber on any tire in the world has been processed on Carrier equipment. Rubber in its raw form has to be cooled and dried, and Carrier will convey it, cool it, and dry it for further processing.

Two of Carrier's major and longterm handling projects involve gathering, classifying by weight and size, and determining the amount of heat needed to burn scrapped tires, and the elimination and subsequent recapturing for further use of excess nitroglycerine in ammunition propellants.

The tire-burning project, designed to create energy for a California power company as well as rid the world of mounds of used tires, features conveyor equipment that will move and orient the tires from a pile three-quarters of a mile long, 500 feet deep, and a half-mile wide to an elevation of about 450 feet and a distance of approximately one mile before being deposited in a furnace.

The nitro problem came with nothing more than the acknowledgment that there was excess nitro on each pellet that goes into propellant. Carrier equipment now can dry the pellets and recapture the excess nitro for reuse. That not only created a savings but also eliminated a potential explosive situation.

Carrier Vibrating Equipment, Inc., a firm of approximately 120 employees, subcontracts most of its manufacturing, keeping much of it local. That gives the firm hands-on control, it is much less expensive, and the quality meets standards, DeSpain explains. The subcontractors may make parts, subassemblies, or the entire piece of equipment.

Collaborating with Louisville firms and institutions includes a close association with the Speed Scientific School, the engineering arm of the University of Louisville. The company generally has at least two engineering students from Speed's co-op program in training throughout the year. DeSpain believes that through the use of that resource (Speed School), Carrier also is giving something back by helping train engineers. "For every 20 students that come through here, we might hire one," he notes. "So we're training a lot of engineers for other people."

Civic ties to the community are strong as well. Says DeSpain, "We encourage ourselves and our employees to get involved in civic affairs. We feel that it is necessary to give that back to the community."

Perhaps the corporation's most telling connection to the community is its dedication to its heritage and its determination to remain a locally owned organization. "A company is just as good as its roots," avows DeSpain. "If new people you hire are not just as proud of the company and its history as I am . . . they can't take it forward. We have already committed . . . when we get to the point to sell this operation, it will be to the employees. We are very committed to that. We put it in writing."

The employees, no doubt, think that's a fair shake.

Vibrating spiral elevators heat, cool, dry, or moisten in the processing of crumb rubber, plastics, pharmaceuticals, ores, metal parts, candy, and pet food.

223

IN CELEBRATION OF LOUISVILLE

DEVOE & RAYNOLDS CO.
DEVOE MARINE COATINGS CO.

Devoe & Raynolds and Devoe Marine Coatings Co. can cover you from A to Sea.

The "A" stands for architectural paint, that which goes inside and outside homes, and the "Sea" refers to the Devoe Marine Coatings Co., a division of Grow Group, Inc., and Devoe & Raynolds' sister company. Louisville serves as the national headquarters for the architectural paint firm and world headquarters for the marine coatings division.

Devoe & Raynolds is the nation's oldest paint manufacturer, having started as William Post's paint shop in 1754 in the colonial burg of New York. Devoe Marine Coatings Co., meanwhile, has become one of the world's leading producers of coatings protecting ships, offshore drilling rigs, and platforms.

Devoe Marine Coatings Co. is one of the two largest firms in the United States in the marine coatings business. Providing protection to commercial ships and naval vessels is a large part of its operation.

"I believe we are the largest supplier of sophisticated, heavy-duty coatings to the U.S. Navy," says Joseph Quinn, president of Devoe Marine Coatings. "We're basically in commercial shipping, the offshore oil industry, and the Navy."

Although the offshore oil business is in a recession, Devoe Marine Coatings can still point to major contributions to the industry. For example, Quinn notes, the most modern drilling rig in the world is coated 100 percent with Devoe products. The protection goes from top to sea bottom for these rigs, according to Quinn, supplying "corrosion control and fouling control, fouling being marine growth on the underwater portions" of the rig.

For more than 20 years Devoe's coatings have stood the test of protecting the nation's submarine fleet under the most demanding of conditions. In addition, aboard aircraft carriers the company's flight deck nonskid coatings are expected to withstand more than 5,000 flight operations without significant maintenance.

Devoe's marine manufacturing operations extend worldwide, manufacturing more than 800 products requiring 1,000-plus raw materials. The formula for each of Devoe's marine products is carefully developed and tested at the technical center in Louisville. It was in the Louisville laboratory that what is believed to be the first synthesis of epoxy resin was accomplished in 1939, Quinn says. "Since then, of course, epoxies have gone in many directions as adhesives and structural compounds. The bulk of our coatings technology is based on epoxy."

What can Devoe's coatings do for a ship's bottom? Quinn gives this example: While 20 years ago ships tended to go into dry dock practically every year for inspection, cleaning, and painting, he knows of at least one Navy ship with Devoe paint on its bottom that had not been dry-docked in more than six years.

Although Devoe Marine Coatings has virtually no customers in Louisville, Quinn praises the city as a fine place to live, and believes the company's laboratory, which sets the industry standard in coatings, is a feather in Louisville's cap.

A recent addition to marine and corrosion control for the Grow Group is Napko Corporation, which manufactures high-performance paints and coatings for the petroleum, chemical, power generation, offshore, and heavy-duty industrial markets. Napko was merged with the existing industrial paint company to form Devoe Napko Protective Coatings.

The architectural side of the business, commonly known as Devoe Paint, has experienced a steady rise

This well-stocked, attractive Devoe paint store is a far cry from William Post's paint shop, predecessor to Devoe & Raynolds, founded in 1754 in colonial New York.

Rich red paint is mixed during operations in Devoe & Raynolds' Louisville manufacturing plant.

MANUFACTURING

in its competitive position over the past six years, in part through a strategy that calls for cultivating independent dealers and the painter maintenance trade, and developing each new market in clusters. This means going into some new areas, as well as continuing the aggressiveness in the Louisville market that began with the appointment of J.R. "Bob" Desjardins as president of the nationwide organization.

Devoe's dealer network includes paint and decorating centers, hardware stores, commercial paint outlets, and building- and farm-supply outlets. Part of Devoe's marketing thrust involves the incorporation in such things as store planning, site selection, advertising, training, and merchandising. Even so, the company's efforts are heavily pointed toward the contractor trade.

Devoe is credited with such industry advances as printing the complete formula and a money-back guarantee on its cans of premixed paints, the two-coat exterior house paint to replace the earlier four-coat variety, the epoxy resin that revolutionized industrial coatings, and the Color Key Color System, which allows a store owner to stock a few basic colorants and bases that can be mixed into hundreds of paint colors.

Vats of paint and boxed cans ready for shipping are part of the day's work at the Devoe Paint plant.

Every Devoe paint must pass at least 29 tests before it is sent into the marketplace. Approximately 33,000 tons of pigment are mined annually for Devoe plants to make their 1,200 products available. Devoe's warehouses and distribution centers nationwide stock more than 2.5 million gallons of paint.

Just as the quality of its coatings has been instrumental in the firm's success, so has the quality and stability of its work force. Says Desjardins: "In Devoe, we have a family of people that is just outstanding. The average time of employment of our people is in excess of 16 years." He believes that is a reflection of the pride that has characterized the company since its founding.

Devoe Marine Coatings are applied from top to sea bottom on offshore drilling rigs.

IN CELEBRATION OF LOUISVILLE

E.I. DU PONT DE NEMOURS & COMPANY

Giving most of the bounce to Louisville's so-called Rubbertown area is the E.I. du Pont de Nemours & Company plant, known in the Du Pont manufacturing family as the Louisville Works. The facility is the world's largest and longest-operating producer of Neoprene synthetic rubber.

The Du Pont plant operates around the clock with a work force of more than 700. Recognizing the need to be good corporate citizens, Du Pont and its employees promote and participate in all manner of civic, social, and cultural activities in the community. In 1986 Louisville Works employees donated $60,000 to the Metro United Way, and they continue to be active in local and state government, school boards, and youth, civic, and church organizations.

Also in 1986 Du Pont added to Louisville's economy more than $38 million in salaries and wages, as well as approximately $175 million in the purchase of goods and services.

It seems only natural that there be a Du Pont industrial presence in Louisville, as there once was a strong presence in the community of a branch of the family—which left its mark through establishing a public transit system, financing the building of Du Pont Manual Training High School, and helping to create Central Park.

Du Pont's discovery of Neoprene came in the Great Depression year of 1931, and it was priced at one dollar a pound—20 times that of rubber—however, the product, through its resistance to influences that deteriorated natural rubber, caught the eye of rubber producers. Its versatility, elasticity, strength, and toughness led them to pay the premium price.

Neoprene was never intended as a substitute for rubber, but as a product that would lead to many applications beyond the capabilities of rubber. Prime among the qualities setting it apart from natural rubber is its resistance to permanent defor-

Neoprene is the major product manufactured at the Louisville Works of E.I. du Pont de Nemours & Company. The plant is located in the Rubbertown area of the city, near the Ohio River.

mation, high and low temperatures, and the deteriorating effects of oil, sunlight, chemicals, abrasion, oxygen, and ozone.

Industrial uses for Neoprene include highway seals, bridge pads, collapsible containers, O-rings, jackets and inner liners of fuel hoses, compressed air hoses, and gas service station hoses. Also, it protects telephone and power cables and is often preferred in conveyor and power-transmission belting. Another use of

Harold L. Dey is plant manager of the Louisville Works.

the product is its application as a protective paint coating for metal structures exposed to severe weather or corrosion.

In the automobile, it is used for such things as ignition cables, gaskets, radiator hoses, engine mountings, spark plug coverings, fan belts, and the white sidewalls of tires. At home, Neoprene is found in sponges, dress shoulder pads, adhesive strips in disposable diapers, mattresses, dish drainers, garden hoses, shoe soles, and electric extension and telephone cords.

In sports, Neoprene running shoes make their rounds on Neoprene-coated tracks; divers in Neoprene wet suits head for the deep in Neoprene life rafts; and other adventurers head for the wild blue yonder in Neoprene-coated balloons.

Neoprene's staying power is exhibited in these examples:

—A waterproofing adhesive installed in New York's Lincoln Tunnel in 1936 is still in place.

—An indoor running track has shown no deterioration after nearly 20 years and the pounding of millions of footsteps.

—For more than 30 years a Neoprene conveyor belt has hauled coal daily to a northeastern U.S. power plant.

—Glazing seals have weathered

MANUFACTURING

more than 30 years of sun, wind, rain, and snow at a General Motors Technical Center.

The Louisville plant's first Neoprene unit was begun in the summer of 1941, but before it was brought into production for Du Pont, World War II intervened. Consequently, the plant was acquired by the U.S. government for wartime production, and Du Pont was asked to operate it. So important was Neoprene production that it was the only nonmetallic product to be put on the government's priority materials list, and each pound of the synthetic rubber was carefully allocated for essential civilian and military use.

Following the war the plant was purchased back from the government, and operated for the first time as a Du Pont facility on January 1, 1949. Located on the west side of Louisville near the Ohio River, the plant covers more than 140 acres and includes an administration building, maintenance and service areas, and a laboratory. In addition to Neoprene it produces Freon®, which is used in refrigeration and air-conditioning, and vinyl fluoride, which is used to produce Tedlar®, a tough inert film with outstanding weather resistance.

The Louisville Works produces Neoprene as a raw material in either dry, solid form or as a liquid latex. It is then sold to manufacturers of rubber products, where it is compounded with other ingredients and processed to make a variety of products.

In the first manufacturing step, the plant produces Neoprene latex, a milky-white liquid with the rubber dispersed in water. The Neoprene can either be shipped in that form or frozen onto a large metal drum, a so-called "freeze roll," and turned into a solid. In that process the film forms a continuous, super-thin rubbery sheet that is washed to eliminate impurities and then dried, compressed into a rope, and cut into chips for bagging and shipping.

Throughout its history, the Louisville Works has produced more than 8 billion pounds of Neoprene. In 55-pound bags set end to end, that volume would reach from Miami to Seattle and back.

Liquid latex is turned into this super-thin, rubber sheet after being frozen onto a large drum. It then is washed, dried, formed into a rope, cut into chips, and packaged for shipment.

One of the many uses for Neoprene is as glazing seals for the windows in high-rise buildings.

Liquid Neoprene leaves the plant in tank trucks heading for manufacturers of rubber products.

227

IN CELEBRATION OF LOUISVILLE

SEAMCO

Right now, in plants across the United States and the world, major appliances, packages, trucks, automobiles, cigarettes, alcoholic beverages, and countless other items are moving. They're moving overhead, on the ground, and around corners on SEAMCO-engineered material-handling systems. They are systems that were designed and fabricated expressly for a specific application in the company's 96,000-square-foot plant in Louisville, Kentucky.

Moving things has always been SEAMCO's business plan. Since its start in a barn in 1956, SEAMCO has provided systems that enable other businesses to move, assemble, package, and ship products.

How did SEAMCO grow from a fledgling operation to a successful company? It grew through a commitment to quality and service, a commitment that can be found in SEAMCO's philosophy, people, conveyor systems—even in its location.

A lot of businesses might agonize over a corporate philosophy. For president Sheeran Howard, SEAMCO's philosophy is quite simple and direct: Provide quality service and build a quality system, one that is ideal for each client's needs.

That philosophy means tailoring custom conveyors for automotive, industrial, or package-handling use. Applications involve either turnkey operations—where SEAMCO designs, engineers, fabricates, and installs the entire project, or engineered systems—where SEAMCO builds and installs conveyors according to clients' specifications.

It's also a philosophy that amounts to much more than words. It is a way of doing business. In SEAMCO's case, it's a way that enabled its customer base to grow from regional to international. And accompanying the growth in size and scope are customers who are exceptionally satisfied with their investment. More than 90 percent return to do repeat business.

The engineers and designers at SEAMCO see material-handling systems as more than a means to transfer objects from point A to point B. They view industrial conveyor systems as an engineered solution to a problem. From that standpoint, each situation must be analyzed in its own light, with such variables as line speed, distance traveled, and product size and weight considered.

In the end the SEAMCO-installed system isn't just a compilation of machinery. It's really a product of craftsmanship and intelligence welded together to meet a customer's specific requirements.

The person responsible for seeing that those requirements are met is the SEAMCO project manager. The project manager follows each job from drawing board to installation. He or she knows precisely where a job stands in relation to its construction deadline. For SEAMCO customers, the project manager delivers the attentive service a customer must have during the development of a material-handling system. Facts, figures, answers to questions—whatever a customer needs to know is easily attained by contacting one source. And that's part of SEAMCO's commitment to service.

Philosophy and people play critical roles in a company's success, but without meeting a customer's specific needs, no company can survive—let alone prosper. That's why SEAMCO designs conveyors to outperform and outlive the competition.

SEAMCO incorporates the latest technology, and only premium materials are used.

And does SEAMCO believe in the systems it installs? One way to measure the firm's confidence would be to examine the warranty behind each project. SEAMCO backs every one of its conveyors with a one-year warranty, a program unique in its

SEAMCO quality and service started in a small barn in Louisville in 1956.

MANUFACTURING

industry.

When SEAMCO employees numbered 150 in six different buildings in 1986, the company decided it was time to search for a new headquarters that would afford it the efficiency of a consolidated operation.

It was determined that the ideal site had to meet strict prerequisites. SEAMCO did not want to make any sacrifices in quality or its ability to service conveyors. The firm required a geographically central location that had a solid labor base and skilled draftsmen. But it needed more than that. The company also needed an interstate highway network to get raw materials in and finished materials out. After considering locations in several states, the best area for relocation was found right in its backyard—Louisville, Kentucky.

For one thing, Louisville met every qualification the firm had established. For another, Louisville's central location put SEAMCO close to its customers' headquarters, while the city's Standiford Airport enabled SEAMCO personnel to reach virtually every client's facility both in the United States and abroad.

What's more, the city also fit in with SEAMCO's commitment to quality. The firm wanted its employees to have an enjoyable city in which to work and live. With Louisville, it got exactly that.

SEAMCO has installed new con-

A special combination of the right people, philosophy, product, and location set SEAMCO's growth into motion.

By 1986 SEAMCO reached 150 employees and was installing material-handling equipment for regional, national, and international industries.

veyor systems and improved existing ones for companies that manufacture products that are diverse in size. Each of these companies has presented SEAMCO with a new set of challenges and obstacles. Some have been easy, some complex, but each has been different and required different answers—answers that have been found through a commitment to quality and service.

If a company has a unique set of material-handling needs, SEAMCO has just the philosophy, the people, the conveyors, and the location to help get things moving.

SEAMCO's current headquarters and plant was selected after research found Louisville to be the best site. Manufacturing facilities worldwide are served from this one location.

IN CELEBRATION OF LOUISVILLE

LOUISVILLE MANUFACTURING COMPANY, INC.

When someone says "Hats off to Louisville Manufacturing," there's a good chance the hat that goes off came from that company—which has been making them since 1940, when it began producing helmet liners for the U.S. military.

There was a time when the firm's largest seller was its patented fatigue cap worn by U.S. troops around the world, but in 1960 the company became a pioneer in designing and producing promotional or "advertising" caps. Those caps generally carry a corporation's message of pride, performance, teamwork, or goals.

Who can ignore caps that bear the John Deere, CAT, and NAPA insignias, for instance? Louisville Manufacturing has had a Deere connection for more than 20 years; Caterpillar, another longtime customer, estimates there are more than 10 million of its CAT caps generating corporate goodwill around the world; and NAPA has been heads-up to more than 5 million caps since 1975. Louisville customers include Porter Paint, Brown & Williamson, Brandeis Machinery Company, Kosair Shrine, and Whayne Supply.

Add to those examples the fact that Louisville Manufacturing is an official licensee for the Kentucky Derby, the Super Bowl, and National Football League teams, as well as the designer and producer of such

Mickey (left) and Ted Heideman beam with pride in the Sales Aids Showroom of their family-owned business.

novel headgear as a Hershey's Kiss and a Big Mac. In fact, just about any idea that can come off the top of the head usually will wear well on somebody else's.

However, business is not just a head game for the company. Over the past 20 years, and especially in the past five years, it has expanded into full-service promotion—not only in wearable items such as caps, T-shirts, jackets, sweatshirts, and sweaters, but also in such sales aids as pens, pencils, desk accessories, flashlights, drink holders, clocks, umbrellas, coolers, calendars, key chains, drinking vessels, and lapel pins.

The organization has about 48,000 customers, and a normal sales week on caps alone numbers about 84,000. All the designing and production are done by the approximately 300 employees at the Louisville production plant and another in nearby Salem, Indiana.

Mickey Heideman, president, and Ted Heideman, chairman of the board, concur that Louisville Manufacturing owes its success to quality and consistency and a staff they consider more creative, more helpful, and more dedicated than a customer can find anywhere else, evidence of why the firm has clients going back as far as 30 years.

Mickey Heideman believes his company "changed the whole apparel-advertising industry," and an employee gives credence to that by saying, "Some folks never get to see what happens to their work. Not me. I can turn on TV or go to the grocery and see my caps comin' and goin'. I feel good knowing people like what I make."

Maybe, then, it should be "Hats on" instead of "Hats off."

During an equipment demonstration at Caterpillar Tractor Proving Grounds in Litchfield, Arizona, a sea of "Cat Power" caps, produced by Louisville Manufacturing Company, covered the heads of thousands of Caterpillar dealers.

MANUFACTURING

WHIP MIX CORPORATION

An internationally recognized leader and pioneer in the manufacture of high-quality dental materials and equipment, Louisville's own Whip Mix Corporation continues to set the standard by which all others in the industry are measured.

Founded in 1919 by E.A. Steinbock, Sr., the company was originally set up to manufacture and nationally market the first complete dental inlay casting unit. This innovative unit featured a mechanical spatulator, a glorified "egg beater" that whipped and mixed better than any similar product on the market and thus became the basis for the fledgling company's name.

Through an unwavering commitment to research, development, and testing, Whip Mix has created and perfected a number of specialized products, including the most complete line of casting investments in the dental specialty field, all of which are renowned for their quality and dependability. The world leader and expert in the manufacture of dental-casting investments and gypsum materials, the firm also produces and markets dental waxes, dental plasters, vacuum-mixing equipment, cast trimmers, grinders, and precision-crafted articulators.

Today, under the direction of Allen Steinbock, the third generation of the family to lead the firm, Whip Mix is expanding its sales, its expertise, and its product lines, while preserving its high standards of quality.

Internally, machine automation and a unique employee training program have yielded dramatic increases in production, enabling more efficient order processing. And advanced computer information systems have enhanced billing, shipping, inventory, and quality-control procedures.

On the new product front, Whip Mix has most recently bolstered its fine product line with the corporate acquisition of C.F. Price, Inc., of Los Angeles, another manufacturer of quality dental lab equipment. This expanded product line provides additional purchase opportunities to Whip Mix's loyal customer base.

Whip Mix pioneered the exporting of dental equipment and was the first dental company so recognized by the U.S. Department of Commerce with the president's "E" and "E-Star" awards. Abroad, the respected Whip Mix name enjoys ever-growing popularity and demand. International exports now account for more than 40 percent of total sales and are expected to increase.

Immediate plans call for the construction of an on-site research laboratory expansion, educational conference center, and dental history museum. Later expansion will add 65,000 square feet and 10 acres to the current plant site.

Firmly rooted in the Louisville community, the firm is headquartered at 361 Farmington Avenue where it enjoys prime accessibility between north/south and east/west interstates, and is located within one mile of Standiford Field, the University of Louisville, the State Fairgrounds, and Churchill Downs.

Though it has been a family-run business since its inception, Whip Mix Corporation credits much of its success to the dedication of its employees and the support of the Louisville community.

Under the direction of Allen and David Steinbock, the family-run business operates state-of-the-art packaging and check-weighing equipment to maintain productivity levels.

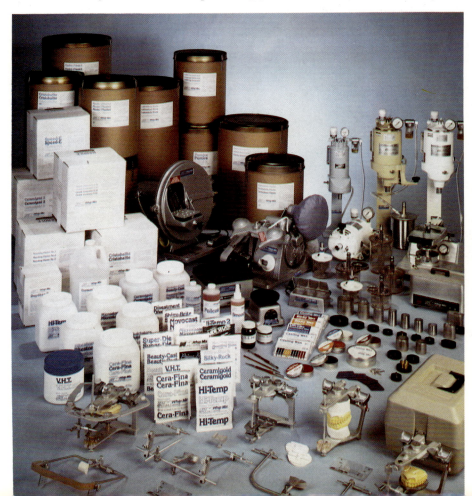

Whip Mix manufactures a broad line of dental laboratory equipment and supplies such as articulators, grinders, trimmers, vacuum-mixing equipment, waxes, plasters, gypsum materials, and casting investments.

LOUISVILLE STONEWARE COMPANY

In this age of high technology and automation, a hands-on business that is still going strong is Louisville Stoneware Company.

Maker of a multitude of pottery items that include plates, cups and saucers, platters, all sorts of cooking vessels, refreshment mugs, personalized gifts, and a huge variety of specialty and ornamental works, Louisville Stoneware and its antecedent, Louisville Pottery Company, trace business and artistic roots to 1905.

Throughout its existence the firm has counted on hands as the most important tools in this classic and ancient art, gliding hands that form, shape, sponge, and brush as molds spin. No machines, save a version of the potter's wheel, repeat the processes; only hands create the pieces that speak of Louisville and Kentucky in eloquent, unique ways.

Louisville Stoneware's niche is to create stoneware that is reminiscent of simpler times, and that's the way it's been since the beginning. Its patterns include bachelor button, country flower (in green, blue, or gold), oak and acorn, and such animal designs as pigs and geese. Because the firm's products fairly shout Louisville and Kentucky, they find their way into homes across the United States as gifts from friends and relatives in the commonwealth and as mementos of visits in the area, both helping to enhance further the organization's national reputation.

Louisville Stoneware supplies dinnerware to many fine retail shops nationwide as well as to Hallmark, Neiman-Marcus, and the Smithsonian Institution. The company's wares also are displayed at numerous gift and trade shows across the nation where store buyers view and select lines. Two of Louisville Stoneware's specially commissioned items, reproductions of the White House and the Executive Office Building in Washington, D.C., have been used as presidential favors for visitors. The roofs lift off so they can be used for stationery, mail, cookies, or such.

Stoneware is much like chinaware in that its properties and end uses

Pictured are a few of the stoneware pieces from the broad line of thousands of products made by Louisville Stoneware Company—a wine cooler, napkin ring, candlesticks, and a pipkin-style dish.

The forming of the clay into the shape for a casserole is done through a spinning mold and tool process, with the hands also acting as a tool.

are closely related—but whereas chinaware is man-made by being formulated from numerous clays and minerals, stoneware is derived from a single naturally occurring clay. Louisville Stoneware's pieces are fired at 2,350 degrees Fahrenheit, thus ensuring strength and a tough, durable glaze—so tough, in fact, that during World War II the company's ware was used as chemical jars and also for holding battery acid in tanks.

That kind of rugged, front-line duty speaks to the strength of the firm's products, but they also can claim a certain rugged beauty that have made them appealing. Much of that beauty is created by the artists who hand-paint the designs on each piece, in contrast to the use of stenciling and decals on most foreign and other domestic ware.

The company says little doubt is left as to whether the pieces are hand-painted: The color application can be felt by the hand, and brush marks are evident to the eye. The colors are underglaze colors painted on the clay with brushes and then covered over by a white overglaze.

MANUFACTURING

A Louisville Stoneware artisan shapes a mug handle just after it is attached to the soft clay cylinder.

During the firing the colors mingle further and bond permanently into the body.

The whole process starts with good clay, mostly from southern Indiana, which is ground, screened, and mixed until it's deemed to be at the right consistency. Then so-called "jiggermen" toss a gob of clay onto a spinning, somewhat jerky molding wheel for forming and shaping the dinnerware pieces, readying them for the eventual air-drying stage.

Pieces of uncommon shapes, such as pitchers, teapots, and the like, are formed in plaster casts prior to the artistic touches and the firing. Those pieces that need handles, such as pitchers and mugs, find their way into skilled hands for what's called the "pull" and "press" process that puts an almost-perfect handle on the item. Not being machine-perfect is a goal at Louisville Stoneware, thereby emphasizing its handmade quality and giving each item a special distinctiveness and charm. The company says a buyer should expect slight variations in the pieces purchased as a result of the technique, but acknowledges that most people consider that as part of the uniqueness of the ware and look on it as added value.

The pieces then move to the artists and on to a 14-hour firing in room-high, 300-cubic-foot kilns that are lined with refractory wool, a soft material that is effective as insulation, rather than the traditional brick.

The story of Louisville Stoneware is much more than just one of a longtime Louisville institution. It's also one of a love of pottery and chinaware by John and Vivian Robertson. John is a ceramic engineer who came to Louisville in 1952 to work with American Standard, and Vivian is an interior designer. When Louisville Pottery chose to close in 1970 rather than relocate under urban renewal, they saw a chance to reshape their careers in a mold that had fit them all the while. The basic policy was from the beginning to revive a community tradition and to maintain respect and concern for the employees who create the products.

So, a business was saved for bigger and better days—and Louisville Stoneware Company intends to keep its hands gently caressing clay and sending out to the rest of the world a distinctive and unique product of the Bluegrass State.

The artist's brush glides over the surface of the clay, in this case a potbellied canister, in the creation of the many colorful decorations.

IN CELEBRATION OF LOUISVILLE

BROWN-FORMAN CORPORATION

Since its beginning in 1870 there have been two constants at Brown-Forman Corporation: family pride and quality products. They go together, and because of them Brown-Forman today is a top-of-the-line *Fortune* 500 company and a leading corporate citizen of the Louisville community.

That commitment to quality started with the founder, George Garvin Brown, and was passed along to his son, Owsley, in this crisp admonition: "We will make quality whisky (the Browns have always spelled it without an e) to sell at quality prices for quality profits. It is a good rule to follow." Carrying on that tradition, Owsley in turn bequeathed the company to sons Lyons and Garvin. Today Lyons' eldest son, W.L. Lyons Brown, Jr., is chairman of the board. He has been chief executive officer since 1975.

With Brown-Forman, quality is not something on which to build slogans. It is, instead, an article of company faith, an accepted characteristic of each product, a part of the firm's basic nature. In the beginning it was the complaint of a physician friend that he couldn't buy whiskey of high and consistent quality for patients that prompted George Garvin Brown and early partner George Forman to enter the whiskey business, and quality has been the backbone of the company philosophy ever since.

That philosophy lives on, not only in the organization's early brand names but also in the careful acquisitions it has made over the years. In fact, what was originally a whiskey company based on Old Forester and Early Times grew first into a wider purveyor of quality spirits and wines, and then grew again into a consumer-goods firm through the acquisition of Lenox, Incorporated, designer and manufacturer of china and crystal products, and Hartmann Luggage, a Lenox subsidiary, which is considered a premier brand in the upper-end American market.

While the Lenox acquisition, Brown-Forman's first venture outside the beverage industry, has brought dramatic changes in the business, changes came to Brown-Forman's Kentucky whiskey foundation as early as the mid-1950s, when it acquired—quality, remember—Jack Daniel's Distillery in Lynchburg, Tennessee, home of the famed Tennessee sour mash "sippin' whiskey."

Since then the company, which now employs 1,200 people in its Louisville operations and approximately 5,600 worldwide, has added these other quality brand names: Canadian Mist; Southern Comfort; Korbel champagnes and brandy; Bols Liqueurs; Bushmills Irish Whiskey; Martell Cognac; Bolla, Cella, and Fontana Candida Italian wines; Parducci California wines; California Cooler; Noilly Prat Vermouth; and Black Bush Special Irish Whiskey.

Lenox, which has about 4,000 employees at sites in several countries, including its headquarters in Lawrenceville, New Jersey, has been the producer of the official White House china since Woodrow Wilson's days as president. On the local level, Lenox has presented the City of Louisville with an official china service.

Lenox continues to solidify its position as the leading marketer of fine china in the United States. Its sales are expanding through new distribution channels, including outlet stores in several states and a highly successful direct mail and media marketing organization known as Lenox Collections. The fundamental strategy for all Lenox products is to design, manufacture, and market quality-crafted products that will provide the consumer an assurance of excellence and good taste.

Also in the realm of good taste, Brown-Forman's first bourbon whiskey, Old Forester, continues to be the cornerstone of the beverage group, even if only for sentiment's sake. George Garvin Brown himself bottled the first Old Forester, and named it. The proud guarantee of its quality that appeared on the first

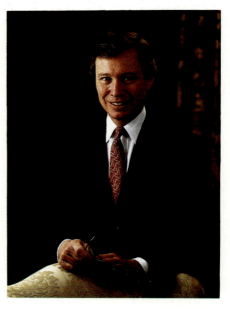

W.L. Lyons Brown, Jr., chairman and chief executive officer of Brown-Forman Corporation.

Owsley Brown Frazier, vice-chairman of Brown-Forman Corporation.

bottle, in his own handwriting, still graces the label of each bottle produced. Although it's not the firm's largest seller, it is a leader among premium bourbons. The importance to Brown-Forman of Early Times is symbolized by the water tower shaped in the form of a giant Early Times bottle that stands as a landmark above the bottling plant, just

MANUFACTURING

William M. Street (left), corporate vice-chairman and president of Brown-Forman Beverage Company, and Owsley Brown II, corporate president and chairman/chief executive officer of the Beverage Company, in front of the corporate headquarters building.

across the street from the headquarters building on Dixie Highway west of downtown Louisville.

In 1986 Brown-Forman dramatically reshaped its wine and spirits organization by merging four separate divisions into one called Brown-Forman Beverage Company. The new structure is unique to the industry and offers the scale, influence, and efficiency of a consolidated company while retaining marketing focus through specialized sales teams within each of 14 geographic business units. Brown-Forman Beverage Company is one of America's largest wine and spirits firms, with annual sales of more than one billion dollars. It represents 19 quality brands to wholesalers and retailers nationwide.

Quality at Brown-Forman doesn't just apply to its products. It covers its leadership, too, starting with the Brown family, four generations of which have been at the helm of the company for practically all of its years. Today Owsley Brown II, younger brother of Lyons Brown, Jr., is corporate president and chief executive officer of the beverage company. William M. Street, whose father was the first non-Brown to be president of Brown-Forman, is a corporate vice-chairman and president of B-F Beverage Company. Owsley Brown Frazier, whose mother was a Brown, is also a corporate vice-chairman. Brothers Robinson Brown III and J. McCauley Brown, whose father was board chairman before Lyons Jr., also hold important positions with the firm.

Brown-Forman's decentralized management system holds the company's divisions and subsidiaries responsible for day-to-day operating decisions, enabling it to respond quickly to the changing demands of the marketplace. An example is

California Cooler is the corporation's entry in the wine cooler market.

235

Early Times is a big seller among the company's whiskies.

Lenox china and crystal continue the corporation's tradition of quality products, and put it in a broader consumer market.

Brown-Forman International Ltd., the firm's export division, under chairman and chief executive officer E. Peter Rutledge, destined to play a vital role in the future as consumers worldwide discover the B-F line of quality beverages.

Brown-Forman is a marketing-oriented company with the leadership and direction that have prompted Wall Street analysts to call it "one of the best managed companies in America." *Forbes* magazine, in its 40th Annual Report on American Industry, credits B-F with the best current record of return on equity and of sales growth in the alcohol beverage business.

In fact, sales growth is a time-honored Brown-Forman tradition. With the increase to $1.4 billion in fiscal-year 1988, B-F net sales had increased annually for 29 consecutive years. All signs point to continued increases in the future.

Another tradition at Brown-Forman is a deep and lasting involvement with its hometown. Strong financial support of numerous civic, educational, cultural, and charitable causes, both corporately and individually, is again a reflection of Brown-Forman's concern with quality—this time, it's the quality of life of its neighbors. In its own "California" neighborhood, it supports a program called Adopt-a-Neighborhood, whereby the company provides seed financing for the rehabilitation of homes for low-income families.

The company's physical presence in West Louisville is another sign of its commitment—to remain in what's been its home area since the 1920s. When the time came to build a new headquarters building, rather than move to a location downtown or in the suburbs, Brown-Forman Corporation chose to erect a colonial-style building just across Dixie Highway from the historic buildings on Howard Street that house so many of its operations. Through renovation and conversion, several of those buildings, including an old icehouse and barrel warehouses, have become handsome office structures that, while having some modern touches, still retain their historic flavor.

Hartmann luggage and leather goods also bear the mark of excellence that has always been a hallmark of Brown-Forman products.

MANUFACTURING

KURFEES COATINGS, INC.

In business, the beauty of being number one has always been a subjective thing—in the eye of the beholder, so to speak.

For some it has to do with assets and revenues; for others, the number of jobs; and for still others, branch offices and employees. However, for Kurfees Coatings, Inc., it's believing that it sets the quality standard for the paint industry.

As Donald B. Kurfees, the fourth-generation Kurfees to carry the title of president, tells it: "Our approach has been to have the finest quality on the market, to be known as the quality leader in the industry. We test our products against other [competitors'] paints, and we come out on top. We may not sell as much, but we're going to be the best quality we can be."

That doesn't mean the company, founded in 1897, is not a market force. On the contrary, it ranks "probably in the top 30" in sales, says Kurfees, who has been with the organization since 1955. He estimates there are hundreds of small paint firms in the industry doing a fraction of what Kurfees sells annually.

The corporation markets products under three labels: Kurfees, which is sold directly to paint-specialty stores, building-materials dealers, and hardware stores in about 18 states; Fixall, which is sold through wholesale hardware distributorships in 26 states; and Panoramic, which is produced for and sold to the outdoor advertising (billboards) industry.

Architectural paint (for inside and outside homes) makes up approximately 90 percent of Kurfees' business, with most of it being sold to painting contractors and do-it-yourselfers. The rest is sold as industrial coatings and furniture finishes and coatings for the gate-manufacturing industry.

Kurfees' annual paint manufacturing generally comes to about 1.5 million gallons in about 3 million containers—some of which are of the

Kurfees brings computer technology to color matching at the retail level.

quarter-pint variety, making the company one of the few that still packages paint in that quantity.

The firm employs nearly 90 people in its plant, administration, sales, and three warehouses in Louisville, Chicago, and Charlotte. Kurfees proudly says his company has done away with "adversary postures" in personnel relations. "We do not refer to employees here," he says. "We call each other associates." A couple of

Kurfees Coatings, Inc., is represented in the paint marketplace by three labels: Kurfees, Fixall, and Panoramic.

those associates, his son and daughter, give the promise of a fifth generation of family ownership.

That feeling of community extends even into the greater community of Louisville. The corporation participates in several charitable and civic endeavors, chief of which is the Cabbage Patch Settlement, one of the largest and oldest charitable institutions in Louisville. Kurfees currently serves as president of the Cabbage Patch organization.

Kurfees views the future for his industry in hues of success. There will be some consolidations, he says, even some liquidations, "but we anticipate being around for the count" right into the twenty-first century.

IN CELEBRATION OF LOUISVILLE

DIGITAL EQUIPMENT CORPORATION

What does Hong Kong's Mass Transit Railway Corporation, England's Unilever Corporation, Italy's Ferrari auto manufacturers, West Germany's Citicorp Investment Bank, and America's General Electric Company have in common?

The answer is Digital VAX computers, perhaps the most sophisticated in the world. More than 100,000 are in use worldwide.

Digital Equipment Corporation, headquartered in Maynard, Massachusetts, is the world's leading manufacturer of networked computer systems and associated peripheral equipment, and is the leader in systems integration with its networks, communications, services, and software products. The VAX systems are used in scientific research, communications, education, data analysis, industrial control, commercial data processing, graphic arts, word processing, personal computing, health care, and engineering.

Digital, founded in 1957 and with more than one million network users at more than 8,000 customer sites, in a recent ranking placed 44th on the list of *Fortune* 500 companies. At its fiscal year-end in 1987, the corporation had revenues of $9.4 billion, up 24 percent from the 1986 figures; net income of $1.1 billion, up 84 percent over the previous year's figures; and

Digital Equipment Corporation is one of the world's largest manufacturers of networked computer systems and associated peripheral equipment, and the leader in systems integration with its networks, communications, and software products.

per-share earnings of $8.53, up 77 percent from 1986.

The Louisville office—which includes sales, software, and service departments—is located in the Forum Office Park and employs approximately 80 people. It's part of the corporation's East Central area, which is based in Farmington Hills, Michigan, and encompasses Kentucky, Indiana, Michigan, Ohio, western Pennsylvania, and West Virginia. Digital employs more than 2,000 people in the East Central area.

The corporation pioneered the concept of distributed computing and manufactures and sells the VAX family of computers, which offers the broadest range of compatible systems in the computer industry. Digital also maintains the world's largest private, nondefense electronic mail system network.

The organization operates more than 650 sales, service, manufacturing, administrative, and engineering facilities in 60 countries. World wide,

Digital's products are used worldwide in a variety of applications and programs, including scientific research, computation, communications, education, data analysis, industrial control, graphic arts, word processing, health care, instrumentation, engineering, simulation, and commercial data processing.

it employs more than 110,500 people.

Digital was the first computer systems manufacturer to tailor such systems to specific customer applications. The Detroit Application Center for Technology, located at the Farmington Hills site, opened in July 1986 and was the first such facility to allow present and potential customers to simulate and analyze their specific computer needs using the latest in technology. The center specializes in the automotive and related industries and—by simulating the factory, office, and numerous other business environments—allows customers to run a broad range of applications without having to

MANUFACTURING

The main computer room at Digital's Detroit Application Center for Technology (ACT) links the company's top-of-the-line equipment with a single operating architecture. This includes the VAX 8974, the highest-performance computer system ever produced by the company. The ACT, one of more than 20 worldwide, allows customers to simulate actual office and factory computer uses before purchasing equipment.

first purchase the equipment.

The Detroit center focuses its expertise in six major areas: discreet manufacturing, mechanical engineering, data base applications, office applications, networking, and work stations.

Louisville has been fairly fertile ground for Digital systems—the most prominent of customers being General Electric's Appliance Park, where the computer system has helped the giant appliance maker create the industry standard for dishwashers and the production patterns that go with that standard.

Another major installation in Louisville is at E.I. du Pont de Nemours, a producer of synthetic rubber located in the Rubbertown section of the city. Du Pont became the first to own the $3-million VAX 8974 computer, Digital's largest, that was introduced in January 1987. The computer is expected to be used by at least 405 people for such things as information storage, word processing, order processing, and product testing.

A computer in the Kentucky Department of Vital Statistics in Frankfort was the first business venture into the state by Digital, and it has proved its worth by helping to find at least five missing children since 1985. In one case the computer balked at a mother's request for a copy of her child's birth certificate. When state officials used the computer to call up birth records, it was noted that the child was missing.

On further investigation, it turned out the mother requesting the information had kidnapped the child, fled to Florida, remarried, and changed the child's name. A Kentucky State Police officer said they probably wouldn't have found the child had it not been for the computer.

In routine business in the vital statistics office, responding to requests for birth records and the like now takes about three to five days to process instead of the six weeks under the previous approach.

So, whether checking birth records, running a mass-transit system, or helping a company make the top-rated dishwasher in the nation, Digital Equipment Corporation's computers stand as marvels of the modern world with the capability of reaching to the frontiers of future technology.

Digital supplies industry standard state-of-the-art computer terminals and peripherals along with its computer systems and services.

IN CELEBRATION OF LOUISVILLE

GE APPLIANCES

General Electric Co.'s Appliance Park, headquarters for the industrial giant's appliance business, has been a massive presence, both physically and economically, in Louisville since 1953.

The huge facility, just to the southeast of the Louisville city limits, has approximately 160 acres under roof, including some 6.5 million square feet of plant space and about 600,000 square feet of office space. There is a 48-acre warehouse, 20 miles of in-plant railroad, and 12 miles of paved road at Appliance Park, where GE produces refrigerators, ranges, washers, dryers, and dishwashers.

GE, as the region's largest private employer, operates Appliance Park with more than 13,000 workers, whose annual payroll runs to approximately $380 million, covering both production and administrative personnel.

To enhance the ability to keep pace in the highly competitive appliance industry, GE plans to introduce work efficiencies throughout all operations while continuing to reduce salaried personnel at a rate of roughly 5 percent per year over the next several years.

Specifically designed for the custom-kitchen market, a line of "Monogram" built-in units is offered by GE Appliances.

While GE has had positive impact on Louisville, the business faces difficult challenges—in consolidating manufacturing operations, and modernizing local and satellite facilities. At two of its five plants at Appliance Park, major investments have been scheduled. Central in that modernization is the approximately $60 million revamping and automating of the dishwasher operation, which was designated by *Fortune* magazine as one of the 10 best managed manufacturing operations in the country in a 1984 article. The dishwasher project has become a model of excellence in overall industry, while providing a specific format for change in other GE manufacturing plants at Appliance Park.

Responsible for the success of GE's appliance business, senior vice-president Roger W. Schipke (center, sixth from left) reviews competitive strategies with members of his staff.

Under way now, for instance, is a $100-million-plus project to modernize the manufacturing equipment for refrigerator lines. The project includes the introduction of a new and more efficient refrigeration compressor.

To show its enthusiasm and appreciation for GE's presence in Louisville, and to infuse that same enthusiasm and appreciation in the people of Jefferson County, the county government made a $2-million grant to the facility to be used for the training of refrigerator-production workers on the new, automated equipment.

The format for change triggered by the dishwasher project has created some significant updating at Appliance Park. State-of-the-art technology, including robots, helps create a higher-quality, lower-cost dishwasher—cutting internal-failure costs in half. In turn, quality enhancement has dramatically reduced the service-call rate. Employees have contributed strongly in planning work environment improvements as well as quality-driven changes in factory procedures. All of these efforts have won GE a greater

MANUFACTURING

Module One, the first completed segment of GE Appliances' local investment in the refrigeration project, is expected to exceed $100 million. Dishwasher modernization at Louisville preceded the refrigerator-upgrade program.

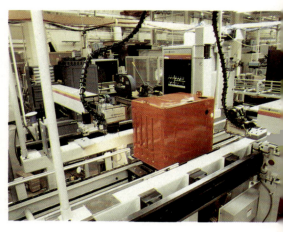

Using laser vision technology, this robotic inspection system, developed by GE's company-wide Advanced Technology/Automated Assembly Application Center at Louisville, gauges the points critical to quality on electric range oven cavities, manufactured locally.

share of market sales and more production jobs.

Other modernization projects have affected the manufacture of electric ranges as well as washers and dryers.

GE Appliances has an overall investment plan for almost one billion dollars during the decade of the 1980s—with consolidation decisions affecting local and satellite plants—based on global efforts to compete. Quality and productivity are both mandatory, and dedicated, individual effort is both vital and critical to the business. These factors set out by Roger W. Schipke, the GE senior vice-president in charge of GE Appliances, indicate that these elements must permeate efforts at successful operations headquarters at Appliance Park and elsewhere—at satellite plants and field offices.

Speaking to the early fear among workers that automation would take away their jobs, Schipke explains, "I think everybody understands now that the best job security is being a very profitable . . . world competitor." He encourages all managers and employees to become a profitable world competitor through modernizing, automating, and performing competitively as a part of an enlightened, enthusiastic work force.

Such a realization is being understood by union leaders, also, where many, though fearing automation, are fearing the alternative—shutdown—even more. Instead of taking jobs at GE, automation in the dishwasher operation actually was a major factor in adding employees.

In addition, change will allow employees to act as quality inspectors, thus improving chances for making the quality products that enhance market position and, in turn, solidify job security. Already they can stop an automated production line long enough to be sure the part being made is free of defects. A nod to automation came from a worker who was quoted in the *Fortune* article as asking, "Have you ever tried to thread a needle in motion?" That is what it was like, she said, to put screws into a dishwasher's timer prior to automation.

All of GE's activities do not go on inside the production walls. The

Engineers with GE's company-wide Plastics Applications Center at Louisville check specifications for a 5,000-ton injection molding machine, largest in the United States, which is used by GE to mold plastic parts for use in automobiles, aircraft engines, and appliances.

company and its employees are active in community affairs, supporting the cultural, civic, and charitable life of the area. In charitable donations alone, the employees and the company together contribute more than $2 million annually to area groups. A number of individuals have been singled out in a GE Is ME advertising campaign for their work with youth, the needy, the aged, infirm, or handicapped.

Though seldom is anything absolute in the world of business, a revitalized GE, at age 35, while facing stiff challenges with difficult decisions affecting Louisville, is devoted to remaining a leader in the appliance industry.

241

IN CELEBRATION OF LOUISVILLE

BORDEN CHEMICAL

Typically Borden is depicted by Elsie the cow. Condensed milk and other dairy and food products have always been the most recognizable face of Borden.

However, just as important—though not as old—is Borden Chemical. Oddly enough, the chemical business grew out of Borden's dairy expertise where casein, the principal protein in milk, became the foundation for the first good, cold-water-soluble, water-resistant wood glue.

Gail Borden, Jr., seemingly a man for all seasons whose bywords were "I tried and failed, I tried again and again, and succeeded," founded his condensed-milk company in 1857 at the age of 56. If that seems old for such an undertaking, it needs to be understood that the man of great persistence already had made several careers for himself—riverman, schoolteacher, surveyor, government official, newspaper publisher, and inventor.

As a Texas publisher he is credited with coining the phrase "Remember the Alamo." As a surveyor he laid out the northern Kentucky city of Covington. He invented the "prairie schooner," the "lazy Susan," and something he called the meat biscuit that was a staple for California Gold Rush miners in 1849.

So it's little wonder the restless and enterprising Borden pursued

All the formaldehyde and urea-formaldehyde produced at the Borden Chemical plant in Louisville come out of this production unit.

another career at what was surely considered advanced age in those days. His condensed milk was accomplished by evaporating the water in milk in a vacuum pan under low heat. What he didn't realize was that he actually was "pasteurizing" his

Quality-control supervisors, such as this one monitoring test information, keep a close eye on production at the plant.

milk—long before Louis Pasteur was credited with the discovery.

Borden died in 1874, 25 years before Borden Chemical was born through the purchase in 1899 of Casein Manufacturing Company in Vermont. From that somewhat sticky beginning has grown a chemical-producing firm that ranks in the top 25 in the United States, producing its own basic chemicals for a wide range of chemical specialty and consumer products.

Louisville's Borden Chemical plant, which includes three operations plus a research and development center, began operating in 1971 with the completion of a formaldehyde production plant and a river terminal for delivery of methanol by barge from the Gulf Coast. Later that year a urea-formaldehyde resin reactor was in operation, bringing the total capital investment to nearly $4 million. Sixteen people worked at the site at that time. In December 1976 a $1.1-million hot-melt adhesives plant was completed, and in September of the following year the $1.6-million, companywide research and development laboratory began operating. A $14-million phenolic resin plant went into operation in May 1978. There was further expansion in 1980 and 1984.

MANUFACTURING

The plant—tucked away on 94 acres of land along the Ohio River in what's known as Rubbertown in southwest Jefferson County—employs approximately 140 people, including about 40 in research and development, and has experienced dramatic growth through the 1980s.

The Louisville plant is responsible for a number of products with a number of applications in industry. Major among the products are urea-formaldehyde resins, which are prime factors in the wood industry, particularly with plywood and particleboard, acting as bonding agents. In addition, the same resins are used in fertilizers and in other lawn-care and weeding items. "Most people don't realize our products are in their homes or on their lawns," says Charles Stevens, Louisville site manager.

Phenol-formaldehyde resins come in both liquid and powder form, and all of these are unique in the Borden family to the Louisville plant. Some phenolic resins can be used as binding materials for home and commercial insulation. These resins give insulation its pink or yellow color, thus helping to make the "Pink Panther" by Owens Corning, or Manville "Gold" of insulation commercials possible.

Another phenolic resin is used in paper impregnation, giving it the rigidity necessary for automobile oil and air filters, and also for production of countertop materials.

Powdered phenolic resins have application as friction materials in the motor-vehicle industry for such products as brake blocks and clutch facings for cars, trucks, and buses. The resins act as adhesives to hold together the friction materials.

Another application for phenolic powder is fiber bonding for car insulation, being found under the hood, under the floor mat, and as the headliner. Basically, these insulations serve as sound deadeners between the engine and the passenger compartment.

In the hot melt adhesives plant,

This sign leads the way to the plant that is tucked away in one corner of the Rubbertown section of western Louisville, near the Ohio River.

various grades of waxes and tackifying materials are melted together and then packaged, with ultimate destination and application in the bookbinding industry and as sealers on cases and cartons prior to shipping.

Though Borden Chemical is something of a Johnny-come-lately in regard to longevity in Louisville as measured against other major chemical plants in the area, it feels confident about its place in Louisville's industrial family and looks forward to many more years of productive life in the area.

All the phenolic resins produced at the Louisville plant come to life in this manufacturing unit.

243

IN CELEBRATION OF LOUISVILLE

DCE, INC.

"Excuse my dust," suggested Dorothy Parker as her epitaph.

With all due respect to the late outstanding twentieth-century author and member of the celebrated gathering of wits and artists known as the Algonquin Roundtable, DCE, Inc., couldn't do that.

The firm is in the business of controlling dust, making an old movie title—*Dust Be My Destiny*—much more appropriate.

DCE, which, not so surprisingly, stands for dust-control equipment, designs and manufactures industrial dust collectors for application in practically any industry, and for customers large and small who require state-of-the-art solutions and equipment. The organization has been in the Louisville area only since 1976, and although it is part of the DCE Group of the United Kingdom—which gives it a long record of expertise in the business—it is nonetheless an American company dealing for the most part with American industry.

In fact, according to president Richard Dodson, DCE, Inc., is now the second-largest firm in its parent group, and "we colonists," as he kiddingly puts it, are pushing to be number one.

At its Louisville headquarters, which has been home to the com-

An employee works with a piece of machinery that is part of the forming operation for dust-control equipment.

Headquarters and the production plant for DCE, Inc., are located in this building in the eastern part of Jefferson County.

pany since October 1981, DCE manufactures two types of dust collectors—one for continuous duty and another for intermittent duty. The former is much larger than the latter and runs continuously in industries with heavy dust loads such as chemicals, tobacco, paint spraying, plastics, mineral processing, and paper products and metalworking. The latter is smaller and is used at the time work is being done at specific work stations such as saws, grinders, blenders, crushers, drills, lathes, mixers, and polishers.

DCE products, confirms Dodson, have some features that set them apart from competitors' equipment. Chief among those are an automatic cleaning process, front access to the dust collector, downflow design, and easy access to and emptying of the dust bin in smaller collectors.

The downflow design, which takes an opposite flow from many competitors' products, combines with the inherent nature of gravity to collect and bring the dust into the machine from above, filter it out of the air as it travels downward, and then exhaust the air. The continuous-duty equipment can be massive because of the immense job of gathering dust from a large area. The dust-filled air is moved to the collector by a powerful fan.

Front access to the equipment allows easy cleaning without getting into the area where most of the dirt

MANUFACTURING

is, and means the unit doesn't have to have as much head room as those collectors that have bags hanging from the top of the unit and must be removed through the top.

In the intermittent-duty operation the unit is self-contained with a fan and controls, and works only when it's turned on. When the job is done the unit is turned off, but before the motor stops it shakes the unit's dust bag and automatically reconditions the bag, sending the debris into a bucket-like dust bin, another feature that DCE thinks is superior to competitors' designs. A lever releases the dust bin and allows it to be dumped easily and with little chance of scattering the dust as in the case of a drawer-like dust bin.

Dodson, president since 1985, says DCE—which had been doing business in the United States for some time and decided it should form a company in this country—chose Louisville because it was the site already of some dust-control firms, is centrally located, is a growth area in an industrial part of the nation, and has a good work force. Though the firm is a subsidiary of the giant British conglomerate BTR (British Tire & Rubber) Group, it is incorporated in Kentucky and concentrates on business in the United States and Canada.

Since the company is relatively young, the work force is young, also. In fact, Dodson mentions that working at DCE is a first job for many employees. Plant workers are involved in manufacturing equipment from the ground up; no subcontracting of components is done. That keeps the quality control in the hands of DCE, which is the way the firm and—from comments received—customers like it. "We're a young company," Dodson says, "and not as well known as many of our principal competitors, but those customers who have our equipment speak highly of it. We are known as a quality supplier, and that's what we're going to grow on."

Dodson stresses that DCE is not just an equipment manufacturer, but a problem solver as well. The corporation has the resources to analyze a dust problem, engineer the best solution, and install and maintain its custom-made equipment. "We are a customer-oriented, problem-solving organization, drawing on more than 60 years' experience," Dodson emphasizes. That mission doesn't figure to be diminished either; the parent company has been generous in its capital-investment program in Louisville, and Dodson expects that to continue.

Responding to its local success DCE, Inc., has taken on quite a bit of community involvement, including membership in the Louisville, Jeffersontown, and Kentucky chambers of commerce, and participation in Junior Achievement, the Metro United Way, the American Red Cross bloodmobile, the Boy Scouts of America, and the Jeffersontown Vocational School. "We try to give back to our community what we get from it," Dodson says.

Research and testing on ways to vent a dust explosion away from workers and equipment is shown in the sequence before, during, and after.

This is a general view of where work goes on in the DCE, Inc., manufacturing plant.

245

IN CELEBRATION OF LOUISVILLE

AMERICAN AIR FILTER

American Air Filter, headquartered in Louisville, is a worldwide manufacturer of products and systems that condition, improve, and control the environment.

American Air Filter can trace its roots to 1921, when a resourceful entrepreneur who operated an automobile paint shop in Louisville prevented dirt particles from settling on freshly painted surfaces by inventing a filter made of steel wool dipped in oil, held in place with chicken wire, and contained in a wooden frame. It worked so well that he got out of the auto painting business to manufacture and sell his filters.

The entrepreneurial spirit continues today with an air of innovative and imaginative approaches to problem solving throughout the organization. The firm employs more than 3,000 people worldwide, with nearly 500 people in the Louisville headquarters and manufacturing facility. In addition, there are 11 other plants in the United States and Canada and six international facilities.

The company, the world's largest manufacturer of air-filtration products and systems, is a market leader in virtually all of its product lines. Worldwide sales are in the neighborhood of $300 million.

The slogan "Better Air Is Our Business" describes the activities of American Air Filter. AAF's products and systems clean, move, cool, heat, and control the temperature, humidity, and noise level of ambient air. These products and systems can be selected individually or in combinations to create a controlled environment suited to the various needs of people and machines.

American Air Filter's business can be divided into four major segments:

—Air filtration products consist of air filters for use in homes, office buildings, hospitals, schools, sewage-treatment facilities, and in a wide range of manufacturing facilities such as electronics, automotive, and pharmaceutical plants.

—Air-pollution-control products include large and small dust- and fume-collection devices for a wide variety of industrial applications, such as automotive, foundry, and metalworking.

—Machinery intake filtration products provide air-filtration devices for use on gas turbines and other internal combustion engines, and air compressors, to reduce erosion and fouling of internal components. AAF products are found on railroad locomotives, work boats, offshore oil rigs, and oil and gas pumping stations.

—Heating, ventilating, and air conditioning products consist of air conditioning products and systems for a wide range of commercial and institutional buildings, such as schools, hotels and motels, nursing homes, and office buildings.

In Louisville, the manufacturing operation is a metalworking plant producing the firm's larger models of air cleaning equipment requiring a high degree of welding and fabrication skills and sophisticated quality-control techniques. Plant personnel range from semi-skilled to highly skilled, many with more than 30 years' service.

Being a good citizen is important to American Air Filter and its employees. That includes active company and employee participation in local charities, minority programs, and the arts. AAF employees take particular pride in their involvement in the Derby Festival Parade, where the employee-sponsored float has been a prize winner.

At American Air Filter there's an air of enthusiasm for Louisville, for AAF, and for the future.

Headquarters for American Air Filter, a worldwide manufacturer of air-cleaning products, is in Louisville.

LOUISVILLE BEDDING COMPANY

"You've made your bed, now sleep in it" generally is not a pleasant thought, because it usually means one has done something that is not beneficial to his or her well-being.

However, if you're associated with Louisville Bedding Company, you'd probably not have much trouble with the statement—as long as there was one of the firm's mattress pads on the bed.

Its products, plus a long history and a stable work force, have given Louisville Bedding Company a solid place in the city's business community.

The organization, which registered sales of $65 million in 1986, was incorporated in 1903 as the Louisville Pillow Company, the successor to a partnership formed in 1889. It changed its name to Louisville Bedding Company in 1917. The firm has manufacturing facilities in Louisville and Munfordville, Kentucky, and distribution centers in Louisville and Los Angeles. It's a business that sells its products nationally to most major retail chains, bed and bath boutiques, and regional linen shops.

The company also markets napkins, place mats, table runners, and chair pads through its Reed Handcrafts trade name, a result of the acquisition of Reed in 1971. In recent years place mats—of which Reed is the largest manufacturer in the country and the acknowledged leader—have been a strong product, but in 1986 it was unseated as the corporation's second-best-selling item by chair pads. Reed considers itself a fashion leader of traditionally styled, high-volume products designed to retail in an intermediate- to high-price category. In addition, the firm manufactures a line of pads for the moving and storage industry.

The company's quilted mattress pads are manufactured both for its own brand and for private labels in fitted, contoured, and anchor-band styles in various sizes. The pads are made for the medium- to high-price range, and produced from high-quality fabric, which has been bleached, preshrunk, and treated with various finishes, depending on the final product.

Generally, the mattress pads are constructed of polyester filler, for ease of care, and of both conventional and ultrasonic sewing methods. The organization markets a full line of pads and is a national leader in deluxe quilted pads. A complete line of dust ruffles and pillow shams also is produced.

The work force of approximately 800 at its various locations is one of experience and a solid work ethic, both of which are reflected in the many long employment histories among the employees. They are considered a major resource of Louisville Bedding Company, and one that is expected to carry the firm forward in the industry.

The corporate offices and the main distribution center for Louisville Bedding Company are housed in this masonry, one-story building containing approximately 120,000 square feet.

Louisville Chamber of Commerce 250

Citizens Fidelity Bank and Trust Company 251

Future Federal Savings Bank 252-253

BATUS, Inc. 254-257

Commonwealth Life Insurance Company 262-263

Great Financial Federal 264-265

Health Data Network 266-267

The Cumberland Federal Savings Bank 258-259

Capital Holding Corporation 260-261

Chapter XI
Business

Louisville's business and financial institutions offer a strong base for the city's growing economy.

Cowger & Miller Mortgage Company 268-269

William M. Mercer Meidinger Hansen, Incorporated 270-271

Photo by Quadrant

IN CELEBRATION OF LOUISVILLE

LOUISVILLE CHAMBER OF COMMERCE

The link between a new idea and a new enterprise. The collective voice of the business community. The spark that helps a small company grow. Since 1949 the Louisville Chamber of Commerce has been this, and more, to businesses throughout the Louisville region. And now, under the energetic leadership of president James O. Roberson, the chamber has strengthened ties with government and business leaders to forge a consensus on what is most important in Louisville's continued economic development.

"Louisville has kept its competitive edge in a time of economic shifts by bringing together resources available in the community," Roberson says. "Now this region is ready to take the lead in economic development, with the support of a $10-million Campaign for Greater Louisville that draws heavily upon the strong relationship between public and private partners."

Today Louisville enters its third century with a renaissance in pride that is built on its newly forged partnerships and its traditional role as the commercial hub of the region. And, to a large degree, Louisville is what it is today because of the individuals who make up its chamber of commerce.

The Louisville Chamber of Commerce boasts 2,500 members, more than 40 employees, and an annual budget of approximately $2 million. Six departments—Government Affairs, Economic Development, Center for Small Business, Member Services, Communications, and Executive—are dedicated to voicing business concerns to the people who form public policy, and to giving members the educational support they need to succeed. Programs include educational workshops, data on the latest business trends, consistent interaction with government representatives, and extensive networking opportunities.

In addition, four related organizations operating under the auspices of the chamber offer services ranging from matching up minority vendors with large corporate buyers to locating capital for start-ups and expansions.

Despite their variety, all of the chamber's programs are aimed at one goal—making a difference in Louisville by making it an even better place to live and do business. Each department charts its course by gauging how its programs will help shape the business climate of the community. Each program is designed according to how it will encourage economic development in the Louisville region.

From the smallest seminar to the numerous committee meetings to an economic development campaign that will take Louisville to the nation, the Louisville Chamber of Commerce is committed not only to sustaining Louisville's growth, but also to quickening it by attracting new businesses and nurturing businesses already here.

The chamber helps its member businesses to increase their markets in a number of ways, including an annual trade show where members promote their goods and services to other members.

As president, James O. Roberson is at the helm of the Louisville Chamber of Commerce.

BUSINESS

CITIZENS FIDELITY BANK AND TRUST COMPANY

Although it traces its roots back 130 years, Citizens Fidelity Bank and Trust Company stands as one of Louisville's "newer" financial institutions because of recent regional acquisitions and a merger with a gigantic Pittsburgh bank holding company.

Citizens Fidelity banks can be found throughout the Louisville area and, beginning in 1985, in several other Kentucky and southern Indiana communities.

The merger in February 1987 with PNC Financial Corporation of Pittsburgh added strength to both institutions. Total assets of PNC Financial at the end of 1987 were $36.5 billion, and the assets of Citizens Fidelity Corporation were more than $6.1 billion.

Citizens has grown up with Louisville, developing a pride in performance stemming from its founding institution, Merchants Deposit Bank, which was established February 17, 1858. That was just 80 years after George Rogers Clark's party of soldiers and pioneers settled the Louisville area.

Merchants Deposit Bank had offices on Main Street on land once owned by Henry Clay, and its first president was W.B. Belknap, founder of Louisville's historic Belknap Hardware. The institution became Citizens Bank during the Civil War, and on July 15, 1874, joined the national banking system.

Several other predecessors helped give Citizens the foundation for its present financial structure. One was Union National Bank; another was Fidelity Trust Company, the first such organization west of the Alleghenies; and still another was Columbia Finance and Trust Company. The two trust companies merged in 1912 and the two banks did likewise seven years later.

As the controlling stockholders of the merged trust companies were essentially the same as those of the Union bank, the operations immediately became affiliated. In 1922 the bank's new headquarters home, the Inter-Southern Building (now Kentucky Home Life Building), was dubbed by *The Louisville Times* as "The Cathedral of Commerce."

The bank and the trust company were unified in 1944 as Citizens Fidelity Bank and Trust Company. Twenty-seven years later, in 1971, the institution moved into a new cathedral of commerce—across Jefferson Street from its previous headquarters—at 30 stories the tallest building in Kentucky at the time.

The bank's 10 floors in Citizens Plaza give it a massive physical as well as financial presence in the center of the city's business and financial district.

Citizens Fidelity Bank and Trust Company's commitment to service is matched by its support of Louisville's quality of life. That includes financial donations to the United Way, substantial investments in educational institutions, and significant contributions to arts, civic, and charitable organizations.

A banker's lamp and a calculator symbolize much of the work that is done by employees of Citizens Bank and Trust Company.

Citizens Fidelity Bank and Trust Company is at home in Citizens Plaza in the center of Louisville's financial and business district.

251

FUTURE FEDERAL SAVINGS BANK

Future Federal Savings Bank is one of Kentucky's most aggressive and competitive banks. Located throughout the Louisville and Glasgow areas, Future Federal offers most all the banking services that consumers desire in their financial institutions.

Future Federal's roots trace back to 1926, when Leo P. Kaufman spearheaded formation of an organization to make home buying affordable for Louisville area residents. The now-Future Federal opened its doors as Louisville Home Building Association and was located in the old Louisville Trust Building.

Louisville Home quickly outgrew these quarters and in 1929 moved to 116 South Fifth Street, where it remained for the next 12 years. In this time span the institution gained membership in the Federal Home Loan Bank system, and in May 1935 became a fully insured member with the FSLIC. With federal affiliation the name was changed to Louisville Home Federal Savings and Loan Association. C.D. Harris was its first president. Under his and the board's leadership, Louisville Home grew and the office was moved to 130 South Fifth Street in 1941.

Louisville Home's participation in the postwar G.I. home-loan program made otherwise unobtainable home purchases available to hundreds of Louisville area veteran families. Following a post-World War II boom, new quarters were found at Fifth and Market in the recently vacated office of the Federal Reserve Bank.

In 1980 Home Federal Savings and Loan Association of Versailles

Future Federal opened in 1926 and now has offices throughout the Louisville and Glasgow areas.

Future Federal's customer service department is one of the nation's most efficient and has served as a model for many financials across the country.

BUSINESS

merged with Louisville Home, and that same year a new name and identification for the institution were sought to reflect its statewide growth. The name was changed to Future Federal, and a readily identifiable rainbow was selected for the logo.

Also during 1980 Jefferson Federal Savings and Loan Association merged with Future Federal; the move was followed by two additional mergers in the next two years. Southern Federal Savings and Loan, based in Louisville, and First Federal Savings and Loan of Glasgow merged with Future Federal in 1982.

Future Federal's corporate office was moved from downtown in November 1982. Its corporate home base is now the totally remodeled and updated facility that formerly housed the Greathouse School. Located in suburban Louisville, Future Federal again has the room for the growth it anticipates.

Throughout its history Future Federal has always been known as an innovator by offering new customer-oriented financial products and services. Future Federal was one of the first savings and loan associations to acquire federal insurance, and was also one of the first associations to build branches in its community. When Individual Retirement Accounts, Keogh Accounts, and Home Equity Loans became available to the general public, Future Federal was one of the first banks in the country to offer these programs. Innovation continues today as Future Federal offers INVEST, an in-house franchise stock brokerage. In addition, many financials nationwide have come to study Future's Customer Service Department, one of the country's most efficient customer-relations departments.

One of Future Federal's specialties has been in the lending area. Since its beginning Future Federal has been committed to making home mortgage loans. Today the bank still makes mortgage loans, but has aggressively expanded its loan services to commercial real estate lending, and also provides all types of personal and consumer loans to individuals.

The overriding corporate objective of Future Federal centers around providing products and services at the greatest possible value to its customers and to the communities it serves. In so doing, Future

The management of Future Federal, headed by Joey Bailey (left) as president and Don Bennett (right) as executive vice-president, has fostered an innovative approach to reach the objectives set forth in the bank's mission statement.

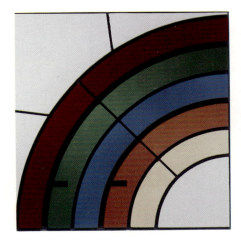

Future Federal's logo, the rainbow, is symbolic of the many positive things happening for its customers.

Federal has gained and holds customer confidence, respect, and loyalty. This has made the bank a profitable, well-capitalized, multi-service consumer banking institution. The management at Future Federal, headed by Joey B. Bailey as president and Don Bennett as executive vice-president, has fostered innovation and creativity. "We allow the individual employee freedom of action in attaining well-defined objectives," says Joey Bailey. Don Bennett adds, "We're proud of the employees at Future; their performance and positive attitude toward their job is evident in the results we expect and receive."

Future Federal's powerful logo, the rainbow, is symbolic of the many positive things happening for its customers and the bank, and reflects the promise of a great future.

IN CELEBRATION OF LOUISVILLE

BATUS INC.

Louisville is the headquarters of BATUS Inc., a diverse, multi-billion-dollar company with a nationwide network of businesses in tobacco paper, and retailing, including Louisville's own Brown & Williamson Tobacco Corporation.

BATUS was founded in 1980, and is the holding and management company for the U.S. business interests of B.A.T Industries p.l.c., London, England, one of the world's largest industrial enterprises.

From offices on the 19th and 20th floors in the Citizens Plaza building at Fifth and Liberty streets in downtown Louisville, a small group of BATUS executives and staff give strategic direction to a diverse group of businesses across the United States.

In addition to Brown & Williamson Tobacco Corporation, which has had its headquarters in Louisville

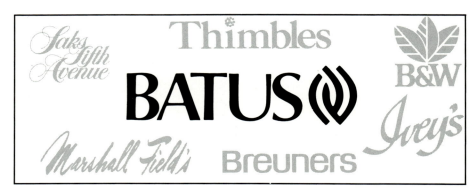

Henry F. Frigon (left), president and chief executive officer, and Wilson Wyatt, Jr., vice-president of corporate affairs, are part of the small group of executives that plots strategic direction for BATUS businesses.

since 1929, other BATUS subsidiary firms are:

—Appleton Papers Inc., headquartered in Appleton, Wisconsin. The world's largest producer of carbonless paper, its sales in 1987 were more than $700 million. It has 3,800 employees at eight locations in four states.

—Saks Fifth Avenue, the nation's leading high-fashion retailer, with 44 stores in 30 markets in 18 states and sales of more than one billion dollars per year. The retailer, with more than 10,000 employees, has been a BATUS subsidiary since 1973.

—Marshall Field's, a Chicago landmark with 25 stores in three states and a 130-year-old American shopping tradition, which has sales approaching one billion dollars annually. Acquired as a BATUS subsidiary company in 1982, Marshall Field's is capturing new market share with quality merchandise, innovative management and superior performance.

—Ivey's, a department store positioned between a full-line traditional department store and the more narrowly focused specialty store. It is a 24-unit department store tradition in North Carolina, South Carolina, and Florida, and is positioned to take advantage of expansion opportunities in the Southeast. Ivey's, a BATUS subsidiary since 1982, has 5,000 employees.

BUSINESS

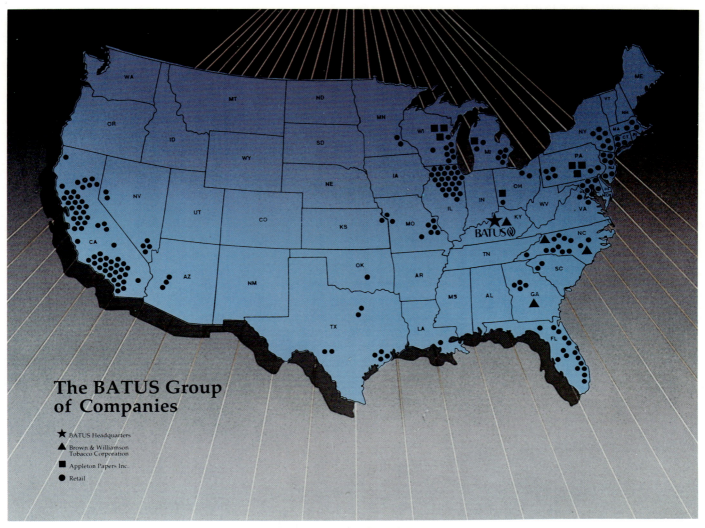

The BATUS Group of Companies

★ BATUS Headquarters
▲ Brown & Williamson Tobacco Corporation
■ Appleton Papers Inc.
● Retail

Locks Mill, Wisconsin, paper plant is one of eight facilities operated by BATUS subsidiary Appleton Papers Inc.

—Breuners, a quality home-furnishing retailing business comprising 17 home-furnishing stores and 40 furniture-rental stores in California.

—Thimbles, the youngest and smallest of the BATUS group of companies, which holds promise as a specialty store for women. There are 57 stores in the chain located in 15 selected metropolitan areas across the country.

Consolidated annual sales for this diverse group of BATUS companies were approximately $5.8 billion for

This map shows locations for BATUS headquarters, and Brown & Williamson Tobacco Corporation, Appleton Papers Inc., and retail facilities around the country.

1987, and trading profit has been increasing at a compound growth rate of more than 12 percent. Total employment nationwide is approximately 40,000. In Louisville, the 125-member BATUS staff provides strategic corporate planning for the BATUS group of companies.

B.A.T Industries has operations in some 90 countries, employing more than 300,000 worldwide. It is involved in four major business areas: tobacco, paper, retailing, and financial services.

B.A.T Industries is listed on the London Exchange and traded in the United States on the American

Stock Exchange in the form of American Depository Receipts. If BATUS were ranked with publicly traded firms, it would be listed among the top 100 companies in the United States.

Explains Henry F. Frigon, president and chief executive officer, "BATUS is the focal point for the strategic development, financing,

A Saks Fifth Avenue shopper admires high-quality goods in this specialty department store in midtown Manhattan. Saks Fifth Avenue is the nation's leading high-fashion specialty retailer.

and management of B.A.T Industries' current and future direct investments in the United States. As such, we are responsible for the performance of B.A.T's U.S. businesses."

Brown & Williamson, the largest of the BATUS subsidiary ventures and which had sales of more than $2.4 billion in 1987, has been a major

Brown & Williamson has a diverse group of products, including its flagship brand, KOOL, one of the most popular menthol cigarettes in the world. CAPRI is B&W's newest brand.

One example of Brown & Williamson's involvement in the community is its funding for computers and computer laboratories in the Jefferson County school system's New Kid on the Block program.

employer in Louisville for a half-century. The organization is headquartered in a 26-story glass tower at Fourth and Liberty streets, anchoring the downtown's Galleria retail and office complex, a sparkling symbol of a downtown resurgence in business and retailing.

As the nation's third-largest tobacco company, B&W employs about 1,000 people in Louisville. Throughout its history in the city, the firm has been an active investor in the community's welfare.

Regardless of form, from funding for the arts to employee civic involvements, community contributions by Brown & Williamson and BATUS are investments made with an eye toward the eventual dividend—an improved quality of life to sustain an environment that is good for business growth.

Community involvement focuses on four primary areas of support: education, the arts, civic, and health and welfare.

Strong educational programs are vital to a community's development. Over the years contributions to local education have served as building blocks for future growth. Examples include the strong tradition of support for the University of Louisville and the United Negro College Fund. Brown & Williamson's participation to provide computers for public schools and funding for public television are other examples.

Being an active corporate citizen is a responsibility that BATUS, Brown & Williamson, and employees meet with enthusiasm. Looking forward, the companies plan to continue this commitment to help make Louisville an even better community in which to live and work.

Brown & Williamson, in addition to its Louisville-based corporate headquarters, conducts research and development activities at 16th and Hill streets at the I.W. Hughes Technical Center. The corporate headquarters includes executive offices, as well as marketing, sales, advertising, international, and administrative offices.

B&W's flagship brand is KOOL, the fourth-largest-selling cigarette brand in the United States and one of the most popular menthol cigarettes in the world. In addition to KOOL, other B&W domestic brands include BARCLAY, CAPRI, RICHLAND, FALCON, VICEROY, RALEIGH, and BELAIR. The company also markets KENT and LUCKY STRIKE, along with other brands, in a growing number of international markets.

Brown & Williamson's cigarette-manufacturing facility is located in Macon, Georgia. Tobacco-leaf processing takes place in Wilson, North Carolina, and specialty tobacco products, such as Sir Walter Raleigh pipe tobacco, are manufactured in Winston-Salem, North Carolina.

Brown & Williamson, which has total employment of approximately 5,000, became a wholly owned subsidiary of British American Tobacco Company in 1927.

The Brown & Williamson Tobacco Corporation headquarters is located in this 26-story glass tower that stands as one of the cornerstones of the Louisville Galleria, a glistening retailing center in the downtown area.

THE CUMBERLAND FEDERAL SAVINGS BANK

In the late 1970s economic forces and the government changed the rules of the savings and loan game. Now, after an eight-year shakeup—and shakeout—created by government deregulation, the ledger on the savings and loan industry reads like Darwin's survival of the fittest. Only those financially healthy enough to acquire others who were not as fortunate survived to combine their home-based business with the new world of retail banking opened to them by deregulation.

The Cumberland, the largest publicly held thrift based in Kentucky, was one of those. It took a further step in this direction when, under new leadership, it decided in late 1986 to leave its mutual status of 100 years and convert to stockholder ownership. Today, following its conversion in the spring of 1987, the organization that now goes by the name The Cumberland Federal Savings Bank is well prepared for the challenges of the new marketplace.

The conversion nearly doubled its capital base from $26 million to about $50 million. That brings a smile from H. David Hale, president and chief executive officer since 1986. "Few companies in our business can claim that much equity," he says. "Our job now is to get our earnings up and keep things steady for a couple of years to show our shareholders that we can perform." Then it will again be time to look around for expansion possibilities, according to Hale, who came from a banking career in West Virginia.

Although he is confident of success, Hale is not thinking of expansion just for the sake of size, especially when his business is already in the neighborhood of one billion dollars. That is especially encouraging for the 27-office thrift that saw adverse times from 1981 to 1985 as it experienced deterioration in assets due to inflation and overall economic forces.

However, Hale knows that success is not going to be an overnight occurrence. "Our biggest challenge is to bring a good return to our shareholders and an increase in the price of our stock. This presents a new challenge for The Cumberland," he says. It means the bank's approximately 400 employees have to consider the needs of their investors as well as those of the community and the customer.

The Cumberland Federal Savings Bank chairman and president, H. David Hale.

The Cumberland's roots go back to the Louisville of the 1880s, when, in 1886, the Home and Savings Fund Company (later Avery Federal Savings and Loan Association) was formed to give employees of the B.F. Avery Plow Works a place to save and eventually buy a home. As de-

Cumberland employees constantly work to keep product information up to date.

BUSINESS

Friendly, knowledgeable customer service is an ongoing goal at The Cumberland.

posits mounted, every so often a loan would be made for that purpose. In 1889 another association was formed in the Portland section of Louisville and became, appropriately, Portland Savings and Loan Association.

They both enjoyed steady, if not spectacular, growth through the years, and thousands of Louisvillians benefited through home mortgages. Boom times followed World War II and continued into the 1970s. However, at that point inflation, high interest rates, other disruptive economic factors, and deregulation combined to send much of the industry to the wrong side of the ledger. The weak fell or were merged with only slightly stronger savings and loans, most of whom eventually weathered the storm.

The first of seven mergers to affect what in 1982 became The Cumberland was completed in 1981, when Fidelity Federal of Bowling Green merged into Portland Federal. The following year Avery merged with Portland to become Portland/Avery Federal Savings and Loan Association, and most of the others that now make up The Cumberland joined that same year.

Hale is prepared to meet head-on The Cumberland's need to develop continuity in its financial picture. "We're a lot better prepared to make money now than we were three or four years ago," Hale says—underlining that belief with the facts that mortgage loans have been steady of late, and that the institution has aggressively diversified its asset portfolio.

As a savings bank, The Cumberland offers most banking functions: savings and checking accounts, credit cards, consumer loans (for cars and home equity, for instance), money machines, and, of course, home loans; however, it leaves large commercial accounts to the commercial banks.

Hale expects growth through inflation, new locations, and possibly even further mergers. He expects growth to continue in what he calls the "I-65 and I-64 corridors," the major east-west and north-south interstate highways in the commonwealth. The growth potential and the "economic action" are in the corridors cited, he believes. That means the Louisville area, western Kentucky, and the Frankfort/Lexington area.

In Louisville, which he calls a lovable city, Hale expects continued steady growth. "It's not a boom economy," he says, "but we have less worry about major employers closing down now." There have been some major adjustments over the past several years in just what kind of economic city Louisville is, moving from a heavily blue-collar, industrial working environment to one of a more service-oriented atmosphere. Hale calls it a gray-collar city—reflecting the growth of white-collar workers, pushed along by the swift growth of the service sector, including the health care industry in the city.

After looking inward for most of the past two years, Hale recognizes that now looking outward should be on his and the institution's agendas. He likes the leadership atmosphere in Louisville and is making plans to take on more community responsibilities for himself and The Cumberland Federal Savings Bank.

State-of-the-art equipment is used in originating and processing mortgage loans.

IN CELEBRATION OF LOUISVILLE

CAPITAL HOLDING CORPORATION

Newcomers to Kentucky may be surprised to discover a $10-billion diversified financial services corporation in the heart of downtown Louisville.

Capital Holding is one of the nation's 10 largest stockholder-owned life insurance organizations, with $43.8 billion of life insurance coverage in force, and is Kentucky's third-largest publicly held company. It is also one of Louisville's largest employers, with 1,500 area employees and a local payroll of $47 million.

Under the bold leadership of chairman Tom Simons and his designated successor, Irv Bailey, Capital Holding has metamorphosed from a regional insurance marketer to a diversified and innovative financial services institution of national stature. Building on its strong base of regional life insurers, the corporation has diversified through acquisition of direct-response life and health and property and casualty operations, and a consumer banking operation. Its broad range of financial services and products are sold in all 50 states through agents, direct-marketing media, investment professionals, and retail locations, and in the Far East through operations in Hong Kong.

Affiliates include Commonwealth Life Insurance Company and Capital Initiatives Corporation, both in Louisville; First Deposit Corporation, in San Francisco, California; National Liberty Corporation, in Valley Forge, Pennsylvania; Peoples Security Life Insurance Company, in Durham, North Carolina; and Worldwide Insurance Group, in St. Louis, Missouri.

Perhaps even more significant to the Louisville community is Capital Holding's innovative and energetic involvement in the area's economic development, to which the company's leadership is staunchly committed.

Capital Holding is a major participant in the Broadway-Brown Partnership—developer of Theater Square on Louisville's Fourth Avenue Mall, anchored by the recently refurbished Brown Hotel. In 1989 Capital Holding will begin construction of a new, $66-million office complex adjacent to its current headquarters next to Theater Square. And Bailey, president and chief executive officer, is chairman of the Broadway Project Corporation, which is spearheading redevelopment of the 33-acre area at the southern end of Fourth Avenue.

The corporation's community interest extends well beyond its front door: Capital Holding also contributed substantial financial and human resources to help lure the Presbyterian Church (U.S.A.) headquarters to Louisville. That relocation effort is expected to create as many as 700 new jobs for Louisville-area residents.

Capital Holding lends strong support to health, social, and recreational youth projects; education; arts and culture; environmental programs; minority affairs; and activities for the elderly. Some grant recipients are Spalding University, University of Louisville, and Bellarmine College; Cedar Lake Lodge, a care facility for the mentally handicapped; Brooklawn, a rehabilitation center for young drug and alcohol abusers; Actors Theatre, Louisville Ballet, and the Kentucky Opera Association; Channel 15 public television; and the Museum of History and Science and the Kentucky Derby Museum.

According to Simons, "The contributions we make are a part of Capital Holding's efforts to play an important role in Louisville's development. We have a responsibility to be a good corporate neighbor and to do our part to help improve the quality of life for the people in our community."

The dynamic growth of Capital Holding took off when Simons joined the company in 1978 as chairman and chief executive officer. The firm then was an old-line insurance organization facing a mature market, rising costs, and flat earnings.

Irving W. Bailey II, president and chief executive officer of Capital Holding.

Armed with a mandate for change, Simons took several decisive moves to achieve Capital Holding's current status as a major financial services intermediary.

His first step—to diversify into national direct-response marketing—raised eyebrows within the conservative insurance industry, but its success has since spurred many major insurers to follow suit. In 1981 Capital Holding acquired National Liberty Corporation, the nation's largest marketer of life and health insurance through television and print advertising. The company subsequently acquired First Deposit Corporation in 1984, a consumer lending and credit card business that uses direct-response marketing techniques, and two years later acquired Worldwide Insurance Group, a direct-response property and casualty company.

Capital Initiatives Corporation was created in 1986 to develop new markets and distribution channels for accumulation and insurance products. It subsequently opened an office in Hong Kong from which it markets a unique, short-term indexed product to institutional investors in the Far East.

Capital Holding has explored other nontraditional marketing avenues. It has established 21 financial centers at Kroger grocery stores in Kentucky, Ohio, Alabama, and Tennessee, and soon will expand into Florida, South Carolina, and Virginia. Through a joint venture with CUNA Mutual, the company markets insurance products to 750,000 credit union members.

Simons also assembled a talented senior management team to carry his visions to successful fruition. Bailey joined Capital Holding in 1981 as chief investment officer and is largely credited with building Capital Holding's top-notch investment area. He was responsible for the acquisition of First Deposit Corporation, moving the corporation even more squarely into financial services.

"I retire in complete confidence that what we've built together is in fine and capable hands," said Simons. "Irv Bailey has demonstrated that he has the ability and the drive to take this organization into a new phase of growth and development.

"Irv also shares my commitment to Louisville. I have every confidence that he will continue to work for the revitalization of downtown and the city's economic vigor."

In addition to its leadership role in the Broadway Renaissance, Capital Holding's commitment to Louisville's development includes support for health, social, cultural, educational, and recreational projects.

261

IN CELEBRATION OF LOUISVILLE

COMMONWEALTH LIFE INSURANCE COMPANY

The life and times of Commonwealth Life Insurance Company go back to June 5, 1905, when the company sold its first life insurance policy—to one of its own employees.

The firm derived its name from the Commonwealth of Kentucky and adopted the state's seal and motto—United We Stand, Divided We Fall—for its own. The fledgling company operated from two rooms in a building on Main Street.

That's a far cry from the 21-story Commonwealth Building that also serves as headquarters for Capital Holding. Today, Commonwealth Insurance is Kentucky's largest life insurance operation, with more than $2 billion in assets and $11.6 billion of insurance in force.

Still, personal service is a continuing tradition at Commonwealth Insurance, which has expanded its home-service base by opening Financial Centers in 21 Kroger grocery stores in Kentucky, Alabama, Tennessee, and Ohio. The company offers an array of life insurance products including whole life, term, universal life, and single-pay premium, as well as cash-accumulation products such as flexible- and single-premium annuities. Commonwealth Insurance also offers insurance for car and home, and health insurance covering major medical, small group medical, Medicare supplement, and catastrophic illness.

It has received an A-plus rating from A.M. Best Insurance Report and an AAA rating from Standard and Poor's for its financial stability and ability to pay claims.

Commonwealth's first president, Colonel Joshua D. Powers, is described in a company history as a man of "sterling integrity, fine business judgment, and high character" who founded several businesses before coming to Louisville in 1902 from western Kentucky. Joining Powers in directing the firm through its early years was Darwin W. Johnson, who served as secretary treasurer and later as president. Johnson, whose early experience had been in the tobacco trade, is characterized in the same history as "a true Kentuckian steeped in the traditions of the Old South of tobacco, race horses, and mint juleps."

Success came quickly. By the end of 1909 the firm had $9.6 million of insurance in force from its sales of weekly premium and ordinary life insurance. Premium payments were steady in those days but weren't always made in cash, sometimes taking the form of chickens, eggs, or vegetables. Even so, the company prospered, and in 1912 purchased a plot of land for $48,000 that became the site of Commonwealth's home office for the next 43 years.

The World War I years and the influenza epidemic of 1918 created

Pegasus Pride, an inflated version of the mythical horse, leads the Kentucky Derby Festival's annual Pegasus Parade, sponsored by Commonwealth Insurance.

BUSINESS

Derby Week fever runs high just before the running of the Kentucky Derby as the Pegasus Parade takes over the downtown area. The parade route runs past the Commonwealth Building, whose parking garage usually is packed with onlookers.

some problems for the firm, but it still increased its in-force insurance to $29 million by the end of 1918. Despite the recession of 1921, the company fared well through the postwar years, particularly through the late 1920s—a time that saw a $200,000 remodeling of the headquarters building, higher salaries for officers, and fewer working hours and better pay for clerical employees.

The early years of the Great Depression brought major losses through 1932; however, the organization made a remarkable comeback over the next three years, building its in-force business to $130.5 million by 1935. A leadership struggle followed the death of Johnson in early 1936, but the choice of Homer Ward Batson as a compromise candidate settled disagreements.

Aware of difficult times, Batson reduced all officers' salaries, beginning with his own—from $22,000 to $15,000. Other economies included turning off unnecessary lights and requiring clerks to use pencils until they were uncomfortably short. Batson also consolidated field offices and eliminated problem debits. These efforts during his five-year tenure put the firm on solid ground for the next president, Morton Boyd, architect of the company's greatest growth.

That growth began after the end of World War II. In a stockholders' report in 1945 Boyd said: "The end of the war finds this company in the full vigor of its development and in the strongest financial condition of its history." By the end of 1946 Commonwealth Insurance had $308.8 million insurance in force on 636,631 policies. The impact of that growth can be seen in these facts: It took the firm 22 years to reach its first $100 million in force, and 16 years to reach its second $100 million. It took less than four years to reach the third.

Even more impressive is that it took the company only five more years to increase its in-force business another $200 million to become, in 1951, a half-billion-dollar company doing business from the Great Lakes to the Gulf Coast. The success also meant the firm needed more space, which came in the form of the $8-million Commonwealth Building at Fourth and Broadway in 1955.

Capital Holding Corporation was created in 1969 in order for the company to expand through acquisitions. The newly acquired companies would retain their names and identities.

Like Capital Holding, Commonwealth Insurance is a prominent supporter of its community. Perhaps its most visible effort is its sponsorship of the annual Pegasus Parade, the premier event of the week-long Kentucky Derby Festival. In addition, Commonwealth Insurance joins Capital Holding in contributing to such organizations as the Hindman Settlement School, an old and well-known school in eastern Kentucky; the Kentucky Vietnam Veterans Association; the Old Kentucky Home Council of the Boy Scouts of America; and Simmons Bible College in Louisville.

Some exciting architectural designs will be incorporated into Commonwealth Insurance's new downtown complex. The conceptual design calls for a low-rise structure with a large central atrium. Escalators will be used to promote the feeling of open space.

GREAT FINANCIAL FEDERAL

The optimism of an ambitious young man along with the partners in a legal firm, coupled with an intrinsic belief in advertising and a carefully directed appeal to the small- and medium-wage earner, represent the cornerstones upon which Great Financial Federal has built one of the most successful savings and loan associations, not only in Kentucky but throughout the United States.

The ambitious young 20-year-old man, a native of Shelby County, Kentucky, was Gustav Flexner, and the attorneys were L.A. Hickman and L. Frank Withers, who together founded the Greater Louisville Savings and Building Association on October 2, 1915. Flexner's previous employment had been as a stock or packaging employee in a Louisville department store.

From the beginning emphasis was placed in attracting small- and medium-wage earners to save systematically. Many accounts were opened whereby savers deposited as little as 10 cents a week to their accounts. However, a number of responsible local citizens did invest substantial amounts, and several of these larger account holders were placed on the initial board of directors.

Although business in general was not considered good in 1915, Flexner and his associates had the vision of the growth of Louisville and that their institution could benefit the community by financing home purchases for their members originally, and later the general public.

The initial 10-foot by 10-foot office on the sixth floor of what was then named The Louisville Trust Building, located at the southwest corner of Fifth and Market streets, served as headquarters until 1919, when resources had grown to one million dollars and the office was moved to the north side of the 400 block of West Market Street.

Although Greater Louisville Savings and Building Association was not the oldest savings and loan in Louisville, its steady growth over the years allowed it to surpass other local institutions in assets. During the late 1920s and early 1930s all financial institutions were affected by the Depression; however, the Greater Louisville continued to operate and retain the confidence of its savers and investors. In 1933 the Home Owners Loan Act was passed. In March 1934 the Greater Louisville became federalized, obtaining insurance of accounts later that year through the Federal Savings and Loan Insurance Corporation. With the addition of the insurance of accounts feature, the association continued to grow along with its expansion of advertising through newspapers, radio, and, in the late 1940s, television.

This is the corporate jet that has been used mostly by Lincoln Service Corporation, a wholly owned subsidiary of Great Financial Federal based in Owensboro, Kentucky.

One of the organization's innovations by the savings and loan was the Greater Louisville Savings Post, which was dedicated to the teaching of thrift among the children of the community. This proved to be very successful and was in operation at the same time as "T-Bar-V," a popular children's television program sponsored by the association. During the years of the Savings Post, the main office was open on Saturdays. Local musical celebrities were engaged on this weekend day for the purpose of entertaining the young savers while they were visiting the office.

Although it was considered somewhat unethical for a financial institution to solicit funds, Flexner believed that advertising was important to the success and growth of a competitive business. His judgment as to the value of advertising proved correct, and at the time of his death in 1960, Greater Louisville had grown to be the largest savings and loan in the State of Kentucky and one of the largest in the United States.

Having operated from one downtown location, the management had the foresight to apply to the Federal Home Loan Bank for permission to open a branch office in Shively in 1953 and, upon approval, was the

The home office of Great Financial Federal sits in the 400 block of West Market Street downtown and covers 40,000 square feet of work space on two levels and parking capability for 200 automobiles. The building is highlighted by four corner towers faced in Dakota mahogany granite.

first savings and loan to establish a branch. The selection of this site proved wise inasmuch as this branch office has the most deposits of any office in the association's branch network.

The company remained in its five-story building at 417 West Market Street for more than 30 years, at which time a new home office was constructed on the same site plus an adjoining tract, which extended to the corner of Fourth and Market. During the construction in the early 1970s the headquarters was temporarily located in the 400 block of South Fourth Street. In November 1974 the home office was completed and occupied. In addition to approximately 40,000 square feet of office space located on two levels, the home office also has a three-tiered parking facility for more than 200 automobiles.

The decade of the 1980s brought about deregulation, mergers, and additional services to customers. It also brought about a change in the corporate name to Great Financial Federal. In recent years the association has expanded outside of the Louisville metropolitan area with offices in Shelbyville, Danville, Liberty, Springfield, and Henderson, and two offices each in Owensboro and Lexington. Collectively the firm has an ever-expanding customer base of more than 100,000. Management will continue to be involved in merger acquisition and branching opportunities in order to expand customer service territory throughout Kentucky.

In addition to the normal functions of a savings and loan association, Great Financial Federal has two wholly owned subsidiary service corporations. Alpha Advertising is the advertising agency arm of the association. Lincoln Service Corporation is a mortgage banking operation and ranks among the nation's top 40 in size. These companies operate in more than 40 states nationwide, from Annandale, Virginia, to San Diego, California, while servicing several billion dollars in mortgage loans for investors.

The original building on the present headquarters site was located at 417 West Market Street and is the cornerstone of two extensive remodelings that have resulted in the present facility.

While this phenomenal growth and expansion of activities started in 1915 with a $26,000 deposit base, the association's assets have now reached in excess of one billion dollars with reserves and surplus totaling in excess of $80 million, while continuing to remain a mutual savings and loan association instead of having converted to a publicly held stock company.

In addition to being a safe depository for funds such as passbook savings, certificates of deposit, individual retirement accounts, and checking and money market accounts, customer services also include construction and permanent financing of residential and commercial investment real estate and home improvement loans.

It generally takes many deposit accounts to provide one mortgage loan to a home purchaser. Over the years the savings programs offered to customers, encouraging them to systematically save, have made funds available for home ownership for thousands of families in the communities Great Financial Federal serves. For more than 70 years the association's mission has been to promote thrift and home ownership, and it will continue to be so in the years ahead.

The intermediate step in the evolution of Great Financial Federal's presence in downtown Louisville was the refacing and refurbishing of the original building.

IN CELEBRATION OF LOUISVILLE

HEALTH DATA NETWORK

Computer technology has a way of changing like chain lightning.

Although its growth is evolutionary, the speed of that evolution tends to leave all but the experts' heads spinning. Geologic time frames are measured in millions of years; in computer time, mind-boggling change often occurs in the blink of an eye.

In the midst of this evolution—and doing things that could not be done as recent as 20 years ago—is Louisville's Health Data Network, an around-the-clock, seven-day-a-week record keeper and information dispenser to several hospitals and approximately 90 physicians locally and elsewhere in Kentucky.

Services to hospitals include patient registration, bed management, nursing order management, laboratory reporting and management, accounting and billing, electronic filing of insurance claims, medical records reporting, and full-service financial systems.

For physicians, HDN offers a practice management system that provides patient account and clinical information via direct access to the hospital data base. Through HDN network links, test results from hospital labs can be printed out in distant physicians' offices as soon as tests are completed.

Since its founding in 1970 as a subsidiary of Baptist Hospitals, Inc., HDN has established itself as a leader in the field of health care information systems, consulting, and management services. The firm's evolution has pretty much followed a course charted by Bill W. Mathis, its president, centering on these criteria: Information must be available whenever and wherever needed; control of (and responsibility for) that information must rest in the hands of health care personnel; and the information management system must reflect what happens at the time it happens.

In the beginning, according to Mathis, the idea was to develop this system for the Baptist hospitals and

The custom-designed headquarters of Health Data Network, one of the premier computer facilities in the Southeast. Hospital and physician clients are linked to the Louisville-based company via minicomputers and more than 1,000 miles of private data lines.

share the system with others, which it has accomplished. It serves hospitals and physicians in Louisville, Lexington, Corbin, Paducah, Henderson, and Morganfield with this stated mission: to assist the network's hospital personnel and physicians in managing resources to provide better patient care. HDN employs 75 people, including electronics engineers, systems analysts, programmers, computer operators, and administrative support personnel.

Mathis, who has spent most of his professional life in computer technology with a generous dose of health care experience, was involved from the outset, beginning in 1969 by conducting a feasibility study and making recommendations to the

Computer operators Donna Staser and Derrick Booker monitor the huge, multiunit mainframe computer from the central console. Behind them is the control center for the communications network serving HDN clients.

BUSINESS

hospital corporation's board in August 1970. The first computer was delivered on December 26, 1970. "We started in January 1971 . . . with the first piece of production, which was the payroll for three hospitals all at once," Mathis says. Acknowledging that his plan was revolutionary, he explains with a chuckle that it was known elsewhere in the industry as "Mathis' folly."

Just how revolutionary was it? "The problem we had in those days," Mathis says, "was that everybody was using yesterday's systems concepts, and nobody was looking at where a hospital would need to be five to eight years down the road. It's fairly commonly accepted today, but when we put on-line terminals in the admitting offices in 1971 and 1972 in Louisville as well as in Lexington and Paducah, it was nothing short of chaos and revolution."

The network hospitals are linked through minicomputers and more than 1,000 miles of data lines to the central computers at HDN. A physician's office can be tied directly to the central system, or connected to distributed minicomputers.

On the business side, HDN can provide an electronic link to an automated bank clearinghouse for direct payroll deposit, and insurance claims processing can be accomplished through similar links with insurers. The business services department provides financial management support to its hospitals and full-service accounting to its physician clients, including internal accounting, tax preparation, and financial planning. In addition, the department provides the microfilming of medical records for hospitals, physicians, and health care providers.

One of the firm's largest departments is the systems services department, whose members keep more than 2,000 dynamic computer programs running. The department's team includes consultants, design analysts, software and data base specialists, and communication systems specialists.

As a direct result of what HDN is doing, Mathis believes, the time is coming when there will be regional medical data bases. If a person

HDN customer services representative Kimentha Autumn, R.N. (standing), helps a nursing unit receptionist with an information request at a nursing station in one of HDN's client hospitals.

moves, for example, to California, that person could take a computer diskette containing an HDN medical profile and deliver it to the regional data base in California—and any health care center in the region could have access to the data. "We built this (the HDN system) with that in mind," explains Mathis, who expects Louisville to be a regional data bank someday.

Could HDN, in the year 2000, handle 50 hospitals, 500 doctors? At that point, Mathis expects a more integrated approach to health care, making the regional medical data bank a necessity. "I think at that time the measure of Health Data Network will not be how many hospitals and how many physicians, but how much population it can keep the records on . . . and with the building we have built and the room that we have in the computer room . . . I think we will be able to handle a large portion of the mid-America region."

"I would say a practical number would be in the five-million range," he added.

That potential, those early critics must admit, is anything but folly.

HDN president Bill Mathis (left, foreground) explains the workings of the network to a delegation from Montpellier, France, during their tour of Health Data Network. The group visited Louisville as part of the Sister Cities exchange program.

IN CELEBRATION OF LOUISVILLE

COWGER & MILLER MORTGAGE COMPANY

Nelson Miller's office is as much a salute to the Thoroughbred as to his company's lofty perch in the mortgage-banking business. He is among photographs, paintings, castings, and practically all manner of decor—all relating to the horse.

His favorite—a bronze casting of a racehorse and jockey in full flight to the finish—symbolizes the way Miller feels about his business, now in its 17th year. It exemplifies the hallmarks of a winner—strength, speed, and staying power, a combination that gives the horse and, he believes, Cowger & Miller Mortgage Company the ability to go the distance.

This is not idle fascination for the horse. Miller, who breeds and races thoroughbreds, uses it as a means of reflecting the sense of purpose, of competitiveness, of the commitment to a winning tradition that marks the performance not only of the equine breed but also of his breed of mortgage banking.

Miller, chairman of the board and chief executive officer, founded the organization with his good friend, William O. Cowger, a former mayor of Louisville and a U.S. representative, in 1971. Cowger died that same year, just as the venture was getting into stride, but the depth of that friendship has led Miller to keep Cowger's name on the firm. He says, with feeling, "I would never change the name of the company. In fact, I think it motivated me more to try to make Cowger & Miller a success just because of my thoughts for Bill."

That success has put the firm at the billion-dollar-servicing plateau and among the nation's leaders in mortgage lending. Miller, in another horse-racing analogy, likes to think that just as the classic twin spires of Churchill Downs point to the sky, his company is heading that way, too.

In that respect Cowger & Miller has chalked up dramatic gains over the past few years, beginning, particularly, in 1983 and 1984. During that period the firm began branching into other areas, until it now is represented in at least 17 other states and approximately 40 cities.

Miller, who says less than 50 percent of the organization's business is done in Louisville, is particularly proud of a strong presence in northern Florida, Maryland, northern Virginia, and Washington, D.C. Still he is in no way ready to settle for his present track record, saying in a company publication, "We recognize a continually changing business environment and welcome the challenges of the future with a spirit of optimism, enthusiasm, and determination."

Those challenges include stepping into the Atlanta market, which, Miller notes, has about 175 mortgage

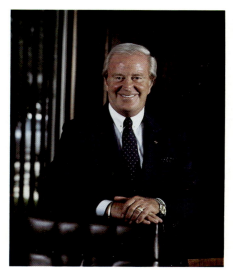

Nelson Miller, chairman of the board and chief executive officer.

Nelson Miller's fascination with the Thoroughbred racing horse is exemplified in this bronze casting, which symbolized "strength, speed, and staying power... the ability to go the distance."

Nelson Miller (standing) with Edward W. Humphries, president (left), and Wesley E. Schissler, executive vice-president.

BUSINESS

Senior vice-president and servicing manager Janet Broady reviews computerized data.

self in lending for such commercial ventures as hotels, apartments, and office buildings, the latter being especially attractive in Louisville today.

Miller's business philosophy can be summed up in these words: "I just try all the time to be honest, forthright, and try not to gouge." Amplifying that, he says, "If we make a deal with an investor and the market turns, we have on many occasions gone back and said—especially if it's an investor we have done business with before— 'We want to change this deal; the market has turned and we don't want it to be bad for you.' And we've had investors do the same thing for us."

The entrepreneur credits an excellent relationship with the real estate industry, permanent investors, and the commercial banking industry for much of his firm's success. Also fitting into that mix is the stability among the employees, from the seven who started with the two friends in 1971 to the approximately 175 now. Four of the originals are still with the company, and there are many 10-year veterans on the staff, indicating the staying power of a winner.

However, the race continues, and no one knows better than Miller what it takes to win. Front running often can be disastrous, both in a horse race and in business, but if the pace is to one's liking and the staying power is there, the stretch run can be joyous. Miller is banking on his company's speed, strength, and ability to go the distance—right to the winner's circle.

bankers. That does not deter him, however, as Cowger & Miller has had some experience with that in the Tampa and Orlando markets, where there were about 150 mortgage bankers in each city that Cowger & Miller entered. "If you're good at what you do," he says, "a firm can get established. The more competition there is, you usually find yourself doing better."

Miller believes, also, that Columbus, Ohio, and Nashville—both listed by *Fortune* magazine as cities on the upswing—are in his firm's future. In Ohio, Cowger & Miller already is doing well with an office in Cincinnati.

In a look a little farther down the track, Miller, pointing out that the company has a young president and an equally young staff, sees the potential for doing business in all 50 states. Make that 49. "California is probably a little too fast for us," he says with a smile.

Although home mortgages are what keeps Cowger & Miller on the right track, the firm also involves it-

Cowger & Miller—a breed ahead in mortgage banking.

IN CELEBRATION OF LOUISVILLE

WILLIAM M. MERCER MEIDINGER HANSEN, INCORPORATED

The employee benefit consulting business is one of the nation's fastest-growing and most dynamic industries. In the past 50 years the world has changed enormously—and few areas have been so affected as the relationship between employers and their employees. Changing demographics, economics, individual attitudes, and family patterns have made it critical for organizations to manage their human resources wisely.

During the last half-century businesses and other organizations have looked to independent outside advisers to help with the increasingly complicated field of benefits, compensation, and other aspects of the employment relationship. At the forefront is William M. Mercer Meidinger Hansen, Incorporated, the largest consulting firm in the fields of employee benefits, compensation, asset planning, and human resource management in the United States.

Until 1984 the company was three firms, not one, and each had a respected name and long history in the field of employee benefit consulting. Bill Mercer founded William M. Mercer Limited in 1946 in Vancouver; Bernard Meidinger founded Meidinger, Inc., in 1936 in Louisville; and Arthur Hansen founded A.S. Hansen, Inc., in 1930 in Chicago.

In 1984, however, the Mercer and Meidinger organizations merged, and three years later the Hansen firm joined the Mercer organization. Today the firm has more than 3,000 employees in 48 offices in the United States.

More than 280 employees, or one-seventh of Mercer Meidinger Hansen's employee base, is in Louisville. The Louisville operations include the local consulting office, corporate computer center, Social Security resource, and publications units in Meidinger Tower, one of the twin office buildings that anchor the Louisville Galleria.

The Mercer companies around

William M. Mercer Meidinger Hansen, Incorporated, is the major tenant in Meidinger Tower, a cornerstone of the Louisville Galleria office/retail complex.

the globe make up the world's largest consulting firm in the field, with more than 5,000 employees and offices in 96 cities. The firm serves more than 16,000 clients in every sector of business, industry, government, and nonprofit operations.

Mercer is part of Marsh & McLennan Companies, Inc. The Marsh & McLennan family includes specialized financial consulting and service firms in a number of related fields. One of its subsidiaries, Marsh & McLennan, Inc., is the world's leading insurance broker.

"Underlying all our growth is the belief that our clients want service as close to home as possible—service that is of exceptional quality," explains William B. Alexander, Jr.,

BUSINESS

The firm is one of the nation's largest employee benefit and compensation consulting firms, and a leader in technology in its field.

head of Mercer Meidinger Hansen's Louisville office, "and we try to provide a full range of consulting services within each office. Of course, we also have the resources that only a large firm can marshal—in people and the diversity of their skills and experience, in geographic reach, in technology and information, that can be called upon as needed."

Mercer Meidinger Hansen's services can be grouped in five areas.

Employee benefits design and administrative services can help attract, motivate, and retain employees. These services can involve group benefit programs, flexible benefits, pension and profit-sharing plans, and benefit administration and record keeping.

Health care cost management helps employers ensure that employees receive quality health care at a reasonable cost. This can involve evaluating and negotiating alternative delivery systems, utilization management and peer review consulting, health service organization structure and management, claim audit and management services, and wellness and preventive programs.

Compensation systems, organizational design, and job planning helps employers reward employees for performance, set up effective work patterns, and stay competitive in the marketplace. Consulting in this area involves wage and salary administration, executive compensation and incentives, employment practices, compensation surveys and research, and performance appraisal systems.

Communication and human resource management can help employees identify with management objectives. This involves employee research and surveys, compensation and benefit communication, personalized communication, and human resource planning and development. Other key activities in this area include assisting employers with human resource strategic planning, new plant start-ups, organizational development, and the training and development of human resource systems to achieve employee productivity.

Funding and financing of compensation and benefit programs help employers control costs and offer the widest range of options to employers. This involves actuarial services, analysis and forecasting of benefit costs, evaluation of funding and asset alternatives, investment manager and trustee selection and evaluation, and monitoring and evaluation of investment performance.

Recent employer interest locally has been in flexible compensation, a program that offers employees choices rather than a set package of benefits and compensation. Alexander expects the Louisville office to be at the forefront of this trend since Mercer Meidinger Hansen is a national leader in this important benefit development. Louisville's interest in flexible benefits mirrors that nationally, as employers seek to maintain and improve employee morale, satisfaction, and productivity, while maintaining or reducing benefit costs.

"Just as the area's employee population continues to grow through change and innovation in the city and county's economic structure, we, too, expect to continue our growth," Alexander says. "Mercer Meidinger Hansen has consistently allocated resources for research and development of new systems and tools—we're leaders in technology in our field—and we're always looking for new areas to extend our range of consulting services. These are plans made for the long term—we continue to build an ever more solid foundation in Louisville for the successful years we see that lay ahead for both the city and our local consulting office."

Mercer Meidinger Hansen professionals consult with clients about benefits, compensation, and other aspects of the employer-employee relationship.

271

Photo by Michael Brohm/Nawrocki Stock Photo

Photo by Mark E. Gibson

Photo by Ted Wathen/Quadrant

Photo by Nawrocki Stock Photo/Michael Brohm

Wyatt, Tarrant & Combs
278-279

Eskew & Gresham,
PSC 280-281

Chapter XII
Professions

Greater Louisville's professional community brings a wealth of service, ability, and insight to the area.

Peat Marwick Main & Co.
282-283

Goldberg & Simpson
284-285

Stites & Harbison 286-287

Barnett & Alagia 288-289

Brown, Todd &
Heyburn 290

WYATT, TARRANT & COMBS

Tradition has always meant a great deal to the social, political, and economic fabric of Louisville, and nowhere is that more in evidence than in the law firm of Wyatt, Tarrant & Combs, located high in Citizens Plaza in downtown Louisville.

But no ivory tower that. It's a place that bustles with the legal toil of nearly 90 of the firm's approximately 140 attorneys operating in four locations—Louisville, Lexington, and Frankfort in Kentucky, and just across the Ohio River in New Albany, Indiana. The practice of the firm, Louisville's largest, covers every corner of the law save immigration and naturalization and patents, neither of which is a factor in the Mid-America river city.

Helping to set the pace, or at least to serve as a beacon for their colleagues, are the three name partners, still in the firm's offices and working regularly. Bert T. Combs does most of his work in the Lexington office; John E. Tarrant, 88, shows up every day in the Citizens Plaza stronghold; and Wilson W. Wyatt, Sr., 80, is just as regular. They boast twice as many years as the early forties of the average colleague.

A Wyatt, Tarrant & Combs brochure has this to say: "The practice of law requires expert advice, prompt service, vigorous advocacy, thoughtful counseling, and attention to detail." These have been bywords throughout its long history, which has included merging with other law organizations.

The major force of Wyatt, Tarrant & Combs grew out of the merger of the practices of the Louisville firms of Tarrant, Combs & Bullitt and Wyatt, Grafton & Sloss in 1980. Orbison, O'Connor, MacGregor & Mattox of New Albany joined in 1984 and Brown, Sledd & McCann of Lexington in 1985.

Tarrant, Combs & Bullitt had roots to 1812 with the formation of the Bullitt law firm that, in the intervening 168 years, also practiced under the name of Bruce & Bullitt and later as Bullitt, Dawson & Tarrant.

The presiding partners in Tarrant, Combs & Bullitt were John E. Tarrant and Bert T. Combs, a former governor of Kentucky, U.S. circuit judge, and judge of the court of appeals, then Kentucky's highest court.

Wyatt, Grafton & Sloss was founded in 1947 as Wyatt & Grafton. The presiding partners were Wilson W. Wyatt, a former mayor of Louisville, eventual lieutenant governor of Kentucky, and an adviser to presidents Harry S. Truman and John F. Kennedy, and Arthur W. Grafton, Sr., a former state senator.

The public offices held by Combs and Wyatt are typical of the tradition of involvement for the barristers of this historic firm. Going back to the seed of the organization, the Bullitt family traces its roots to pre-Revolutionary War days. William Marshall Bullitt was solicitor general of the United States under President Howard Taft. In the words of Gordon B. Davidson, the current managing partner of Wyatt, Tarrant & Combs, "Historically, this firm has always had as its partners people prominent and active in government and who have grown up with Louisville . . . Whatever Louisville was doing, we were doing."

Another partner, A. Wallace Grafton, Jr., expands on that theme by pointing out that Wyatt, Tarrant & Combs represents more public bodies than any other law firm in the area, handling bond financing for Jefferson County, representing the county's school system, the City of Louisville and the State of Kentucky, and governors John Y. Brown and Martha Layne Collins in landmark cases dealing with their authority during their respective terms of office.

Grafton, who finds himself in New York quite often in his specialty of municipal bonds, proudly says that his firm can do things just as well as the big New York firms: "The practice of law in Louisville is highly sophisticated and professional. It's a good bar," he says confidently.

Part of the client list for Wyatt, Tarrant & Combs reads like a who's who of Louisville and Kentucky: Brown & Williamson Tobacco Corp. and its parent, BATUS, Inc.; Churchill Downs Inc.; Citizens Fidelity Bank & Trust Co.; Capitol Holding and Commonwealth Life Insurance Companies; *The Courier-Journal*; E.I. du Pont de Nemours and Co., Inc.; Heaven Hill Distilleries; South Central Bell; Kentucky Hospital Association; Louisville's Jewish Hospital; Norton Hospital; Kosair Children's Hospital; Joseph E. Seagram & Sons, Inc.; WHAS and WHAS-TV; and the Louisville operations of Ford Motor Company and General Electric.

Although Kentucky law doesn't certify specialties of legal practice, Wyatt, Tarrant & Combs considers certain fields as areas of special expertise: banking, communications, construction, disaster litigation, energy, mineral and environmental law, health care, public finance and tax-exempt bonds, and governmental agencies.

However, a young lawyer's early days with the firm are spent getting a taste of general practice, with the prospect of specializing waiting in the legal wings. Davidson emphasizes that Wyatt, Tarrant & Combs is one of the few law firms left in the country that seldom hires for specialties. "Very few young lawyers know what they really want," he says. "They usually think they like subjects that their favorite professor taught." From a general pool at Wyatt, Tarrant & Combs young associates draw general assignments. A committee sees to it that they get a little of everything. Then they can make an informed choice. The choice of a field of practice usually comes in about a year, and in another two to three years the young lawyer usually is qualified to practice in the chosen area.

The backgrounds of the firm's lawyers can be painted with a broad brush—from rich and poor beginnings, black and white, men

PROFESSIONS

and women, Christians and Jews, Democrats and Republicans, a true cross-section of Americana. Wyatt, Tarrant & Combs is looking for academic excellence in its prospective newcomers from the college ranks, but it also considers strongly personality and diverse backgrounds that can mean new views and perhaps fresh approaches to otherwise standard fare.

And, as is the tradition with the firm, prospects are judged on their seeming interest in getting involved in the community—such things as support for the arts, youth programs, education, volunteer work, any facet that will have a positive effect on the community. "We want our people to be an asset to the community," Davidson says.

The community has prospered socially, economically, and educationally through various leadership roles taken by members of the Wyatt, Tarrant & Combs firm. Aside from the political, judicial, and professional leadership given by its name partners, other partners have made major contributions in all areas of community commitment, from leading the Louisville Chamber of Commerce and the United Way to heading up the boards of trustees at the University of Louisville and Bellarmine College to practically every facet of the arts community.

The firm's versatility was further illustrated when, in the early 1960s, it represented the Louisville Sponsoring Group in signing then-Olympic gold medal winner Cassius Clay to a professional boxing contract. The group was composed of leading Louisville business executives dedicated to helping secure the future of the young Louisville boxer. For six years the Louisville Sponsoring Group, with Davidson as counsel, guided the career of Muhammad Ali to the world heavyweight championship.

As Kentucky's largest law firm, Wyatt, Tarrant & Combs continues to be intimately involved in the growth of Louisville and its region.

The name partners in Louisville's historic Wyatt, Tarrant & Combs law firm are (from left) Wilson W. Wyatt, Sr., John E. Tarrant, and Bert T. Combs.

IN CELEBRATION OF LOUISVILLE

ESKEW & GRESHAM, PSC

Although based on a heritage that reaches back 66 years, the public accounting firm of Eskew & Gresham, PSC, is working on a ledger that has changed dramatically in the decade of the 1980s.

Not only have techniques been speeded up through the explosion of technology but some of the strategies, and, most of all, the people and the way they do things have changed. Still, serving the client's best interests—a hallmark of Eskew & Gresham since its beginning and one that has given the firm an impeccable reputation—remains standard.

These changes led Gary L. Stewart, president, to say, "We are one of the oldest accounting firms in the Commonwealth of Kentucky, and yet we are a very young firm, making almost a complete change in ownership in the late 1970s as most of the older partners decided to retire and turn things over to younger partners."

The transfer of leadership went smoothly, and Eskew & Gresham made a new entry in its historic ledger—one that has met successfully the challenges of the 1980s. The way the older partners helped in the transition was a major asset, Stewart says admiringly of his mentors.

"It could have been a difficult time," he says, noting that often when such transitions are made, accounting firms begin losing business or find themselves subjects of mergers. "Clients who have dealt with the same accountants for many years find themselves feeling unsure of things when their old associates begin to turn things over to young people who they (the clients) might feel aren't dry behind the ears," Stewart says. "But we were very fortunate—because at the same time, many of these businesses were moving into a new generation of leadership. The new leadership on both sides got along fine."

Since the late 1970s the number of employees at Eskew & Gresham has more than doubled. During that same period its gross fees nearly tripled. The firm has offices in Louisville, which serves as headquarters for the operation, and in Lexington, in the Bluegrass section of Kentucky.

Eskew & Gresham is the successor to a public accounting practice begun in 1922 by Samuel W. Eskew, who was joined in the early 1930s by Austin H. Gresham, a young man who came out of Salmon, Idaho, to earn a degree at the University of Kentucky in 1931. Both men worked long and diligently on the state and national levels to help set the standards of public accounting that remain today.

In the firm's early years it became involved with the humble beginnings of many Louisville businesses, some merely storefront operations, that now stand as major, multi-million-dollar successes—and continuing clients. Eskew & Gresham has grown right along with them, and the long association has allowed the accountants to gain the experience and knowledge that allows them to meet client needs in today's changing business environment.

In a time when mergers and franchised operations are common in

Computer graphics are an important tool in the accounting business.

Gary Stewart, president, leads a workshop on audit procedures with an audience of bank directors at the Kentucky Bankers' Association Bank Directors' Conference.

PROFESSIONS

business, Eskew & Gresham, a closely held, almost family-type organization, has retained most of its original character. The ownership opportunities in the firm have gone to only a select number of people over the years. Currently there are four shareholders in Louisville and two in Lexington.

Everybody in the firm is a "roll-up-the-sleeves, let's-get-the-job-done person," says Stewart. Those on the shareholder level generally have 20 years' or more experience, and supervisors and managers offer six to 10 years' experience. "We want to have the best, most experienced people on the job," Stewart advises. "This gives our younger people the opportunity to watch them in action and to gain the expertise they'll need as they go along."

Because of the complexities of the times, developing specialties is all-important—a switch from the generalists of Eskew & Gresham's first 50 years. Widespread regulation of industries and the uniqueness of so many industry problems have created the need for specialists. Explains Stewart: "Clients now are asking, 'Can you speak my language?' or 'What do you know about my business?' Because of this, our clients help us shape our specialties."

However, it is not a hit-or-miss situation. Five years ago the leaders at Eskew & Gresham sat down and took stock of their practice. What they came up with was a strategy for growth that centered on being strong in the industries that were the core

The equine industry is one of the core groups that have contributed to the success of Eskew & Gresham, PSC, along with construction, financial institutions, and small businesses. Photo by Dell Hancock

of their success at the time: financial institutions, the equine industry, construction, and small businesses.

Along with this, they decided, it would make dollars and good sense to be on the creative, innovative side of the ledger rather than merely be-

The Eskew & Gresham staff at work on financial projections.

ing on the reaction side—to become involved with clients in their professional groups and to some degree in their social groups, so the client could consider Eskew & Gresham a part of the business team.

Technology has helped expand business as well, mostly through reducing the time it takes to compile statistics—thus allowing more time to pursue other facets of the client's business, such as planning, acquisitions, financing, and budgeting. "It used to be that projections would take days to accomplish, and then the client might say, 'What if?' and the whole thing would have to be changed and more time would be needed," says Stewart. "With computerization the changes can be made in a matter of minutes. It has made analysis and decision making far more effective, and you no longer have downtime while moving numbers around."

The bottom line for Eskew & Gresham, PSC, is to keep those numbers moving in the right direction—upward and onward.

PEAT MARWICK MAIN & CO.

"Peat Marwick Main is determined to be the leading professional accounting and consulting firm in the world by providing our clients with superior service and our people with opportunities for personal growth and economic reward."

Lofty goals such as these generally inspire equally lofty accomplishments.

Pursuit of its goal already has put the accounting and consulting firm at the top of the ledger as the largest in the United States, with approximately 1,850 partners, a total staff of 18,325 in 137 offices, and fiscal 1986 revenues of $1.35 billion.

In addition to being the leading firm serving mid-size and growth organizations, Peat Marwick is auditor to more of the *Fortune* 1,000 companies than any other firm. Nationally, it maintains a preeminent position in several industry sectors, including banking, thrifts, insurance, health care, real estate and construction, state and local government, and high technology.

Throughout company literature the theme of "excellence" prevails—and so it is in Louisville, where Peat Marwick Main & Co., with a professional staff of 84 and an administrative staff of seven, services clients in Kentucky and in southern Indiana, across the Ohio River from Louisville. Banking makes up a large portion of the firm's practice, though no portion is more than 15 percent of the corporate pie.

Clients include Liberty National Bank and Trust Company; Dairy-

Louisville's Peat Marwick Main & Co. serves clients in Kentucky and southern Indiana with a staff of dedicated professionals.

men's Inc., one of the largest agricultural cooperatives in the country; Falls City Industries; General Electric, locally; and several firms in the transportation, coal, and thoroughbred breeding and racing fields. The fastest-growing segment of the business has been generated by the many Japanese corporations that have moved into the region in recent years. Peat Marwick has 12 Japanese clients.

The company's presence in Louisville goes back to 1921, when a Marwick Mitchell venture located in the community. That firm left later, but returned in 1954 and has prospered.

What can a client expect from Peat Marwick? Says Douglas Sumner, managing partner in the Louisville operation: "Our clients can expect the highest-quality individuals, dedicated professionals to

assist and aid them in business development." That doesn't mean just accounting and auditing. "Our firm does business planning, tax planning, structuring of tax compliance, audits, and helps in installing computer systems," Sumner explains. Each client is assigned both a manager and at least two firm partners.

The company's policy requires a change in managers every seven years and in partners every five years for publicly held clients. Changes are less frequent for private, closely held companies.

In recruiting young professionals, Sumner says, Peat Marwick looks first at academic accomplishments, and then at campus activities, motivation, and an obvious interest on the part of the person to come into the accounting business. "A world of opportunity awaits anyone coming into our firm," Sumner states. "The variety of experiences a young professional gets here can't be touched anywhere else in the business community. Young professionals coming to work for us may see the workings of 20 to 30 companies in their first year."

Training, on which Peat Marwick spends $50 million per year nationally for its people, is the first thing that awaits a newcomer. In three weeks, after learning about the organization's goals, and about client orientation and relationships, the newcomer is in the field working with managers and partners. Something they find out quickly is that, while most classroom study is applicable, things are not always black or white.

Louisville's Peat Marwick Main & Co. recruits almost entirely in Kentucky and Indiana, mining the business schools at the universities of Louisville, Kentucky, and Indiana; Bellarmine College in Louisville; Indiana University Southeast (in nearby New Albany); Western Kentucky University; and Eastern Kentucky University. However, that doesn't preclude people from other areas being on the Louisville staff, or

A young professional gains a variety of experiences that "can't be touched anywhere else in the business community."

from local people going to other areas. The mix in Louisville, for instance, also includes graduates from Wake Forest, Notre Dame, and the universities of Alabama and North Carolina.

Being a good corporate citizen rates high on the Peat Marwick spreadsheet, and in Louisville that means people who are active on the boards of Bellarmine College, PBS Channel 15, hospitals, and the Boy Scouts. Corporate and individual support also are given to Metro United Way, Junior Achievement, the Younger Woman's Club, and Fund for the Arts. According to Sumner, the firm supports with time and funds those organizations in which its people show an interest.

What of the future for Peat Marwick in Louisville? "We see great things here," says Sumner. "We are pleased with our progress; we have grown rapidly and expect to continue. We have a good client mix and a good client base: diverse, solid clients."

Sumner also believes that Louisville is making great strides now toward reaching the potential that so many of its natives and newcomers believe is there. Perhaps, after more than 30 years, some of the Peat Marwick Main & Co. mission has rubbed off.

IN CELEBRATION OF LOUISVILLE

GOLDBERG & SIMPSON

"The law is merely a reflection of the current ethics of our society," attorney Fred M. Goldberg, one of the name partners in Louisville's Goldberg & Simpson law firm, has been quoted as saying.

"The law will expand as human relations expand," he continues. "It has from Sinai to today, and there isn't much reason not to believe that 3,300 years from today that that body of law we understand today will be as miniscule as the Ten Commandments appear to us."

That seems to be part and parcel of what Goldberg considers the organic nature of the law; it's living and changing, ever moving forward, ever responding to society. "The organic nature of the Constitution dictated by [Chief Justice of the Supreme Court] John Marshall is what has led it to be the great instrument that it is today," he says. "If it doesn't respond, you have anarchy. The civil rights movement is a good example; if the law hadn't responded, there would have been war in the streets."

Goldberg believes it is his firm's understanding of the nature of the law and its clients' needs that keep it growing and progressive, dedicated to providing total-service law to a diverse group of clients from the conference room to the Supreme Court of the United States.

Through a merger, Goldberg & Simpson assumed its current configuration in 1974, but Goldberg's practice goes back beyond that date. The firm has evolved from eight lawyers in 1981 to its present 25—with a projection of an addition of three or four each year. Goldberg prefers controlled expansion that centers on quality, and expects the growth to be warranted by client load.

The firm has clients throughout the nation and in parts of Canada, primarily those in the banking, insurance, construction, and health care businesses. In Louisville, the company's operation is broad based, and it makes up the major portion of business done. Even so, says Goldberg, the firm has some lawyers who are on the move nearly full time.

Though Kentucky law doesn't certify specialties of practice, certain members of the firm concentrate on such areas as employee relations, commercial law, construction law, insurance, domestic relations, health care law, communications law, and corporate and tax law. Litigation probably is the largest part of the firm's practice, Goldberg says, particularly in the fields of business, bankruptcy, tax and estate planning, real estate, arson defense, construction, and personnel relations (formerly labor law).

Goldberg believes strongly in the value of the team concept in serving a client, stating that when the firm receives "a piece of work, we build a team. That team exchanges ideas, develops a plan of attack and a strategy, all in consultation with the client . . . there's a lot of input, even from law clerks. Then we synthesize the overall MO [modus operandi], into which we plug strategy and how to execute the strategy."

Preparation then is done by those who are considered most adequate to prepare it and execute it. Hourly

Fred M. Goldberg and Edward L. Schoenbaechler symbolize the relationship the law firm of Goldberg & Simpson has with the health care industry in Louisville.

The team concept is illustrated in this negotiating session by Goldberg & Simpson personnel involved in the field of labor law.

PROFESSIONS

rates for those people often are not the highest in the firm, Goldberg says, so the client gets more for the money. Goldberg swears by the concept, which for him goes back to his early days as a lawyer.

In recruiting young lawyers, Goldberg & Simpson, unlike some other major law firms, has found success without going too far afield—the majority of those in the organization being University of Louisville Law School graduates. When reviewing applicants, the firm considers class standing a clear bellwether of a person's ability, enthusiasm, and capacity for work. In addition, compatibility with the firm and aggressiveness in a gentlemanly manner are considered prime qualities. Of the latter Goldberg cautions young lawyers that they "are an advocate, not justice personified...part of the machine that grinds out justice." On several occasions those serving as law clerks while pursuing a degree have joined the firm upon graduation.

With so many members of the firm being University of Louisville graduates, it's only natural that they

On-site discussions with builders and developers help to nurture expertise and are an integral part in Goldberg & Simpson's approach to construction law.

would build quite a record of achievement for supporting civic affairs. They have been involved with such diverse groups as the Greater Louisville Fund for the Arts, the Louisville Theatrical Association, the American Jewish Committee, Channel 15 public television, the Louisville Free Public Library, Leadership Louisville, Metro United Way, and the Catholic Archdiocese of Louisville.

On the professional level, Goldberg & Simpson attorneys are active in the Kentucky, Louisville, and American bar associations; the Fellows of the American Bar Foundation; the Kentucky Defense Council; and the Women Lawyers Association.

Goldberg & Simpson has developed and maintains its own computerized litigation-support system, putting the firm on line with the technology revolution and giving its attorneys who are working with volumes of legal documents immediate access to a massive cataloging and retrieval system. However, at Goldberg & Simpson technology is merely the bridge to efficient case management. Technology supports the firm's innovation, but doesn't infringe on the all-important attorney-client relationships. Personal, individualized client service is and always has been at the heart of the Goldberg & Simpson practice. No amount of technology will change that.

The vitality and initiative of youth lends to the innovative atmosphere that the firm relies so heavily on.

IN CELEBRATION OF LOUISVILLE

STITES & HARBISON

The favorable mention of any attorney in *The New Yorker* these days is unusual. When Stites & Harbison's Lively Wilson was described as "redoubtable" and "one of the best defense lawyers in the country" in a recent *New Yorker* series on asbestos, however, his partners and their clients were not surprised. Wilson's abilities are legendary. Those abilities also reflect the growing scope and sophistication of this 156-year-old firm's practice and of the growing national reputation it enjoys.

The firm's 100 lawyers practice from offices in Louisville, Lexington, and Frankfort, Kentucky, and Jeffersonville, Indiana, a town across the Ohio River from Louisville. These four locations function as a single operation through the use of high-tech word-processing and data-retrieval systems, telephone conferencing, facsimile transmission, telex equipment, and Lexis and Westlaw computerized legal research systems. The firm's practice encompasses all major areas of the law, including corporate and securities, banking and finance, municipal bonds, construction, admiralty and general litigation, environment, mineral and real estate, health care, tax planning, employment law, employee benefits, estate planning and probate administration, equine law, antitrust, commercial and product defense litigation, and public utility regulation.

Approximately one-half of Stites & Harbison's lawyers are involved in civil and administrative litigation. They have represented the firm's clients in asbestos cases on a national basis; in the defense of PVC cases, another national representation; in cases arising from several multifatality fires in the region; in complex product liability litigation for products ranging from ladders to pollution-control equipment; in employment matters; and in complex corporate and securities cases. The rest of the firm concentrates on business, real estate, banking, and tax law, representing a variety of clients from large, publicly held corporations to small, closely held businesses.

Much of Stites & Harbison's work is done through client teams that cut across legal specialties to provide continuity and ensure that a client's legal matters are handled by attorneys who not only concentrate on the substantive matter at hand but who also understand the particular business of the client. Each team is directed by a supervising partner who provides legal services to the client in his or her area of concentration and also acts as coordinator of all of the client's work.

Lively Wilson is the latest member of Stites & Harbison to attain national prominence, but he is not the first. One of its early partners, James Speed, was Abraham Lincoln's attorney general, and its alumni include a sitting federal district judge, a sitting federal court of appeals judge, a former chief justice of the Kentucky Supreme Court, numerous retired federal and state trial and appellate judges, and several law professors. Its current partners include a former lieutenant governor and attorney general of Kentucky, a former Kentucky Court of Appeals judge, five past presidents of the Kentucky Bar Association, and five fellows of the American College of Trial Lawyers.

Contrary to what might be expected from such an old firm, its current composition is quite young. Most of the partnership is under 50 years of age, including the firm's management committee and its managing partner, David C. Brown. This fact may account in some part for the innovative, efficient service that is a hallmark of the firm's practice.

Stites & Harbison produces two quarterly publications to keep its clients abreast of developments in the law: *Banking & Finance Report* and *Kentucky Litigation Quarterly*.

The firm's historic nineteenth-century Louisville home features this five-story atrium.

A reception area in the Louisville office.

PROFESSIONS

A client team prepares for trial.

Both are provided free of charge. In addition, the firm serves as the Kentucky editor for the *Martindale-Hubbell Law Summary,* of the U.S. Corporation Company's *Kentucky Corporate Law Guide,* and of the Probate Directory's *Kentucky Probate Law Digest.*

The attorneys at Stites & Harbison also have a commitment to civic affairs in keeping with the firm's tradition of involvement in the communities it serves. The firm's long-standing view is that the legal profession involves a personal and professional responsibility to the public, which is best served by attorneys choosing for themselves community activities about which they feel strongly. That attitude has served both the firm and its communities well, and reflects the religious and ethnic diversity of its lawyers as well as the diversity of their interests.

Stites & Harbison was instrumental, for example, in the movement that resulted in the national Presbyterian Church's decision to move to Louisville. Its lawyers have also been involved in community activities as diverse as the Board of the Louisville Symphony Orchestra, the Jewish Community Federation, and the Louisville Rape Relief Center.

It is no secret that the legal profession is currently undergoing changes that have altered many of its traditional ways of doing business. Stites & Harbison is ready for these changes and accepts the challenges they offer with enthusiasm, looking forward to the future with confidence.

Six conference rooms in the Louisville office allow for plenty of work space.

IN CELEBRATION OF LOUISVILLE

BARNETT & ALAGIA

Bernard Barnett and D. Paul Alagia, Jr., founded the Barnett & Alagia law firm of Louisville 14 years ago.

True to the teenage years in life, Barnett & Alagia seems always to be reaching for new experiences and new worlds to conquer. That attitude is reflected in something one of the young lawyers has said: "You know what I like about it here? This is one of the few successful law firms with a sense of adventure. The people here aren't afraid of things, so you're not bound by standardized approaches."

For Barnett & Alagia that sense of adventure has been one of the driving forces behind the firm since its birth in 1974, when the two name partners merged their small firms to tackle the future with about 15 lawyers. Over the following 10 years a regional practice was put together through offices in Washington, D.C.; Atlanta, Georgia; Nashville, Tennessee; Miami and Palm Beach, Florida, as well as the home office in Louisville and offices in New Albany, Indiana, and Frankfort, Kentucky. Despite its broad regional nature that includes more than 100 lawyers and expertise that might be located in one office but can be used throughout the system, the two principal partners still influence significantly the firm's philosophy and its activities.

For example, here are a few thoughts from Barnett:

Success, he says, is

to mean not only financially rewarding but personally gratifying. And the secret is this—a firm has got to move. It has to feel itself moving with the times. It has to have a direction and energy beyond simply getting bigger or richer. There has to be

D. Paul Alagia, Jr., calls the Louisville office his home base.

Donald F. Mintmire is the partner in charge of the Washington operation, the firm's second-largest office.

some genuine appreciation for new ideas . . . Innovation and creativity aren't words that just apply to the making and selling of computers and soap.

What of his legacy?

. . . What I'd hope my legacy would be is an attitude . . . What does a law firm have to offer except the intellect and experience of its lawyers? The trick is to keep people stimulated so that they do the best job possible . . . The law may change, our areas of practice may change, the firm's leadership may change, but I'd hope that a stimulating environment would continue.

Alagia offers these thoughts:

In regard to the firm's regional nature versus huge, national firms, he says those firms

may be more inflexible in changing their directions when the need arises . . . We're able to adjust quickly. If something develops tomorrow, we could call a management committee meeting and change the direction of the firm . . . And let me add another thing: Legal counsel is still a personal relationship. We think clients

D. Paul Alagia, Jr., and Malcolm Y. Marshall, a longtime partner in the firm, meet in the Louisville office's reception area.

PROFESSIONS

A.W. Sandbach serves as the legal administrator for the firm's eight offices.

like to know where they fit into the scheme of things. They like to know that when they come back next week, the same person is going to be there, that their lawyer hasn't moved somewhere else.

We have a mixture of large, medium, and small corporations as well as individuals. That's a mix we like and intend to continue. We represent large, corporate clients, but we want to remain very approachable to smaller concerns and individuals, because they have a way of keeping your legal life varied and changing.

Two of the younger partners in the firm are A. Paul Prosperi (right), and Charles Barnett, son of the late Bernard Barnett, one of the founders.

The firm's practice includes such areas as agriculture, antitrust and trade regulation, banking and financial institutions, bankruptcy, corporate, domestic relations, employee benefits, estate planning, government contracting, health care, immigration, insurance, international trade, labor and employee relations, legislation, litigation, mergers and acquisitions, real estate, regulatory matters, securities, taxation, and white-collar crime.

The firm represents clients in the energy, defense, construction, telecommunications, food-processing, banking and financial, insurance, agricultural, utility, real estate, health care, and manufacturing industries; in international trade; and in the professions. Those clients include individuals, cooperatives, and domestic, foreign, and multinational corporations.

Joseph M. Day, managing partner in the Louisville office, expresses the firm's attitude when he says, "We are a service organization. As a team, our number one priority is to serve our clients, whatever their needs may be."

The Louisville office is the largest; the Washington office—formed in 1975 to serve clients who wanted a Washington presence and to bring to the firm some lawyers with heavy-duty, substantive skills in the tax, securities, and antitrust fields—is the next largest, with 30 lawyers. Barnett & Alagia was one of the first out-of-town firms to come to Washington, says Donald F. Mintmire, the managing partner in that office. Many others have come and gone over the years, he adds, but Barnett & Alagia is there for the long haul.

Barnett & Alagia has established a Far Eastern presence, also. An associate, who is a former Thai ambassador to the United States, spends six months a year serving clients from an office in Bangkok, and the other six months in Washington. The firm also has had contacts in Singapore, Japan, and Korea. Some legal exploration also is going on in China.

The Far East connection fits in with the firm's desire to move into the international field, a longtime interest for Barnett and a new one for Alagia. They consider it a fertile field, with many potential clients in matters of trade and investment and acquisition.

For the future, Mintmire sees a number of areas of practice that will expand, and probably will mean more work in governmental affairs for the firm. He believes there will be a resurgence in law enforcement activities in the securities and antitrust fields, and more work in the areas of trademarks, patents, and copyright infringements. Immigration, a matter that could expand the firm's international emphasis, will be a growing field, he believes, not only because of the new immigration law but also because so many foreign countries are investing so heavily in the United States.

Whatever the future holds, Barnett & Alagia—firmly planted on regional ground, and with its continuing sense of adventure—is prepared to, as Alagia says, "deliver a quality product in a timely fashion for a reasonable fee."

Joseph M. Day, partner in the Louisville firm.

BROWN, TODD & HEYBURN

Brown, Todd & Heyburn, a full-service law firm consisting of more than 100 attorneys, 19 paralegals, and a support staff of 120-plus people, serves domestic and international clients engaged in a myriad of business transactions.

In spite of the impressive number of attorneys in its offices in Citizens Plaza in downtown Louisville, and its offices in Lexington and across the Ohio River in New Albany, Indiana, the firm has not forgotten that it stemmed from three small Louisville firms whose members' legacies of practicing law dated back to the early 1900s.

Realizing the need to expand their capabilities, the firms of Brown, Eldred & Bonnie; Marshall, Cochran, Heyburn & Wells; and Brown, Ardery, Todd & Dudley merged in 1972 to form Brown, Todd & Heyburn. The joining of these practices allowed the firm to offer more specialized services to its rapidly growing and diversified client base. The merger of these organizations gave the fledgling Brown, Todd & Heyburn a total of 22 attorneys.

Through the years Brown, Todd & Heyburn has continued to expand its services and capabilities. The firm has represented thousands of corporate clients in its domestic practice, but it also reaches out internationally, serving several European manufacturers with operations in the United States, and, specifically, in the Midwest.

The firm's varied practice is pursued in several major sections that in turn have subsections that form highly concentrated practice groups involved in specific areas of the law.

While some business transactions are simple and involve only one area of the law, others are complex and require the input and knowledge of a number of different lawyers. By working with lawyers from other practice groups, Brown, Todd & Heyburn lawyers have the ability and resources to handle projects of the most complicated nature.

The firm practices in the areas of corporate tax, mergers and acquisitions, securities, limited partnership offerings, commercial lending, bonds, commercial and tax-exempt equipment leasing, commercial and residential land development, mineral resources, environmental regulation, labor relations, immigration law, estate planning and probate, health care, transportation regulation, bank and savings and loan regulation, employee benefits, the equine industry, public utilities regulation, creditors' rights, bankruptcy reorganizations, and all types of civil litigation, including antitrust, disaster, complex tort, products liability, workers' compensation, securities and RICO, asbestos, other toxic exposure, and general casualty litigation.

Brown, Todd & Heyburn lawyers represent more than 20 top law schools nationwide. They are high achievers, team players, and well-rounded individuals who aren't afraid to roll up their shirtsleeves to get the job done for the client.

In addition to their legal responsibilities, Brown, Todd & Heyburn lawyers give freely of their time and talent in many areas of public service, including serving on the boards of more than 100 business, charitable, political, and community organizations. The firm's commitment to its region also shows up in sponsorship of law school scholarships at both the University of Louisville and the University of Kentucky.

The Brown, Todd & Heyburn Louisville office overlooks the Ohio River and downtown skyline.

Photo by Bill Benoit/Nawrocki Stock Photo

NTS Corporation 294-297

Brandeis Machinery & Supply Corporation 298

RESCO 299

Henderson Electric Company Inc. 300-301

Silliman Development Company, Inc. 308-309

Ready Electric Company, Inc. 310-311

C&I Engineering, Inc. 312-313

US Ecology, Inc. 314-315

Hilliard Lyons 302-303

Sturgeon-Thornton-Marrett Development Company 304-307

Paragon Group, Inc. 316-317

Harold W. Cates & Co., Inc. 318

Chapter XIII
Building Greater Louisville

From concept to completion, Louisville's building industry shapes tomorrow's skyline.

Photo by C.J. Elfont

IN CELEBRATION OF LOUISVILLE

NTS CORPORATION

What do thousands of home owners, apartment renters, businesses, employees, and consumers in Louisville's East End have in common? They live, work, or shop in properties built by NTS Corporation, Louisville's premier real estate developer.

NTS, a major force in transforming much of eastern Jefferson County into an economically robust residential and business center, was founded in Louisville by chairman J.D. Nichols and Richard Thurman.

Although NTS' development activities extend far beyond Louisville, the company's roots are firmly planted in the River City. A couple of fairly recent Louisville successes, the residential developments of Owl Creek and Lake Forest, are considered two of the corporation's greatest accomplishments.

Says John R. Davis, president of NTS, "Our constant aim is to build each new development to be better than the last. No matter how well we do it, we like to do it better the next time. In our residential communities that means more than just developing homesites. It means creating a life-style—with tennis, swimming, lakes, jogging trails, and clubhouse facilities. What makes NTS unique is that we go the extra mile."

Going that extra mile is not new to NTS. Over its more than 20 years as a growing part of the real estate development and management industry, the company has always pursued excellence and elegance in its developments. In Louisville, NTS' residential projects such as Oxmoor Woods, Stonebridge at Anchorage, and The Willows of Plainview apartments; and commercial developments, such as the Atrium, Triad North, NTS Plaza, and Plainview Point, all attest to the quality that has built the firm's reputation for superiority in development.

Nichols began his building and development business with something less than a vast background in construction. Originally in the restaurant business, his recipe for suc-

The Atrium Center is part of the more than one million square feet of office space in the Plainview Office Park, developed by NTS.

cess as a developer included these ingredients: a law degree and some former high school chums with a tax problem as a result of their home-building business. While trying to help them overcome their problem, Nichols got a taste of the construction business—and redirected his goals.

He subsequently formed a partnership with friend and builder Thurman, and NTS was born. A small apartment community in South Louisville was their first venture. After that they developed a major East End apartment complex: LaFontenay. They soon began building what were then called office

NTS business centers, such as Blankenbaker Business Center, combine office, showroom, distribution, and storage space all in one attractive location.

BUILDING GREATER LOUISVILLE

warehouses, and for the first time went outside Louisville to build.

Following some active home building in the upscale Hurstbourne area of eastern Louisville, NTS struck the development gold mine that was then the huge Plainview Farms dairy area. Plainview proved to be the catalyst for the firm's rapid expansion.

Purchasing Plainview Farms wasn't considered a sound move by everyone in the real estate development arena in Louisville. In fact, NTS principals remember that a sales manager with a local real estate company "thought we were absolutely crazy to buy Plainview," and predicted that it would never go.

Here's how it did go: Well over one million square feet of office space in the Plainview office park, approximately 200,000 square feet of shopping area, nearly 800 single-family homes, more than 800 rental apartments, and almost 600 condominiums. Also, there's room to build an additional half-million square feet of office space, which, according to Burt Deutsch, senior vice-president/operations, will be done. Plainview is home to the NTS headquarters, whose employees constitute more than half of the 300 working for the organization nationwide.

By 1987 NTS had developed more

NTS was a leader in establishing the flexible business center design that appeals to tenants who require both tasteful offices and functional service space, such as is located in Commonwealth Business Center.

than 6.5 million square feet of residential and commercial space and more than 6,000 acres of land, with a market value approaching a half-billion dollars. In addition to Louisville, these developments are located in Lexington, Indianapolis, Orlando, Fort Lauderdale, Atlanta, Birmingham, Cincinnati, Charlotte, Grand Rapids, and the Washington, D.C., area.

"Now Plainview is 15 years old," says Gary Adams, executive vice-president. "We've taken what we learned in Plainview and added to it." The company's award-winning Sabal Point development in Orlando is a good example. Sabal Point features a professional 18-hole golf course, tennis and swim club, expensive single-family homes, luxury apartments, and NTS' Florida headquarters.

One of the corporation's newer developments in Louisville, the Springs, is another good example. Like Plainview, the Springs is a totally planned development, combining homes, offices, and a shopping center on what used to be agricultural land. According to Donald J. Cook, senior vice-president/acquisition and development, "NTS' plan for the Springs began with a vision to build the finest shopping and working environments in Louisville."

There are two fundamental

Microwave ovens, skylights, marble floors, Jacuzzi baths, security systems, and designer interiors are all standard in most NTS apartment communities. This is The Willows of Plainview.

Much of the funding for NTS' income-producing properties, such as Plainview Point Office Center, comes from participants in the firm's public limited partnerships.

IN CELEBRATION OF LOUISVILLE

NTS residential communities, such as Owl Creek, offer a country club life-style in a private, neighborhood setting.

The fastest-growing segment of the NTS empire may be that of single-family residential development.

branches of business conducted within NTS. The first involves all phases of real estate development and management. It falls under the auspices of NTS Development Company, which is led by Davis. The second involves the formation and marketing of public limited partnership investments in NTS' developments. It falls under the auspices of NTS Securities, Inc., which is led by president Richard L. Good, who is also executive vice-president of NTS Corporation.

On the real estate side, NTS has recently stepped up its development in the luxury apartment and business center markets. The corporation believes its apartment amenities are unequaled in the marketplace. Microwave ovens, skylights, Italian marble floors, Jacuzzi baths, security systems, and designer interiors are all standard in most NTS apartments. As in its single-family neighborhoods, the firm's apartment communities also feature a variety of athletic facilities, including tennis and racquetball courts, whirlpools, exercise rooms, and even tanning beds. The result is high rent revenues and strong demand.

The company's business centers, such as Commonwealth Business Center I and II and the Blankenbaker Business Center, are a relatively new entry to the real estate industry. Catering to emerging high-tech and service ventures, these facilities combine office, showroom, distribution, and storage space all in one attractive location. NTS was a leader in establishing this flexible

Elegant brick entryways and lush landscaping are hallmarks of NTS communities.

design that appeals to tenants who require both tasteful offices and functional service space.

Much of the funding for NTS' income-producing properties comes from participants in the organization's public limited partnerships. From 1980 through 1987 NTS brought nearly $140 million from more than 13,000 investors through the Louisville economy. "Rather than borrowing money," explains

NTS has hosted Louisville's Homearama tours for seven consecutive years.

Good, "we raise most of our capital in the public marketplace, through a number of regional securities brokers and financial-planning firms."

In general the NTS approach to its partnerships is a conservative, careful one—especially in a time when competition is fierce and some markets have become overbuilt. The company's investment philosophy centers on these four criteria: design and build top-quality properties, manage every aspect of the construction and operation of those properties, focus on markets with little or no competition for its types of properties, and establish a superior reputation in the communities it serves.

"We're not a tax-shelter type of investment," Good advises. "As a matter of fact, a lot of people say NTS stands for 'Not a Tax Shelter.' It's true. We've never been in the tax-shelter business. Our average limited partner invests about $10,000 for diversification and as a hedge against inflation."

The partnerships are income generators, and NTS' track record has been pretty good. The people who invested in its very first public offering earned 8 percent per year, tax-sheltered, and another 60.5 percent profit when the property was sold in the fifth year. That's an average cash return of close to 20 percent per year.

Though limited partnerships in real estate are fairly common, Good says not many firms are doing it the way NTS is. "We don't charge any syndication fees or take any profit on the front end of the offering itself," he states. "If we earn anything on it, we have to make money for the limited partners first. If we do a good job for them then we get our reward."

However, the fastest-growing segment of NTS' empire may be that of single-family residential development. Eight such communities are in progress in Louisville, where the firm has hosted the city's Homearama tours for seven consecutive years. Three more such developments are in Orlando, where, in 1986, NTS sold 83 homesites to local builders in less than two hours, and a 12th residential community is under way near Washington, D.C. With plans for additional single-family developments in the Midwest and the Southeast, Davis confides that NTS has entertained the possibility of taking this portion of the operation public.

According to Richard K. Johnsen, senior vice-president in charge of single-family developments: "NTS residential developments are typically in the medium-price range on up. We cater to people who buy homes from $120,000 up to more than one million dollars; so, we start at the middle. We don't get into what you would call starter homes. The low end of our marketplace would be the junior executive or young professional. They would probably be young married couples in two-income households. In one of our developments more than 75 percent of the wives work. This is a development where the vast majority would be college graduates."

NTS Corporation's success stems from understanding what this segment of the market wants and being able to deliver it in grand style. A couple of slogans make that point. For the office centers, promotional literature suggests, "Enjoy Going to Work Again," and for the NTS residential communities, "A Great Lifestyle Starts Where You Live."

"We view ourselves as neighbors," says Davis, "not only to those who live and work in our developments, but to the Louisville community as a whole."

"We view ourselves as neighbors," says John R. Davis, president of NTS, "not only to those who live and work in our developments, but to the Louisville community as a whole."

IN CELEBRATION OF LOUISVILLE

BRANDEIS MACHINERY & SUPPLY CORPORATION

The reality of the turn-of-the-century construction boom, plus the founder's vision of an even busier future, put Brandeis Machinery & Supply Corporation in gear in 1908 and on the road to becoming what it is today—one of America's largest distributors of heavy equipment.

It all started in a 2,000-square-foot building with two employees. Their immediate goal was to supply equipment to the construction industry in the blossoming Louisville market. However, founder Robert E. Brandeis saw far beyond the moment, to the days when that construction would usher in industrial growth and improved transportation systems.

As he saw it, Louisville and Brandeis Machinery were ideally suited to grow and prosper together. That suit continues to fit Brandeis, though it has grown in size many times in its 80 years and now serves as the backbone for the corporate body known as Bramco, Inc., which includes other heavy-equipment companies and an equipment-rental business (Resco) of national stature.

Brandeis died in 1924, but through the leadership of J.A. Paradis, Sr.—who had been chief salesman and became owner and president following Brandeis' death —his son, J.A. Jr., and now his grandson, J.A. Paradis III, the company has flourished in line with the founder's vision.

Throughout its existence Brandeis Machinery has been associated with outstanding names in heavy equipment: Ingersoll-Rand, Gorman-Rupp, Coleman, Grove, Barber Greene, and Komatsu. In 1928 the growing firm moved into quarters 20 times the size of the original stand—40,000 square feet in an area near the University of Louisville and on the main line of the Louisville & Nashville Railroad.

The company now resides in a 122,000-square-foot headquarters on the fringe of the Blue Grass Industrial Park in eastern Jefferson County and employs in excess of 300 people in Louisville, Lexington, Middlesboro, and Allen, all in Kentucky, and in Indianapolis and Evansville, Indiana.

The Brandeis Machinery & Supply Corporation's showroom in the firm's early days in downtown Louisville.

The success Brandeis has enjoyed has been accomplished largely through its ability to back up sales with the parts and service to maintain equipment sold. If there are problems with equipment, repair can be made in any of six maintenance shops located strategically throughout Kentucky and Indiana, where mining, construction, and industry are the organization's major markets.

In mining, Brandeis Machinery equipment can be found throughout its two-state service area, which is rich in limestone, coal, lead, silica, iron, zinc, sand, and gravel. Coal is the major mining resource in the region, especially in Kentucky. In line with environmental concerns, the same equipment that takes the minerals from the land is used by mining companies to restore it to its natural state.

In construction, the firm's equipment is used in building highways; site preparation; soil conservation; building and maintaining of dams, levies, and locks; sewer and water lines; and home building. Included in the markets served are those organizations involved in the home appliance, automobile, atomic energy, steel, cement, steam generation, aluminum, and petrochemicals industries.

Just as the stirrings of industrial and commercial growth of Louisville at the beginning of the twentieth century inspired and then fueled the founding and growth of Brandeis Machinery & Supply Corporation, a reawakening of a recently slumbering Louisville area seems to be setting the stage for more dramatic growth as Brandeis looks ahead to the twenty-first century.

An array of some of the major construction and industrial machinery sold and maintained by Brandeis Machinery & Supply Corporation.

BUILDING GREATER LOUISVILLE

RESCO

Just as it did for Brandeis Machinery & Supply Corporation in 1908, the Louisville area produced, in 1966, the correct economic and market environment for the formation of a new firm—Rental Equipment Service Company (Resco). As a sister company to Brandeis Machinery & Supply Corporation (see preceding page), Resco built on Brandeis' knowledge of construction, mining, and industrial equipment to begin serving an emerging segment of those markets—rentals.

The progressive attitude of the Louisville-based customers and their willingness to fill their equipment needs through rentals preceded the national trend by approximately a decade, and is largely responsible for Resco's being the 10th-largest construction and industrial equipment rental company in the United States. Headquartered in Louisville, Resco now has nine branches operating in a six-state area, and there are plans for further expansion.

Through Resco, customers are able to fill their equipment needs by renting late-model, high-quality equipment on a daily, weekly, or monthly basis, with the firm retaining the responsibilities for maintenance and ownership. Resco's customers include all types of construction contractors and industries.

Its products offered include air compressors, pumps, cranes, aerial work platforms, and all types of material-handling and earth-moving equipment. Within the rental industry, Resco is unique in its broad range of equipment offered, an attribute that allows the customer to deal with only one equipment supplier for the entire construction, renovation, or maintenance project.

While Louisville is not the most populous market area in which Rental Equipment Service Company operates, its customers' progressive attitudes provide an ideal environment from which the firm headquarters its vast regional operations.

Headquartered in Louisville, Kentucky, Resco, one of the major equipment-rental companies in the United States, can fill practically any need for a firm in the construction business from any of its nine branches throughout the Midwest.

IN CELEBRATION OF LOUISVILLE

HENDERSON ELECTRIC COMPANY INC.

Henderson Electric Company Inc.—in operation for nearly 70 years—began as a small electrical supply firm, and eventually grew into a massive contracting business of approximately $20 million a year.

The corporation, one of the oldest electrical companies in Louisville and now in its third generation of family leadership, is probably the largest such firm in the city and perhaps the state, according to Rodney Henderson, chairman of the board. He adds that, with offices in Louisville and Lexington, it ranks among the top 60 in the United States.

The organization's roots trace back to 1919, when Henderson's grandfather, Harry, ventured into the fledgling electrical power industry that was growing rapidly in Kentucky. As the new power source became commonplace in the 1920s and 1930s, Henderson Electric moved into the contracting business, and the end of World War II brought rapid expansion.

Henderson provided the labor for the electrical work for a $6-million, totally automated tobacco-handling system for Philip Morris, which was completed in 1985.

The first major strides were made in conversion work, turning war plants into peace plants. Louisville's International Harvester, which had been a Curtiss-Wright airplane factory, is one example; a facility in Rubbertown for Du Pont, which had previously operated the Indiana Army Ammunition Plant, is another.

Although Henderson Electric has not been active in the residential housing market recently, it was prominent in home construction during the postwar building boom in the area. Success in that endeavor helped put the firm into the high-voltage industrial and commercial fields, where it has carved out a major market for itself over the past 30 years. The organization has made its mark by completing major work at General Electric's Appliance Park and the Kentucky Fair and Exposition Center, among others.

Diversification, that old friend of business success, is given much of the credit for Henderson Electric's place among its peers. "Our work," Henderson says, "covers hospitals, schools, university work, government work—federal, state and local—the petrochemical industry, heavy manufacturing, and high-voltage line work." The company's more prominent clients have such easily recognized names as Churchill Downs, General Electric, Ralston Purina, Ford Motor Company, Rohm and Haas, Du Pont, Philip Morris and Dow Corning.

In recalling the list of major clients, Henderson, who was succeeded as president in 1987 by his brother, Bruce, vents one of his pet peeves: "Louisville is perceived in the construction industry as not having the type of contractors who can do big work, but that's not true. We are an example. We feel we can han-

Churchill Downs is the home of the prestigious "Run For The Roses"—the Kentucky Derby. Shown here is the newly completed paddock and tote board located in the clubhouse garden. Henderson Electric has been doing the electrical work for Churchill Downs for more than 30 years, including a recently completed private dining area.

BUILDING GREATER LOUISVILLE

dle just about any job that comes down the pike, and we take pride in saying so: no job too large or no job too small."

One of the company's federal government contracts was with the National Aeronautics and Space Administration for electrical work on a launch gantry for the Gemini space program—not a minor electrical hookup.

Henderson gives substantial credit for the firm's continuing success to the stability of the work force, fostered by the length of service the corporation has given the industry. "Because of our size and because of our length of time in business, we can attract people who know that not only are we going to be here today but we're going to be here tomorrow," he says. The stay of the average employee exceeds the industry average of 11 years.

Henderson, who succeeded his father, Rodger, as president in 1979, encourages longevity from an employee's first day, emphasizing communications and the desire to operate as a small business. "When we hire we like for a person to look at us as a permanent situation, not as a stepping stone," he explains. The organization has approximately 270 employees in Louisville and Lexington, and, according to Henderson, the greatest disruption for the company comes when a personnel change has to be made.

The corporation's work is split almost equally between new work and the refitting and refurbishing of existing buildings. General maintenance of office buildings is another facet of the business, First National Bank and Liberty National Bank being prime examples.

The firm's loyalty to Louisville has been exhibited by the fact that the company, Henderson states, has had several attractive offers to merge with national organizations, but "we (the brothers, who are Louisville natives and graduates of the University of Louisville) intend to stay active and control the business and participate in Louisville's economy. Louisville's a good place to live, and it shows a lot of potential."

Oxmoor Mall, Louisville's premier shopping center, was completed in the mid-1970s. Henderson Electric did the original electric work for what was then a 600,000-square-foot mall and a recent addition of 300,000 square feet.

Hometown pride shows up in the firm's support for community programs, including a $50,000 commitment to the University of Louisville's Quest for Excellence fund drive and continued backing for the city's Fund for the Arts.

In Henderson's view, Louisville will develop further into a service center, due to a cost of living that encourages such industries. Also, it will grow as a distribution center, built on its transportation resources.

Although he does not see any major growth in the industrial arena, Henderson believes local manufacturing workers will begin to take a more responsible leadership role in the community, and that could eventually help to attract new industry and provide an atmosphere for companies already located in Louisville to expand.

The Columbia Steak House, owned by a member of the family that owns the famous Calumet Horse Farm in Lexington, Kentucky, is an example of the type of quality small jobs finished by Henderson Electric Company Inc.

IN CELEBRATION OF LOUISVILLE

HILLIARD LYONS

Capital Ideas

Those are the kind that interest J.J.B. Hilliard, W.L. Lyons, Inc., so much so that the securities firm's slogan is "Creating Capital for You." This is the company's way of saying it is serious about making money for its clients, just as it has been since its founding in 1854.

Hilliard Lyons makes no bones about its mission—to make money. It advertises: "When you profit, we profit." That profit, of course, in turn creates a loyal clientele, people who invest with the firm time and again, year after year. This kind of loyalty is what Hilliard Lyons has built its reputation on. And it has placed them at the center of Louis-

ville's financial community.

To underline this, Hilliard Lyons has moved physically into the heart of the retail and financial district of Louisville by buying the historic Stewart Dry Goods building at Fourth Avenue and Muhammad Ali Boulevard. The move is a reflection of the firm's continued growth and its long-standing commitment to inject the city with financial vitality. It is the third headquarters building for Hilliard Lyons in recent years, the previous two becoming too small for the operation.

The new headquarters building, a sign of the company's keen sense of history and preservation, is the eighth Hilliard Lyons office listed on the National Register of Historic Places. Four of those are in Louisville, three are in other Kentucky cities, and one is in central Indiana. The building, which will have other tenants also, is considered by Hilliard Lyons managers as the centerpiece of what they see as the new Louisville.

While it is often thought of as a Louisville securities firm, Hilliard Lyons goes well beyond that —ranking as the largest Kentucky-based securities firm and operating throughout the Midwest and Southeast with a staff of investment brokers handling in excess of one billion dollars in securities transactions annually. In addition to Kentucky, Hilliard Lyons offices reach from Indiana to Mississippi and from Missouri to North Carolina.

This geographic area is consid-

Offices throughout the Midwest and Southeast.

ered prime wealth and growth territory for the kind of clientele that has always been the business backbone for Hilliard Lyons. Gilbert L. Pamplin, chairman, says, "We are a retail regional firm. Our main thrust is careful attention to investments for individuals and small businesses.

Hilliard Lyons Center corporate headquarters.

BUILDING GREATER LOUISVILLE

Our specialty has always been the individual customer ... this is our niche."

This segment of the United States is the greatest place to be today and, in the future, for those firms specializing in retail business. With this considered as prime territory, Hilliard Lyons has shown little interest in going to such places as California, New York, or New Jersey.

Hilliard Lyons, a member of the New York Stock Exchange and all other major exchanges, brims with the confidence born of financial strength and management ability that has seen the company prosper through wars, panics, and depressions during its history. That confidence continues today in this Hilliard Lyons philosophy: "A retail securities firm that is well-capitalized and has good people will always be successful." When statistics of large New York-based firms and regional firms are compared, historically the good regionals have outperformed the national ones when it comes to return on investment for shareholders and customers alike.

Although operating in somewhat of a conservative mode, Hilliard Lyons has always made room for innovative, creative thinking. Its growth has not been in great leaps, but rather moving in a steady and deliberate pattern. Growth turned a bit up-tempo in 1965 with the merger of J.J.B. Hilliard & Son and W.L. Lyons & Company, bringing together two of Louisville's oldest financial institutions. In 1972 the firm incorporated under its present name, and very significant, controlled expansion has resulted.

Corporate citizenship has always been a concern for Hilliard Lyons. The firm takes great pride in being a good corporate citizen. Its officials spend a lot of time with every new investment broker, stressing the importance of being active in the community. While the company hopes to benefit from the community, it also pursues an active role in community development.

The Hilliard Lyons reputation that has grown through the years is reflected in its vision of the future. The organization is prepared for active, dull, or even disastrous times that may lie ahead, secure in the knowledge that good securities firms are going to survive and prosper. Pamplin says, "One of our strengths has been that we have survived since 1854 through just about every turn and cycle that you can think of, and we've remained profitable through it all."

And that, for Hilliard Lyons clients, is an especially capital idea.

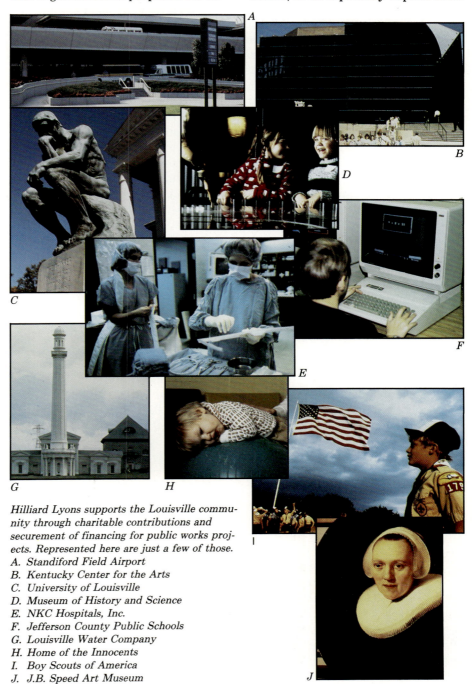

Hilliard Lyons supports the Louisville community through charitable contributions and securement of financing for public works projects. Represented here are just a few of those.
A. Standiford Field Airport
B. Kentucky Center for the Arts
C. University of Louisville
D. Museum of History and Science
E. NKC Hospitals, Inc.
F. Jefferson County Public Schools
G. Louisville Water Company
H. Home of the Innocents
I. Boy Scouts of America
J. J.B. Speed Art Museum

IN CELEBRATION OF LOUISVILLE

STURGEON-THORNTON-MARRETT DEVELOPMENT COMPANY

It's rare when the most appropriate and complete explanation can be given without uttering a word.

When describing the quality of the developments of Sturgeon-Thornton-Marrett Development Company (STM), words seem meager. All one has to do is take a look.

Take a look around the east end of Jefferson County, downtown Louisville, Nashville, Atlanta, Lexington, and Cincinnati. Everything that bears the STM name, whether it's commercial, residential, or industrial, is marked by innovative imagination, meticulous attention to detail, and an aura of elegance. From the moment A. Thomas Sturgeon, Jr., James H. Thornton, and Robert H. Marrett initiate a development, it is destined to be in a class all its own.

High-powered talk? Hardly. Just take a look.

Drive down Highway 42 in Prospect and look at Jefferson County's most exclusive residential community, Bridgepointe. Blasted through a rock cliff along the highway, the entrance to this classic 121-acre development is considered by many to be the most beautiful subdivision entrance in this part of the country. The 100,000 cubic yards of rock removed to create an entrance that preserves the beauty of the eight-acre valley green space was used to build not only beautiful, decorative walls and a gatehouse, but a retaining wall that preserves the natural beauty of the tree-lined area. The cobblestone entrance winds its way up to an upscale residential community complete with clubhouse and junior Olympic pool, and from one corner, a breathtaking view of mile after mile of eastern Jefferson County.

There's the $14.9-million, 200-acre Copperfield community on Shelbyville Road, .75 mile east of the Jefferson Freeway. The site of the 1986 Homearama, this cozy community, which sports a recreational facility for the residents' exclusive use, will have more than 400 homes.

This is STM's Chenoweth community in Nashville, Tennessee. Making a grand entrance is an everyday affair at an STM community.

There's the $200-million Hartland in southern Fayette County that rambles across 500 acres from Tates Creek Road to the Armstrong Mill Road with sections of every type of residential unit, from apartments to spacious estate homes. When complete, STM's largest residential development will include 1,149 living units, a 13-acre tennis and pool complex, and a clubhouse that will provide space for private entertaining. "With Hartland, we presented a community with a level of quality that Lexington has never had a chance to see before," Marrett says. "It's the kind of place that will have an impact on Lexington for years to come."

There's the $250-million Burton Hills planned community in the heart of Nashville, a diverse development of 550,000 square feet of office space and 850 homes sprawled over 192 prime acres in the prestigious Green Hills neighborhood. Viewed as the finest residential community in Nashville, Burton Hills was named the top mixed-use community in the city by the Nashville Home Builders Association's Sales and Marketing Council.

There's the $50-million Hurstbourne Forum Office Park and Retail Center, one of STM's primary commercial thrusts in Louisville. The strategically located development includes a four-building, 300,000-square-foot office complex and a 135,000-square-foot retail area of upscale design and landscaping stretched across 50 acres at the corridor of Hurstbourne Lane and Shelbyville Road. Housing such exclusive tenants as Gidding-Jenny, Talbot's, and two of Louisville's most popular restaurants, L&N Seafood Grill and Ruby Tuesday, the Forum Center is regarded as one of the city's finest retail developments.

There's the Tri-County Business Center, a 125,000-square-foot retail/office warehouse complex in Cincinnati, which is considered state of the art in commercial design. Next door is STM's 105,000-square-foot facil-

STM's Copperfield in Louisville. STM communities are private, inviting, and rich with details that make them an enviable place to live.

ity for the Kroger Company's new wholesale warehouse concept, Price Savers.

There's more than a dozen other residential developments in Louisville, Kentucky; Atlanta, Georgia; Hendersonville and Nashville, Tennessee, where STM hosted the Parade of Homes three of the past four years; and several more commercial developments in eastern Jefferson County and Cincinnati—each with its own unique personality, yet all distinctively marked by STM's commitment to excellence.

And, of course, there's the $46-million Broadway Project, Phase I, part of the Broadway Renaissance that has changed the face of downtown Louisville with the restoration of the Brown Hotel and the Brown office building, a new 50,000-square-foot retail area called Theater Square, a 500-car parking garage, the refurbishing of the MaCauley Theatre, and, of course, the Fourth Street Mall, home to the new trolley that connects the Broadway Renaissance Project to other attractive retail areas in downtown Louisville. In 1986, for its role in the Brown Hotel revival, STM was presented the National Private Sector Initiative Award, a presidential honor sponsored by the National Council for Urban Economic Development.

As its record proves, STM is a name synonymous with quality.

A. Thomas Sturgeon, Jr., the intuitive, industrious chairman of the board of STM, is the personification of all that makes STM such a respected entity in the development business. Intense, yet cool, confident, yet cautious, Sturgeon won't give the nod to any project unless he's certain it will work. The key is, he seems to know exactly what will work.

Sturgeon entered the real estate business in 1971 when he became president of Plainview Farms Development Corp., developer of the 750-acre Hurstbourne Lane community, Plainview.

James H. Thornton is a seasoned,

STM communities offer homes of finest quality built by STM-approved builders.

polished entrepreneur, tempered by years of tremendous success in a wide spectrum of business endeavors, particularly the Thornton Oil Corporation. While Sturgeon and Marrett handle the day-to-day requirements of the business, Thornton works closely with them several days per week, providing insight into the planning of all company projects.

Thornton, the self-professed "dutch uncle" at STM, has an extremely lofty opinion of his partners and gives them all the credit for the success of STM. "Tom Sturgeon is a good leader," Thornton says. "He has a lot of ability, and he has surrounded himself with a lot of capable people, such as Bob Marrett. They complement one another very, very well. The chemistry is good; the intellect is good."

Robert H. Marrett, the dynamic, energetic president of STM, has the

Many STM communities have clubhouses, pools, and tennis courts where life can be as active or relaxing as you like.

Forum One office building is one of four buildings in the Hurstbourne Forum Office Park that is a mixed-use development in Louisville.

kind of firing enthusiasm that leaves little doubt that his lofty goals for the company are much more than mere dreams. Specializing in the residential end of the business, Marrett knows exactly what he wants to see in a residential community, and one can bet he'll see it.

While it's not always easy for a three-way partnership to survive and thrive, STM has only grown stronger since the company began in the early 1980s. "The secret to getting along in business is to have compatible goals and objectives and to have compatible personalities," Sturgeon says. "Our various talents are pretty diverse so we seem to work very well together."

Marrett calls it "hitchhiking" on one another's thoughts. "We will frequently help out one another and overlap in a way that's very constructive," he says. "Our partnership has been very comfortable for all of us." Comfortable and profitable—for the company and for the cities in which STM chooses to locate.

This powerful partnership has orchestrated a dynasty of versatility that has left the STM mark of distinction in several major cities. Building everything from office showrooms, warehouses, office buildings, shopping centers, and parking garages to apartments, estate homes, town homes, residential communities, recreational and public facilities, condominiums, and multiuse developments, STM has just begun to spread that mark of distinction.

"I think STM is a company on the move," Sturgeon says. "As the economy allows, we'll continue to do more and more projects in more and more cities. We have no small plans; our projects are not small projects. We have a lot of diversity, a lot of talent, and a lot of capability. We do a lot of things, and we're going to do a lot more things."

Sturgeon's "we" doesn't mean just himself, Thornton, and Marrett, but all of STM's 150 employees. "What you've got is three smart businessmen who also understand that our company is not just three people," he says. "We have very, very talented people with lots of great experience. They are astute and hard working, and I would say one of our talents is our ability to provide opportunities to others so they can excel."

Marrett agrees. "The secret of STM's success is our clearly defined goals and our ability to work hard and pay the price," he says. "All our employees do pay the price. They are intense; they are committed; they are very methodical and goal-oriented kind of folks."

And every one is committed to the continuance of that tradition of quality, marked not only by state-of-the-art design, but also by precise attention to detail.

From the point where the blue sign introduces a development as

Burton Hills office building, one of five planned office buildings in Nashville.

BUILDING GREATER LOUISVILLE

Uniquely designed office atrium lobbies are a hallmark of STM buildings.

one of Sturgeon-Thornton-Marrett Development Company, every amenity has its own classy style and every feature its own personality. With STM, everything counts—from the subdivision layout to the street signs.

No STM development is without brilliant landscaping of colorful splashes of blooming flowers, verdant shrubbery, thoughtfully placed trees that have been saved from other areas of the land and transplanted, stylish brick or stone entrances, and intense buffer zones of trees and walls. In many areas built-in electronic irrigation systems maintain the landscaping. Even sewage-treatment plants are attractively camouflaged by roofs or walls and hidden by trees.

Stringent architectural control guarantees that site layout plans and home designs are compatible with the natural surroundings of each development. Curbs, gutters, and distinctive, unique street signing mark all STM residential developments. And almost every STM community offers an extensive collection of modern recreational facilities.

"We spend a lot of time in planning and trying to make our projects not only financially successful, but aesthetically pleasing," Sturgeon says. "I think when you look at our projects, you immediately realize that there's a lot of attention to detail, and the STM product is a very high-quality product. Whatever we do, we try to accomplish in a very elegant, upscale way."

First and foremost, however, before beginning any development, STM makes certain the market is there. The STM staff is constantly studying market analyses, a strategy proven effective by the fact that nearly all STM developments are fully occupied within a limited amount of time. Such a remarkable instinct for knowing what needs to be built where has always been one of STM's strongest attributes.

"I think we have a very good understanding of what will and what will not work," Sturgeon says. "We make it a point to understand the market to which we are developing to or building to. That can make the difference between success and failure."

Whatever and wherever a particular market may be, STM is there, molding that market into a successful development, usually with a new twist each time.

"We're constantly fine-tuning our program," Marrett says. "There aren't any two residential projects that are ever alike because we adapt our projects to the circumstances at hand wherever we go. We are gaining little tips of things that work every time out so the accumulation of experience and knowledge and such that occurs is used in each succeeding development. So, in essence, each community gets a little better and better and better.

"One of our cardinal rules is to stay flexible. If a better idea comes along, we're going to seize the initiative and utilize it. I think the secret is the standards that we set for ourselves. There's an old maxim: 'to get the results you expect, you must inspect.' People around our company know our standards and, quite frankly, they have adopted them as their own."

"Such perfectionism," Thornton says, "points to a bright future for STM as it spreads its mark across Kentucky and other states."

"I expect STM to continue to grow at a fairly rapid pace and begin opening offices in additional cities throughout the balance of the 1980s and 1990s," Thornton says. "I expect us one day to have offices in 15 or 20 cities."

High-powered talk? Hardly. Just sit back and watch.

By Shanda Pulliam

Downtown renovation of The Brown Hotel, part of a mixed-use development of the Broadway Project Phase I, in Louisville.

IN CELEBRATION OF LOUISVILLE

SILLIMAN DEVELOPMENT COMPANY, INC.

Enthusiasm plays an important part in any successful effort. For the Silliman Development Company, however, such enthusiasm extends beyond the boundaries of the firm's main interest of developing shopping centers and office buildings in the Louisville metropolitan area.

Thanks to a strong loyalty to his hometown, Michael B. Silliman, president, has concentrated his organization toward developing quality retail and office projects that have a twofold purpose. The first aim is to serve the existing market in Louisville. Equally important, the second aim is to strengthen the city's present and future position in attracting new businesses to locate in the area.

"This is a company dedicated to producing commercial real estate projects that are aesthetically pleasing as well as market sensitive," Silliman says. "We want to see Louisville become nationally recognized as a very viable and attractive city in which to live and work."

The Silliman Company's development record has been of Olympian proportions, well-suited to the president's background as captain of the gold-medal-winning U.S. Olympic basketball team in the 1968 Summer Games in Mexico City. The company's ledger shows more than $75 million in development projects—either finished or under construction. "We have accomplished many things over the past several years," Silliman says. "We are constantly involved with planning new developments as the opportunities become more defined."

In shopping centers, Silliman Development Company counts Herman's Plaza, Hunnington Place, and The Eastgate Shopping Center, all in the burgeoning east side of Jefferson County. Located on Shelbyville Road near the Gene Snyder Freeway, Eastgate is the newest of the trio and promises to have a major impact on one of the fastest-growing sections in the metropolitan area. In addition to its location, the center has a strong attraction because of its retail anchor, a Kroger Superstore, representing one of the largest in the country and a prototype for Kroger stores of the future. The shopping center sits on 30 acres of land and features 175,000 square feet of retail space, in addition to eight frontage sites, for other freestanding buildings.

For suburban office buildings, the company is developing Hunnington Office Park, situated on 20 acres across Bunsen Parkway from the Hunnington Place Shopping Center. The first of four contemporary-style buildings houses the current headquarters for the Silliman Development Company. The firm employs approximately 15 people in administration, finance, leasing, and property management. Silliman says that the number of employees will probably stay steady because the company prefers to go into the community for architecture, construction, marketing, and legal services rather than to have a large in-house staff handling these disciplines.

That philosophy also is tinged with some hometown pride and the opportunity to work with other professionals in the community. "We feel there are some very good, capable, and experienced companies in Louisville that can efficiently perform these tasks," Silliman says.

Located on Hurstbourne Lane across from the Hunnington Office Park, Hunnington Place comprises 113,000 square feet of retail space serving the east side of Louisville.

Glistening in the night lights, this three-story, 69,000-square-foot, contemporary-style office building is the first of four in the Hunnington Office Park.

This artist's rendering shows the Corporate Plaza development at Main and Third streets near Louisville's evolving riverfront.

This approach includes working with the city's banking community for the company's financing needs, which generally exceed $10 million per development.

Another sign of the corporation's enthusiasm for a growing, thriving Louisville is the 23-story One Corporate Plaza, a major-league office tower that Silliman and his associates expect will galvanize future activity along the city's booming riverfront, perhaps providing a beacon for drawing new businesses to the city. The sleek granite-and-glass structure blends in with the eclectic style of Louisville's downtown, but at the same time puts forth a tasteful design of its own.

Silliman believes One Corporate Plaza, which in the near future will be joined by Two Corporate Plaza, will help fill the need for first-class office space in the downtown area, a need that has been growing over the past several years and is expected to continue to grow. "We think the building itself," he says, "will add a great deal of excitement to downtown development and will, hopefully, spur further development of the riverfront area."

Silliman, a firm believer that real estate plays a major role in a city's growth and the attitude of its citizens, states that the company's philosophy is simply to build the best

The 175,000-square-foot Eastgate Shopping Center is located on Shelbyville Road near the Gene Snyder Freeway, a rapidly growing area of eastern Jefferson County.

buildings in the best locations that can be found. "We try to enhance our developments with a high quality of design, interior finish, and state-of-the-art building systems. We are delivering a value-added service to our clients as well as to the community in general."

Louisville has tremendously improved its air service and terminal facilities that have helped to attract new businesses to the community. Its educational systems are sound and are highlighted by the University of Louisville, which provides a young, well-educated work force from which business can draw. Considering these and other positive aspects of Louisville, Silliman views the future with enthusiastic anticipation. "Looking toward the 1990s and further, we see a great potential for this city," he convincingly states. "Most of us [in the company] are from here or have been here for a long time. We are working hard to create some exciting things in Louisville."

As for Silliman Development Company, Inc., which doesn't expect to make any major expansion into other markets anytime soon, Silliman says: "We think Louisville offers enough opportunity to keep us quite busy."

IN CELEBRATION OF LOUISVILLE

READY ELECTRIC COMPANY, INC.

"Ready or not, here I come."

Most anybody would remember that cry from the children's game of hide and seek. There's an electrical contracting company in Louisville that believes in being ready—and it's no children's game.

Ready Electric Company, Inc., is a nationwide contracting and engineering firm that was founded in Louisville in 1949 and has established itself as a leader in full-service work with major credits across the country as well as in the immediate region. The company has also completed projects in Canada and Puerto Rico.

Despite the national scope of the corporation, Stanley E. Windhorst, president, says the firm has never forgotten that its roots are in Louisville, where it all started when his father, Ollie Sr., replaced a fuse as the company's first job. A dedication to quality and the tenacity and skills to accomplish goals have been the guiding lights for Ready Electric ever since.

Windhorst, joined in the business by two brothers and an average of 200 to 250 employees, beams with pride when he talks of his late father and his legacy, adding that "the principles of professionalism and total dedication are as prevalent today as when our company was founded."

It wasn't an easy start. In those early days the founder, without a car or truck, rode public transportation to and from his jobs. He was loaded down with tools, lunch bucket, and conduit that had to be cut in half because of a transit rule.

Later he turned a room in his mother's house into something of a shop, with tools, equipment, and supplies piled all around. Subsequently moving his one-man business into a one-room facility, the entrepreneur eventually relocated to a shop in the Crescent Hill district of Louisville—the site of Ready Electric's permanent home.

"That's the way this company started," says the younger Windhorst, in obvious pride over his father's indomitable spirit. "He was always very professional. He built a good reputation for finishing jobs on time and on budget, as well as for quality."

Ready Electric Company, Inc., continues to follow the tenets of its founder, Ollie H. Windhorst, Sr.

Ready Electric, always trying to see the light a bit sooner than others, has helped blaze the trail in the design-build concept that has become more popular over the past 10 years. Ready moved into that field, where it serves both as engineer and contractor, 30 years ago. In such a project, Windhorst says, "We are the engineer and we are also the contractor, seeing the project through to completion as part of a design-build team. The job is done in an efficient manner, on budget, and often completed ahead of schedule."

In 1987 Ready Electric was again on the list of the top 100 electrical contracting firms in the country. Ready counts commercial and industrial work as its prime fields, though it also does a great deal of work in institutional and governmental fields as well as some residential work. While much of its work is done outside Louisville, Windhorst says the firm stays "respectably busy" in its hometown.

Of particular note in recent years is Ready Electric's massive presence in the refurbishing and building anew of Louisville's downtown. In fact, Windhorst states without reservation, "We have had more to do with new construction and the revitalization of downtown than any of our competitors."

The list of the firm's work is something of a what's what downtown: Citizens Plaza; University Hospital; Kentucky Towers; the Galleria, where the corporation had as many as 125 electricians on the project that included two 26-story office towers, a parking garage, and retail center all going up at the same time; the Hyatt Hotel; and the Crescent Center, a complex of high-rise and low-rise condominiums and apart-

Another of Ready Electric's major projects in recent years called for the firm to have as many as 125 electricians working to construct the Louisville Galleria.

BUILDING GREATER LOUISVILLE

Miles of electrical wire went into Ready Electric's work at the Kentucky Center for the Arts, which includes controlling all lighting and special effects onstage.

The giant Toyota automobile assembly plant in central Kentucky contains more than 500,000 feet of Ready Electric conduit carrying more than 6 million feet of the company's wiring for the plant.

ments and a retail center that are all part of Phase 2 of the Broadway Project.

Two very special—and very complicated—projects that inspire extra pride in the Ready people are the Kentucky Center for the Arts in downtown Louisville and the new Toyota auto-assembly plant in Georgetown, Kentucky, about 75 miles from Louisville.

In the former, Ready was responsible for all the electrical work, but special skills went into the systems, made up of miles of wire that not only light the theaters but also control all the lighting and special effects on the stage of each of the center's theaters. "That," Windhorst says, "sets off a professional electrical contractor from a wire puller."

At Toyota, just the immensity of the complex, which has 87 acres under roof covering several buildings, was a considerable challenge as Ready installed the systems for fire alarms, intercoms, paging, building security, master clocks, nurse call, closed-circuit surveillance, and telephone distribution. There is more than 500,000 feet of conduit in the ceiling carrying more than 6 million feet of wire.

Though jobs can be immense and business can flourish, Windhorst says his firm never loses sight of the importance of its employees, "our most important asset." He believes the company has a good mix of employees—field-trained electricians who have progressed from an apprenticeship program through supervisory ranks, estimators and project managers, professional engineers, and other workers with engineering backgrounds.

Windhorst sees Ready Electric continuing to be active as a corporate citizen in such civic endeavors as support for Kosair Hospital, the University of Louisville, the local school system, and the Metro United Way.

Of Louisville's future, Windhorst is encouraged though admitting only to cautious optimism. "We've been here all our lives, and the city is very important to us," he says. "I see good things coming. I think Louisville is on the threshold of a big move."

His company, of course, is ready to turn on the lights.

A complex of high-rise and low-rise condominiums and apartments and a retail center make up Crescent Center, another downtown project for Ready Electric.

IN CELEBRATION OF LOUISVILLE

C&I ENGINEERING, INC.

C&I Engineering, Inc., has grown from the internationally known C&I Girdler Co., a long-running company in Louisville that was closed by its parent firm, leaving many veteran employees to ponder their future.

For many of those that future turned out to be C&I Engineering, which has grown dramatically in its short life and has helped eliminate the uncertainty that struck those lives just five years ago. Of the first 70 employees who came to work for C&I, 90 percent had worked for the shut-down C&I Girdler Company.

The presence of people experienced in engineering and in working with each other has forged a team that has built the company steadily since its beginning in 1983. Billings increased from $1.4 million in 1984 to $6.7 million in 1987, and the number of employees went from three at its formation to 125 in two offices at the end of 1987. The projection for employees by mid-1988 is 140.

C&I, which stands for chemical and industrial, provides a full range of technical engineering, including chemical process design, project engineering, mechanical engineering, material handling and packaging, energy conservation, piping layout, building and structural design, and electrical power and control systems design. In addition, the firm provides project management, construction management, capital-goods procurement, project scheduling, and cost estimating.

The organization services clients in the chemical process and manufacturing industries, including companies that manufacture plastics, coatings, fertilizers, agricultural chemicals, and petrochemicals. In the consumer products area these include tobacco, foods, beverages, and health care products. The heavy industrial area includes aluminum fabrication, printing, and power-generation facilities.

One of C&I's niches is the augmentation of trimmed-down internal engineering staffs of many operating companies, often working on site. In this mode, C&I can do small and medium-size jobs with a high level of technical skill but low overhead. Many smaller firms don't have the technical capability, and a larger company brings high overhead to such a job. For these endeavors C&I engineers serve as project managers, senior engineers, construction managers, planners, and construction engineers.

There's no clash with the client's engineering department employees. Instead, they often have more work than they can handle and welcome help from outside. In fact, C&I makes the point to its customers that C&I people get paid for their work, and when they're no longer needed they can be reassigned to other work by C&I—providing an organization with the optimum level of support staff at all times.

The company specialties are chemical process plant design; specialty chemicals (low-volume, high-value chemicals that have narrow uses); food and beverages; dry-material handling; packaging technologies, especially in consumer products; and computerized control

To assist clients in evaluating alternate layouts of their facilities, C&I frequently makes a model of the processing area, in this case a consumer products packaging facility.

C&I performed the engineering in support of Pyrochem's permit submittal for a chemical hazardous-waste incineration facility in Mason County, West Virginia.

C&I designed this high-speed conveyor system at a primary processing plant for a major tobacco company.

of production processes. Clients include Procter & Gamble, Colgate-Palmolive, Ashland Oil, and Shell Chemical, all outside Louisville; and American Synthetic Rubber Corporation, Ralston-Purina, Louisville Gas & Electric Company, B.F. Goodrich, Du Pont, Interez, United Catalyst Company, and Rohm and Haas, all in Louisville.

Though the company does much work in Louisville, it cannot survive on that business alone. It must work on a regional basis. Its focus essentially is in the Midwest... companies that have a corporate engineering operation or a plant operation in the Midwest... Cincinnati (where C&I has its other office), St. Louis, Cleveland, southern Michigan, Indianapolis, West Virginia. For the future, C&I may look also to western Tennessee.

The bulk of C&I's clients are those who usually have many projects that fit into the less-than-$10-million range and frequently in the one-million-dollar to $5-million arena. Its business strategy is to forge continuing relationships, and the company has been pretty successful at that. Its top 10 clients have been with the firm since its first year. The corporation estimates that 80 percent of its work is repeat business.

How does a company create such repeat business? Clear understanding of clients' needs, planning the work well, providing the best technical quality it can bring to bear, meeting the work schedule, treating clients' budgets as if they were its own, and operating as a team—that kind of attention creates client confidence and repeat business.

While repeat relationships are prime for C&I, new business relationships are not only inevitable but necessary to continued growth.

This is a latex chemical reactor for producing feedstock for adhesives and plastic coatings for W.R. Grace in Owensboro, Kentucky.

C&I-designed piping and automatic controls for the addition of flavorings, aromatics, and seasonings at a food-product plant installation that met the latest requirements of the Food and Drug Administration.

IN CELEBRATION OF LOUISVILLE

US ECOLOGY, INC.

There are those who would dispose of hazardous wastes the easy way: stop creating them. However, this solution is not as simple as it sounds.

Here are just a few of the consumer products that generate chemical wastes: medicine, clothing, automobiles, soap and detergents, paint, shoes and other leather goods, radios, and television sets.

Low-level radioactive wastes are generated through 80 million to 100 million nuclear-related medical procedures annually that benefit one out of every two hospital patients, including anyone who undergoes what would seem to be a harmless series of blood tests. In addition, low-level radioactive wastes are created in the production of clocks and watches, color television sets, photographic devices, agricultural research, packaging of agricultural products, and nuclear power.

Modernization has dictated much of the waste Americans generate every year, and who's willing to forego progress? Hazardous waste, then, is the price Americans pay for their high standard of living.

Fortunately, there are waste-management firms to deal with the estimated 2,400 pounds of hazardous waste that each resident has to share in each year because of using the products that create that waste. One of those waste-management firms is US Ecology, Inc., of Louisville, whose parent company is American Ecology Corporation of California.

US Ecology, which has been in business since 1952, has its corporate headquarters in Louisville, and also operates its analytical chemical laboratory locally. The laboratory's job is to sample, analyze, and verify physical and chemical properties of society's manufacturing by-products to assure that they are suitable for disposal at US Ecology sites. The company operates two of the nation's three disposal facilities for low-level nuclear waste in Beatty, Nevada, and Richland, Washington; chemical-waste-disposal facilities in Robstown, Texas, and Beatty, Nevada; and a warehouse for temporary storage of low-level nuclear waste in Pleasanton, California.

Company employees install an 80-mil synthetic liner in the bottom of this trench at the Robstown, Texas, facility.

In addition, the organization, which employs nearly 200 people in Louisville and at its other locations, has an operation in Tipton, Missouri, for the draining, flushing, and disposal of polychlorinated biphenyls (PCBs) transformers and their waste materials. Transportation of all waste materials is handled by the US Ecology truck fleet or by common carrier.

Although the company has more than 3,900 customers in 48 states, it does little business with Louisville firms due to the geographic location of its facilities, except on what's known as a "milk run" basis, meaning that pickups are made only periodically for transport to the appropriate disposal site. Among its customers nationwide are universities and colleges, auto and auto-parts manufacturers, hospitals and medical laboratories, power-generating companies, government agencies, general manufacturers, and chemical industries.

US Ecology emphasizes that while it handles more than half of the nation's low-level radioactive waste clients, that does not include the highly radioactive fuel elements and assemblies from nuclear reactors. Instead, the items handled are, typically, contaminated tools, clothing, cleaning wastes, and filter materials from nuclear power plants; medical materials from hospitals and laboratories; and industrial waste from both research and the production of many consumer goods. These materials require little shielding and no cooling.

BUILDING GREATER LOUISVILLE

US Ecology's 2,200-ton mobile supercompactor is capable of reducing dry active waste volume by 90 percent.

Disposal is done in landfills that are designed using one or more of the following: clay, soil, gravel, silt, or synthetic liners that safely encapsulate the nuclear or chemical wastes. When filled, trenches are covered with engineered caps, some containing synthetic materials, to impede infiltration of rainfall.

The company equips the landfills with surface and subsurface monitoring systems that can assist in identifying any potential problems. Samples taken from these systems are analyzed regularly both by the corporation and by regulatory agencies. Monitoring and maintenance of chemical landfills must be performed for a minimum of 30 years after a site is closed and low-level radioactive waste facilities for 100 years after closure.

Ever cognizant of the growth in waste material, US Ecology operates the most powerful mobile super-compactor in the nation. The 2,200-ton super-compactor is capable of reducing dry, active waste by as much as 90 percent. The machine, which is operated by a special team from US Ecology, also compacts steel pipe, valves, clothing, paper, and concrete blocks—eliminating the need to sort waste. It can be used anywhere in the United States, which yields a savings to the customer in transportation, disposal, and storage costs.

Future technology is pointing toward new recycling techniques to help reduce wastes, above-ground facilities that will feature disposal cells inside concrete-block buildings, chemical neutralization of wastes, and incineration, which would leave a nominal amount of residue to be buried.

Development of these technologies will help US Ecology, Inc., to underline the theme of one of its publications: "Protecting the environment today for tomorrow."

PARAGON GROUP, INC.

Paragon: A model of excellence.

That is exactly what the Paragon Group has tried to build during its rise in a little more than 20 years from its founding in Dallas by Bill Cooper to a top-10 position among privately held commercial and residential developers in North America. Its portfolio stands at more than 25,000 apartments and more than 12 million square feet of office and commercial space, with an asset value in excess of $2 billion.

In Louisville, that image has been reflected in the development of nearly 300,000 square feet of office space and more than 1,500 apartments. That comes to approximately $100 million in development over the 14 years that the firm has been operating in Louisville and Jefferson County.

Little wonder, then, that Brian F. Lavin, the energetic Paragon vice-president in charge of Kentucky operations, says proudly, "We like to feel we've helped in the growth of Louisville." That help also takes the form of using local builders and suppliers almost exclusively, Lavin says.

The growth he speaks of centers on such apartment communities as Sundance, a 1974 venture that was Louisville's first all-adult apartment community; national award-winning Post Oak; the prestigious Hurstbourne Apartments; contemporary Copper Creek; distinctive Deerfield; and the luxurious Glenridge layout.

The group's office buildings in the area are characterized by flowing, horizontal architecture creating dramatic office environments. Dynamic design, rich materials, sensitive site planning, and extensive landscaping are the trademarks of such Paragon office developments as Paragon Place and Paragon Centre, both located in the prestigious corridor in eastern Jefferson County. From the firm's Paragon Place headquarters for Kentucky operations (which includes Lexington, about 75 miles to the east), the management, leasing, and maintenance people who make up the Paragon team make plans for the future and carry out the day-to-day functions of the development and property management.

The Deerfield Apartments are just one of the Paragon Group's several apartment communities in Louisville.

Paragon, since its beginning, has had the goal throughout its 50-city, 15-state network of long-term ownership of prime properties, and the company believes management of those properties is paramount to reaching that goal. This means that Paragon not only tries to build the highest quality product in the high end of each local market, but it, unlike many developers, is in the race for the long run, continuing to own and operate its properties.

By managing its properties, Paragon believes it is able to maintain them in a way that enhances their value as income producers and as assets. As a result, according to a Paragon report, the firm has enjoyed asset appreciation, sustained growth, and stability—even through the roller-coaster market of the past couple of decades. Lavin puts it very directly, "We're a profitable group, and we make no apologies for that."

Operating in the upper strata of a market naturally brings the frequent objection that the price is too high, but Lavin says that objection is only effective if the firm hasn't "built value. If we're just trying to sell shelter, we're going to lose," he continues. "We don't want to sell shelter or basic office space, we want to create a life-style both residentially and commercially; we want to create value." One component of this

One Paragon Centre is a recent addition to the Paragon presence in Louisville.

Copper Creek Apartments, Louisville.

sense of value lies in Paragon's commitment to responsive management. The firm's service-oriented philosophy assures long-term satisfaction by both residents of its apartment communities and tenants of its office buildings.

The Paragon business style is to give its regional management teams the authority for making decisions. The Dallas headquarters sets the tempo, Lavin says, but the local offices do their own scouting and carry through on all the details. That means site selection, placing the land under contract, negotiating any necessary rezoning, dealing with architects and engineering firms, overseeing the hiring of contractors, capitalizing the project, and managing it.

All of this follows some extensive research in which the area's demographics are analyzed, and a judgment is made as to what is not addressed in that particular market. From there a project is designed and carried through to fit the neighborhood and market Paragon is pursuing. "We like to be market specific and sensitive," Lavin says, referring to some developers' penchant for building prototype projects and then plugging them in whether they fit the market or not.

Real estate development in a community is not all work. Becoming actively involved in the community is extremely important to Lavin. "Paragon and our employees actively support several community activities and civic institutions," says Lavin, who has been in Louisville approximately 12 years. "We feel it is important to contribute to, as well as receive from, the many benefits of Louisville." Paragon's corporate culture in Louisville includes support for the University of Louisville, Churchill Downs, public television, the Louisville Ballet, and other arts and civic endeavors.

A look into the future for the Louisville real estate market by Lavin brings many positive aspects to light. In his view, he expects the steady growth that has characterized the area for several years to continue. "Louisville may not experience the dynamic growth of some other cities, but consequently it also doesn't have the downside that many other cities have. That will be important for our industry in upcoming years," says the native of St. Louis.

Louisville community leadership is stronger than ever, according to Lavin. "The city and county governments are working together to generate significant and lasting changes to the metropolitan area." That, according to Lavin, will build a better community. "Louisville offers a tremendous quality of life, and is a great place to do business. We are obviously committed to the area on a long-term basis, and view Louisville as an outstanding opportunity for continued steady growth."

Paragon Place, in the bustling Hurstbourne area, houses the group's headquarters for Kentucky development.

HAROLD W. CATES & CO. INC.

"We're known as an aggressive firm. I've had people say to me, 'I understand you're very aggressive' as if it's a negative thing. I thank them for the compliment. We're not the type of firm that puts a sign up and waits for the phone to ring."

So says Harold W. Cates, president and founder of Harold W. Cates & Co. Inc., Louisville's specialist in office leasing and management, a market that has been growing for the 11 years that Cates has been active—make that aggressive—in it.

The firm handles a large percentage of the city's leasing and management activity, with almost equal division between downtown and the suburbs, and 95 percent of its business is local.

The company usually represents building owners or tenants, and often acts as a consultant on design and marketability, as in the case of two office towers planned near Louisville's City Hall, but its cornerstone is winning the space race from the ground up.

When Cates returned to his hometown several years ago, he brought with him marketing and sales skills developed during a successful tenure with IBM in Kentucky and Tennessee. He put his expertise to work first for several real estate developers and then in his own business. His venture has leased close to 2 million square feet of space in Louisville and its environs.

Deeply involved personally as well as professionally in the renaissance of the Main Street district of downtown Louisville, Cates has represented, among his other clients, many buildings on Main Street—including First National Tower, which gained him an office-leasing reputation. At the time—about 11 years ago—the 40-story building was still one-third empty, and Cates was engaged to fill it up in 2.5 years. He did it in one year, and his company expanded from that effort.

In the suburbs the firm represents a number of office parks and the three office towers in Watterson City.

Market Square is an example of the quality and style the office leasing and management firm enjoys representing.

Cates proclaims the office market healthy. "Space is being leased in both the downtown area and the suburbs," he notes. "By the time the new office parks and towers come on line, we will essentially be out of 'A-class' space." Occupancy has been running at about 90 percent downtown, and 85 percent in the suburbs.

"I'm optimistic about Louisville," Cates adds. "We're a city that doesn't grow fast—but we grow." Naturally, he would like to see that growth include more organizations with office-space needs.

According to Cates, "Louisville is one of the best-kept secrets in the United States. It's a great place to live, but nobody knows about it." He thinks that is beginning to change, a change that he believes will give the city a different kind of lease on life.

Standing in front of one of his past successes, First National Tower, Harold W. Cates looks ahead.

Photo by John Nation

Photo by Quadrant

Dept. of Surgery, U. of L. School of Medicine 322-323

University of Louisville 324

Chapter XIV
Quality of Life

Medical and educational institutions contribute to the quality of life of Louisville area residents.

Bellarmine College 325

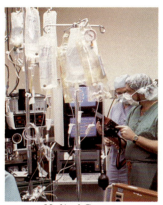

Medical Center Anesthesiologists 326-327

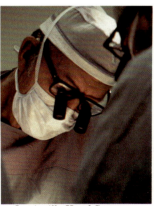

Louisville Hand Surgery 328-331

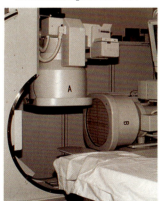

Medical Imaging Consultants 332-333

University Medical Associates, PSC 334-335

IN CELEBRATION OF LOUISVILLE

DEPARTMENT OF SURGERY, UNIVERSITY OF LOUISVILLE SCHOOL OF MEDICINE

In 1837, when Louisville was a bustling river town and the gateway to the western frontier, the University of Louisville Department of Surgery was created with a staff of three surgeons.

Medical education was as primitive as the times themselves. Students completed two years of classwork, then finished their training by informally following physicians on their rounds. It was an inauspicious beginning for what has become one of the most respected academic surgical programs in the world.

Today surgical "firsts" continue to characterize the achievements of the U of L Department of Surgery faculty.

In 1984 the first adult heart transplant in Kentucky was performed by Dr. Laman Gray, Jr. Two years later one of the first pediatric heart transplants in the nation and the world was performed by U of L surgeon Dr. Constantine Mavroudis. In 1987 the first successful pancreas transplant in the region was performed by Dr. Neal Garrison's U of L surgical team.

Doctors Serge Martinez and Michael Nolph pioneered the development of the cochlear implant (Ineraid), also known as the artificial ear. Other surgeons in the department also are renowned for special techniques in plastic surgery, spine surgery, lithotripsy in the treatment of kidney stones, complex heart surgery in the newborn, and surgical approaches to epilepsy.

The 46 faculty members in the department represent specialties in general, oncologic (cancer treatment), neurological, otolaryngologic (ear, nose, and throat), pediatric, plastic and reconstructive, cardiovascular, and urological surgery, as well as audiology and speech pathology.

The leadership and achievements of the faculty and resident staff members underscore the department's dedication to medical excellence. Faculty members consistently serve in leadership roles in national, regional, and specialty societies. No fewer than 10 major national surgical groups have been presided over by U of L Department of Surgery faculty in the past five years.

Faculty members continue to be recruited by many of the most distinguished medical schools in the United States and abroad. In fact, four recent former faculty or residents serve as chairpersons of other major medical school surgery departments.

That's why it's not surprising that the department's residency program is one of the most difficult in which to gain admittance. More than 700 students representing the country's finest medical schools apply annually for the 16 first-year positions available.

U of L students and residents consistently achieve superior scores on national board and in-training examinations, with more than 95 percent of them becoming certified by the American Specialty Boards.

Medical research continues to be an integral part of the Department of Surgery's teaching program. The Price Institute of Surgical Research, created by the Price family trust, provides the department with its own departmental bench laboratory research program, which is often shared by other university departments. Research fellows from leading institutions throughout the world have come to the Price Institute for advanced study.

The production of more than 300 publications each year reflects the highest quality inquiries into basic surgical pathophysiology. Faculty members have published medical journal articles that have become the standard on trauma and burns, laser use in the treatment of cancer, surgical management of reflux esophagitis and complicated hiatal hernia, and selective surgical treatment of melanoma (skin cancer).

**DEPARTMENT OF SURGERY EDUCATIONAL PROGRAMS
UNIVERSITY OF LOUISVILLE AFFILIATED HOSPITALS**

SPECIALTY	Humana Hospital University	Veterans Administration Medical Center	Norton Hospital	Kosair Children's Hospital	Jewish Hospital	Other
General Surgery	●	●	●	●	●	Trover Clinic
Neurological Surgery	●	●	●	●		
Orthopaedic Surgery	●	●	●	●	●	
Otolaryngology	●	●	●	●	●	
Communicative Disorders	●	●	●	●		Hazelwood Hospital
Pediatric Surgery	●			●		
Plastic & Reconstructive Surgery	●	●	●	●	●	
Microsurgery	●	●	●		●	
Surgical Oncology	●	●	●	●	●	J. Graham Brown Cancer Center
Thoracic & Cardiovascular Surgery	●	●	●	●	●	
Urology	●	●	●	●	●	

QUALITY OF LIFE

The faculty makes one of its most significant contributions in the area of patient care. With professional affiliations at five "teaching" hospitals, U of L surgeons bring the medical advances learned in the classroom and laboratory to the patient.

At Humana Hospital University the surgical faculty has taken the lead by extending private patient care in this modern and complete treatment center. Long-standing relationships also exist at The Norton Hospital, Jewish Hospital, Kosair Children's Hospital, and the Veterans Administration Medical Center.

The treatment of both inpatients and outpatients is provided, regardless of the individual's ability to pay. The amount of unreimbursed care provided by the faculty during a recent five-year period reached $12.8 million for inpatient care and $2.8 million for outpatients. These contributions reflect the dedication of the faculty members, who have underwritten the financial component of outpatient indigent surgical care at the Ambulatory Care Building.

The Emergency Surgical Services within the university's medical complex provide the only full-service, Level 1 trauma unit in the region. Clinical results for trauma injuries and burns, including lacerations to the bowel, pelvic fractures, and vascular injuries to the extremities are superior to any results reported in the world. The clinical results for other types of injuries match those of major trauma centers in this country.

The faculty also takes a major patient care and research role at the James Graham Brown Cancer Center with its Breast Care Center, considered the busiest such unit in the region.

At the University of Louisville there traditionally has been a close relationship among a distinguished surgical faculty, medical students, and the city's university hospitals—where indigent patients receive the best in medical care. This relationship has resulted in a world-recognized surgical program; dedicated medical care for the citizens of Louisville and the region, regardless of their ability to pay; and the education of thousands of medical students who serve the needs of all people, whether they live in Louisville or elsewhere in the nation.

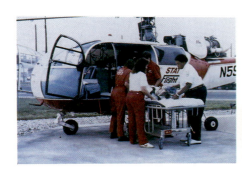

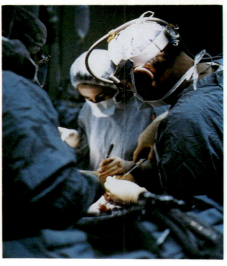

IN CELEBRATION OF LOUISVILLE

UNIVERSITY OF LOUISVILLE

Scarcely 10 years away from beginning its third century, the University of Louisville stands as one of the oldest urban universities in the United States.

However, the university—founded in 1798, when the city was only 20 years old and the Commonwealth of Kentucky only six—does not just point to that venerable heritage. It lives it, and its pursuit of excellence in education and concern for urban living is emphasized in president Donald C. Swain's comment: "Our objective is to become one of the best urban universities in the country."

All of its schools and colleges contribute to its "urban mission" that links the university to the business, educational, intellectual, and cultural aspects of the Louisville area. The university is deeply involved in economic development activities to benefit all of Kentucky. It is one of Kentucky's two major research universities.

Beyond the classroom and laboratories, the university's ties to the urban area are evident in numerous individual contributions of time and resources to the fabric of life. The most visible contribution in 1987 was Swain's term as president of the Louisville Chamber of Commerce, something of a rarity for a university president.

Adding important dimensions to life in Louisville are the schools of medicine, dentistry, and law, all among the oldest west of the Alleghenies. The medical school, the oldest of the three, celebrated its 150th anniversary in 1987. The impact of these schools' graduates on Kentucky is reflected in these figures: 42 percent of the state's physicians, 81 percent of its dentists, and 34 percent of its lawyers.

U of L, which joined the state's public system in 1970 after years as an independent, municipally supported institution, also boasts excellent programs in education, arts and sciences, urban affairs, business, nursing, music, and engineering—where its Speed Scientific School has national standing and supplies Kentucky with 48 percent of its engineers. An equine industry program, the first in the heart of the racing and breeding industries, has just been inaugurated.

The university—second largest in the state, with more than 20,000 students—offers 36 degrees and certificates in 146 fields of undergraduate, graduate, and professional study. There are three campuses: Belknap (main campus), about two miles

The Speed Scientific School, U of L's School of Engineering, features state-of-the-art facilities and equipment.

Rodin's The Thinker *sits in front of the University of Louisville's Administration Building. This cast of the statue was personally supervised by the artist and first appeared in this country at the 1904 World's Fair in St. Louis.*

from downtown; the Health Sciences Center in the downtown medical complex; and Shelby, home for the National Crime Prevention Institute and continuing education. Educational centers also are located in downtown Louisville and at Fort Knox.

One of the high points in U of L's recent history came with the establishment in 1985 of the University of Louisville's Grawemeyer Awards. The first was for music composition, and it included an annual $150,000 cash award endowed by alumnus H. Charles Grawemeyer. This is the largest such prize in the world, and has been described as the equivalent of the Nobel Prize. Beginning in 1988, two new annual awards will be awarded for great ideas in education and international affairs.

In the 1980s the University of Louisville gained further recognition by winning national collegiate championships: two in basketball under coach Denny Crum, continuing a tradition that goes back more than four decades, and two in intercollegiate debates.

QUALITY OF LIFE

BELLARMINE COLLEGE

"Learn to make a living. Learn to make a life."

That is the thrust at Louisville's Bellarmine College, founded in 1950 by the Louisville Catholic Archdiocese and now the largest private college in Kentucky. Although still Catholic in spirit, Bellarmine became independent several years ago.

The college's student profile shows a strong hometown flavor, but Bellarmine has set as one of its goals a broader student geographic area, while in no way disturbing its Louisville base. Enrollment, hovering around the 2,700 mark, is expected to grow at an annual rate of 3.5 percent in the next several years. Dr. Eugene V. Petrik, president, envisions the eventual growth of the student body to approximately 4,000.

The 16-building campus—located about five miles from the center of Louisville in the picturesque, residential Highlands area—sits amid 120 rolling acres, and that means it is blessed with plenty of room for expansion. Some of that has been accomplished in this decade through construction of five handsome teaching and multipurpose buildings.

Bellarmine prides itself on a faculty in which more than 80 percent hold the highest degree in their field, as against a national average of 60 percent. Since becoming president in 1973 Petrik has scoured the country in order to build a faculty that is diverse enough in background to offer what he considers a cosmopolitan view to students.

The students, who have the opportunity to study in 40 undergraduate and graduate programs, are a bit special themselves. In a typical freshman class, 40-45 percent come from the top 10 percent of their high school senior class, and 70-75 percent are in the top 25 percent. Success at graduation is reflected by 100-percent teacher placement for its education graduates, the acceptance of more than 90 percent of its applicants to law and medical schools, and the fact that accounting

graduates earn CPA status at a rate well above the national average.

Bellarmine is organized into a College of Arts and Sciences; the W. Fielding Rubel School of Business; and the Allan and Donna Lansing School of Nursing, Education, and Health Sciences. It has the largest graduate programs in Kentucky in nursing and business. Although the college offers the full range and quality of academic services of a larger, research-oriented university, it retains the intimate size and feeling of the classic liberal arts college with a student to faculty ratio of 15 to one.

Beyond all this, Bellarmine College serves the community through its Small Business Development Center and the Entrepreneur Society to help meet the area's needs to

Bellarmine, sitting on 120 rolling acres, is the largest private, independent college in Kentucky, having an enrollment of about 2,700 students, most of whom are from the Louisville area.

spawn and nurture businesses, through its huge holdings of business periodicals (one of the largest in the nation), through its professors and staff serving as consultants to businesses and service agencies and on more than 100 community boards, and through its frequent cultural events that are open to the public.

Students can study in more than 40 undergraduate and graduate programs in Bellarmine's College of Arts and Sciences and its schools of Business, Nursing, Education, and Health Sciences.

IN CELEBRATION OF LOUISVILLE

MEDICAL CENTER ANESTHESIOLOGISTS

Responsibility exists in all facets of human life. In the medical profession, responsibility refers to patients' lives and well-being. This characteristic is no more acutely visible than in the practice of anesthesiology. Safely guiding a patient through the complex changes in his or her physiology that occur during an operation is the job of the anesthesiologist.

In the United States approximately 20 million operations are performed each year. That volume of surgery is distributed over the practicing anesthesiologists and certified registered nurse anesthetists providing anesthesia care in this country.

The anesthesiologist is responsi-

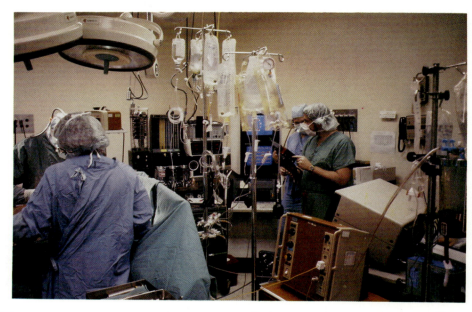

Patients are carefully monitored with state-of-the-art anesthetic management by Medical Center Anesthesiologists during the course of their surgery.

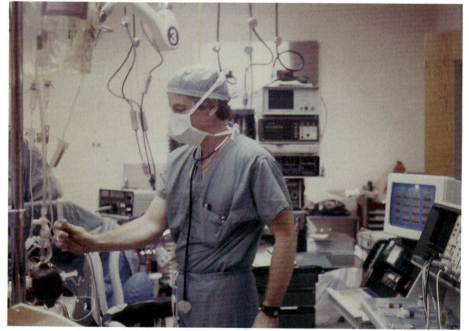

ble for a preoperative visit and medical assessment, intraoperative care, and the postoperative pain management and stabilization in the recovery room of each patient.

The anesthesiologist, in his preoperative assessment, must evaluate the suitability of the patient's physical condition for the surgical procedure and the anesthetic stress that that patient will experience. The choice of the anesthetic technique is made at this time, in consultation with the patient. Many patients who have not experienced surgery believe that general anesthesia, i.e., "going to sleep," is the best anesthetic for any surgical procedure. It is the role of the anesthesiologist to inform patients that general anesthesia is not always the best anesthetic for a particular operation.

Once the choice of anesthesia has been made, the major part of the care of the patient (the surgical time period) is handled on a minute-to-minute basis by the anesthesiologist. Changes in the patient's status during surgery occur at a much more rapid rate than they occur even in the intensive care unit. Medical Center Anesthesiologists has utilized the

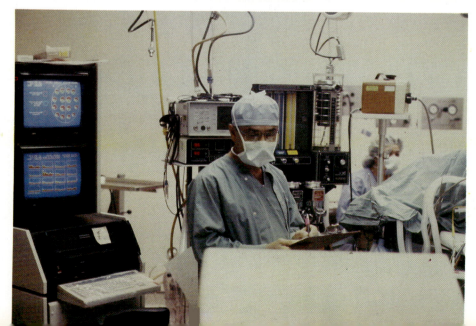

"anesthesia care team" concept to manage patients in this rapidly changing environment. A physician anesthesiologist and a nurse anesthetist participate in the care of patients in surgery.

Fourteen physicians and 27 nurse anesthetists comprise Medical Center Anesthesiologists, a group founded 25 years ago. Its practice is based at Louisville's Jewish Hospital, its Outpatient Care Center, and the Humana Heart Institute International at Humana Hospital Audubon. The anesthesia for all the cardiac heart transplants done in Kentucky has been given by this group. All three Kentucky recipients of the Jarvik-7 mechanical heart received their anesthesia from Medical Center Anesthesiologists.

Regional anesthesia, the administration of nerve blocks for hand surgery, is a specialty of Medical Center Anesthesiologists. One of the largest hand surgery practices in the nation is centered at Jewish Hospital. The refinement of nerve block anesthesia for hand surgery has meant that many patients are able to leave the hospital immediately upon completion of their surgery and have a pain-free day. The administration of the nerve block allows a patient to have a relatively stress-free surgical experience. The insult to the body is minimized by blocking the effect of pain upon the patient. This method of reducing the stress response of surgery allows the patient to have a smoother course in the postoperative period.

Because of its experience with cardiac and regional anesthesia, Medical Center Anesthesiologists has been able to accumulate information and initiate some research that has been beneficial to the overall specialty of anesthesiology. Accomplishing research in a private practice is atypical in the United States. Medical Center Anesthesiologists has shown initiative in this area, which has garnered the organization a national standing in its specialty. In hand surgery, Medical Center Anesthesiologists is recognized as having expertise in the anesthetic management of hand replantations. The anesthetic conduct of complex, lengthy surgical procedures is also an area of expertise for this group. In cardiac surgery, the group has done original work in monitoring the brain during open-heart surgery. These ventures into research have benefited the patients by affording them state-of-the-art anesthetic management.

In the area of education, a close tie with the University of Louisville and appointments to the clinical faculty of the Department of Anesthesiology have allowed this group to participate in residency training and afforded the opportunity to present regional seminars in anesthesia. These educational programs have allowed the group to pursue goals (remain inquisitive) and to attract top-notch recruits to the group.

Dramatic advances have been made in anesthesiology in the past 20 years, beginning with just making sure that the patient didn't move,

All three Kentucky recipients of the Jarvik-7 mechanical heart (shown here) received their anesthesia from Medical Center Anesthesiologists.

didn't remember, and didn't feel pain to the point where incredibly ill patients can survive very complex operations. Maintaining clinical expertise at the cutting edge of medical science allows the anesthesiologist to care for and safely protect even the most seriously ill patients more easily. It is the effort by this anesthesia group to maintain its knowledge at the highest level that enables it to routinely care for seriously ill patients and to have the ability to adjust to any untoward event that occurs in the healthy patient with ease.

It is the responsibility accepted by this professional team, the anesthesiologist and nurse anesthetist, to care for and protect the patient from the stresses of a surgical procedure.

Inherent in this responsibility is the maintenance of skills and the knowledge necessary to utilize those skills to deliver a safe anesthetic. As the conquest of outer space occupies the minds of many at the threshold of the twenty-first century, there are others (anesthesiologists among them) who are more concerned with the conquest of inner space—that place where all of those magnificent working parts run the landlocked spaceship we call the body.

IN CELEBRATION OF LOUISVILLE

LOUISVILLE HAND SURGERY

The hand is truly one of humanity's most remarkable gifts. It is a bone and sinew machine excelling the most precious of those born of the Industrial Revolution or of more recent times. It is a flexible, grasping mechanism that can handle almost anything of comparable size that's within its reach. It can dial a telephone, write a letter, wrap a birthday gift, plant a flower, type this article—or touch another hand. Its index finger can turn pages, indicate direction, and stab the air as the symbol of athletic superiority.

Though these abilities are taken for granted by most people, there are those who find them either painful or beyond their reach because of severe hand or arm injuries or a disabling disease such as rheumatoid arthritis.

In Louisville there is a surgical group called Louisville Hand Surgery that is dedicated to the treatment of such injuries and disabilities and, by the best means possible, to the restoration of the use of the hands, arms, and shoulders. The

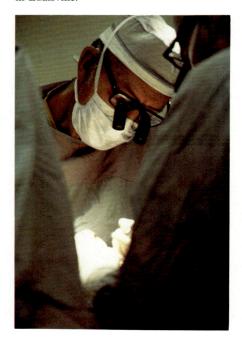

Dr. Harold E. Kleinert, facing camera, founder of Louisville Hand Surgery and a pioneer in microsurgery, performs surgery several times each week at Jewish Hospital in Louisville.

A shield for a finger is prepared for a patient by one of the members of Louisville Hand Surgery's orthotics departments.

band of eight surgeons has gained international stature through its success, its innovative techniques, its mastery of microsurgery, and the seemingly endless line of skilled surgeons it turns out for the rest of the world through its teaching/fellowship program.

The founder of the group is Dr. Harold E. Kleinert, who began taking fellows in hand surgery in 1960 and took his first partner, Dr. Joseph E. Kutz, who had been one of the early fellows, in 1963. The other partners, as of 1987, were doctors Erdogan Atasoy, Thomas W. Wolff, Tsu-Min Tsai, James M. Kleinert, Luis R. Scheker, and Warren C. Breidenbach.

This partnership, from its beginning, has encouraged teamwork, the sharing of ideas, research, and a dedication to both excellence and continued innovation. In addition, the Christine Kleinert Fellowship in Hand Surgery, named in honor of Kleinert's mother, brings surgeons from around the world to train with the partners in the free world's largest hand clinic.

Kleinert, who decided he wanted to be a doctor while growing up in a tiny Montana town with the colorful name of Sunburst, came to the University of Louisville School of Medicine in 1953 to do general surgery. He was put in charge of vascular surgery, directed the university's mobile cancer clinic, and started a hand surgery clinic. The hand practice got so large that he had to give up his teaching position, and that's when he began the fellowship program that has since trained more than 500 doctors in hand and microsurgery—the latter developing just since the early 1970s.

The clinic takes 16 fellows each year, eight Americans and eight foreigners, out of an average 50 to 70 applicants who have finished earlier training in either orthopedics, general surgery, or plastic surgery. The fellowship year in hand surgery qualifies a surgeon in that specialty.

Where do the foreigners come from? "Some come from Japan, they come from China [both Taiwan and the Mainland], Germany, England," Kleinert says. "We've probably trained most hand surgeons in England . . . some from Iron Curtain countries such as Poland . . . We've had quite a contact with Yugoslavia . . . Singapore pays their own fellow, and we have agreed to take their top person each year."

The bulk of the clinic's patients come from the Louisville metropolitan area and communities through-

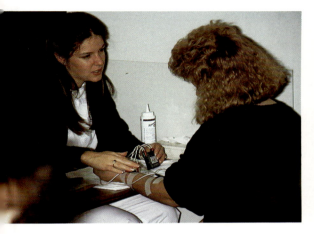

A recovering patient spends time in Louisville Hand Surgery's physical therapy department.

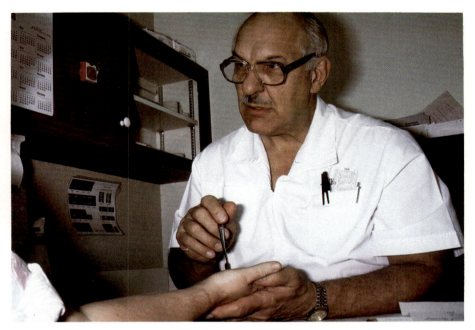

Dr. Kutz spends time each week in the group's offices, seeing patients on a regular basis.

out Kentucky, Indiana, Tennessee, West Virginia, Ohio, Illinois, and Missouri, but others come from practically every state and from many foreign countries. New patients at the clinic, located near the giant medical complex just east of downtown, usually number about 8,500 a year. Approximately 6,500 patients each year undergo surgery performed by the group's surgeons, usually at nearby Jewish Hospital. As many as 300 rheumatoid arthritis reconstructions, 90 replantations of amputated upper and lower extremities or parts thereof, 25 toe-to-hand transfers, and 60 free flaps (muscle, bone, or skin-tissue grafts) may take place in a given year.

In the surgeons' work, which includes probably more replantations than have been done anywhere in the world and among the first in the world performed by microsurgery, there is an air of supreme confidence and professionalism as well as an intense concern for the patient. Precision is one of the keys to success in the operating room because in many cases the surgeons are dealing with the tiniest of body parts—a nerve graft, for instance—where the work can be done only under magnification and with sutures that can hardly be seen with the naked eye.

"We have changed the hand-surgery world," says Kleinert. "As a matter of fact, the method that is now used all over the world to repair flexor tendons [those that bend the fingers] was developed here. Before they were infrequently repaired primarily . . . [but now] are repaired at the time of injury under magnification, using dynamic splints afterward. Other things that we're known as pioneers for are helping to develop the replantation field, and the use of microsurgery."

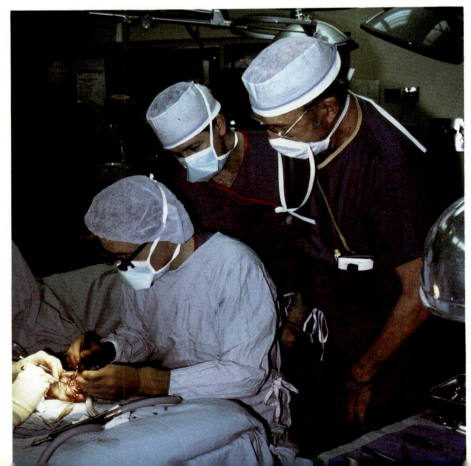

There always seems to be a team of Louisville Hand Surgery surgeons scrubbed and at work in the operating rooms at Jewish Hospital, located in the city's giant medical complex near downtown.

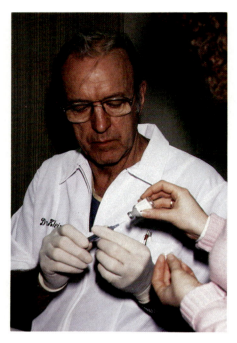

Dr. Kleinert prepares to administer an injection while seeing patients in his office during times when he's not in surgery.

In addition to the flexor tendon repair, other major accomplishments of the group include the world's first bilateral arm replantation, the first reported repairs on digital arteries, the first vascularized epiphyseal bone transfer, and one of the first complete hand transfers. Since so much of their work is innovative, the group's doctors also have contributed mightily to their specialties by creating, for microsurgery, an operating microscope and microsurgery instruments and sutures, and, for regular hand surgery, special instruments that serve them better than ordinary surgical instruments and splinting techniques that have advanced the specialty greatly.

However, the doctors' truest measure of value to their fellow man is the consistency of their work, and the untiring dedication to bettering the life opportunities for patients who come to them with injuries or disabling problems. Their response to emergencies is immediate and with professional precision, whether it be the replantation of a severed finger of Neil Armstrong, the first man on the moon, or care of a person injured in a farm, industrial, home, sporting, or highway accident.

Along with that there is the constant scheduled surgery for their general patients with similar problems, a schedule that finds all the partners and fellows in the operating room several days a week. Then, of course, there's the followup appointments and the appointments of new and continuing patients, both of which keep the offices and waiting rooms full most of the time. The patient load ranges from professional athletes such as former Cincinnati Bengals quarterback Ken Anderson during his playing days, and several St. Louis, Cincinnati, and Pittsburgh baseball players, to those with minor hand disorders, injuries, nerve damage, congenital deformities, rheumatoid arthritis, and other crippling diseases.

After the surgical work is done, many patients are involved with the group's Therapy Services, established in the 1970s, for therapy, rehabilitation, and joint-protection and back-to-work programs. Like the surgeons, the group's Therapy Services staff is in the vanguard in its field—using programs supported by testing, education, counseling, and advanced technology. The therapists are involved in research on such things as the measurement of function and the most effective ways to implement home exercise. In addition, they have pioneered the use of nerve-stimulation technology.

In physical therapy the patient is guided through an individualized series of exercises to increase strength, range of motion, and physical function, and several tests and biofeedback are used to monitor the patient's condition and progress. Also, patients may undergo physical reeducation of muscles and nerves, as well as pain control—all a part of returning to a fruitful life.

In occupational therapy, patients receive functional training and testing, and sensory reeducation in preparation for meeting the demands of daily work life. In the back-to-work program, an injured worker is made ready for a return to employment through these steps: a job analysis, an evaluation of the patient's work capacity, exercise (known as work hardening) in which the patient tackles the demands of his or her pre-injury job, and job placement. In the work-hardening phase, the therapy unit offers work simulators for, among others, such things as driving a bus, car, or truck; digging a ditch; swinging a hammer; swinging a golf club; using a trowel; and throwing a ball.

In the event an injured worker cannot return to his or her previous employer, a rehabilitation counselor analyzes the patient's work skills to identify realistic job alternatives, and then Louisville Hand Surgery assists in the search for a suitable job and helps the individual make full use of available state and private re-

Dr. Joseph E. Kutz, the first of Dr. Kleinert's partners, stays busy in surgery, as do all the group's partners and fellows in training.

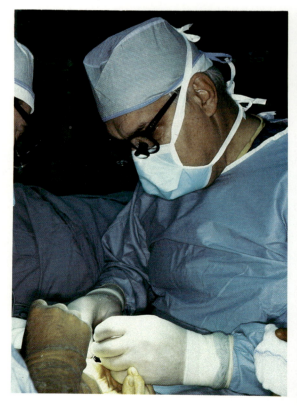

QUALITY OF LIFE

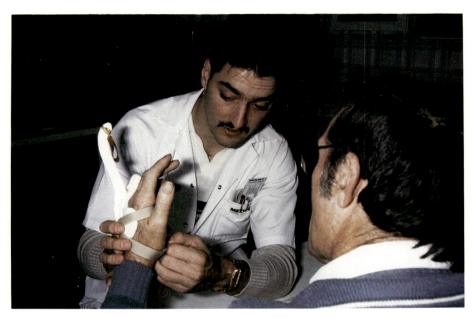

Patients sometimes need hand braces during their recovery, and those devices are designed and created in the orthotics department.

sources while seeking employment.

In the group's joint-protection program, which falls into the preventive-medicine category, patients with rheumatoid arthritis are trained in techniques they can use every day to protect joints from flare-ups and further deformity. A therapist designs individualized exercise programs to help these patients increase flexibility and strength, and maintain maximum joint health.

Because the healing of a hand or arm often requires that it be held in a set position and yet allowed to move in a way that promotes recovery, braces and other adaptive aids are needed. The group's Orthotics Department designs and crafts these braces and aids so they not only meet the requirements but harmonize with the individual's health requirements and life-style. Neither artistry nor science is taken for granted as orthotists work closely with surgeons, referring physicians, and therapists in crafting each brace and aid and then train each patient in their use.

To enhance Louisville Hand Surgery's already glittering record in research, development of techniques and procedures, training of other hand-care professionals, and education, the group formed the Christine M. Kleinert Institute for Hand and Microsurgery in 1987. The focus of the institute is threefold:
—To conduct research that will significantly expand the frontiers of hand surgery and microsurgery;
—To put research findings in a form that doctors may readily be put to use in bettering patient care; and
—To train surgeons and physicians from around the world in the latest developments in both the theory and practice of hand surgery and microsurgery.

Several of the group's preexisting departments have joined the institute in an effort to achieve the stated goals. Among them are the fellowship program, the associates' residency program, the physicians' observer program, the research department, and media services—which includes photography, medical illustration, display, and video services.

Partners in the Louisville Hand Surgery group consist of (seated, from left): Joseph E. Kutz, M.D.; Harold E. Kleinert, M.D.; and James M. Kleinert, M.D. In the back row (from left): Thomas W. Wolff, M.D.; Tsu-Min Tsai, M.D.; Luis R. Scheker, M.D., and Warren C. Breidenbach, M.D. Not present is Erdogan Atasoy, M.D.

IN CELEBRATION OF LOUISVILLE

MEDICAL IMAGING CONSULTANTS

If you could take an X-ray of Louisville's medical community, you would find a picture of robust health, with signs of unlimited growth potential and a tendency to be on the cutting edge of dramatic breakthroughs in technology.

It is very likely you would choose Medical Imaging Consultants to read that X-ray and diagnose the patient.

Medical Imaging Consultants, with 15 radiologists, is the largest group of its kind in Kentucky, having started as a small partnership but incorporating in 1968 at Louisville's St. Joseph Infirmary, a hospital founded in 1836 by the Sisters of Charity of Nazareth, Kentucky.

Some of the members of the group trace their association back to residency days at St. Joseph, and recall fondly Dr. Sidney Johnson as their mentor and example in the field of radiology. He was a professor of anatomy and radiology at the University of Louisville School of Medicine, and director of the radiology department at St. Joseph from 1926 to 1961.

Dr. Johnson was succeeded by Dr. Edward Maxwell, his first associate at St. Joseph. Under their direction, 26 residents completed training at St. Joseph, many of whom practice in Louisville and nearby communities in Kentucky and southern Indiana. In 1970 St. Joseph Infirmary was purchased by Extendicare, later to become Humana, and was operated for 10 years before being replaced by Humana Hospital Audubon.

Medical Imaging Consultants currently provides radiology coverage to Humana Hospital Audubon; Humana Hospital Suburban, constructed in 1973; and Our Lady of Peace Hospital, a psychiatric hospital. The group offers a full range of service, including regular X-ray, CT scans, Ultrasound, Mammography,

Dr. Sidney Johnson founded the partnership that has grown into Medical Imaging Consultants and still serves as something of a spiritual leader to the group.

Angiography, and Magnetic Resonance Imaging at the Humana hospitals, and Louisville Imaging Services, an outpatient imaging center.

Radiology is not just a picture show. It is a highly technical and integral part of the health-sciences scene, a diagnostic field that requires its specialists to be acutely aware of all the functions of the body and its health needs. Says Dr. Bernard F. Sams, a spokesman for the group: "Many of us choose radiology because it lets us stay in all areas of medicine—internal medicine, obstetrics, pediatrics, orthopedics; not being limited to just one segment makes it more fascinating. We like the diagnostic end of medicine, trying to determine what's wrong with the patient, and are less interested in the treatment area." Even though they do not treat a patient, the radiologist often has input with the physician on the course of treatment, says Dr. Maxwell, the senior member of the group.

Members of the group, many of whom are graduates of the University of Louisville School of Medicine and have associations with the school for teaching, find themselves in specialties within the radiology field. Dr. John Rice, one of the group's three neuroradiologists, was instrumental in getting magnetic

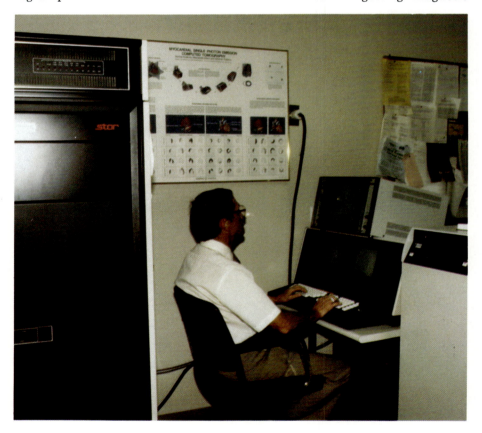

Dr. Burke Casper uses equipment that reflects the latest in diagnostic means in nuclear cardiology.

Magnetic Resonance Imaging is one of the major advances of recent years in the radiology field.

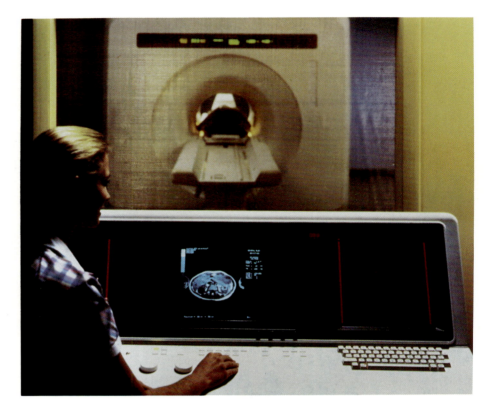

resonance equipment at Humana Audubon's Neuro-Science Center of Excellence, putting it in the forefront of that means of diagnosis.

Drs. Curry and Meyers point out that mammography and ultrasound, two of the many special procedures, are finding increased applications. The former is particularly useful in early detection of breast cancer, and the latter has expanded far beyond its early value in studying early pregnancy into such things as evaluating blood vessels and masses of all kinds in the abdomen. Also, ultrasound is used in blood-flow studies on aged people who may be having small strokes.

Radiology calls for looking at the big picture, says Dr. Sams. "I've always felt that the difference between the radiologist and the other subspecialists who learned radiology (e.g. the orthopedist, whose interest is in the bones, or the pulmonary specialist, who is focusing on the lungs), is that the radiologist is responsible for the entire film from margin to margin, which crosses every section of specialties."

"We may be looking at the bone for a fracture, but we're also looking at the entire region on the film for anything else we can detect—foreign bodies, calcifications, anything suspicious... obviously, if we find anything unusual, we inform the physician."

Because it lends itself so well to a marriage with computerization, radiology is expected to grow as fast if not faster and more technically than its compatriot specialties. "This is a very technically oriented specialty," explains Dr. Sams, "with CT scans and magnetic resonance leading the way in that regard. X-ray images are being digitalized, and this technique will be used more and more in routine X-ray interpretation," he says.

In the future radiologists can expect digitalized images on a screen or on photographic plates instead of the films that are now used. "These techniques," he adds, "promise a much broader background image, one that will show soft tissue in one instant and, with the turn of a knob, the bone structure in another."

Dr. Sams envisions the day when a radiologist will sit before a bank of television monitors bringing up images and dialing through them for study and interpretation before they are stored on magnetic tape. It is a picture that promises more success for the health sciences.

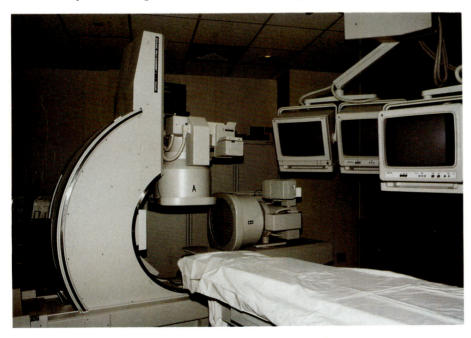

Study of a patient's blood flow in the brain is done in a neurovascular suite.

333

IN CELEBRATION OF LOUISVILLE

UNIVERSITY MEDICAL ASSOCIATES, PSC

In a city that boasts an impressive medical community, University Medical Associates, PSC, is a young, aggressive, and innovative group of physicians who are also full-time faculty members of the Department of Medicine in the University of Louisville's School of Medicine—they play a leading role in the health of the greater community of Louisville and Jefferson County.

The group, which represents the largest internal medicine specialty and subspecialty practice in Kentucky, has a full-service orientation. Its practice encompasses medical care in all aspects of clinical medicine: cancer medicine, cardiology, endocrinology, gastroenterology/hepatology, general internal medicine, hematology, infectious diseases, nephrology, pulmonary medicine, and rheumatology. Basically, the physicians are involved in tertiary care, the person a family doctor turns to when he or she has a very sick patient, such as one with heart trouble or cancer.

There are 75 physicians associated with the group, which was founded in 1976 under another name and renamed University Medical Associates in 1982. Requirements for being a shareholder include being a physician and a member of the full-time faculty at the University of Louisville. Its uniqueness stems from its relationship with the University of Louisville, which allows close ties between the medical research going on at the University and the application of that research in patient care.

This association with the University of Louisville School of Medicine is consistent with the University's tradition for helping to serve the health needs of its community, as well as the entire Ohio Valley and beyond to major cities across the country. The Medical School has educated countless physicians and surgeons, many of whom have chosen to practice in the area, making it one of the region's finest for health care. It has even moved some to say if a per-

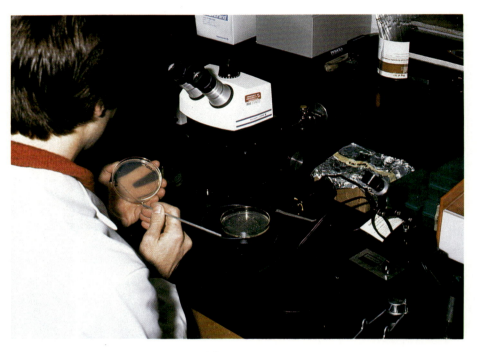

Clinical laboratories perform many specialized services.

son is going to get sick, Louisville is the place to do it because there are so many skilled doctors locally.

With most of its offices in the Ambulatory Care Building, the group's physicians are near enough to the heart of Louisville's downtown medical center to keep in touch with the pulse of health care in the area. Nephrology specialists are located in the nearby Kidney Disease Program Building, and those practicing in cancer medicine have offices in the James Graham Brown Cancer Center (across the street from the Ambulatory Care Building).

The group is heavily involved in subspecialty work at Norton Hospital, including noninvasive and inva-

Research laboratories help improve disease detection, diagnosis, and treatment.

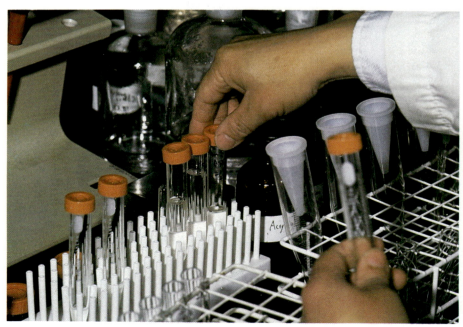

QUALITY OF LIFE

sive cardiology, infectious diseases, and cancer medicine. It's involved in Jewish Hospital's large organ-transplant program, in all medical facets of Humana Hospital-University of Louisville, and in the lipid clinic at Humana Hospital Audubon. Almost all of the Associates have appointments to practically every hospital in the city, especially to each of the downtown hospitals.

Because of the consultative nature of its practice, the University Medical Associates' location in the medical center is prime to the practice. "We have to be able to go when another doctor feels he has a patient sick enough to be seen by us," says Dr. Joseph C. Allegra, Chairman of the Board and President of University Medical Associates. "We are a service-oriented group," he continues, "and we think we add significantly to the quality of life of the people living in Louisville."

That factor has a bit of a twist to it, he believes. "It's sort of like [Kosair] Children's Hospital in that you know it's there, but you hope you never need to use it—but it's comforting to know that it is there," he says. "We think that we sort of fit into that category in the sense that we offer full-service, state-of-the-art medicine to the citizens of Louisville, so that if they get a significant illness, they don't have to travel to New York or to Texas or to the Mayo Clinic or the Cleveland Clinic for treatment. They can get just about anything that they might need with the same degree of expertise right here in Louisville."

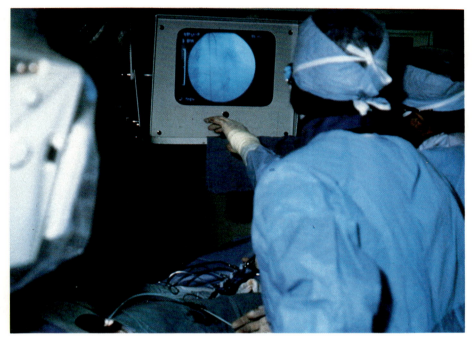

Cardiology physicians performing a cardiac catheterization.

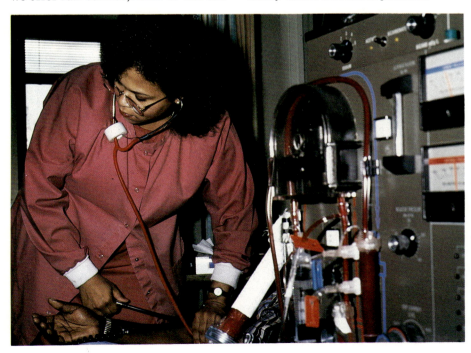

Chronic dialysis treatment for patients with kidney disease and related problems.

As if meeting the health needs of Louisville and area citizens isn't enough, members of University Medical Associates and/or their spouses are heavily involved in community, civic, and charitable projects. Among them are service on a number of boards tied to the arts community, the Kidney Foundation, and the Arthritis Foundation; contributions to the arts; support for the area's schools; and support for the county's very successful Junior Achievement program aimed at teenagers with designs on entrepreneurship.

So, while University Medical Associates can help write prescriptions for the good health of the community, it also sees a need to get involved in the greater health of Louisville and its environs with an eye toward helping to fulfill the future promise of the Associates' chosen hometown. That kind of involvement has a promise of its own: an infusion of energy and enthusiasm that should help Louisville grow, prosper, and gain the strength to flex its economic and life-style muscles in a way that will beckon new blood to the area.

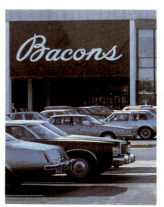
J. Bacon & Sons
Company 338-339

Hunt Tractor, Inc. 340

Kroger Company 344-345

Kentucky Fried Chicken
346-347

Photo by Mark E. Gibson

Chapter XV
The Marketplace

Louisville's retail establishments, service industries, and products are enjoyed by residents and visitors to the area.

Galt House 341

Fashion Shops of Kentucky 342-343

Ehrler's Stores 348-349

Winn-Dixie Stores, Inc. 350-351

The Paul Schultz Companies 352-353

A. Arnold & Son Worldwide Moving & Storage 354

IN CELEBRATION OF LOUISVILLE

J. BACON & SONS COMPANY

PAST:

The organization, a vital part of Louisville's commercial life since its founding as J. Bacon & Sons in 1845 by Jeremiah Bacon, operates five stores in the area (one is across the Ohio River in Jeffersonville, Indiana), and will soon add a sixth as part of the company's renovation and expansion plans for 1988 and 1989. Remodeling of two of its existing outlets also is part of that program.

Location was a major concern of Jeremiah Bacon, too. Before opening his store he made a careful survey of all the turnpikes and roads leading into the city from the east, and chose a site that afforded him the opportunity to capitalize on the heaviest traffic. As stagecoaches and the like gave way to public transportation, the entrepreneur's little retail venture prospered so that he had to add several stories to the original operation.

That growth continued at such a rate as to inspire Bacon to build a duplicate addition to the old store in 1876 and merge the two into one large emporium, in which he added a thriving wholesale operation to his already hardy retail business. Eventually the enterprise even outgrew those quarters, requiring the construction of a more spacious store—which opened in 1901 on Market Street near Fourth Street.

However, Bacon's three sons, who then were running the business, tired of the huge organization, sold the company, and retired from retailing in 1903. In 1914 Bacons was acquired by Mercantile Stores Company, Inc., of Wilmington, Delaware, making the store group the oldest Mercantile division in the United States.

Bacons is the major retailer in the Louisville Galleria, the focal point of a rebounding downtown business area.

PRESENT:

Bacons stores are strategically located in the Louisville area. Those locations are in the busy, sparkling, $50-million Louisville Galleria that has revitalized retailing downtown; Shively, which serves south-central and southwestern Jefferson County; St. Matthews, for the near East End; Bashford Manor Mall, in southeastern Jefferson County; and the soon-to-be-opened store in the Mall in St. Matthews, which is located farther out in the East End.

In 1987 Bacons acquired the L.S. Ayres store in the Mall in St. Matthews. The 125,000-square-foot store will be completely remodeled and expanded, and will open in the fall of 1988.

The merchandise in this store will be devoted solely to menswear, ladies' sportswear, dresses, lingerie, cosmetics, shoes, and accessories. This will be the largest store in the metro Louisville market to feature

THE MARKETPLACE

For the Bashford Manor Mall in eastern Louisville, Bacons is a major attraction and home to the chain's administrative offices.

only ready-to-wear merchandise. This space will serve to offer the largest array of merchandise catering to all life-styles.

The existing St. Matthews store will be totally remodeled and open in the spring of 1989 as a Bacons Home Center. The home center will feature a furniture gallery, linens, draperies, housewares, china, luggage, gifts, carpeting, lamps, stationery, and custom window draperies.

Upon completion of St. Matthews Home Center, the Bashford Manor Store will be completely updated, featuring a major expansion of the ready-to-wear departments that include menswear, ladies' sportswear and dresses, children's wear, ladies' shoes, lingerie, cosmetics, and accessories.

Bacons' upscaling strategy is a dramatic departure from its beginnings, when it operated as a major dry-goods store of its day. However, keeping pace with Louisville has always been central to the merchandising philosophy of Bacons, the oldest retailing name in Kentucky. That philosophy, combined with sound policies and an intense interest in good personnel and customer relations, has earned J. Bacon & Sons Company the kind of deep and lasting acceptance that doubtless will carry it into a third century of service to the community.

The Bacons store is the cornerstone of a large shopping center in Shively, a heavily populated southwestern suburb of Louisville.

339

IN CELEBRATION OF LOUISVILLE

HUNT TRACTOR, INC.

Although its roots are "down on the farm" "downtown" will always be home to Hunt Tractor.

In the early 1940s, faced with a move from rural Meade County dictated by annexation of the family farm and business site into the sprawling Fort Knox military complex, the Hunt family seized the opportunity to bring their Case agricultural machinery franchise to Louisville. This decision proved to be an important first step in response to a developing market. As anticipated, the site selected near the bustling Bourbon Stock Yards delivered a dependable flow of prospective customers. An increasing demand for improved automation and tractive power to upgrade rapidly expanding tillage and harvest operations fueled the Hunts' determination to provide quality equipment supported by concerned and competent service.

Ensuring such support then, as now, Hunt Tractor emphasizes to its clientele active owner involvement and accessibility. "We recognize that our capacity to successfully effect small or large equipment transactions is a function of our sensitivity to each individual customer's concerns." This expressed philosophy of Roy Hunt and his son, Scott, remains constant despite significantly extended product lines and a diversified customer base. As family farms gave way to subdivisions and industrial parks, the "Tractor" with Hunt came to refer predominantly to excavating and trenching equipment. Currently more than 90 percent of the firm's annual volume is generated by the sale and rental of construction-related machinery.

Hunt's affiliation since 1922 with the J.I. Case Company underscores its flexibility and responsiveness to a changing market. Originally acclaimed for development of the threshing machine and agricultural applications of the steam engine, Case presently ranks as the second-largest producer of construction equipment in the United States.

The vast majority of Hunt's business is generated from the metro area and surrounding counties in Kentucky and southern Indiana. It is that factor, unlikely to change in the foreseeable future, that sustains Hunt Tractor's earnest commitment to downtown Louisville. "The additional space requirements of separate facilities for construction machinery rentals and turf-maintenance equipment demanded we consider relocating out of the downtown area. Ultimately however, neither logic nor inclination would allow such a move," Roy explains. "We have uncongested access to three major interstates, and we're across the street from our primary financial partner, Stock Yards Bank. Plus, there's the invaluable recognition and continuity inherent with more than 40 years in the same location."

A recent major renovation and 13,000-square-foot addition to its main building at 1000 East Market Street confirms Hunt Tractor's physical and fiscal commitment to the area. Scott's third-generation outlook is emphatic. "We consider our downtown tradition a significant asset well worthy of reinvestment," he says. "This is where we want to be."

Forty years at the same East Market Street location assures Hunt Tractor customers of the firm's reliability and continuity when buying or leasing construction or agricultural machinery.

THE MARKETPLACE

GALT HOUSE, GALT HOUSE EAST, EXECUTIVE INN, EXECUTIVE WEST

It is said that one cannot be everything to everybody. However, as in the George and Ira Gershwin composition: "It ain't necessarily so."

Examples include the Galt House, the Galt House East, the Executive Inn, and the Executive West.

These hotels, constructed and owned locally by The Home Supply Co., comprise a total of more than 2,200 sleeping rooms and have become a force in Louisville's economy and convention-city reputation since 1963. The Executive Inn was opened that year just in time for the NCAA's Final Four basketball tournament being played at Freedom Hall, a marriage of Louisville's love of the sport and its need for a new hotel.

Following that opening in the Standiford Field/Kentucky Fair and Exposition Center area, the Galt House opening in 1972—only a short walk from Commonwealth Convention Center—helped trigger a revival of Louisville's riverfront, the Executive West joined the Executive Inn in the airport/exposition center corridor, and the all-suite Galt House East was erected across the street from the Galt House.

The four hotels are within six or seven miles of each other by interstate highway, and have carved out market niches that touch just about any type of customer, says Paul Luersen, general manager of the units.

He explains: "For example, the Executive Inn and Executive West are basically airport hotels, but at the same time we are the headquarters hotel for the Kentucky Fair and Exposition Center. And at the same time the Executive Inn's Empire Room has been one of the leading hotel restaurants in the community for 25 years. Executive West, with its 600 rooms, has a nice share of the large-meeting market, with a ballroom that can feed 1,200 ... also both are suburban hotels."

Of the 1,200-room Galt House complex, Luersen notes, "We are in prime position to capture national conventions that need 1,100 rooms, plus banquet, meeting, and exhibition space." The Galt House East grand ballroom can host 2,500 people for a dinner, and a ballroom at the Galt House can accommodate 1,200. Being on the riverfront in the downtown area and near popular restaurants and cultural centers give the Galt houses additional appeal.

It is not only the buildings that make the hotels special, Luersen says. Something he calls "Louisville sincerity" has contributed to the facilities' success. "Our people are friendly enough to be your next-door neighbor," he says, noting also that being independent and locally owned eliminates the bureaucracy plaguing chain hotels and creates a more stable work force (some have been employees for 20 years or more).

In that respect, Luersen recalls a remark by a guest: "Your beds sleep as well as any other hotel's, but your people are so friendly—and in doing business with your hotel, I feel like I'm doing business with a friend."

That is the idea, emphasizes Luersen.

Galt House

Executive Inn

IN CELEBRATION OF LOUISVILLE

FASHION SHOPS OF KENTUCKY

"Business in millions, profits in pennies."

That is the billboard message that caught the eye and the fancy of Clarence Benjamin many years ago during a New York City visit. He liked the idea so much that it has been the wellspring from which he and his family have quenched the thirst for style and value in women's wear for nearly 60 years.

At 23 years of age the entrepreneur opened the first Fashion Shop, a women's clothing store, in 1930 in New Albany, Indiana, just across the Ohio River from Louisville, following an apprenticeship in the family's original business—a coat-manufacturing firm founded, also in New Albany, by his father, Louis, in 1910. Benjamin has seen the family's business move into its fourth generation, with a daughter and son and grandchildren now involved.

From that single store, which the octogenarian still operates in addition to two others, has grown a chain of 15, primarily in the Falls Cities area. Benjamin's son, Clarence Jr., has a store in downtown Louisville, and the latter's two sons have four stores in central Indiana. However, the major part of the family-business story revolves around Benjamin's daughter, Ann B. Levine, and her four children, who operate Fashion Shops of Kentucky—composed of five stores in Louisville, two in Lexington, and one in Elizabethtown.

Following most of the retail philosophies she learned from her father, especially the need for giving women a large selection and savings in price, Mrs. Levine, president, has built a chain that has sales volume in excess of $30 million and 325 employees working in retail and distribution. The merchandise, most of which is American-made, includes many nationally known labels, in petite, junior, regular, and plus sizes. Prices at the self-service Fashion Shops range from 20 percent to 50 percent below those on the same merchandise at large department stores.

Clarence Benjamin (seated) opened the first Fashion Shop in New Albany, Indiana, in 1930. Today the same tradition of family management is carried out by Ann Benjamin Levine (standing), daughter of the founder and president of Fashion Shops of Kentucky.

Ann Levine has said that the venture, which she began with her former husband in the early 1960s, is a success because it adheres to her father's formula of being family managed—including responsibilities of finances, buying, and advertising. This factor makes for low overhead, and that savings is passed along to the consumer, she notes.

In addition, the businesswoman credits loyalty among customers for a great deal of the success. "Many customers have moved out of Louisville," she says, "but they come back twice a year and go from store to store to buy things." Sometimes those return trips are on New Year's Day, pioneered by Fashion Shops as a business day in Louisville.

Many of her employees work in the corporate headquarters and warehouse building in a giant industrial park on the eastern edge of Louisville. The vivacious Ann Levine is proud to say that the family touch in her firm goes well beyond her children and father. "This is not a very sophisticated setup," she explains. "We have a family atmosphere throughout the organization. We train a lot of people and promote from within, constantly offering a career opportunity. I am very accessible... we're on a first-name basis. And I am in every store at least once a week."

However, there is nothing unsophisticated about the way her company operates in the marketplace:

THE MARKETPLACE

searching and buying in the New York, Atlanta, Los Angeles, and Dallas merchandise marts. The corporation buys from more than 3,000 vendors, and it has four trucks always rolling toward appointed rounds—where merchandise is either loaded at the warehouse or delivered to outlets.

According to a magazine account of a few years ago, Ann Levine characterized the teamwork of her employees thusly: "When something we've been waiting for comes in, even if it's a holiday, we summon everybody—family and staff—to mark the goods and get it to the stores promptly. My children and I have even helped load the trucks."

It has not always been jingling cash registers for Levine and her family. As recent as 1980, when she became sole owner of Fashion Shops of Kentucky, the chain was in substantial debt. Showing the same determination that brought her father

Ann Benjamin Levine (seated) and Clarence Benjamin (with telephone) are joined by (from left) David Levine, Benjamin Levine, Vycki Goldenberg, and Laurance Levine, sons and daughter of Mrs. Levine and all actively involved in the business.

back from the disaster of the 1937 flood, Levine pulled the business together and "paid off every dime in 18 months." She shares the credit for that with her family, workers, and customers.

Aiding her at the helm of the operation are her eldest son, David L. Levine, a graduate of Tulane University and vice-president; and her daughter, Vycki Goldenberg, a graduate of the University of Denver and of a training program with the May Company, who serves as secretary. Two younger sons, Laurance and Benjamin, recent graduates of Indiana University and the University of Colorado, respectively, also work in the business.

Ann Levine sees larger Fashion Shops in the future, but the Benjamin basics will still serve as the cornerstones of those stores: Business in millions, profits in pennies.

The Fashion Shops of Kentucky feature name-brand women's merchandise at attractive prices. Here, the quality is checked by David and Laurance Levine, and Vycki Goldenberg.

IN CELEBRATION OF LOUISVILLE

KROGER COMPANY

The Kroger Company is not waiting for the next decade. As far as the company is concerned, the 1990s are here because it already has what it calls the "Store of the 1990s," an all-purpose, complete store catering to practically every taste and most needs of any family.

In 1987 Kroger, whose home base is in Cincinnati, Ohio, just a little more than 100 miles to the northeast of Louisville, opened its first three Louisville "future stores," and eight more are planned for the area in 1988. Kroger in Louisville believes its early move into the 1990s coincides with the on-the-move stance the city has developed over the past few years. That puts Kroger right in step with the city, company officials believe.

Kroger's Store of the 1990s is easily recognizable from the moment one walks through the door, thanks to a decor that features the high-technology neon and contemporary design that provides a futuristic feel. Each store gives the shopper the impression of a small city, with 300 to 400 employees and more of what are being called by Kroger "full-service shoppes" than any of its competitors in the area.

These shops, also dubbed "Shoppes To Go," invite a shopper to come into the store, go to the shop of his choice, buy what is needed or wanted, and leave the store easily, without waiting in the normal grocery checkout lines. The individual shops include a full-service pharmacy; gourmet foods; a large restaurant; soft-serve frozen yogurt; a New York-style delicatessen; cheeses; custom-made pizza; pastry; European crusty breads; salad bar; produce; a floral shop featuring worldwide delivery; a nutrition center; fresh seafood; custom-cut meat; card and party department; books and magazines; general merchandise; film and video, including movie rental; a financial center; and a customer-service center.

These stores have been several years in the planning, with scru-

Hundreds of people lined up for the opening of one of three "Stores of the 1990s" that Kroger opened in Louisville in 1987.

pulous attention paid to detail and convenience. It is the store that customers have said they want, based on needs, a Kroger official says. Research has shown that 80 percent of Kroger customers are women, and 50 percent to 60 percent of them work, making the idea of "one stop does it all" particularly enticing, Kroger officials believe. The days of shopping around appear to be gone.

Alysheba, winner of the 1987 Kentucky Derby, wore the first blanket of roses created by Kroger for a Derby winner.

Aside from grocery and general-merchandise items, the Kroger stores that have financial centers give the shopper another dimension to his or her time pushing a grocery cart. That is where the shopper can sign up for home or automobile insurance, IRAs, or annuities.

As proud as Kroger is of its Stores of the 1990s, the firm is just as proud of its massive involvement in and commitment to the Louisville community. Carrying its overall slogan of "Expect The Best" way beyond the doors of its stores, the company takes part in myriad community and charitable activities every year, putting Kroger in the position it thrives on: being a major force in Louisville's forward movement into the 1990s and beyond.

THE MARKETPLACE

The Kroger float is one of the fixtures in each year's Pegasus Parade as the Kentucky Derby approaches.

Since the Kentucky Derby is the major event of the year for the city, it is only natural that Kroger would choose that as one of its major functions every year. For Kroger, Derby involvement starts long before the race; it starts with the annual sponsoring of the Kentucky Derby Festival's theme song, which is sung live for the first time for an audience at the "They're Off!" luncheon that inaugurates each year's Derby Festival.

Kroger enters a hot-air balloon in the race that has become a popular fixture during Derby week. As the week rolls on, Kroger is represented in the colorful and creative Pegasus Parade that helps raise Derby fever not only among visitors to Louisville but also among the home folks. The company float, which each year includes a group singing the Derby Festival theme song that Kroger commissioned, has won major awards in the annual parade.

In 1987 and 1988 Kroger, the world's largest florist, supplied the blanket of roses that goes to the winner of the Kentucky Derby. For the first time, only Kentucky roses were used in its construction. Kroger hopes to continue making the blanket, which is put out for bid each year, for many more Derby winners.

Beyond the Derby, Kroger supports Churchill Downs as a major corporate sponsor during the race track's two meets each year. Also in the sports realm, Kroger is a major sponsor and supporter of University of Louisville basketball and football programs, promoting the sports in television commercial spots, and of Louisville's American Association professional baseball team, the Redbirds.

In other community involvement Kroger is a major sponsor for the annual Kentucky State Fair; works closely with the City of Louisville's beautification program, Operation Brightside; supports Dare to Care, a food-distribution program to help the needy; and aids the Coalition for the Homeless, Wednesday's Child, fund-raising efforts of the Muscular Dystrophy Association, and Channel 15 educational television. In addition, each Kroger store in the area is a member of the Safe Place program.

Kroger Company's involvement in Louisville goes far beyond cash registers, produce displays, and shelves of groceries. It goes to the heart of the community.

The company enters a hot-air balloon each year in the popular balloon race that usually gets Derby Week soaring.

KENTUCKY FRIED CHICKEN

Any argument over which came first, the chicken or the egg, would surely be settled in favor of Colonel Harland Sanders' feathered friends. After all, in a marriage with 11 herbs and spices to make his Original Recipe Chicken, they have winged their way to practically all corners of the earth, leading a Kentucky Fried Chicken company publication to dub it "the empire that never sleeps" and one on which "the sun never sets."

It all started with a struggling service station and tiny restaurant tucked away in the southeastern Kentucky town of Corbin during the Great Depression in the 1930s. That was long before Sanders became known as a colonel and his white suit, black string tie, and white mustache and spiked goatee became a living trademark for "finger-lickin' good" chicken.

Although The Colonel died in 1980, the company, now part of the Pepsi Generation as a result of its purchase for $841 million in 1986 by PepsiCo, Inc., still looks on The Colonel as its mentor and inspiration—so much so that it has a Colonel Sanders Museum in its headquarters and several art objects depicting The Colonel. In addition, the firm has constructed a six-story Colonel Sanders Technical Center adjacent to its world headquarters, dubbed the "White House," that sits just beyond the Henry Watterson Expressway in southeast Louisville.

The Colonel's secret formula is still a secret even within the organization, which includes more than 7,500 restaurants worldwide (57 countries) and more than 120,000 employees doing more than $4 billion in business for the 1987 calendar year. The secret is entrusted only to two people, and it is kept safe by using two suppliers, each of whom mixes his part of the recipe independently.

But what The Colonel did to chicken with those 11 herbs and spices and a pressure cooker is no secret. He originated his recipe in the late 1930s, and expanded to a few franchisees in the early 1950s. He sold his restaurant in 1956 and took

Extensive training for employees is conducted in the technical center.

his "finger-lickin' good" chicken on the road to encourage more franchising. When he sold his business for $2 million in 1964 to a group that included a future governor of Kentucky, John Y. Brown, Jr., he had 600 KFC restaurants in the United States and England.

In 1971 KFC was acquired by Heublein Inc. and subsequently became a subsidiary of R.J. Reynolds Industries, Inc., and then PepsiCo.

According to a company brochure, "The Colonel was always the company's conscience and critic. Perfection was the only acceptable level of performance for a Kentucky Fried Chicken restaurant. Any employee who didn't meet his standards . . . would receive a lecture and a cooking demonstration. The Colonel would take off his white coat, roll up his sleeves, put on an apron, and show the staff how to do chicken right."

Apparently those lessons were learned well: KFC restaurants worldwide serve more than one billion meals annually, which comes to about 4 billion pieces of chicken from about 475 million chickens. Laid head to claw, KFC chickens consumed would stretch 246,497 miles—circling the earth 9.5 times at the equator. Also, that is a lot of mashed potatoes, gravy, slaw, and biscuits, all part of the basic meal.

KFC employees are mostly young people who live in the neighborhood in which they work, and many of the

An aerial view of the Kentucky Fried Chicken complex in Louisville shows the headquarters building in the foreground and the technical center in the background.

THE MARKETPLACE

dollars earned are spent in the neighborhood. The restaurants often offer teenagers their first job and just as often help provide funds to further an employee's education, thus enriching the youths and their neighborhoods even further.

KFC goes beyond being an equal-opportunity employer. The firm offers a minority-franchising and loan-guarantee program, and it is a model for the quick-service-restaurant industry in this respect.

The future of Kentucky Fried Chicken is housed in the Colonel Sanders Technical Center, packed with high-tech equipment and plucky ideas. It is a place where employees are developing ideas for new products, worldwide technology, training, information resources, and engineering programs, all of which assure the chain's competitiveness and continuing growth around the world. The center was completed in 1986. The building contains about 200,000 square feet of offices, laboratories, kitchens, computer facilities, training restaurants, classrooms, and libraries. Total cost, including all equipment and furnishings, was $23 million.

Perhaps the heart of the technical center lies in worldwide technology and training. The technology function is broken into four disciplines: research and development, equipment technology, operations engineering, and technical services, all of which are concerned with product, process, and equipment development and performance. The training department, which handles approximately 4,500 students a year, trains people who take company procedures all over the world. There are two complete restaurants at the center, each with seating for 40. Trainees prepare food and provide customer service to approximately 270 customers during two hours on Sales and Service days, equivalent to the customer count in a $2-million-per-year restaurant operation.

Where it all started—The Harland Sanders Restaurant at Sanders Court in Corbin, Kentucky, in the southeast part of the state.

Appropriately, Colonel Sanders' secret blend of 11 herbs and spices embedded in 11 test vials are sealed in the center's cornerstone. There could not be a more fitting site for the ingredients that form the foundation of Kentucky Fried Chicken.

For an international flavor to The Colonel's secret recipe of herbs and spices, what could be better than Tokyo, Japan, with snow-capped Mount Fuji in the background?

The spirit of Colonel Harland Sanders lives on through this statue of the founder that graces a gallery area between the headquarters building and the technical center.

347

EHRLER'S STORES

Picture a child with his or her first ice cream sundae—piled high with ice cream, delicious chocolate syrup, whipped cream, perhaps nut chips, and topped with the shiny delight of a cherry.

Eyes swell to saucers of joy and adoration for dad or mom, the mouth flashes a crescent smile, and cheeks pooch out with maybe just a little larger bite than should have been attempted.

Remember? Ehrler's does, because the people at Ehrler's have been seeing that for generations in Louisville. Those same generations have been watching Ehrler's, under the familiar green-and-orange cow and windmill sign, grow and prosper and become a Louisville folkway—a scoop of local culture, so to speak.

Ehrler's began as a dairy in 1867 when a Swiss immigrant named Joseph Ehrler settled in the Louisville area, and starting in 1924 built a strong home-delivery presence in the area for more than 50 years. The operation, which was purchased in 1977 by Dairymen's Inc., continues to carry a full line of dairy products, though its presence now is almost entirely in retail stores, and its emphasis is on dairy treats—ice cream and soft frozen yogurt.

It's those dairy treats that

Adults who have grown up with Ehrler's and its ice cream delights can be found sharing goodies, such as this banana split, at a neighborhood ice cream store.

Ehrler's, which has 150 employees in delivery, store management, store personnel, accounting, and administration, believes will help it maintain its heritage that was built on high quality and being an important part of the local community. In fact, the company's theme line now is "old-fashioned Louisville goodness since 1867." "There's a pride here that we're still in the dairy-products business," says Barry Kinslow, general manager. "We don't intend to turn ourselves into a brand-new plastic ice cream parlor. That's not in our heritage."

What is in Ehrler's heritage is a bright attitude toward customers that transcends all age groups, friendly service, fun, value for the money, and three treats that Ehrler's people believe they do better than anybody in the Louisville area: milkshakes; banana splits; and tortoise sundaes, a delectable combination of vanilla ice cream, hot fudge syrup, caramel syrup, and pecans. Louisvillians have responded annually by roughly these numbers: one million ice cream cones, 500,000 milkshakes, and 350,000 sundaes. In addition, Ehrler's is the area's leading seller of frozen yogurt, and its half-gallon cartons of ice cream remain the best seller in the area.

Since 1980 ice cream has been produced for the Ehrler's stores at a

Half-gallon containers of ice cream continue to bear the orange and green logo-type theme that has graced Ehrler's products for years.

THE MARKETPLACE

Keeping pace with the tastes of the 1980s, this neon sign promotes the company's frozen yogurt as well as its ice cream.

Dairymen's Inc. facility in Alabama; however, in the near future the company anticipates returning the ice-cream production to the Louisville Ehrler's plant located on Poplar Level Road; it could be in operation as early as the fall of 1988. This move will help Ehrler's maintain and enhance its historic position in Louisville.

Since its beginning in 1867 Ehrler's has always been involved in the community and community activities. However, over the past two years, through its 17 stores across Louisville and the surrounding communities, the firm's concession trailers, and its community-oriented advertising and marketing programs, Ehrler's has reasserted itself as more of a neighborhood partner than just being part of an industry. The company, not satisfied to sit on that gain, intends to expand its community orientation and activity through its concessions trailers—which serve as mobile stores at countless neighborhood fairs and other functions, fund-raising and charitable affairs, the Kentucky State Fair, and during Kentucky Derby Week.

These concessions trailers offer all the dairy treats that are available in a store: sundaes, milkshakes, sodas, ice cream cones, and frozen yogurt. "We've been able to go out and help neighborhoods and organizations have successful events," Kinslow says. For example, Ehrler's has helped the Leukemia Society raise funds by taking its trailers to businesses where personnel departments have promoted the appearance, and the profits from sales have gone to the charity. "This helps the society and helps Ehrler's," Kinslow says. "It tells them that we're a local company, and we care for this community."

Other groups benefiting from similar functions include the Kidney Foundation and the Art Association. In addition, Ehrler's feted several hundred youths who had taken part in Operation Brightside, a city beautification program in the summer of 1987.

Perhaps the major factor in community involvement is what employment at Ehrler's has meant to thousands of youths in the area. For many it was a first job that provided spending money through the middle and late teen years, perhaps even cars and a portion of college expenses. Those things continue to be a source of pride for the company's officials, who can say without question that what a youth does at work at Ehrler's can affect the rest of his or her life.

Frozen yogurt has become a popular item with Ehrler's customers.

349

IN CELEBRATION OF LOUISVILLE

WINN-DIXIE STORES, INC.

Perhaps unwittingly, a retail food industry executive somewhere in the past gave Winn-Dixie Stores, Inc., a full-throated battle cry for the present and the future when he said of the corporation: "The only change [at Winn-Dixie] is that they've gotten better at it."

"Getting better at it" is exactly what Winn-Dixie pursues each day as it opens its doors to the shopping public in 1,271 stores over a broad swath of the United States that includes 13 southeastern and southwestern states, making it the largest food retailer in the Sun Belt section of the country. All of that got its start in 1925 in a 2,800-square-foot retail grocery store in the Miami suburb of Lemon City.

In Louisville, Winn-Dixie, with its slogan "The Beef People," is represented by 30 stores in the metropolitan area—which includes several surrounding counties and reaches into southern Indiana—and the divisional headquarters for all of Kentucky, a portion of southern Indiana, and a part of northern middle Tennessee. The Winn-Dixie presence in greater Louisville includes 3,000 employees and four stores operating in the firm's new type Marketplace format.

These "stores of the future" are already making a present impact with their array of services that include all the normal grocery store fare such as meat shops, deli-bakeries, boutiques, seafood shops, and nutrition centers, plus full-service pharmacies and complete floral shops. These stores are approaching the 50,000-square-foot category, making them considerably larger than their 30,000- and 35,000-square-foot little brothers.

In addition to its stores in the area, Winn-Dixie, which came to Louisville as a result of buying out the Steiden stores in 1953, has divisional headquarters and a giant warehouse and distribution center on the same site as the administrative offices. For the division, whose vice-president is W.C. Calkins, the

Inside the bright, modern Marketplace, shoppers enjoy a variety of services and grocery departments such as this Prestige Meat Shoppe.

W-D brand reaches into 63 store locations in the three-state area and makes its way across the landscape via the truck fleet that supplies its stores.

Teamwork and team spirit have always been a major factor in the Winn-Dixie operation, so much so that its 80,000 employees are designated in the organization's printed material as associates. Helping to build and intensify that team spirit is an active and thorough training program for all associates, so they can carry out the company's stated commitment to customer satisfaction in modern, clean, and conveniently located supermarkets that offer a complete line of quality products at competitive prices.

Formal training programs have been developed for each department: grocery, produce, meat, bakery, deli, and general merchandise. In addition, there are programs for cashiers, department managers, and location management. Always with an eye to the future, not only in customer needs or wants but also in those that impinge on associates, Winn-Dixie conducts a management skills training program with three primary objectives: to improve customer relations, to improve associate

THE MARKETPLACE

skills, and to improve associates' decision-making.

All these skills are considered particularly valuable as the food-retailing giant heads for the twenty-first century with its eye on one-stop shopping in its huge new combination stores. It's here, W-D officials believe, where consumers will shop through the departments of the stores for fresh-cut flowers, plants, or garden accessories and supplies; vitamins, natural foods, and low-sodium and low-sugar foods from the nutrition shops; and hot entrees, desserts, and party platters from delicatessens.

Shoppers will also be able to get oven-fresh breads and hot sweet goods in the bakeries, fresh fish and seafood in that department, domestic and imported cheeses in the cheese shops, and a greater variety of general merchandise, ranging from auto supplies to kitchen wares to greeting cards, books, and magazines.

Even with all those attractions the retail business is still a people-to-people matter, and Winn-Dixie promotes the idea that mutual trust, confidence, and strong interpersonal relations directly benefit customers, associates, and the communities the corporation serves. Winn-Dixie, corporately and through its associates, annually contributes millions of dollars to charity. Most popular among the associates is the company's Matching-Grants Program, whereby the firm matches contributions made by associates to qualified, tax-exempt charitable, educational, cultural, or civic organizations.

In Louisville, says divisional advertising director Mel Kline, approximately 25 charities and other nonprofit organizations, including the Metro United Way, Urban League, American Red Cross, American Heart Association, and March of Dimes, are beneficiaries of W-D individual and corporate giving.

With a growing Louisville and a growing Winn-Dixie Stores, Inc., as major possibilities for the future, it wouldn't be out of the question for the people of the region to hope that the market giant and the entire area will be "getting better at it" on the way to the 1990s and beyond.

The wave of the future is already here for Winn-Dixie Stores in the form of its new Winn-Dixie Marketplace format.

IN CELEBRATION OF LOUISVILLE

THE PAUL SCHULTZ COMPANIES

The Catalyst.

Webster's defines it as a substance that initiates a reaction or something that provokes significant change. The Paul Schultz Companies in Louisville fits the bill in both instances. The firm has the perfect chemistry for creating significant positive change in retail merchandising and marketing programs.

The organization actually is two companies—Paul Schultz Catalogs, the founding division, and Paul Schultz Marketing Group. Each division has its own field of expertise and can operate independently. But working together, they form a synergism that produces high-quality and innovative techniques in marketing, merchandising, graphics, and consulting. All these services are used to promote the sale of their clients' products on a local, regional, or national basis.

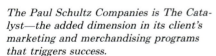

The Paul Schultz Companies is The Catalyst—the added dimension in its client's marketing and merchandising programs that triggers success.

The Paul Schultz Companies has the ability and studio facilities to photograph anything from a full room setting to the latest fashion.

The Paul Schultz Companies specializes in the creation and management of publications, vendor development programs, and syndications. The firm has the unique skill to create retail promotional programs that can be used by more than one client, thereby sharing costs and increasing profitability.

Paul Schultz Catalogs is a merchandising and marketing group for catalog showrooms. It was founded by Paul Schultz in 1968, and right from the start it stood out as an innovator and leader in the catalog showroom industry. Today the firm is guided by Schultz' sons, Steve and Richard. Paul Schultz Catalogs has changed the whole concept of the showroom catalog from preprinted pages submitted by manufacturers, to a selectively merchandised and graphically customized selling tool.

The organization's reputation grew and so did business, based to a large extent on the firm's ability to lead in a changing marketplace. Through the years the Paul Schultz Catalogs division has become preeminent in the field, and is today considered twice as dominant as its nearest competitor.

Paul Schultz Catalogs works with a large number of independent catalog-showroom "members," tying them together under one umbrella and representing them in the marketplace. This provides the cooperative-style buying power needed to be competitive with the large national firms. "All merchandise is evaluated by us, picked by us, recommended by us, and negotiated by us," says Steve Schultz. That merchandise is then featured in the annual catalog and flyer program, created and produced by Paul Schultz Catalogs to drive sales. The member showrooms stock the merchandise, and it is available for purchase by consumers nationwide.

And purchase they do—to the tune of about $700 million worth of retail goods per year, according to Steve Schultz. "We understand what it takes to move a product to a consumer," he says. "We're not just

Bringing the consumer and the product closer together is the first step. But the Paul Schultz Companies keeps working until it finds the key that will turn those shoppers into buyers.

trying to create a sizzle—we're in business to sell a product."

While the past has relied heavily on the catalog side of the companies, the future may be in the hands of the innovative Paul Schultz Marketing Group. The four-year-old division—whose clients typically are manufacturers, retailers, and direct marketers—is presently involved in producing publications such as catalogs, flyers, and newspaper inserts. When appropriate, the division also uses the broadcast media to create powerful and effective programs designed to sell products and maximize profits.

A great push in this division involves an intensification of the corporation's syndication philosophy. It is currently involved in several forms of publication, multimedia and event syndications. One example is the firm's successful retail jewelry promotion, now in its third year of national syndication. This experience will allow the company to move into other market segments where it can put together a preselected merchandising package for a large group of retailers. The packages will be heavily promoted with materials produced by Paul Schultz, including four-color publications and television presentations.

These syndications are directed at independent retailers who lack the resources and the expertise to produce professional promotions on their own. Syndication can provide a group of common retailers with a cost-effective promotional program and allow them to compete with heavily advertised national firms. Syndication can also give them the cooperative buying power needed to ensure competitive pricing.

Another strong area for the Marketing Group is vendor development programs. Working with clients, typically large multioutlet retail businesses, Paul Schultz solicits marketing funds from national manufacturers of branded merchandise. These funds are used to produce multimedia promotional programs

Successful syndicated promotional programs for jewelry stores and other retailers are a specialty at Paul Schultz.

to drive sales at the retail level. These targeted, local-level promotions have been very successful for both the retailer and the manufacturer.

Though the Schultzes are not native Louisvillians, they have taken the city to heart. It is a true family business for the former Chicagoans—a business that has grown from a time when Paul Schultz was the president, his wife, Sylvia, was the secretary, and their younger son, Richard, ran the copying machine. Today the Paul Schultz Companies has 150 full-time employees and has expanded its operations to include the opening in 1987 of an additional photography studio and sales office in Richmond, Virginia.

The Paul Schultz Companies is committed to the Louisville downtown renaissance and, as part of a city industrial bond issue, moved in 1982 to its present Broadway Street location. In 1984 the organization purchased and renovated adjacent nearby property, doubling its square footage. And, as of January 1988, the firm completed construction and moved into a third building, connecting the two original structures.

The Paul Schultz Companies, in addition to being deeply involved in a variety of civic, charitable, and professional endeavors, is also acting as a catalyst in yet another arena—the potential for Louisville's continued growth and the promise of brighter days ahead.

IN CELEBRATION OF LOUISVILLE

A. ARNOLD & SON WORLDWIDE MOVING & STORAGE

A. Arnold & Son Worldwide Moving & Storage has a message for families, individuals, businesses, organizations, and corporate decision makers: "Don't make a move without us."

Since 1905 A. Arnold & Son has been providing safe, reliable moving and storage for people and businesses on the move. In those 80-plus years the Louisville-based firm has gained a reputation for quality service in handling moves from across town or even halfway around the world.

The company was founded by Alous Arnold and his son, Carl, who began by delivering purchases from the local Haymarket. Their care and professional approach has been handed down through the organization, much like the many cherished belongings the firm is asked to move for its customers.

Corporate president Bill Arnold, great-grandson of the company's founder, explains that the A. Arnold tradition is something of which the firm is very proud. Many families and businesses, in fact, have moved with A. Arnold two and three times, one generation after another.

From its early beginnings the company has expanded its range of services and operating area many times over. No longer just a local moving company, more than 50 percent of A. Arnold's business does not have Louisville as either the origination or destination point. And not only has A. Arnold moved tons and tons of earthly possessions, it was also responsible for moving the Apollo 13 capsule from NASA to its permanent home at Louisville's Museum of Natural History.

Training is the key to A. Arnold's reputation for quality service. Because moving personal household goods has always been the backbone of its business, A. Arnold places special emphasis on teaching "people skills" to its approximately 160 employees. The result is a highly skilled "personal moving team" that handles the job from packing to final delivery, beginning to end, with no outside intervention.

Another area of concentration for A. Arnold is corporate moving. Not only does the firm move office furnishings and equipment but personnel as well. Corporations that transfer and relocate executives and other personnel on a frequent basis trust A. Arnold to ease the transition by providing prompt, competent service for their employees from coast to coast. Among A. Arnold's customers are Brown & Williamson Tobacco Corporation, Brown-Forman Corp., Humana, Inc., Humana Hospital-Audubon, and Norton and Kosair Children's hospitals, among others.

The firm has three locations, with headquarters situated on 18 acres in eastern Jefferson County. In addition to moving, A. Arnold & Son Worldwide Moving & Storage, as the name implies, also offers electronically secured storage areas for warehousing goods and storing records.

In business since 1905, A. Arnold & Son's president and chief executive officer Bill Arnold is the fourth generation to lead the company.

Quality and damage-free packing are assured as all employees attend the company's exclusive training school.

Photo by Chuck Elfont

Photo by John Beckman/Quadrant

Photo by John Nation

Churchill Downs 358-359

Kentucky Fair & Exposition Center
Louisville Convention and Visitors Bureau 360-363

Louisville Downs 364

Chapter XVI
Recreation and Leisure

Thoroughbred and harness racing, major college and professional sporting events, conventions, concerts, and the annual Kentucky State Fair — all are at home in Louisville.

IN CELEBRATION OF LOUISVILLE

CHURCHILL DOWNS

It had been 17 years since Proud Clarion had won the Kentucky Derby when another, not-so-proud, clarion sounded over ancient Churchill Downs—the home of the greatest two minutes in sport, on the first Saturday of each May.

It was a clarion call to action, and it has been heeded by a group of business and management thoroughbreds who have helped turn what had become a drab and dreary old patriarch of American racing into a sparkling, renovated, revitalized entertainment place. It's now a good bet to be one of the finest racetracks in North America.

The old, tradition-rich racetrack is building a new tradition under leaders who took over in 1984, following a couple of poor financial years and a growing lethargy among track officials and workers that had tarnished the luster the track could count on each spring at Derby time. Now that luster is returning, not only at Derby time but throughout the track's spring and fall racing meets.

The revitalization has been generated by a brighter, fresher face, both on the track's buildings and its people; by greater cordiality, better service, more entertainment opportunities, and fine dining; and by a gleaming paddock and walking ring and a fine turf course. The paddock

One of Churchill Downs' additions in 1987 was the plush Turf Club for members.

and the turf course, in particular, have helped Churchill Downs—founded in 1874 as the Louisville Jockey Club and brought to world prominence by such men as Colonel Matt Winn—return to a preeminent position among American racetracks.

The turf course, in particular, acted as a special magnet in the track's successful pursuit of the 1988 Breeders' Cup races that this year will give Churchill Downs the double-barreled promotion of the first Saturday in May and the first Saturday in November, Breeders' Cup day.

The paddock and the turf course make up the largest part of a $25-million capital-improvement program that was started after the

The parade to the post at the Kentucky Derby, the first Saturday in May, is the highlight of the racing season for Churchill Downs and the racing and breeding industries. The beautiful Matt C. Winn Turf Course is inside the main track.

naming of Thomas H. Meeker as president and Gerald Lawrence as vice-president and general manager in 1984 and the elevation of longtime board member Warner L. Jones, Jr., to chairman, giving the board—which hadn't spent $25 million in the previous 50 years—a new aggressive spirit that responded to Meeker's plans. Other improvements include the creation, through renovation, of a new, private-membership Turf Club, a superb dining area known as the Eclipse Room, balconies that overlook the track's tailored gardens and paddock, a club-like spot called Silks, and a beer-garden-style grandstand pavilion.

Through all of this, according to architect Dennis DeWitt, "Our intention was to make Churchill Downs more exciting, vibrant, and entertaining, while maintaining the character that is so much a part of the Churchill Downs experience."

That's exactly how Meeker sees it. "Churchill had suffered two years of losses, bad racing, the plant was in disrepair, and morale was low," he says. "All of that was manifested in

RECREATION AND LEISURE

The Eclipse Room is a public dining room located in the clubhouse area of the historic racing facility.

poor service . . . we changed the way we operated . . . we developed a target marketing plan . . . targeting groups and individuals in the community and elsewhere. Hand in glove with that went a move to identify our products: dining, pageantry, and fun."

A key factor in the change was the need for making the employees realize the role they play in the success of the track. "We got together with all groups [at the track] and laid down some tight rules," Meeker explains, "and we preached to them the good to come from customer service. And they all understood that."

In the mind's eye of many, especially outsiders, Churchill Downs is Kentucky and Louisville—and racing—and the track management recognizes that as a considerable responsibility. "Unlike most public corporations," Meeker says, "we have an obligation beyond return on investment to shareholders. Because everything we do as an institution manifests Kentucky, we have an obligation, also, to the public . . . Many of our decisions are tempered by the recognition that we can't do anything that would harm the community in terms of image."

The feeling for the community goes well beyond that. Acknowledging that Churchill Downs seemed an island unto itself in years past, Meeker and his staff have moved in a number of ways to reestablish its nexus with the community. For instance, it's the site of the Old Kentucky Home Council Scout-O-Rama and the United Way Kick Off/Run, and was host to a social event for the 1987 Southern Governors' Conference. In doing these things, Meeker says, the racetrack is a community asset that can be relied on.

As bright as the recent past has been, Churchill Downs looks forward to an even brighter future. The track expects to sound the call to the post in the Breeders' Cup every few years on a rotating basis among tracks in New York, California, Kentucky, and perhaps Florida. Meeker is not one of those who wonders if the Breeders' Cup will harm the Triple Crown races—the Kentucky Derby, the Preakness, and the Belmont Stakes. Quite to the contrary, he calls the Breeders' Cup races the most innovative thing that's come to racing in a long time. He believes the Breeders' Cup and the Triple Crown support all of racing. "The Triple Crown series creates racing stars," he says, "and the Breeders' Cup needs racing stars. We kind of hold the whole of racing together."

An enhancement of the fall racing meet is expected also, with a possible series of major races for fillies and colts, particularly two-year-olds that might be looking ahead to the following year's Derby. Ever thinking of the first week in May, Meeker also envisions—in 1989 or 1990—an Alumni Derby for four-year-olds and up.

It's safe to say now that whatever the clarion call from the future, Churchill Downs is on track to hear it, act on it, and take it to the wire a winner.

This 20-percent larger-than-life bronze statue of Aristides, the first Kentucky Derby winner, graces the Paddock Garden in the clubhouse area of the historic racetrack.

Another of the major accomplishments of the multimillion-dollar improvement program in recent years is the bright paddock, where horses are saddled and walked prior to each race.

IN CELEBRATION OF LOUISVILLE

KENTUCKY FAIR & EXPOSITION CENTER
LOUISVILLE CONVENTION & VISITORS BUREAU

The Louisville area is home to nearly one million people on a daily basis, but over any year's time it is a short-term home to thousands more because of its popularity as a convention and tourist city.

The center of activity that brings people and the potential for economic vitality is conventions, major trade shows, tourism, the annual Kentucky State Fair, and other special events.

Tying much of this together in a neat, attractive package are the Commonwealth Convention Center, the Kentucky Fair & Exposition Center, and the Louisville Convention & Visitors Bureau. Although separate organizations, their staffs work together to promote Louisville and its facilities. The sales and marketing staff of the two centers promote the facilities to potential clients.

At the same time the Convention & Visitors Bureau is singing the praises of the city in general, with strong emphasis on its ability to handle gatherings of just about any kind or size.

Much of that ability rests within the walls of the Kentucky Fair & Exposition Center and Commonwealth Convention Center, two of America's major convention halls. Even though Louisville is generally considered to be a second-tier city in relation to New York, Chicago, Los Angeles, San Francisco, and Dallas, it has been able to compete in the first tier and holds a strong place in the national picture. The 1986 Louisville convention of the National Education Association is a prime example. This was the first time that the NEA had met in a second-tier city. NEA was just one of the 600-plus conventions held in 1986 for an economic infusion of $207 million.

While not a convention, the return to Louisville of Kentucky's Sweet 16 state high school basketball tournament has been a major tourism advance for the city. Sixteen state high school teams and their ardent fans mean a great deal economically and image-wise.

What makes Louisville so appealing to the conventioneer and visitor? Location is one thing: It is within a day's drive for half the nation's population, and most major airlines offer daily flights from all sections of the country. The facilities are out-

Excitement mounts as the thundering herd turns the bend at the Kentucky Derby at Churchill Downs.

Colorful flags welcome shoppers and browsers alike to the bustling downtown Louisville Galleria shopping mall.

standing, food and lodging are cost effective, and there are ample hotel rooms in the immediate area of both the Kentucky Fair & Exposition Center and the Commonwealth Convention Center.

By one measure, service to its clients, Louisville ranks among the top 10 in the country. Helping to maintain that level of service are frequent post-convention reviews with the goal of continued improvement. That, no doubt, has helped Louisville sport a Golden Key Award for its conventions and meetings, and to enjoy such repeat business as the International Lawn, Garden, and Power Equipment Expo, which has booked Louisville through 1991.

The convention bureau and the centers are already working several years in advance in order to fill up future calendars with conventions and trade shows that characteristically spend three to four days in the city. The staffs are projecting into the mid-1990s, and there are even some bookings in the year 2000 and beyond.

Courting potential conventions and trade shows is not a hit-and-run affair. Staff members sometimes

RECREATION AND LEISURE

spend up to 10 years grooming a potential client to choose Louisville, with the average time spent being approximately six years. In 1986, 615 future meetings were scheduled, accounting for 845,100 room nights, a 50-percent increase over 1985. That, figured on an average $50-per-night rate, makes those meetings worth more than $42 million in room revenue alone.

Each year the Louisville Convention & Visitors Bureau sponsors familiarization tours, the 1986 tours netting decision makers from 16 cities. Also, site inspections were made by representatives of 82 other organizations considering Louisville as a meeting site. In addition, the city was represented in 1986 at major industry functions that could lead to future conventions.

Aside from its convention facilities, Louisville offers a number of attractions tied to the nation's history, and, of course, Churchill Downs—home of the Kentucky Derby and the Derby Museum—is a major drawing card. The sternwheeler *Belle of Louisville* plies the Ohio River on summer cruises, the Louisville Zoo offers a walk on the wild side, and the arts community is active throughout the year.

These features are not exclusively for conventioneers, however. They beckon the regular tourist, whether just on a day trip or staying for several days. In the tourism arena, Louisville has become very aggressive in its competition with St. Louis, Cincinnati, Nashville, Indianapolis, and Lexington.

The visitors bureau's tourism efforts are directed at several markets, with motor-coach tours and individual family leisure travel being just two. The bureau has printed 500,000 visitors guides, and has received 106,000 tourist inquiries in 1986. Senior-citizen groups, who are ardent travelers, are one of the major markets.

In 1986 the Louisville visitors bureau initiated the Bluegrass Triangle Tours of Kentucky, the state's first collaborative tour packages, with fellow bureaus in Lexington and northern Kentucky. Continued aggressive promotion of Louisville as a leisure destination practically ensures that the 50-percent increase in telephone inquiries in 1986 will continue to accelerate.

Those in the business of promoting the city for conventions, shows, and tourism by no means take all the credit for the increase in Louisville's stature. Instead, they are generous with their praise of the city's people, who, they say, have helped build Louisville's reputation as a "city that loves visitors." Many clients have given the city a "10" for the way it handles visitors and conventioneers.

With its promotion campaigns, its friendly people, and its massive capacity for special events, Louisville plays host to people from around the world.

The largest and most versatile host, of course, is the Kentucky Fair & Exposition Center, just six miles from downtown. It serves as a site for everything from mammoth trade shows to mini-conventions, from concerts to rodeos, from the State Fair to a three-ring circus. The center, whose initial build-

Everything is beautiful at the Louisville Ballet.

Like a big blue ribbon the Ohio River winds through the modern, vital city of Louisville, still escorting the proverbial steamboat during summer tourist season.

IN CELEBRATION OF LOUISVILLE

Commonwealth Convention Center, located in the heart of downtown Louisville, has 100,000 square feet of column-free exhibit space and 36 meeting rooms. It is within walking distance of 3,000 hotel rooms, several restaurants, and a major shopping area.

Aside from Freedom Hall coliseum and Cardinal Stadium, the breakdown of the facilities shows this:

—West Exposition Wing provides 177,000 square feet that allow for 900 10- by 10-foot booths. A pavilion that adds 75,000 square feet is attached and provides space for another 375 booths of the same size.

—East Exposition Wing is a marvel of vastness, containing 212,000 square feet of floor space that can easily accommodate 1,125 10- by 10-foot booths. With six overhead entrance doors, air conditioning, loading docks, unlimited floor load, and more than 1,000 fluorescent light fixtures, the wing can handle trade shows of any size.

—West and East exhibit halls are identical layouts that are attached to the East and West exposition wings. Each has 32,000 square feet of exhibit space that can accommodate 160 10- by 10-foot booths, and three multipurpose rooms of 6,000, 5,400, and 5,200 square feet divisible into 10 soundproof meeting rooms.

—Newmarket Hall is an air-conditioned, 600-seat amphitheater that lends itself ideally to small variety and fashion shows, lectures, demonstrations, and livestock sales. It is connected to the pavilion by enclosed passageways and to the West Wing by covered walkways.

—Broadbent Arena offers permanent seating for 5,250 people and with portable floor seating is expandable to 6,600 on 39,000 square feet of floor space with unlimited load. It is air conditioned and has been home to the Louisville Thunder professional indoor soccer team.

ings were completed in 1957, consists of 700,000 square feet of air-conditioned space under one roof, including two exposition wings and Freedom Hall, which can accommodate 20,000 people for concerts, 20,500 convention delegates, and 19,500 for basketball games as home to the University of Louisville Cardinals.

In addition, the multistructure complex offers 24 meeting rooms, a ballroom, mirror-image exhibit halls, a large pavilion, a 600-seat amphitheater, a livestock arena, and a 35,000-seat stadium that is home to the American Association Louisville Redbirds baseball team and the University of Louisville football team. Parking is provided for 15,000 vehicles.

Steamboating on the Belle of Louisville as she churns the waters of the Ohio River is one of the many summer pleasures to be found in Louisville.

RECREATION AND LEISURE

The mammoth Kentucky Fair & Exposition Center near downtown is home to the University of Louisville Cardinals basketball team, and is host to everything from conventions and trade shows to concerts, rodeos, and the state fair.

A master facilities development plan that was just completed projects for the year 2000 a fairgrounds complex that is 80 acres larger, has several thousand more parking spaces, 600 more horse stalls, a recreational-vehicle park, a 50,000-seat stadium, and a 400-room hotel. State officials have already begun to focus on the short-run addition of 200,000 square feet of exhibit space and 75,000 square feet of support facilities for the East Wing. Officials expect to ask the 1988 Kentucky Legislature to fund the $25-million project.

Complementing the fairgrounds layout is the downtown site of Commonwealth Convention Center, where versatility is a key to success. The center, with 100,000 square feet of column-free exhibit space, is large enough to handle about 90 percent of the nation's conventions and trade shows. At the same time its design makes it adaptable for comfortable settings for smaller meetings, conventions, and exhibitions.

The exhibition hall can be divided into three smaller areas of 50,000, 30,000, and 20,000 square feet. In addition, there is a 9,600-square-foot ballroom that can also provide theater-style seating for 1,200 people, there are 37 meeting rooms for groups from 25 to 1,200 people, and banquet accommodations for as many as 6,000.

As Louisville's downtown continues to be revitalized, the Commonwealth Convention Center will be a vital link in that new vigor.

363

LOUISVILLE DOWNS

Louisville Downs is one of the most exciting attractions in the Ohio Valley. Open eight months a year, the track is an entertainment highlight in Louisville.

Visitors from the local area and all parts of the country pass through its gates each year. Louisville Downs accounts for more than 50 percent of the attendance and pari-mutuel handled in the state's standardbred industry. In 1986 more than 340,000 people pushed more than $30 million through the betting windows.

The sport of standardbred racing features trotters and pacers, with the purists in the sport preferring the trotters because of the beauty of their square-gaited stride. While the trotters are beautiful to watch, the pacers are known for their speed. Some pacers have been clocked at 40 miles per hour and can sustain speeds of up to 30 to 35 miles per hour.

At Louisville Downs, both the grandstand and clubhouse are air conditioned in the summer and heated in the winter for the comfort of the patrons. Many racing fans enjoy the action from the grandstand for its up-close vantage point, while others enjoy the clubhouse, where beverages and sandwiches are served in the Niatross Room.

The clubhouse at Louisville Downs boasts one of the finest restaurants in the South. The Directors' Room offers formal dining in an elegant atmosphere. The Directors' and Niatross rooms can accommodate approximately 500 people and offer a variety of special menu selections.

Louisville Downs was founded in 1966 and has flourished since. Starting with 51 racing nights that year, the track has expanded its potential to allow a total of 177 race nights in 1988. It offers wagering opportunities ranging from the traditional win, place, and show and the daily double to the challenging Superfecta. The latter can return as much as $50,000 or more, depending on the carry-over pool.

In addition to the regular racing, the highlight of the season is the Kentucky Pacing Derby. In 1987 the purse for the classic was $575,000, the first time in its 10-year history it has gone beyond a half-million dollars. The best two-year-old pacers are eligible for the classic, and no fewer than eight world records have been set in years past.

Louisville Downs also hosts approximately 15 Kentucky Sire Stakes that are restricted to horses bred in the state. The total purse money available each year at these events is approximately $300,000.

Louisville Downs is open the day after Christmas through April, racing each Tuesday through Saturday. A second meeting runs from July through early September on a Monday-through-Saturday schedule, and a third runs from late September through October, again Tuesday through Saturday.

President and general manager William H. King and vice-president Joyce Jennings, King's daughter, own 80 percent of Louisville Downs.

The clubhouse at Louisville Downs boasts one of the finest restaurants in the South.

Patrons

The following individuals, companies, and organizations have made a valuable commitment to the quality of this publication. Windsor Publications and the Louisville Chamber of Commerce gratefully acknowledge their support of *In Celebration of Louisville.*

Mayor Jerry E. Abramson
American Air Filter*
American Synthetic Rubber Corporation*
ANDALEX Resources, Inc.
A. Arnold & Son Worldwide Moving & Storage*
J. Bacon & Sons Company*
Barnett & Alagia*
BATUS, Inc.*
Bellarmine College*
Borden Chemical*
Brandeis Machinery & Supply Corporation*
Brown-Forman Corporation*
Brown, Todd & Heyburn*
C&I Engineering, Inc.*
Capital Holding Corporation*
Carrier Vibrating Equipment, Inc.*
Harold W. Cates & Co., Inc.*
Cellular One
Churchill Downs*
Citizens Fidelity Bank and Trust Company*
Commonwealth Life Insurance Company*
Corhart Refractories*
The Courier-Journal*
Cowger & Miller Mortgage Company*
The Cumberland Federal Savings Bank*
DCE, Inc.*

Department of Surgery, University of Louisville School of Medicine*
Devoe & Raynolds Co.*
Digital Equipment Corporation*
E.I. Du Pont de Nemours & Company*
Ehrler's Stores*
Eskew & Gresham, PSC*
Fashion Shops of Kentucky*
Future Federal Savings Bank*
Galt House, Galt House East, Executive Inn, Executive West*
GE Appliances*
Goldberg & Simpson*
Great Financial Federal*
Greenebaum Doll & McDonald
Health Data Network*
Heck Equipment Company, Inc.
Henderson Electric Company Inc.*
Hillhaven Corporation
Hilliard Lyons*
Hunt Tractor Inc.*
Kentucky Fair & Exposition Center Louisville Convention and Visitors Bureau*
Kentucky Fried Chicken*
Kroger Company*
Kunz's Fourth & Market
Kurfees Coatings, Inc.*
Lakeside Corporation
Louisville Bedding Company*
Louisville Downs*
Louisville Gas and Electric Company*
Louisville Hand Surgery*
Louisville Manufacturing Company, Inc.*
Louisville Stoneware Company*
Medical Center Anesthesiologists*
Medical Imaging Consultants*
Mercer Meidinger Hansen, Incorporated*

NTS Corporation*
Paine Webber Inc.
Paragon Group, Inc.*
Paramount Plywood Products, Inc.
Peat Marwick Main & Co.*
Philip Morris U.S.A.*
Porter Paint Co.*
Raque Food Systems, Inc.
Ready Electric Company, Inc.*
Reliance Universal Inc.*
RESCO*
Rohm and Haas*
The Paul Schultz Companies*
SEAMCO*
Silliman Development Company, Inc.*
South Central Bell*
Stites & Harbison*
Sturgeon-Thornton-Marrett Development Company*
Tarrant Parts
Tarrant Service Agency
Tumbleweed Mexican Food & Mesquite Grill
United Catalysts Inc.*
University Medical Associates, PSC*
University of Louisville*
US Ecology, Inc.*
WAVE 3/Cosmos Broadcasting Corp.*
WHAS-TV*
Whip Mix Corporation*
Winn-Dixie Stores, Inc.*
WLKY-TV*
Wyatt, Tarrant & Combs*

*Partners in Progress of *In Celebration of Louisville.* The stories of these companies and organizations appear in Part Two, beginning on page 188.

Bibliography

Bates, Alan L. *Belle of Louisville*. Berkeley, Calif.: Howell-North, 1965.

Boyer, Richard, and David Savageau. *Places Rated Almanac*. New York: Rand McNally & Company, 1985.

Crews, Clyde F. *The Faithful Image*. Louisville, Ky.: n.p., 1986.

Davis, Billy. *40 Years of Aerial Photography Over Kentucky*. Louisville, Ky.: The Courier-Journal and The Louisville Times, 1981.

Flood Plain Information Study: Ohio River, Clark County, Ind. Louisville, Ky.: U.S. Army Corps of Engineers, 1972.

Flood Plain Information Study: Ohio River, Jefferson County, Ky. Louisville, Ky.: U.S. Army Corps of Engineers, 1973.

Herr, Kincaid A. *Louisville & Nashville Railroad, 1850-1963*. Louisville, Ky.: Louisville & Nashville Railroad, 1964.

Hilton, George W. *Monon Route*. Berkeley, Calif.: Howell-North Books, 1978.

Inter-City Cost of Living Index, 1986. Indianapolis, Ind.: American Chamber of Commerce Researchers Association.

Jefferson County, Kentucky Soil Survey. Washington, D.C.: U.S. Department of Agriculture, 1966.

Johnson, Leland R. *The Falls City Engineers*. Louisville, Ky.: U.S. Army Corps of Engineers, 1974.

Johnson, Leland R. *The Falls City Engineers ... 1970-1983*. Louisville, Ky.: U.S. Army Corps of Engineers, 1984.

Kentucky Demographics: The 1980 Census of Kentucky. Louisville, Ky.: University of Louisville Urban Studies Center, 1982.

Klein, Maury. *History of the Louisville & Nashville Railroad*. New York: Macmillian Publishing Co., 1972.

Landau, Herman. *Adath Louisville: The Story of a Jewish Community*. Louisville, Ky.: n.p., 1981.

The Large Employers Directory. Louisville, Ky.: Louisville Chamber of Commerce, 1986.

Leibowitz, Irving. *My Indiana*. Englewood Cliffs, N.J.: Prentice-Hall, 1964.

Louisville Area Directory of Manufacturers, 1979-80. Louisville, Ky.: Louisville Area Chamber of Commerce.

Louisville Economic Inventory. Louisville, Ky.: Louisville Area Chamber of Commerce, 1981.

Louisville Fact Book. Louisville, Ky.: Louisville Chamber of Commerce, 1987.

Louisville, Ky.-Ind., 1970 Census of Population and Housing. Washington, D.C.: U.S. Department of Commerce Bureau of the Census, 1972.

Louisville Statistical Abstract, 1986. Louisville, Ky.: Louisville Chamber of Commerce, 1986.

Louisville Survey Central & South Report. City of Louisville Community Development Cabinet, 1978. Historian, Carl E. Kramer.

Louisville Survey East Report. City of Louisville Community Development Cabinet, 1979. Historian, Carl E. Kramer.

Melham, Tom. *John Muir's Wild America*. Washington, D.C.: National Geographic Society, 1976.

Mueller, William A. *A History of Southern Baptist Theological Seminary*. Nashville, Tenn.: Broadman Press, 1959.

1985-86 Louisville Business Trends. Louisville, Ky.: Louisville Chamber of Commerce, 1986.

Powell, Richard L. *Geology of the Falls of the Ohio River*. Bloomington, Ind.: Indiana Geological Survey, 1970.

Sanders, Robert Stuart. *History of Louisville Presbyterian Theological Seminary, 1853-1953*. The Louisville Presbyterian Theological Seminary, 1953.

Sanders, Scott Russell. *Audubon Reader: The Best Writing of John James Audubon*. Bloomington, Ind.: Indiana University Press, 1986.

The Shotgun House. Louisville, Ky.: Preservation Alliance of Louisville and Jefferson County, 1980.

Stover, John F. *History of the Illinois Central Railroad*. New York: Macmillan Publishing Co., 1975.

Sulzer, Elmer G. *Ghost Railroads of Indiana*. Indianapolis, Ind.: Vane A. Jones Co., 1970.

Thom, James Alexander. *From Sea to Shining Sea*. New York: Ballantine Books, 1984.

Thomas, Samuel W. *Louisville Since the Twenties*. Louisville, Ky.: The Courier-Journal and The Louisville Times, 1978.

Thomas, Samuel W. *Views of Louisville Since 1766*. Louisville, Ky.: The Courier-Journal and The Louisville Times, 1971.

Thomas, Samuel W., and William Morgan. *Old Louisville: The Victorian Era*. Louisville, Ky.: The Courier-Journal and The Louisville Times, 1975.

Twain, Mark. *Life on the Mississippi*. New York: Harper & Row, n.d.

Vlach, John. "Shotgun Houses," *Natural History* (February 1977).

Yater, George H. *Two Hundred Years at the Falls of the Ohio: A History of Louisville and Jefferson County*. Louisville, Ky.: The Heritage Corporation, 1979.

Top: Photo by Mark E. Gibson

Above: Photo by John Nation

367

Index

PARTNERS IN PROGRESS INDEX
American Air Filter, 246
American Synthetic Rubber Corporation, 220-221
Arnold & Son Worldwide Moving & Storage, A., 354
Bacon & Sons Company, J., 338-339
Barnett & Alagia, 288-289
BATUS, Inc., 254-257
Bellarmine College, 325
Borden Chemical, 242-243
Brandeis Machinery & Supply Corporation, 298
Brown-Forman Corporation, 234-236
Brown, Todd & Heyburn, 290
C&I Engineering, Inc., 312-313
Capital Holding Corporation, 260-261
Carrier Vibrating Equipment, Inc., 222-223
Cates & Co., Inc., Harold W., 318
Churchill Downs, 358-359
Citizens Fidelity Bank and Trust Company, 251
Commonwealth Life Insurance Company, 262-263
Corhart Refractories, 212-213
Courier-Journal, The, 204
Cowger & Miller Mortgage Company, 268-269
Cumberland Federal Savings Bank, The, 258-259
DCE, Inc., 244-245
Department of Surgery, University of Louisville School of Medicine, 322-323
Devoe & Raynolds Co., 224-225
Digital Equipment Corporation, 238-239
Du Pont de Nemours & Company, E.I., 226-227
Ehrler's Stores, 348-349
Eskew & Gresham, PSC, 280-281
Fashion Shops of Kentucky, 342-343
Future Federal Savings Bank, 252-253
Galt House, Galt House East, Executive Inn, Executive West, 341
GE Appliances, 240-241
Goldberg & Simpson, 284-285
Great Financial Federal, 264-265
Health Data Network, 266-267
Henderson Electric Company Inc., 300-301
Hilliard Lyons, 302-303
Hunt Tractor, Inc., 340

Kentucky Fair & Exposition Center Louisville Convention and Visitors Bureau, 360-363
Kentucky Fried Chicken, 346-347
Kroger Company, 344-345
Kurfees Coatings, Inc., 237
Louisville Bedding Company, 247
Louisville Chamber of Commerce, 250
Louisville Downs, 364
Louisville Gas and Electric Company, 202-203
Louisville Hand Surgery, 328-331
Louisville Manufacturing Company, Inc., 230
Louisville Stoneware Company, 232-233
Medical Center Anesthesiologists, 326-327
Medical Imaging Consultants, 332-333
Mercer Meidinger Hansen, Incorporated, 270-271
NTS Corporation, 294-297
Paragon Group, Inc., 316-317
Peat Marwick Main & Co., 282-283
Philip Morris U.S.A., 215
Porter Paint Co., 214
Ready Electric Company, Inc., 310-311
Reliance Universal Inc., 208-209
RESCO, 299
Rohm and Haas, 210-211
Schultz Companies, The Paul, 352-353
SEAMCO, 228-229
Silliman Development Company, Inc., 308-309
South Central Bell, 192-193
Stites & Harbison, 286-287
Sturgeon-Thornton-Marrett Development Company, 304-307
United Catalysts Inc., 216-219
University Medical Associates, PSC, 334-335
University of Louisville, 324
US Ecology, Inc., 314-315
WAVE 3/Cosmos Broadcasting Corp., 194-197
WHAS-TV, 198-199
Whip Mix Corporation, 231
Winn-Dixie Stores, Inc., 350-351
WLKY-TV, 200-201
Wyatt, Tarrant & Combs, 278-279

GENERAL INDEX
A
Abrams, Mark, 154
Actors Theatre, 47, 71, 93, 94
Airco Carbide, 178
Airports, 36, 38, 55, 57, 63-65, 172; see also Standiford Field and Bowman Field
Alcan Aluminum, 180
Algonquin parkway, 150
Ali, Mohammad, 132
Almstedt Brothers Building, 166-167
American Commercial Barge Lines, 62
American Institute of Steel Construction, 48-49
American Public Radio, 97
American Revolution, 27-28
American Standard, 180
American Tobacco Company, 182-183
Anchorage, 41, 85
Appleton Papers Incorporated, 160
Archdiocese of Louisville, 130
Armour meat packing, 183
Arts and entertainment, 34, 47; dance, 95; drama, 31, 38, 93-96; music, 47, 94, 112; visual arts, 98-99
ArtsSpace, 101
Associated Advertising Clubs of America (Better Business Bureau), 159
Audubon, John James, 21, 25, 85
Audubon Park, 24-25, 85, 148
Avalon (steamboat), 106
Ayers stores, L.S., 161

B
Bakery, Confectionery and Tobacco Workers International Union, 183
Ballard High School, 119
Banks and banking, 157, 158, 166-168
Baptist Hospital East, 164, 166
Baptist Hospitals of Louisville, 166
Baptists, Southern, 104
Bardstown Road, 85
Baryshnikov, Mikhail, 95
BATUS Incorporated, 159
Beargrass Creek, 28, 60, 139, 158
Beargrass Park, 150
Belgravia Court, 83
Belknap, Jonathan, 159
Belknap Inc., 46; Belknap Hardware and Manufacturing Company, 159
Bellarmine College, 130, 131

Bellarmine Medal, 131
Belle of Louisville (steamboat), 56, 57, 79, 106-107, 143, 144, 148, 184-185
Belvedere, 144
Bernheim Distillery Company, 178-179
Better Business Bureau, 159
Bingham, Barry, Sr., 79, 113, 168
Bingham, Mary, 79
Bingham, Robert Worth, 168
Bingham Endowed Series, 113
Bingham Fund, 113
Birdsall, Frederick, 43
Blacks, 31; improving opportunities for, 37, 118; *see also* Desegregation and racial justice
"Bloody Monday," 32, 104
Bluegrass Industrial Park, 85
Bluegrass Music Festival, 47, 148
Bluegrass State Poll, 118
Board of Health, 75
Bowman Field, 62-63, 65
Boyce Bible School, 134
Brennan House, 106, 107
Breuner's furniture stores, 160
Bridges, 23, 26-27, 33, 34, 37, 48-49, 52-53, 55, 58, 59, 60, 69
Broadway, 34, 36, 72, 73, 75, 76, 77, 144
Brodhead, Daniel, 159
Brown, J. Graham, 36
Brown, John Y., Jr., 162
Brown & Williamson Tobacco Corporation, 160, 173, 182
Brown & Williamson Tower, 76
Brown Hotel, 35, 76, 77
Browning, Pete, 181
Buckley, William F., 131
Buechel, 85
Bunton Company, 180
Burgoo, 87
"Burnt Knob," 148; *see also* Iroquois Park
Business First, 168
Bus service, 36
Butchertown, 67, 82, 102, 109, 148
Butchertown Candle Factory, 180

C
Campbell, John, 158
Canals, 31, 33, 36, 50
Capital Holding Corp., 168
Carrier Vibrating Equipment, 174
Catholic Archdiocese of Louisville, 103
Catholic church, 103-104

Catholic schools and colleges, 103, 129-132
Cave Hill Cemetery, 85, 151
Central Colored School, 121
Central Park, 83
Charitable activities, 112-115
Charlestown, IN, 38, 172
Cherokee Park, 12-13, 105, 150, 151
Cherokee parkway, 150
Cherokee Triangle, 85
Cherokee Triangle arts & crafts fair, 141
Chesapeake & Ohio Railroad, 55
Chi-Chi's Mexican-style restaurants, 163
Churches: first church (Methodist), 103; first Catholic, 103; St. Joseph's Catholic Church, 82
Churchill, Henry, 146
Churchill, John, 146
Churchill Downs, 55, 136-137, 143, 144, 146, 153
Citizens Fidelity bank, 166-167, 168
Civil War, 33, 52
Clark, George Rogers, 27-28, 109, 159
Clark, William, and Meriwether Lewis, 146
Clark Bridge, George Rogers, 23, 60, 69
Clark County Airport, IN, 65
Clark Maritime Centre, 65
Clarksville, IN, 29, 33, 151
Clemens, Samuel L. (Mark Twain), 49
Coburn, D.L., 93
Colgate-Palmolive, 183
Commission on Interracial Cooperation, 37
Commonwealth Building, 42, 73, 168
Communities and neighborhoods, 67-87; downtown, 67-77; historic, 79-85; riverfront, 77-79; second wealthiest ZIP code area, 69; Southern Indiana, 86-87; suburbs, 85-86
Connolly, John, 158
Conrail bridge, 52-53
Corbin, 162
Corn Island Storytelling Festival, 148
Council on Higher Education, 127-128
Courier-Journal, 168
Crescent Hill, 186-187
Crimes of the Heart, 93
Croghan, Major William, 109
Cronkite, Walter, 131
CSX Transportation, 60-61, 62, 173
Culbertson Mansion, 12-13, 109

Cumberland Coffee Concerts, 113

D
Dairymen, 183
Dams, 36-37
Danville (Kentucky) Theological Seminary, 134
DeAndrea, John, 99
Delta Queen (steamboat), 56, 143, 144
Depression, the Great, 37
Desegregation and racial justice, 42-44, 120-124, 130; *see also* Blacks
DeVoe & Raynolds, 179
Dickens on Main Street, 148
Distilling and brewing, 34-35, 36, 37, 38, 46, 172, 173, 178-179, 180, 181, 182, 183
Distinguished Achievement in Theatre (Tony), 94
Dixie Highway, 85
Downtown, 34, 36, 41, 189
Druther's International, 163
Duerr, Rev. Thomas, 130
Dupont de Nemours & Company, E.I., 178
Durkee Foods, 174

E
Early Times distillery, 181
Eastern parkway, 138, 150
Eclipse (steamboat), 87
Economic adaptation, 159-160, 171-172, 174, 175, 177, 182-183, 186
Edison House, Thomas, 109
Education and schools, 117-135; business, 117; Catholic schools, 117, 129-132; colleges, 117, 127-133; magnet programs, 124; primary and secondary, 44; private, 117, 130; public, 117-120; seminaries, 117, 134-135; universities, 117, 124-129, 132-134; vocational, 117
Enterprize (steamboat), 30
Environmental issues: air pollution, 44-46; river, 44-46
Ethnic diversity: heritage festivals, 88-89, 91, 92; politics, 93
Explorers and early settlers, 27, 28
Extendicare Inc., 166

F
Fairdale, 85
Faith Channel, 103
Falls of the Ohio, 21, 23, 25, 27, 29, 36, 46-47, 49, 51, 55, 64; coral reef, 23, 25

Farm Credit Banks, 69
Farmington, 12, 107
Fern Creek, 67
Festivals: Bluegrass Music Festival, 148; Corn Island Storytelling Festival, 148; Festival of the Dogwood, 141; Harvest Homecoming Festival, 148; Kentucky Derby Festival, 141-146; Kentucky State Fair, 147-148; Light Up Louisville and Dickens on Main Street, 148; Louisville Shakespearean Festival, 92; Oktoberfest, 92, 148; Strassenfest, 92, 148
Fillies Derby Ball, 143
Filson, John E., 111
Filson Club, 111
First Edition Records, 94
First Kentucky National Corporation, 167, 168
First National bank, 166-167
First National Tower, 71, 75
Fischer Packaging Company, 183
Flood of 1937, the, 37, 38-39
Floyd, John, 28
Floyd County Museum, 110, 112-113
Floyds Knobs, 67
Ford Motor Company, 35, 38, 46, 55, 171, 172, 173, 174-175
Fourth Avenue, 11
Fourth Avenue Mall, 160
Fourth Street, 34, 36, 72, 73, 75, 76, 77, 182
Fox, Fontaine, 51
French and Indian War, 28
Fund for the Arts, 114

G
Galleria, 76, 156-157, 160, 182
Galt House Hotel, 75
Gardercourt Mansion, 105
General Electric Appliance Park, 41, 46, 170-171, 173, 175-178
Geology and prehistory, 23-25
German influence, 52, 92
Germantown, 82
Gilded Antlers, 144
The Gin Game (drama), 93
Glenmore Distillery, 183
Glenview, 85
Goodrich, B.F., 178
Graham, John, 110
Grawemeyer Award, 93
Greater Louisville Fund for the Arts, 96

Great Steamboat Race, 106, 143
"grits line," 91

H
Hadley, Mary Alice, 180
Hadley Pottery Company, 180
Hard Scuffle Steeplechase, 96-97, 145, 147
Harrods Creek, 69, 85
Harvest Homecoming Festival, 148
Haymarket, 79
Heart/artificial-heart surgery, 163-164
Henley, Beth, 93
Heritage Festival, 91
Heritage Weekend, 88-89
Heyburn Building, 73
Highways, 39-41, 58-60
Hillerich, John Andrew "Bud," 181
Hillerich, J.A., III, 182
Hillerich and Bradsby, 38, 181-182; Powerbilt golf clubs, 123
Historical research: Filson Club, 111; Photographic Archives, 112; Sons of the American Revolution, 112; University of Louisville Archives, 112
Historic buildings and architecture, 71, 105, 107, 109; *see also* Shotgun houses
Hospitals, 38, 75, 163-166; first established, 31; University of Louisville Schools of Medicine and Dentistry, 75
Hotels: Brown Hotel, 76; Galt House Hotel, 75; Hyatt Regency Louisville, 75; Riverfront Plaza/Belvedere, 75, 79; Seelbach Hotel, 76
Howard, Edmonds J., 110
Howard Shipyards, 110, 172, 173
Howard Steamboat Museum, 110
Humana Building, 71, 73
Humana Festival of New American Plays, 112
Humana Heart Institute International, 166
Humana Hospital/Audubon, 163, 166
Humana Hospital/Southwest, 166
Humana Hospital/University of Louisville, 164
Humana Inc., 46, 157, 159
Hyatt Regency Louisville, 75

I
I.C.H. Corporation, 168
Idlewild (steamboat), 106
Illinois Central Railroad, 28-29, 62

Immigration, 32, 172
Indiana Army Ammunition plant, 179
Indiana University Southeast, 128, 131
Indians, 23, 28
Ingwerson, Donald W., 119, 122
Insurance, 168
International Harvester, 41, 46, 172, 173, 174
Interstate 64, 60
Interstate 65, 60
Interstate 264, 58-59
Interstate 265, 59
Irish influence, 32, 92
Iroquois Amphitheater, 151
Iroquois Golf Course, 155
Iroquois Park, 130, 143, 149, 150
Ivey's department stores, 160

J
Jack Daniel's (whiskey), 157
Jackson, Jesse, 131
Jacob, Charles D., 148
"Jacobs's Folly," 148
James, Jesse, 151
Jeffboat, 62-63, 173
Jefferson Community College, 128, 129
Jefferson County, 67; suburbs, 39, 85
Jefferson County Memorial Forest, 150
Jefferson Mall, 160-161
Jefferson Square Park, 148
Jeffersontown, 85, 148
Jeffersonville, IN, 29, 31, 33, 51, 62, 87, 110, 148, 151, 168, 172, 181
Jewish Hospital, 164
Jones, Alun, 95
Jones, David A., 159-160
Jones Award, Margo 94
Jory, Jon, 93

K
Kallay, Mike, 169
Kaufman-Straus department store, 76
Kennedy Memorial Bridge, John F., 60
Kosair Children's Hospital, 164
Kentuckiana Interfaith Community, 103
Kentuckiana Metroversity, 118
Kentucky Center for the Arts, 71, 93, 96, 98, 114-115
Kentucky Derby, 38, 140, 146-147, 153, 161
Kentucky Derby Festival, 37, 38, 141-146; Fillies Derby Ball, 143; Great Balloon Race, 143; Great Steamboat Race, 56,

106, 143, 144; mini-marathon, 143, 144-145; parade, 143; Pegasus Parade, 120, 144; Ramble for the Roses, 145; Run for the Rodents, 132, 145; Run for the Rosé, 145; "They're Off" luncheon, 143
Kentucky Derby Museum, 153
Kentucky Fair and Exposition Center, 143
Kentucky Fried Chicken, 157, 163
Kentucky Home Life building, 34
Kentucky Industries for the Blind, 101
Kentucky Manufacturing Company, 180
Kentucky National Bank, 71
Kentucky Oaks, 144
Kentucky Opera, 94-95, 147
Kentucky Railway Museum, 57, 60-61, 110
Kentucky's Center of Excellence, 127
Kentucky State Fair, 147-148
King, Martin Luther, Jr., 42
Knobs, The, 21, 23, 24, 85
"Know Nothing" party, 32
Knox, Fort, 35-36, 38, 45
Kosair Shrine, 32-33
Kurfees Coatings Inc., 179

L
Labor climate, 44, 174-175, 177-178, 182-183; *see also* Economic adaptation
Lakeside Club, 147
Lantech Inc., 180
Lemon and Son Jewelers Inc., 160-161
Lenox (china), 157
Levy Brothers, 39
Lewis, Meriwether, and William Clark, 146
Lexington, 31, 51, 53
Liberty National bank, 167
Light Up Louisville, 148
Lincoln, Abraham (grandfather of president), 28
Lindsey Methodist Church, Marcus, 102
Lloyd George, David, 36
Locomotive 152, 106
Locust Grove, 108, 109, 110-111
Lodge, Henry Cabot, 131
Long Run Cemetery, 148
Lorillard, 173, 182
Louis XVI, King of France, 28
Louisville, founding of, 28
Louisville and Jefferson County Riverport, 65
Louisville and Portland canal, 50, 82
Louisville Art Gallery, 99

Louisville Bach Society, 181
Louisville Ballet, 95
Louisville Cathedral of Assumption, 114
Louisville Chamber of Commerce, 169, 186
Louisville Downs, 153
Louisville Edible Oil Products, 174
Louisville Forge and Gear Works, 174
Louisville Galleria, 76, 156-157, 160, 182
Louisville Gas and Electric Company, 36, 45
Louisville Institute for Hand and Microsurgery, 164
Louisville Jazz Society, 98
Louisville Jockey Club, 146
Louisville magazine, 169
Louisville Municipal College, 127
Louisville Museum of History and Science, 109
Louisville and Nashville Railroad (L&N), 31, 38, 52-53, 55, 57, 60, 173
Louisville Orchestra, 47, 94
Louisville Redbirds, 152-153, 154, 182
Louisville Sluggers, 181
Louisville Stoneware Company, 180
Louisville Times, 168
Louisville Water Company, 99
Louisville wharf, 30
Louisville Zoological Gardens, 152

M
Main Street, 34, 69, 71, 72, 75, 79, 109, 114-115, 148, 159
Malls: Fourth Avenue Mall, 77; Galleria, 76, 156-157, 160, 182; Jefferson Mall, 160-161; River City Mall, 75
Manet, Edouard, 99
Manufacturing, 31, 33, 36, 38, 46, 172; appliance, 175-178; auto, 174-175; liquor, 182; military, 172, 179-180; organ, 181-182; pottery and stoneware, 180; sports equipment, 181-182; tobacco, 182-183
Market Street, 158, 166-167
Marshall Field's, 157, 160
McAlpine Dam, 23, 82-83
McAlpine Locks, 82
McDonough, Archbishop Thomas J., 122
Mead Container Corporation, 174
Media, 168-169
Medical Center (downtown), 164
Medical Tower Building, 165

Methodist Evangelical Hospital, 164
Metro United Way, 114
Middletown, 85
Military installations, 35-36, 38, 45, 172, 179-180
Milwaukee Road (railroad), 62
Minton Bridge, 48-49
Mississippi Queen (steamboat), 63
Mississippi River, 30, 33
Monroe, Bill, 148
Morgan, John Hunt, 151
Morris, William Gouverneur, 94
Mother's Cookie Company, 183
Museums: Floyd County Museum (IN), 110; Howard Steamboat Museum, 110; Kentucky Derby Museum, 153; Kentucky Railway Museum, 110; Louisville Museum of History & Science, 72, 109; Portland Museum, 109
Music: Iroquois Amphitheater Association, 96; Kentucky Opera, 94; Louisville Bach Society, 181; Louisville Free Public Library, 96; Louisville Jazz Society, 98; Louisville Orchestra, 94; Louisville Theatrical Association, 96; WFPK, 96; WFPL, 96
"My Old Kentucky Home," 146

N
National Commission on Educational Excellence, 125
National Council of Churches report (1980), 101
National Headquarters of the Presbyterian Church (U.S.A.), 79
National Processing Company, 168
National Public Radio, 97
National Register of Historic Places, 69, 106
National Wildlife Conservation Area, 23, 25
Natural History magazine, 80
Naval Ordnance Station Louisville, 179-180
Nazareth College, 133
NCAA Basketball/Championship, 154-155
New Albany, IN, 29, 30, 31, 34, 51, 86-87, 109, 112-113, 148, 151, 168
Newburg, 85
New Orleans (steamboat), 30
Newspapers, 168-169
New York Central Railroad, 55

Norfolk Southern Railroad, 61
North Western parkway, 150
Norton Hospital, 164

O
Ohio River, 23, 24, 29, 33, 44, 49; see also Falls of the Ohio
Ohio River Bridge, 26-27
Oktoberfest, 148
Old Louisville, 67, 82, 148, 152
Olmsted, Frederick Law, 25, 149
Otter Creek Park, 151
Oxmoor Estate, 14-15
Oxmoor Steeplechase, 141

P
Paducah and Louisville Railroad, 62
Paramount Foods Inc., 183
Parks, 25, 34; Beargrass, 150; Cherokee, 150, 151; Iroquois, 149, 150; Jefferson County Memorial Forest, 150; Otter Creek Park, 151; Pleasure Ridge Park, 85; E.P. "Tom" Sawyer State Park, 151; Shawnee, 150
Pennsylvania, Baltimore & Ohio Railroad, 55
PepsiCo Inc., 163
Petrik, Eugene V., 131
Philip Morris, 182-183
Photographic Archives (U of L), 112
Pillsbury, 183
Pleasure Ridge Park, 85
Porter Paint Company, 179
Portland, 29, 31, 51, 67, 82
Portland Museum, 109
Presbyterian Church (U.S.A.), 104-105, 114-115, 157, 159-160
Presbyterian Synods of Kentucky and Missouri, 134
Presbyterian Theological Seminary, 12-13, 128-129
Presentation Academy, 130
Professional Banking Services, 167
Prohibition, 34-35, 36, 37
Pulitzer Prize, *Courier-Journal*, 93
Purnell Sausage Company, 183

Q
"Quest for Excellence," 120

R
Radio, 35, 169

Railroads, 10, 31, 33, 51-55, 57, 60-62, 172; see also Louisville and Nashville Railroad (L&N)
Ramble for the Roses, 145
Reck, Gottfried C., 180-181
Red Cross headquarters, 164
Reliance Universal Inc., 179
Religious affiliations, 103-105
Rembrandt, 99
Retail trade, 76, 158-159, 160-162
Reynolds Metals Company, 41-42, 43, 180
Riverboats, 28-29, 30, 31, 33, 38, 79, 87, 106; barges, 36, 62; see also Belle of Louisville *and other names of particular riverboats*
River City Mall, 75
Riverfront Plaza/Belvedere, 75, 79
Riverports and river commerce, 28-29, 30, 65; see also Riverboats
River Road, 144
Riverside Drive/Expressway, 23, 58
Robert E. Lee (steamboat), 87
Rohm & Haas Kentucky Inc., 178
Rubbertown, 38, 41, 172, 178, 179
Run for the Rosé, 145
Rutherford, Glenn, 113-114

S
St. Anthony's hospital, 166
St. Catherine Street, 102-103
St. Elizabeth hospital, 166
St. James Court, 83
St. James Court Art Fair, 148
St. Joseph's Catholic Church, 82
St. Joseph's Infirmary, 164, 166
St. Mary hospital, 166
St. Matthews, 67, 85, 148
St. Patrick's Day, 141
Saks Fifth Avenue, 157, 160
Sanders, Col. Harland, 157, 162-163
Sanders, John, 158
E.P. "Tom" Sawyer State Park, 51
Scenic beauty, 21-23
Schnitzelberg, 82
Schroeder, Bill, 163
Scribner House, 109, 113
Second Presbyterian Church, 137
Seelbach Hotel, 11, 34, 76
Seminaries: Danville (Kentucky) Theological, 134; Jefferson Seminary (U of L), 127; Louisville Presbyterian Theological (U.S.A.), 103, 134-135; Southern Baptist Theological, 103-134
Seneca Gardens, 85
Shakespeare in Central Park, 95-96, 151
Shawnee Park, 150-151
Shea, Michael, 168
Shelbyville, 85
Sherman, Gen. William T., 33
Shipping port, 29
Shively, 67, 85, 148
Shotgun houses, 79-82
Shriver, Sargent, 131
Sisney, Sherleen (national teacher of the year, 1984), 118-119
Sisters of Charity of Nazareth, 133
Six Mile Island, 144
Slavery, 31-32, 33
Smith, A. Ray, 154
Snyder's department stores, 161-162
Soo (railroad), 62
Southern Railroad, 53, 55
South Western parkway, 150
Spalding University, 132-134
Speed Art Museum, J.B., 98-99, 101
Speed Scientific School, 125
Stage One: The Louisville Children's Theatre, 95
Standard Gravure, 168
Standiford Field, 62, 63, 65
Starks Office Building, 76
Steiner, Phares, 180-181
Steiner-Reck Inc., 180-181
Stewart Dry Goods Company, 161
Stitzel Distillery, 34-35
Strassenfest, 148
Strathmoor Manor, 85
Strathmoor Village, 85
Stryker, Roy, 112; photographic collection, 112
Suburban Hospital, 166
Suburbanization, 39-41
Sullivan, Danny, 155
Swain, Donald C., 119, 128

T
Taylor, Camp Zachary, 35
Taylorsville, 85
Telephone service, 36
Television, 169
Teresa, Mother
Theatre Square, 76
"They're Off" luncheon, 143
Thimbles fashion stores, 160

Thoroughbred Containers Inc., 174
300 Building (Kentucky National Bank), 69, 71
Tobacco, 172-173, 182-183
Toonerville II (trolley), 51, 162
Transit Authority of River City, 60
Trolley cars, 34
Twain, Mark, 49

U
Union Station, 10
United Catalysts Inc., 178
United Parcel Service, 63-65
University of Kentucky, 128, 155
University of Louisville, 37, 75, 118, 123, 124-128, 153; Archives, 112; Louisville Medical Institute, 127; Louisville Municipal College, 127; NCAA basketball championships, 125-127; Schools of Medicine and Dentistry, 75, 154; School of Music, 125, 181; Speed Scientific School, 125
Urban renewal, 42, 69, 71, 72, 75-85
Ursuline College, 130
Utica, 69

V
Valley Station, 85
Vaughan Memorial Award for Exceptional Achievement, 94
Vlach, John, 80
Vogt Machine Company, Henry, 180

W
Walnut Street Baptist Church, 102-103
WAMZ (radio station), 168, 169
Water Tower, 100, 148
Water Tower Art Association, 99, 144, 152
Watterson Expressway, 58
WAVE-TV, 169
Weather, 24-25, 137, 151
"Wedding cake building," 176
Weekend College, 133
West Buechel, 85
WFPK, 96-98
WFPL, 96-98, 169
WHAS (radio station), 168, 169; Crusade for Children, 115
WHAS-TV, 115, 168
Whiteman's Orchestra, Paul, 36
Whitestone Mansion, 132
Wholesale trade, 162
WKET (public television station), 169
WKPC (public television station), 169
World War I, 33, 35, 36
World War II, 38, 43, 82, 172

Y
Yellowstone Superpops Concerts, 112
Youth Performing Arts School, 120-121, 122
YWCA, 186

Z
Zoo programs, 153

John Nation

John Beckman/Quadrant

John Nation

374

John Nation